DATE DUE

			PRINTED IN U.S.A.

Authors & Artists for Young Adults

ISSN 1040-5682

Authors & Artists for Young Adults

VOLUME 6

Agnes Garrett and Helga P. McCue,
Editors

 Gale Research Inc. · *DETROIT* · *LONDON*

Managing Editor: Anne Commire

Editors: Agnes Garrett, Helga P. McCue

Associate Editors: Elisa Ann Ferraro, Eunice L. Petrini

Assistant Editors: Marc Caplan, Marja Hiltunen, Linda Shedd

Sketchwriters: Catherine Coray, Johanna Cypis, Marguerite Feitlowitz,
Mimi H. Hutson, Deborah Klezmer, Dieter Miller, Beatrice Smedley

Researcher: Catherine Ruello

Editorial Assistants: Joanne J. Ferraro, June Lee, Susan Pfanner

Production Manager: Mary Beth Trimper
External Production Assistant: Mary Winterhalter

Art Director: Arthur Chartow
Keyliner: C.J. Jonik

Special acknowledgment is due to members of the *Contemporary
Authors* Original Volumes and *Contemporary Authors New Revisions* staff who assisted in the preparation of this volume.

The paper used in this publication meets the minimum requirements of
American National Standard for Information Sciences—Permanence Paper for
Printed Library Materials, ANSI Z39.48-1984.   ∞™

Copyright © 1991
Gale Research Inc.
835 Penobscot Bldg.
Detroit, MI 48226-4094
All rights reserved.

Library of Congress Catalog Card Number
ISBN 0-8103-5055-6
ISSN 1040-5682

Printed in the United States of America

Published simultaneously in the United Kingdom
by Gale Research International Limited
(An affiliated company of Gale Research Inc.)

Contents

Introduction

Authors and Artists for Young Adults is a reference series designed to bridge the gap between Gale's *Something about the Author*, created for children, and *Contemporary Authors*, intended for older students and adults.

Authors and Artists for Young Adults is aimed entirely at the needs and interests of the often overlooked young adults. We share the concerns of librarians who must send young readers to the adult reference shelves for which they may not be ready. *Authors and Artists for Young Adults* will give high school and junior high school students information about the lives and works of their favorite creative artists—the people behind the books, movies, television programs, plays, lyrics, cartoon and animated features that they most enjoy.

Although most of the entries in *Authors and Artists for Young Adults* will cover contemporary artists, the series will include artists of all time periods and all countries whose work has a special appeal to young adults today. Some of these artists may also be profiled in *Something about the Author* or *Contemporary Authors*, but their entries in *Authors and Artists for Young Adults* are tailored specifically to the information needs of the young adult user.

Entry Format

Each volume of *Authors and Artists for Young Adults* will furnish in-depth coverage of about twenty authors and artists. The typical entry consists of:

— A detailed biographical section that includes date of birth, marriage, children, education, and addresses.

— A comprehensive bibliography or filmography including publishers, producers, and years.

— Adaptations into other media forms.

— Works in progress.

— A distinctive essay featuring comments on an artist's life, career, artistic intentions, world views, and controversies.

— References for further reading.

— Extensive illustrations, photographs, movie stills, manuscript samples, book covers, and other relevant visual material.

A cumulative index to featured authors and artists appears in each volume.

Highlights of Forthcoming Volumes

Among the authors and artists planned for future volumes are:

Vivian Alcock
Maya Angelou
Isaac Asimov
W. H. Auden
Jean Auel
James Blish
Robin Brancato
Sue Ellen Bridgers
Bruce Brooks
Claude Brown
Agatha Christie
Daniel Cohen
Evan Connell
Thomas Dygard
William Faulkner

Leon Garfield
Jane Goodall
Bette Greene
Constance Greene
Chester Gould
Judith Guest
Deborah Hautzig
Robert Heinlein
Jamake Highwater
Marjorie Holmes
John Hughes
Bob Kane
W. P. Kinsella
Linda Lewis
Lael Littke

Robert Lipsyte
Margaret Mahy
Flannery O'Connor
Jayne A. Phillips
Judith St. George
Ouida Sebestyen
Scott Spencer
Steven Spielberg
Mildred D. Taylor
Edmund White
Simon Wiesenthal
Elie Wiesel
Jack Williamson
Judie Wolkoff
Roger Zelazny

The editors of *Authors and Artists for Young Adults* welcome any suggestions for additional biographees to be included in this series. Please write and give us your opinions and suggestions for making our series more helpful to you. Direct your comments to: Editors, *Authors and Artists for Young Adults*, Gale Research Inc., 835 Penobscot Building, Detroit, Michigan 48226-4094.

Authors
& Artists
for Young
Adults

Brent Ashabranner

Born November 3, 1921, in Shawnee, Okla.; son of Dudley (a pharmacist) and Rose Thelma (a homemaker; maiden name, Cotton) Ashabranner; married Martha White (a homemaker), August 9, 1941; children: Melissa Lynn, Jennifer Ann. *Education:* Oklahoma State University, B.S., 1948, M.A., 1951; additional study at University of Michigan, 1955, and Boston University and Oxford University, 1959-60. *Home and office:* 15 Spring W., Williamsburg, Va. 23185.

■ Career

Oklahoma State University, Stillwater, instructor in English, 1952-55; Ministry of Education, Technical Cooperation Administration, Addis Ababa, Ethiopia, educational materials adviser, 1955-57; International Cooperation Administration, Tripoli, Libya, chief of Education Materials Development Division, 1957-59; Agency for International Development, Lagos, Nigeria, education program officer, 1960-61; Peace Corps, Washington, D.C., acting director of program in Nigeria, 1961-62, deputy director of program in India, 1962-64, director of program in India, 1964-66, director of Office of Training, 1966-67, deputy director of Peace Corps, 1967-69; Harvard University, Center

for Studies in Education and Development, Cambridge, Mass., research associate, 1969-70; Pathfinder Fund, Boston, Mass., director of Near East-South Asia Population Program, 1970-71; director of project development, World Population International Assistance Division, Planned Parenthood, 1971-72; Ford Foundation, New York, N.Y., associate representative and population program officer, 1972-80, officer-in-charge, Philippines, 1972-75, deputy representative, Indonesia, 1975-80; full-time writer, 1980—. *Military service:* U.S. Navy, 1942-45. *Member:* Authors Guild, Society of Children's Book Writers, Children's Book Guild (Washington, D.C.).

■ Awards, Honors

National Civil Service League Career Service Award, 1968; Notable Children's Trade Book in the Field of Social Studies from the National Council for Social Studies and the Children's Book Council, 1982, and Carter G. Woodson Book Award from the National Council for the Social Studies, 1983, both for *Morning Star, Black Sun;* Notable Children's Trade Book in the Field of Social Studies, and one of New York Public Library's Books for the Teen-Age, both 1983, both for *The New Americans;* Notable Children's Trade Book in the Field of Social Studies, and one of American Library Association's Best Books for Young Adults, both 1984, and Carter G. Woodson Book Award, 1985, all for *To Live in Two Worlds;* Notable Children's Trade Book in the Field of Social Studies, 1984, for *Gavriel and Jemal,* and 1990, for *Born to the Land* and *Counting America.*

Notable Trade Book in the Field of Social Studies, 1985, and *Boston Globe-Horn Book* Nonfiction Honor Book, Carter G. Woodson Book Award, one of Child Study Association of America's Children's Books of the Year, and one of *School Library Journal*'s Best Books for Young Adults, all 1986, all for *Dark Harvest*; one of *School Library Journal*'s Best Books of the Year, 1986, and Jane Addams Children's Book Award Honor Book from the Jane Addams Peace Association and the Women's International League for Peace and Freedom, 1987, both for *Children of the Maya*; Notable Children's Trade Book in the Field of Social Studies, one of *School Library Journal*'s Best Books of the Year, and Christopher Award, all 1987, all for *Into a Strange Land*; Notable Children's Trade Book in the Field of Social Studies, 1987, for *The Vanishing Border*; *Always to Remember* was a Notable Children's Trade Book in the Field of Social Studies, American Library Association Best Book for Young Adults, and New York Public Library Books for the Teen-Age, all 1989; *Washington Post*/Children's Book Guild of Washington, D.C. Nonfiction Award, 1990; one of New York Public Library Books for the Teen-Age for *Born to the Land* and *Counting America*, both 1990.

■ Writings

(Editor) *The Stakes Are High*, Bantam, 1954.

(With Russell Davis) *The Lion's Whiskers* (illustrated by James G. Teason), Little, Brown, 1959.

(With R. Davis) *Point Four Assignment*, Little, Brown, 1959.

(With R. Davis) *Ten Thousand Desert Swords*, Little, Brown, 1960.

(With R. Davis) *The Choctaw Code*, McGraw, 1961.

(With Judson Milburn and Cecil B. Williams) *A First Course in College English* (textbook), Houghton, 1962.

(With R. Davis) *Chief Joseph*, McGraw, 1962.

(With R. Davis) *Land in the Sun: The Story of West Africa* (illustrated by Robert William Hinds), Little, Brown, 1963.

(With R. Davis) *Land in the Sun*, Little, Brown, 1963.

(With R. Davis) *Strangers in Africa*, McGraw, 1963.

A Moment in History: The First Ten Years of the Peace Corps, Doubleday, 1971.

Morning Star, Black Sun: The Northern Cheyenne Indians and America's Energy Crisis (Junior Literary Guild selection; illustrated with photographs by Paul Conklin), Dodd, 1982.

The New Americans: Changing Patterns in U.S. Immigration (Junior Literary Guild selection; ALA Notable Book; illustrated with photographs by P. Conklin), Dodd, 1983.

To Live in Two Worlds: American Indian Youth Today (Junior Literary Guild selection; illustrated with photographs by P. Conklin), Dodd, 1984.

Gavriel and Jemal: Two Boys of Jerusalem (Junior Literary Guild selection; ALA Notable Book; illustrated with photographs by P. Conklin), Dodd, 1984.

Dark Harvest: Migrant Farmworkers in America (ALA Notable Book; illustrated with photographs by P. Conklin), Dodd, 1985.

Children of the Maya: A Guatemalan Indian Odyssey (ALA Notable Book; illustrated with photographs by P. Conklin), Dodd, 1986.

(With daughter, Melissa Ashabranner) *Into a Strange Land: Unaccompanied Refugee Youth in America* (Junior Literary Guild selection; ALA Notable Book), Dodd, 1987.

The Vanishing Border: A Photographic Journey along Our Frontier with Mexico (Junior Literary Guild selection; illustrated with photographs by P. Conklin), Dodd, 1987.

Always to Remember: The Story of the Vietnam Veterans Memorial (Junior Literary Guild selection; illustrated with photographs by daughter, Jennifer Ashabranner), Dodd, 1988.

(With M. Ashabranner) *Counting America: The Story of the United States Cenus* (Junior Literary Guild selection), Putnam, 1989.

People Who Make a Difference (illustrated with photographs by P. Conklin), Cobblehill/Dutton, 1989.

Born to the Land: An American Portrait (Junior Literary Guild selection; illustrated with photographs by P. Conklin), Putnam, 1989.

I'm in the Zoo Too, Cobblehill/Dutton, 1989.

Times of My Life, Cobblehill/Dutton, 1990.

Crazy about German Shepherds (illustrated with photographs by Jennifer Ashabranner), Cobblehill/Dutton, 1990.

A Grateful Nation: The Story of Arlington National Cemetery (illustrated with photographs by J. Ashabranner), Putnam, 1990.

An Ancient Heritage: The Arab-American Minority, Harper/Collins, 1991.

Contributor of articles and short stories to periodicals, including *American Mercury, Catholic Digest, Childhood Education, Elementary English, Horn*

Book, Junior Scholastic, Salt, Western Folklore, and *Writer.*

■ Work in Progress

A Grateful Nation: The Story of the Lincoln Memorial, for Putnam; *Still a Nation of Immigrants: America as a Multicultural Society,* for Cobblehill/Dutton.

■ Sidelights

"I have never had any doubt that the books I read as a boy influenced the direction of my life, including my life as a writer. I grew up in a small Oklahoma town, but I was fascinated by books about foreign countries. I devoured Kipling, practically memorized *Beau Geste* (Buccaneer), and lived every moment of the wonderful overseas adventures Richard Halliburton described in travel books, the titles of which I have long since forgotten. For an afternoon of lugging boxes around, I was once offered any book on the shelves by the owner of the tiny local bookstore. I remember that I picked Alec Waugh's *Hot Countries* (Farrar). Waugh was a bit much for a thirteen-year-

The 1982 Junior Literary Guild selection.

old Oklahoma boy, but I had sweated for the book, and I read it.

"I cannot prove that this exotic reading diet was responsible for my having lived and worked much of my adult life in Ethiopia, Libya, Nigeria, India, the Philippines, and Indonesia; but I strongly suspect that Kipling, Wren, Halliburton, and a few other mesmerizing writers about Africa and Asia—including Pearl Buck—made my initial decision to work in foreign assistance programs much easier than it otherwise would have been."[1]

"When I first tried my hand at writing at the age of eleven, the setting was Africa. Under the spell of a book called *Bomba the Jungle Boy,* I decided to write *Barbara the Jungle Girl.* That was not very original, I admit, but at least, like Robert Louis Stevenson, I 'played the sedulous ape' to a writer I admired. In any case, by page three I was hopelessly bogged down in the plot and gave up that effort. When I was in high school I won fourth prize in the *Scholastic Magazine* national short story writing contest, and I never stopped writing after that.

"World War II got me out of Oklahoma and into the Navy for three years. I saw some of the world—Hawaii, the Philippines, Japan—that I had only read about before. After the war, however, I came back to Oklahoma, finished my education at Oklahoma State University, and taught English there for several years. I continued to write and published many stories and articles about the American West. It seemed as if I was settling in for a career of teaching and writing in my native state.

"Then, out of the blue, I had a chance to go to Africa and work in the U.S. foreign aid program. All of the Kipling, Wren, Halliburton, and Edgar Rice Burroughs I had read as a boy came flooding back. With my wife's enthusiastic agreement, we packed our bags, convinced our two young daughters that they were in for a big adventure and headed overseas. We never got back to Oklahoma except for an occasional visit.

"Two years in Ethiopia were followed by two in Libya, working with ministries of education in developing reading materials for their schools.

"But no matter where I was or what I was doing, I always had another life as a writer. The things I felt I was learning about understanding other cultures and about people of different cultures understanding each other seemed worth sharing with young readers....A number of my books for upper elementary, junior high, and high school students deal with complex cross-cultural issues, for example,

DARK HARVEST
Migrant Farmworkers in America

Brent Ashabranner
Photographs by Paul Conklin

The 1985 Dodd, Mead edition.

the gulf separating Arabs and Jews in the Middle East, the adjustment of unaccompanied refugee children to America, the melding of cultures along our frontier with Mexico. I believe such books can be made interesting to young readers because they are about real people trying to cope with very real and serious problems."[2]

During his work with the Point Four foreign aid program in Africa, Ashabranner met Russell Davis, a writer who shared his interest and concern in education. The two decided to embark on a project that would not only help foster the folk tales of African countries, but educate the readers as well. African students would benefit from quality reading materials based on their own experience, while non-African students would learn about those developing countries. The collaboration developed into an anthology of Ethiopian folk tales, *The Lion's Whiskers*, published in 1959. "We have collected folk materials in three different areas—East Africa, North Africa, and Latin America. Methods of collection vary with circumstances. The tape recorder is essential for capturing the manner of delivery and language; but often the tape recorder cannot be used, either because it cannot withstand

the rigors of a rough country or because the storyteller freezes at the sight of such an outlandish gadget. In such cases collectors must record with pencil and paper. Sometimes even the pencil and paper create the wrong mood, and the collector must simply let his man rip, and rely on memory after the session ends. And at times, sadly, some of the best storytellers react to the foreign collector rather than to the magic of the materials. Then narrators either lose their eloquence and lapse into dumb awe, or they posture, and embroider simple materials with elaborate and quasi-learned trivia.

"We were on our way to Aksum, holy city of Ethiopia, and had stopped to make night camp at the edge of *Haik* [a lake in central Ethiopia]. As we unloaded our Land Rover, an old monk from St. Stephen's wandered by and stopped to watch us. We talked to him, and he told us that he was a bird watcher in a monastery corn field nearby. All day long he sat on a little elevated platform in the center of the field and threw rocks to frighten away the marauding birds.

"Here seemed to be just the man we were looking for: one old enough in the area to know its oral traditions, clear-minded enough to remember details, possessed of a certain facility with words, and holding a clear set of belief and values. Such a combination often returns rich dividends for the folklorist.

"Our man was as good as he promised to be. We drew him out slowly; and as shadows lengthened beside our Land Rover, he told us story after story that he had heard since his boyhood. Once he was warmed up, he felt no shyness about talking into the microphone of our battery-run tape recorder. In fact, after he heard his own voice on our playback, he seemed to enjoy himself immensely.

"Inevitably many of his stories dealt with the lake that was so important to the life of the region. He told us of the wicked people who had once made human sacrifices to a huge water serpent which they believed to be the spirit of the lake. He told us of a great holy man who came into the land and was outraged at the wickedness of the lake people. The holy man set the waters of the lake afire to show the people the power of the true God, and from that day they were all Christians and the monastery of St. Stephen's was founded. The old monk told us how the clever monkey had tricked all the other animals into thinking that the lake water was poison so that he could have it all to himself. He not only knew folk stories, but had given some thoughts to the whys and wherefores of the tale.

He said: 'The tale must teach something important or I, an old man, would not bother to squat among noisy children to tell them stories. And then the tale must entertain, or children would not bother to squat down to listen to a dull, old man.'

"Later, as we sat around our campfire, the vividness of the old bird watcher's tales lingered on and sharpened our awareness of the sights and sounds around us—the night cries of unseen animals, the moonlight floating like a golden film on the lake, the dark, crouching bulk of the encircling mountains. The stories became sharp, were more enjoyable for us because we had heard them in their own setting and from the mouth of a man who had known them from childhood.

"This is more than just a recounting of a pleasant experience. To us it illustrates a very fundamental truth about folk tales. Before folk tales can be offered to American children, two distinct and important operations are necessary. First comes the collection and recording of the tales; second comes their translation and re-creation. Our interest here is the collection, or harvest. The winnowing and threshing is another matter.

"Only by experiencing the stories in their environment can the writer appreciate their true flavor. A skillful writer may be able to bring out the universal values in a group of folk stories he knows only from second-hand sources, but he can hope for only meager success in bringing out their elements of uniqueness. And it is in their uniqueness that the major enjoyment in folk tales is to be found.

"We have also found that school children can be a good source of folk material. By asking them to write down a story that they have heard from a grandmother or an uncle, one can often get on the track of a good story. Of course, ninety per cent of all that is collected in this way is worthless, but the other ten per cent can put one on the trail of some excellent tales. The advantage of using local school children lies in getting maximum coverage at minimum expense and time. Some countries have so many diverse languages and cultures that it would take forever to cover them without leads. Taking the tales from children has other advantages for the collector who plans to retell them for children. The collector gets a built-in marketing judgment, because the local child tells the tales he remembers and likes; and children the world over differ surprisingly little in taste.

"Disappointments must be accepted as a part of the game. The storyteller may have to be wooed with persistence and yet circumspection. Even then he may never perform before the visitor. We have spent up to three days in uncomfortable back country villages, wooing the shy narrator, sending various emissaries such as a priest and school teacher, making handsome gifts, and running parties and priming the pump with stories of our own. The real champion almost always rises to such a challenge. If you tell a good tale, he will top it. We once made a long and hard detour from our regular route to locate an old Ethiopian who was reported to be the soul of wisdom and the finest storyteller in that part of the country. When we finally found him—an aged and gentle old man living alone in a spotlessly clean mud hut—we were astonished to hear him address us in Swedish. He had lived and worked almost all of his life as a catechist at a nearby Swedish Mission and when he saw two white men, he naturally assumed that we spoke Swedish. He never did fully understand why we could not. To him, Swedish was the language of white men.

"We talked with the old gentleman for a long time, but we could never get him to tell us any Ethiopian stories. He knew many, he admitted, but it was beneath his dignity to tell them. He simply could not believe that we–two grown men—wanted to hear them. He gave us long discourses (partly in Swedish, partly in Amharic) from the Bible and told us some of the great Biblical stories. But of tales of his own land and people we heard not a one.

"A well-written volume of folk tales requires an unusual effort on the part of the author, but it is worth the time and effort it takes. Such a volume provides a particularly enjoyable way for young readers to get an insight into different cultures in a time when it is increasingly important for everyone to have a growing understanding of the world and the people in it. Good folk tales are not only fun to read, but at their best they reveal a great deal about the lands and people to whom they belong. No one can understand the politics or political history of Ethiopia, for example, without understanding the importance which that country attaches to its own version of the Solomon and Sheba legend. And anyone familiar with the little-known epic narratives of the tribe of Bani Hilal will have a greater understanding of the modern Arab temperament.

"From a literary standpoint, the well-written folk tale also has much to offer. Some of the greatest possibilities in children's literature, for originality of both theme and situation, lie in unexploited

CHILDREN OF THE MAYA

A Guatemalan Indian Odyssey

Brent Ashabranner

Photographs by Paul Conklin

Dust jacket from the 1986 Putnam edition.

veins of folklore. From the Ethiopian story which pictures the lowly earthworm as a powerful creature and agent of God's grace, to the Arab fable of the white mouse who considers herself so beautiful that she will marry only the sun, the best folk tales offer a freshness that only old and diverse cultures can provide today's youngster surfeited with the canned plots and characters of television, movies, and comic books."[3]

In 1961, Sargent Shriver asked Ashabranner to develop the first Peace Corps program in Nigeria, where he was stationed for the Agency for International Development. Later he was transferred to India where he became a director of their Peace Corps program from 1964-1966. "My years with the Peace Corps spanned all of two presidential administrations and the early months of a third. I saw it grow from an idea in a campaign speech to an organization with more than fifteen thousand volunteers working in sixty countries around the world. Over thirty-five thousand volunteers and staff served in it during those eight and a half years, and I knew many hundreds of them personally.

"My own personal Peace Corps contains such memories as that of a volunteer in Nigeria bitten by a green mamba and the tragic death in the Bay of Bengal of one of the loveliest women volunteers I ever knew. I remember my difficult decision to pull our volunteers from Biafra. I vividly recall my tense, prolonged negotiations that determined, in the earliest days of the Peace Corps, whether we would be invited to have a progam in Nigeria, where, in a sense, Shriver's reputation was on the line.

"There are very different kinds of memories. I remember once at the end of a frustrating day of desk work in New Delhi picking up a letter from a schoolgirl in the south Indian city of Visakhapatnam, where we had a volunteer teacher assigned. The letter contained a poem emtitled 'Thank You, America, for Sending Margery Donk.' The iambic pentameter was a bit shaky and the heroic efforts to find words that rhymed with 'Donk' were only marginally successful, but there was no questioning the depth of feeling the girl had for her Peace Corps volunteer teacher.

"Margery changed her name to Mrs. Richard Beeler when she married a volunteer who was teaching in a nearby town. They came to Delhi for the wedding, and I stood in for her father when the moment came to give Margery away. I'm not sure I can remember all of the Peace Corps brides I have given away, but they are a part of emotional investment in the Peace Corps.

"The experiences of a Peace Corps staff person are of course quite different from those of volunteers. He spends his time working with government officials in developing new programs and in trying, with sharply varying degrees of success, to help volunteers in their work. Between these two kinds of work, the staff man probably builds an emotional investment in the Peace Corps that, while different, is equal to that of the volunteer. My point is that, volunteer or staff, the Peace Corps becomes very much 'his' through an accumulation of strongly felt, emotion-charged experiences and not through devotion to some abstract ideals of service."[4]

In 1966, Ashabranner moved to Washington, D.C. and took over as director of all volunteer training. The following year President Johnson named him Deputy Director of the Peace Corps. He chronicled his experience in *A Moment in History: The First Ten Years of the Peace Corps*, published in 1971. "...My interest in writing this book was not to record a personal memoir. Rather it was to chart the growth of the Peace Corps idea. Where stories of my personal experiences appear in the pages ahead, they are not there because they are my experiences but because they illustrate some point about the Peace Corps' development that I could make more clearly than with secondhand material. Fortunately, several memoirs by former Peace Corps volunteers are now in print, and I have not tried to compete with them. I have tried to do what I think has not yet been done: tell the story of the Peace Corps' philosophical and political development."[4]

Although Ashabranner resigned the Corps in 1969, he remained actively involved in overseas education, working for various charitable agencies. From 1972 to 1980, he worked for the Ford Foundation as associate representative and population program officer. "Since leaving the Ford Foundation in 1980, I have spent most of my time writing books for young readers.

"Most of my books for children and young adults, beginning with *The Lion's Whiskers* in 1959, have been about cross-cultural encounters or have explored cultures other than my own. The things I felt I was learning about understanding other cultures and about people of different cultures trying to understand each other seemed worth sharing with young readers. Since returning to the United States to live, I have concentrated on nonfiction and have written mostly about minorities, including Native Americans, and the growing ethnic groups in America. My years of living and working overseas have helped me to understand better their hopes, desires, frustrations, and fears.

"Most of my books for upper elementary, junior high, and high school students deal with complex cross-cultural issues and problems: the changing nature of U.S. immigration in *The New Americans*, the desire of young American Indians to succeed in the dominant white culture while retaining their tribal heritage in *To Live in Two Worlds*, the genocidal threat to Guatemalan Indians in *Children of the Maya*, the melding of cultures along our frontier with Mexico in *The Vanishing Border* (all Dodd).

"Occasionally an adult will express to me some astonishment and—usually tactful—skepticism that young readers can understand or would be interested in such subjects.

"I believe subjects that involve cross-cultural issues and problems can be made interesting to readers of all ages because they deal with conflict on all levels—conflict between people, conflict with a strange environment, conflicting desires within a person. The latter may be the hardest of all to resolve. The poverty-stricken Cheyenne Indian in *Morning Star, Black Sun* must decide between a great deal of money and the destruction of the sacred land of his ancestors. The Korean immigrant in *The New Americans* sees the educational opportunities in America for her children but longs for the familiar traditions, the loved ones, the language of her homeland.

"Paul Conklin's photographs illustrated most of my recent books. Good illustrations are essential to most young readers' nonfiction today. Properly done, they expand the text and contribute to a more interesting, more readable, more informative book. In Paul I have a master who sets the very highest standards for himself. We first met almost thirty years ago when I was starting the Peace Corps program in Nigeria, and Paul was an adventurous young free-lance photographer learning to make a living with his camera. Later he joined the Peace Corps as a staff photographer and visited me in India when I was directing the Peace Corps program there. Paul and I care about the same things. Usually we develop a book idea together, and we always travel together while we collect material, sharing every experience. When the time

Jacket of the 1987 Putnam reissue.

Detail from the jacket of the 1989 Putnam edition of *Always to Remember*.

comes for me to lock myself in my study and write, I have Paul's wonderful black-and-white pictures to help keep mood and memory alive.

"I love the work I do, and there have been few disappointments. Perhaps the only regret I have is that it is difficult to stay in touch with most of the people I write about. Our paths seldom cross again, and these people do not write many letters. But occasionally I do get some feedback, and usually it is heart-warming. When Paul and I were gathering material for *The Vanishing Border,* we had a chance to visit a migrant farmworker family who had appeared in *Dark Harvest* and who were then in their winter home in Texas. In the tiny living room of their house was a small table on which lay the copy of *Dark Harvest* we had sent them. The wife said, 'Our friends'—she meant their migrant farm-worker friends—"'still come to look at the book. They can't believe people like us could be in a book.' I did receive a letter from a young girl who had spent her entire life in migrant camps; she gave me a box number in Florida where I could send a copy of the book, and I did. Her letter, in its entirety, said, 'Thank you for the book. What you wrote is true. I like the part about me best.' *Dark Harvest* received the Carter G. Woodson Book Award and was a *Boston Globe-Horn Book* Honor Book, and I am proud of those awards. But I am at least as proud of that letter from the migrant farmworker girl in Florida.

"No matter what social issues or problems my books may deal with, I have one overriding hope for each of them: that the people I write about will emerge as human beings who have lives that are real and valuable and who have a right to a decent life. If I can get that truth across, young readers will hear it and know what I am talking about."[1]

Most of Ashabranner's books have begun with a social grievance, with such issues as the immigrant, or the financial plight of minorities. "But *Always to Remember* began in my heart. There is no other way to say it. I was walking on the Mall in Washington, D.C., one lovely April day. I knew that the Vietnam Veterans Memorial was there, but I had not yet visited it.

"Then, suddenly, I came upon it: a long, V-shaped black granite wall cut into a small, contoured hill in the quiet, tree-sheltered park called Constitution Gardens. I walked slowly to the place where the east and west wings of the wall intersect. Many people were at the memorial, but it was as if I were there alone. I looked at the names engraved on the wall—the names of over 58,000 young American men and women killed or missing in the Vietnam War. They stretched west toward the Lincoln Memorial, east toward the Washington Monument, in a seemingly endless litany in stone. Tears came to my eyes. I did not know it then, but *Always to Remember* was born at that moment.

"The Vietnam Veterans Memorial, built entirely by private contributions, has been hailed as one of the great war memorials and praised for its 'extraordinary sense of dignity and nobility.' Since its inauguration in 1982, this simple black wall of names has become Washington's most-visited memorial.

"In *Always to Remember* I wanted to tell the human story of the Vietnam Veterans Memorial. It is the story of Jan C. Scruggs, a Vietnam veteran determined that every American man and woman who died in the Vietnam War should have his or her name on a national memorial; he would not listen to those who said it could not be built. It is the story of Maya Ying Lin, an architectural student at Yale, who in a magic half-hour at the memorial site envisioned a design that was chosen over designs by some of America's most famous architects and artists. But more than anything, I hope that my book is the story of millions of Americans who have found in the memorial an emotional meeting ground that has helped to bring a divided nation together."[5]

One of Ashabranner's most recent book also deals with bringing a nation together. *Counting America: The Story of the United States Census*, on which he worked with his daughter, Melissa, was published by Putnam in 1989. "I think my life and work overseas have helped me to be a better writer about my country.

"My wife and I moved to Williamsburg, Virginia. This cradle of American democracy is a quiet and

wonderfully rich place for me to write about my country, which is exactly what I want to do at this point in my life. A delightful bonus is that my family has been able to be a part of my life as a writer. My wife Martha frequently travels with me, helps with interviews, and has taken photographs for some of my books and articles. My daughter Melissa lives in nearby Washington, D.C. We collaborated on *Into a Strange Land,* the book about unaccompanied refugee children, and on *Counting America,* which is about the United States census and its importance. My daughter Jennifer lives in Alexandria, Virginia. She took the photographs for *Always to Remember.*

"I have lived long enough and seen enough of the world to know what a fortunate man I am."[2]

Footnote Sources:

[1] Brent Ashabranner, "Did You Really Write That for Children?," *Horn Book,* November/December, 1988.
[2] "Brent Ashabranner," publicity.
[3] R. G. Davis and B. Ashabranner, "Harvesting Folk Tales," *Horn Book,* April, 1960.
[4] B. Ashabranner, *A Moment in History: The First Ten Years of the Peace Corps,* Doubleday, 1971.
[5] "Always to Remember: The Story of the Vietnam Veterans Memorial," *Junior Literary Guild,* April-September, 1988.

■ For More Information See

American Mercury, August, 1953 (pg. 13ff).
Time, December 14, 1953.
New York Times, August 23, 1954.
Booklist, April 15, 1959.
New York Herald Tribune Book Review, May 10, 1959.
School Library Journal, November 15, 1959.
Horn Book, February, 1960, April, 1961 (p. 142ff), October, 1963.
Saturday Review, February 20, 1960.
Kirkus Reviews, March 1, 1962.
New York Times Book Review, August 5, 1962, April 4, 1971.
Book Week, November 10, 1963.
Library Journal, August, 1971.
Choice, October, 1971.
Times Educational Supplement, January 2, 1976.
Junior Literary Guild, March, 1984, October, 1987-March, 1988, April-September, 1988.
Washington Post Book World, June 8, 1986.

Collections:

Kerlan Collection at the University of Minnesota.

Beverly Cleary

Born April 12, 1916, in McMinnville, Ore.; daughter of Chester Lloyd (a farmer) and Mable (a teacher; maiden name, Atlee) Bunn; married Clarence T. Cleary (an accountant), October 6, 1940; children: Marianne Elisabeth, Malcolm James. *Education:* Chaffey Junior College, Ontario, Calif., A.A., 1936; University of California, Berkeley, B.A., 1938; University of Washington, Seattle, B.A. in Librarianship, 1939. *Address:* c/o William Morrow & Co., 105 Madison Ave., New York, N.Y. 10016.

■ Career

Public Library, Yakima, Wash., children's librarian, 1939-40; U.S. Army Hospital, Oakland, Calif., post librarian, 1943-45; writer for young people, 1950—. *Member:* Authors Guild.

■ Awards, Honors

Young Readers' Choice Award from the Pacific Northwest Library Association, 1957, for *Henry and Ribsy,* 1960, for *Henry and the Paper Route,* 1968, for *The Mouse and the Motorcycle,* 1971, for *Ramona the Pest,* and 1980, for *Ramona and Her Father;* Dorothy Canfield Fisher Memorial Chil-

dren's Book Award from the Vermont Congress of Parents and Teachers, 1958, for *Fifteen,* 1966, for *Ribsy,* and 1985, for *Dear Mr. Henshaw; Jean and Johnny* was selected one of *New York Times* Outstanding Books of the Year, 1959.

South Central Iowa Association of Classroom Teachers' Youth Award, 1968, Sue Hefly Award from the Louisiana Association of School Librarians, 1972, Surrey School Book Award from the Surrey School District, 1974, and Great Stone Face Award from the New Hampshire Library Association, 1983, all for *The Mouse and the Motorcycle;* Nene Award from Hawaii Association of School Librarians and Hawaii Library Association, 1968, for *Ribsy,* 1969, for *The Mouse and the Motorcycle,* 1971, for *Ramona the Pest,* 1972, for *Runaway Ralph,* and 1979, for *Ramona and Her Father;* William Allen White Award from the Kansas Association of School Libraries and the Kansas Teachers' Association, 1968, for *The Mouse and the Motorcycle,* and 1976, for *Socks.*

Georgia Children's Book Award from the College of Education of the University of Georgia, 1970, Sequoyah Children's Book Award from the Oklahoma Library Association, 1971, and Massachusetts Children's Book Award runner-up, 1977, all for *Ramona the Pest;* New England Round Table of Children's Librarians Honor Book, 1972, for *Henry Huggins,* and 1973, for *The Mouse and the Motorcycle;* Charlie Mae Simon Children's Book Award from the Arkansas Elementary School Council, 1973, for *Runaway Ralph.*

Distinguished Alumna Award from the University of Washington, 1975; Laura Ingalls Wilder Award from the American Library Association, 1975, for substantial and lasting contributions to children's literature; Golden Archer Award from the University of Wisconsin, 1977, for *Socks;* Children's Choice Award, second place, from the Children's Book Council, 1978; Golden Archer Award, 1977, and Mark Twain Award from the Missouri Library Association and the Missouri Association of School Librarians, 1978, both for *Ramona the Brave;* Newbery Medal Honor Book from the American Library Association, 1978, for *Ramona and Her Father,* and 1982, for *Ramona Quimby, Age 8; Boston Globe-Horn Book* Honor Book for Fiction, 1978, International Board on Books for Young People Honor Book, Tennessee Children's Book Award from the Tennessee Library Association, Utah Children's Book Award from the Children's Library Association of Utah, all 1980, Land of Enchantment Children's Book Award from the New Mexico Library Association, and Texas Bluebonnet Award from the Texas Library Association, both 1981, and Sue Hefly Award Honor Book, 1982, all for *Ramona and Her Father;* one of *School Library Journal's* Best Books of the Year, 1979, American Book Award, Surrey School Book Award, both 1982, and Buckeye Children's Book Award from the State Library of Ohio, 1985, all for *Ramona and Her Mother.*

Regina Medal from the Catholic Library Association, 1980, for continued distinguished contributions to children's literature; Garden State Children's Choice Award from the New Jersey Library Association, 1980, for *Ramona and Her Father,* 1982, for *Ramona and Her Mother,* 1984, for *Ramona Quimby, Age 8,* and 1985, for *Ralph S. Mouse;* one of *School Library Journal's* Best Books, 1981, American Book Award finalist, 1982, Charlie Mae Simon Children's Book Award from the Arkansas Elementary School Council, Michigan Young Readers' Award from the Michigan Council of Teachers, and Sunshine State Young Readers Award from the Florida Association for Media in Education, all 1984, Buckeye Children's Book Award, 1985, and West Virginia's Children's Book Award from the Wise Library, West Virginia University, 1986, all for *Ramona Quimby, Age 8;* Silver Medallion from the University of Southern Mississippi, 1982, for distinguished contributions to children's literature; *Ralph S. Mouse* was selected one of Child Study Association of America's Children's Books of the Year, 1982, *Dear Mr. Henshaw,* 1983, and *Ramona Forever,* 1985.

George G. Stone Center for Children's Books Recognition of Merit Award, 1983, for collected works; one of *School Library Journal's* Best Books, and Parents' Choice Award for Literature from the Parents' Choice Foundation, both 1982, Golden Kite Award for Fiction from the Society of Children's Book Writers, and California Association of Teachers of English Award, both 1983, Iowa Children's Choice Award from the Iowa Educational Media Association, and Sunshine State Young Readers Award runner-up, both 1985, and West Virginia Children's Book Award, 1987, all for *Ralph S. Mouse;* Parents' Choice Award for Literature, 1983, Silver Medal from the Commonwealth Club of California, one of *New York Times* Notable Books of the Year, and one *School Library Journal's* Best Books, all 1983, Newbery Medal from the American Library Association, and Christopher Award, both 1984, and Sequoyah Children's Book Award, and Massachussetts Children's Book Award from the Education Department of Salem State College, both 1986, all for *Dear Mr. Henshaw;* Hans Christian Andersen Award nominee from the United States, 1984; Golden Pen Award from Young Adult Advisory Committee of Spokane, Washington Public Library, 1984, to "the author who has given us the most reading pleasure."

Everychild Honor Citation for Children's Books from the Children's Book Council, 1985; Parent's Choice Award for Literature, one of *New York Times* Notable Books of the Year, both 1984, and Iowa Children's Choice Award, 1987, all for *Ramona Forever;* CBC Honors Program for Books from the Children's Book Council, 1985; Jeremiah Ludington Memorial Award from the Educational Paperback Association, 1987, for a significant contribution to children and paperback books.

■ Writings

Henry Huggins (ALA Notable Book; illustrated by Louis Darling), Morrow, 1950.
Ellen Tebbits (illustrated by L. Darling), Morrow, 1951.
Henry and Beezus (illustrated by L. Darling), Morrow, 1952.
Otis Spofford (illustrated by L. Darling), Morrow, 1953.
Henry and Ribsy (illustrated by L. Darling), Morrow, 1954.
Beezus and Ramona (illustrated by L. Darling), Morrow, 1955.
Fifteen (illustrated by Beth Krush and Joe Krush), Morrow, 1956.

Henry and the Paper Route (illustrated by L. Darling), Morrow, 1957.

The Luckiest Girl, Morrow, 1958.

Jean and Johnny (ALA Notable Book; illustrated by B. Krush and J. Krush), Morrow, 1959.

The Real Hole (picture book; illustrated by Mary Stevens), Morrow, 1960, reissued (illustrated by Dyann DiSalvo-Ryan), 1986.

Hullabaloo ABC (picture book; verse; illustrated by Earl Thollander), Parnassus, 1960.

Two Dog Biscuits (picture book; illustrated by M. Stevens), Morrow, 1961, reissued (illustrated by D. DiSalvo-Ryan), 1986.

Emily's Runaway Imagination (illustrated by B. Krush and J. Krush), Morrow, 1961.

Henry and the Clubhouse (illustrated by L. Darling), Morrow, 1962.

Sister of the Bride (illustrated by B. Krush and J. Krush), Morrow, 1963.

Ribsy (illustrated by L. Darling), Morrow, 1964.

The Mouse and the Motorcycle (ALA Notable Book; illustrated by L. Darling), Morrow, 1965.

Mitch and Amy (illustrated by George Porter), Morrow, 1967.

Ramona the Pest (illustrated by L. Darling), Morrow, 1968.

Runaway Ralph (illustrated by L. Darling), Morrow, 1970.

Socks (illustrated by Beatrice Darwin), Morrow, 1973.

The Sausage at the End of the Nose (play), Children's Book Council, 1974.

Ramona the Brave (illustrated by Alan Tiegreen), Morrow, 1975.

Ramona and Her Father (ALA Notable Book; *Horn Book* honor list; illustrated by A. Tiegreen), Morrow, 1977.

Ramona and Her Mother (illustrated by A. Tiegreen), Morrow, 1979.

Ramona Quimby, Age 8 (illustrated by A. Tiegreen), Morrow, 1981.

Ralph S. Mouse (illustrated by Paul O. Zelinsky), Morrow, 1982.

Dear Mr. Henshaw (ALA Notable Book; *Horn Book* honor list; illustrated by P. O. Zelinsky), Morrow, 1983.

Lucky Chuck (illustrated by J. Winslow Higginbottom), Morrow, 1984.

Ramona Forever (illustrated by A. Tiegreen), Morrow, 1984.

The Ramona Quimby Diary (illustrated by A. Tiegreen), Morrow, 1984.

The Beezus and Ramona Diary (illustrated by A. Tiegreen), Morrow, 1986.

Janet's Thingamajigs (illustrated by D. DiSalvo-Ryan), Morrow, 1987.

The Growing-Up Feet (illustrated by D. DiSalvo-Ryan), Morrow, 1987.

A Girl from Yamhill: A Memoir, Morrow, 1988.

Muggie Maggie (illustrated by Kay Life), Morrow, 1990.

Cleary's books have been published in other languages, including Danish, Japanese, and Swedish. Television programs have been based on the "Henry Huggins" series. Contributor of adult short stories to magazines, including *Woman's Day* and *Wigwag*.

■ Adaptations

"Henry and the Clubhouse" (filmstrip with cassette), Pied Piper, 1962.

"Ribsy" (filmstrip with cassette), Pied Piper, 1964.

"Ramona and Her Father" (record or cassette), Miller-Brody, 1979, (filmstrip with cassette), 1980.

"Beezus and Ramona" (filmstrip with cassette; listening cassette), Miller-Brody, 1980.

"Henry Huggins" (cassette; filmstrip with cassette), Miller-Brody, 1980.

"Henry and Ribsy" (cassette), Miller-Brody, 1980.

"Ramona and Her Mother" (cassette), Miller-Brody, 1980.

"Ramona the Brave" (filmstrip with cassette; cassette), Miller-Brody, 1980.

"Ramona Quimby, Age 8" (cassette), Miller-Brody, 1981, (filmstrip with cassette), 1982.

"Henry and Beezus" (cassette), Miller-Brody, 1981.

"Ellen Tebbits" (cassette), Listening Library, 1982.

"Runaway Ralph" (cassette), Listening Library, 1983, (television film), ABC-TV, 1988.

"Ralph S. Mouse" (cassette), Miller-Brody, 1983, (television film), ABC-TV, 1991.

"Dear Mr. Henshaw" (cassette), Miller-Brody, 1984, (filmstrip with cassette), 1985.

"Socks" (cassette), Listening Library, 1985.

"Jean and Johnny" (cassette), Listening Library, 1986.

"Emily's Runaway Imagination" (cassette), Listening Library, 1986.

"Ramona Forever" (filmstrip with cassette), Miller-Brody, 1986.

"Siblingitis" (film; based on *Ramona Forever*), Atlantis Film Productions, 1988.

"The Patient" (film; based on *Ramona Quimby, Age 8*), Atlantis Film Productions, 1988.

"Ramona" (ten-part television series; based on *Ramona and Her Mother, Ramona Quimby, Age 8,* and *Ramona Forever*), PBS-TV, fall, 1988.

"The Mouse and the Motorcycle" (two-part television show), ABC-TV, 1986.

■ Work in Progress

Strider, a sequel to *Dear Mr. Henshaw; Patsy's Bedtime Story,* a picture book.

■ Sidelights

"Many words are needed to describe my mother: small, pert, vivacious, talkative, fun-loving, excitable, easily fatigued, depressed, discouraged, determined. Her best features were her brown eyes; her shining black hair, which grew to a widow's peak on her forehead; her even white teeth; and her erect carriage. She had a round nose and a sallow complexion, both distressing to her, but she made up for these shortcomings with her sense of style.

"Mother was born Mable Atlee in Dowagiac, Michigan, and became a classic figure of the westward emigration movement, the little schoolmarm from the East who stepped off a train in the West to teach school.

"From this period of her life [she saved] a copy of *The Biography of a Grizzly,* by Ernest Thompson Seton, which had been sent by friends in Michigan. She told me that after she read the book aloud in Waterville, her pupils told their families about it. People began to come from miles around to borrow the book, which was read until its binding was frayed and its pages loosened, but Mother treasured it and in her old age wrote inside the cover in a shaky hand, 'This book is very soiled because it has been read by many many people, including boys and girls.'"[1]

During a summer trip Cleary's mother met her father: "There, sitting on the steps of the store, was a tall, handsome young man wearing a white sweater and eating a pie, a whole pie. This man was Chester Lloyd Bunn. He and my mother were married on December 26, 1907, in Vancouver, Washington.

"The life of a farmer's wife came as a shock to my small, high-strung mother, ill equipped for long hours and heavy work.

"On April 12, 1916, I was born in the nearest hospital, which was in McMinnville. Mother traveled there by train and lived in a hospital for a week while she awaited my birth. It was wartime, and there was a shortage of nurses, so she busied herself running the dust mop and helping around the hospital until I was born.

"Father was the grandson of pioneers on both sides of his family. All through my childhood, whenever a task was difficult, my parents said, 'Remember your pioneer ancestors.' Life had not been easy for them; we should not expect life to be easy for us. If I cried when I fell down, Father said, 'Buck up, kid. You'll pull through. Your pioneer ancestors did.'

"I came to resent those exemplary people who were, with one exception, a hardy bunch. My Great-grandmother Bunn was rarely mentioned. I pictured them all as old, grim, plodding eternally across the plains to Oregon. As a child, I simply stopped listening. In high school, I scoffed, 'Ancestor worship.' Unfortunately, no one pointed out

Beverly Cleary
HENRY HUGGINS

Jacket of the 1950 award winner.

that some of those ancestors were children. If they had, I might have pricked up my ears.

"The three of us. . .lived or 'rattled around,' as Mother put it—in the two-story house with a green mansard roof set on eighty acres of rolling farmland in the Willamette Valley. To the west, beyond the barn, we could see forest and the Coast Range. To the east, at the other end of a boardwalk, lay the main street, Maple, of Yamhill.

"The big old house, once the home of my grandfather, John Marion Bunn, was the first fine house in Yamhill, with the second bathtub in Yamhill County. Mother said the house had thirteen rooms. I count eleven, but Mother sometimes exaggerated. Or perhaps she counted the bathroom, which was precisely what the word indicates—a room off the kitchen for taking a bath. . . .The house also had three porches and two balconies, one for sleeping under the stars on summer nights until the sky clouded over and rain fell.

"The roof was tin. Raindrops, at first sounding like big paws, pattered and then pounded, and hail crashed above the bedroom where I slept in an iron crib in the warmest spot upstairs, by the wall against the chimney from the wood range in the kitchen below.

"In the morning I descended from the bedroom by sliding down the banister railing, which curved at the end to make a flat landing place just right for my bottom. At night I climbed the long flight of stairs alone, undressed in the dark because I could not reach the light, and went to bed. I was not afraid and did not know that other children were tucked in bed and kissed good night by parents not too tired to make an extra trip up a flight of stairs after a hard day's work.

"In good weather, I followed my father around the farm, listening while he explained his work and taught me the rules I must obey.

"Winter days belonged entirely to Mother and were spent in the kitchen, where it was warm. I stood at the window watching the weather, the ever-changing Oregon clouds that sometimes hung so low they hid the Coast Range, rain that slanted endlessly on the bleak brown fields, stubble stiff with frost, and, sometimes, a world made clean and white by snow.

"Because we were lonely for companionship, Mother talked while she boiled clothes in a copper wash boiler, ironed, baked, or worked at her hated chore, washing and scalding the cream separator. She recited lines she must have learned from an

Cleary's 1955 hardcover edition.

elocution class in Chicago when she was a girl. 'There it stands above the warehouse door'—dramatic pause, thump of the iron on the ironing board—'Scrooge and Marley.' These words from Dickens's *Christmas Carol* to me were mysterious and filled with foreboding.

"My one companion was my cousin Winston; we were 'practically twins' because we were born a month apart. But Winston, who took after my father's side of the family, was large, good-natured, and deliberate in thought and movement. I, who took after Mother's side of the family, was small, impetuous, and quick.

"I longed to play, really play, with other children. A cousin, I somehow felt, did not count as 'other children.'

"My picture books were a book of Jell-O recipes that showed shimmering pastel desserts, and advertisements in the *Saturday Evening Post*, *Ladies' Home Journal*, and *Country Gentleman*.

"I owned two books: the Volland edition of *Mother Goose* and a linen book, *The Story of the Three*

Bears, in which Mother Bear, returning from her walk, carried a beautiful bouquet of purple violets. Mother read both books until I had memorized them."[1]

When Cleary was five, her mother established the first library in Yamhill. "Mother, too, was starved for books, perhaps to take her mind off her worries. 'Yamhill needs a library,' she said. 'There is entirely too much gossip. People would be better off reading books.'

"Somehow, in spite of all her work, Mother summoned energy to start a campaign for a library....She asked for donations of books and a bookcase or cupboard that could be locked. A glass china cupboard was carried upstairs to the Commercial Clubrooms over the Yamhill Bank. The community donated books, boring grown-up books with dull pictures that were a disappointment to me.

"Mother persisted. She arranged a silver tea to raise money for the library, and someone gave a luncheon at which a woman played a saxophone solo. The library now had sixteen dollars! Mother called a meeting for the purpose of securing a traveling state library for Yamhill.

"Crates of books began to arrive from the Oregon State Library in Salem. At last Yamhill had books for children—and what good books there were! The first I recall was Joseph Jacobs's *More English Fairy Tales,* which included a gruesome little tale called 'The Hobyahs.' I was so attached to that story that Mother had to pry the book out of my fingers at bedtime.

"Books by Beatrix Potter were among the many that came out of those state library crates. My favorite was *The Tailor of Gloucester;* not only because I loved the story, but because of the picture of the waistcoat so beautifully embroidered by mice. I studied that picture and knew that someday I wanted to sew beautifully, too.

"That brave little library brightened the lives of many of us that winter, and in the spring, when flowers bloomed again, the library had a hundred and forty-two books in addition to sixty-two state books."[1]

"Then in the early 1920s came a year...when a rich harvest did not bring in enough money to pay the debts and meet the needs of three people—a year symbolized for me by my mother going about her work in rubbers to spare her shoes.

"A decision was made. We would rent the farm and move to [Portland, Oregon] to seek our fortunes—a precarious step, for the children of pioneers, unaware that the world was changing, had educated their daughters but not their sons. My father had been reared to farm the land settled by his grandparents, not to live in the city. To a six-year-old the move meant that at last I would have what I longed for: someone to play with and a big library full of books which I would learn to read."[2]

"I recall my pleasure upon entering the first grade at seeing above the blackboard in room 1 a reproduction of Sir Joshua Reynolds' painting 'The Age of Innocence.' I was filled with admiration for the pretty little girl who was wearing, to my six-year-old eyes, a white party dress. I loved that little girl, but by Thanksgiving my love had changed to resentment. There she sat under a tree with nothing to do but keep her party dress clean. There

Paperback edition of the 1956 novel.

I sat itching in my navy blue serge sailor dress, the shrunken elastic of my new black bloomers cutting into my legs, struggling to learn to read.

"We had no bright beckoning book covers with such words as 'fun,' 'adventure,' or 'horizon' to tempt us on. No children played, no dogs romped, no ships sailed or planes flew on the covers of our schoolbooks. Our primer looked grim. Its olive-green cover with its austere black lettering bore the symbol of a beacon light, presumably to guide us and to warn us the dangers that lay within.

"The sight of that book's olive-green cover still brings back the feelings of bewilderment I experienced that year when I was confined to a city classroom full of strange children after a life of freedom and isolation on a farm; it brings back the anger, guilt, and despair some of us endured that first year of school while the girl in the white party dress sat there smiling serenely above the blackboard.

"The first grade was soon sorted into three reading groups—Bluebirds, Redbirds, and Blackbirds. I was a Blackbird, the only girl Blackbird among the boy Blackbirds who had to sit in the row by the blackboard. Perhaps this was the beginning of my sympathy for the problems of boys. How I envied the bright, self-confident Bluebirds, most of them girls, who got to sit by the windows and who, unlike myself, pleased the teacher by remembering to write with their right hands—a ridiculous thing to do in my six-year-old opinion. Anyone could see that both hands were alike. One should use the hand nearer the task.

"Even Redbirds in the center rows were better off than Blackbirds. To be a Blackbird was to be disgraced. I wanted to read, but somehow I could not. I wept at home while my puzzled mother tried to drill me on the dreaded word charts. 'But reading is fun,' insisted my mother. I stamped my feet and threw the book on the floor. Reading was *not* fun!

"At school we Blackbirds struggled along, bored by our primer, baffled when our reading group gathered in the circle of little chairs in the front of the room to stumble over the phonic lists. 'Sin, sip, sit, red, rill, till, tin, tip, bib, bed.' The words meant nothing.

"Memorizing rules which we chanted in unison was easier, even though we might be too frightened or confused to apply these rules. 'E on the end makes *a* say *a* in cake.' At least we were anonymous. Sounding out words in chorus, *c a t,*

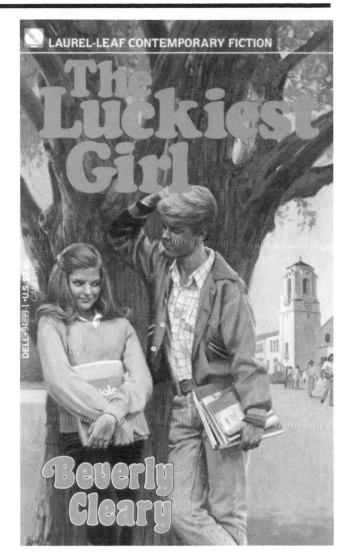

Cover of the Laurel Leaf softbound edition.

our voices mingling with those of the Bluebirds and Redbirds, was less painful than trying to decipher, 'lad, lag, lap' when our turn came in the dreaded reading circle. When a wretched Blackbird lost his place during word drill, he was banished to the cloakroom to huddle among the muddy rubbers and lunch bags that smelled of peanut butter. Once the teacher switched my hands with a bamboo pointer with a metal tip for not paying attention. I was too ashamed to tell my parents.

"In the second grade this Blackbird, although not exactly taking wing, at least got off the ground. No serene little girl in a clean party dress made me feel inferior; Washington crossed the Delaware above this blackboard and apparently did not know that one should never stand up in a rowboat. The teacher was kind and gentle; crowds of children were no longer bewildering. I could tell my right hand from my left, although I was still skeptical about the necessity for doing so. We were not made anxious by bird labels, and probably the former Blackbird had reached that mysterious point in life now known as reading readiness.

"At any rate, I was able to plod through my reader a step or two ahead of disgrace, but here another problem presented itself. Although I could read if I wanted to, I no longer wanted to. Reading was not fun. It was boring. Most of the stories were simplified versions of folk tales that had been read aloud to me many times. There was no surprise left. One story was an exception—the story of Goody Two-Shoes, who tripped about the village with her basket of letters teaching children to read. A former Blackbird was unable to identify with Goody and, in fact, disliked her.

"Then in the third grade, the miracle happened. It was a dull rainy Portland Sunday afternoon when there was nothing to do but thumb through two books from the Sunday-school library. After looking at the pictures, I began out of boredom to read *The Dutch Twins* by Lucy Fitch Perkins. Twins had

Cover of the 1959 ALA Notable Book.

fascinated me as a small child living on a farm where magazines were my only picture books. Each week I had searched the *Saturday Evening Post* for the pictures of the Campbell Soup twins. To a solitary child, the idea of twins was fascinating. A twin would always have someone to play with; a twin would never be lonely. Now here was a whole book about twins, a boy and girl who lived in Holland but who had experiences a girl in Portland, Oregon, could share. I could laugh when the boy twin fell into the Zuyder Zee because I had once fallen into the Yamhill River during a church picnic. Here was a book with a story in which something happened. With rising elation I read on. I read all afternoon and evening and by bedtime I had read not only *The Dutch Twins* but *The Swiss Twins* as well. It was one of the most exciting days of my life. Shame and guilt dropped away from the ex-Blackbird who had at last taken wing. I could read and read with pleasure! Grownups were right after all. Reading was fun.

"From the third grade on, I was a reader, and when my school librarian suggested that I should write children's books when I grew up, I was ecstatic. Of course! This was exactly what I wanted to do."[3]

"When I reported all this to Mother, she said, 'If you are going to become a writer, you must have a steady way of earning your living.' This sound advice was followed by a thoughtful pause before she continued, 'I have always wanted to write myself.'

"My career decision was lightly made. The Rose City Branch Library—quiet, tastefully furnished, filled with books and flowers—immediately came to mind. I wanted to work in such a place, so I would become a librarian."[1]

"And so, with some hardship to my parents, I was sent off to college, not to catch a husband, as was the custom for young women of that time and place, but to become independent. I became a children's librarian, the next best thing to a writer."[4]

"About the time I began to feel I might survive my career as a new children's librarian in Yakima, Washington, a Sister of St. Joseph told me she had in her class a group of boys who were not interested in reading. She thought perhaps the fault lay in their school books. She asked if she might send the boys to the library once a week for help in selecting books that they might find interesting and which would stimulate them to read.

"However, they soon presented a problem I had not met in work with children who came voluntarily to the library—there was very little in the library those boys wanted to read. They all demanded funny stories just as I had demanded funny stories from the children's librarian when I was their age. Like the librarian of my childhood, I was forced to turn to folk tales for easy humor, only to have the boys reject the books I offered.

"'Don't you have any books about kids like us?' they asked. No I did not. The boys compromised by accepting animal stories, and most of those were too difficult for these readers. I consulted lists and catalogs and concluded there were very few right books for these children.

"For the first time I began to question the books published for children....Where were the funny stories for children past picture books? Why were there almost no stories, lively and easy to read, about ordinary middle-class children and ordinary middle-class pets? Why did book dogs always live in the country? Why were all the stories about the Pacific Northwest pioneer stories? Didn't authors know the West had been won and that Oregon and Washington had been settled long enough to have cities? Where were the books about children who attended parochial schools? (I still wonder about this.) And why did children in books have to reform at the end of the story? These were questions the non-readers forced me to consider, questions that took me back to my own childhood reading.

"I found disappointing, even objectionable, any book in which a child accepted the wisdom of an adult and reformed, any book in which a child reformed at all, any book in which problems were solved by a long-lost rich relative turning up in the last chapter, any book in which a family was grateful for the gift of a basket of groceries, usually on Christmas Eve, or any book in which a child turned out to be lord of the manor or heir to a fortune. These things did not happen in my neighborhood. Neither did I want to read about a noble dog who died in the last chapter after a long journey home on bleeding paws nor any book in which a pioneer girl ran through the forest to warn settlers of Indians.

"Ten years after leaving Yakima, I finally sat down to write the children's book I had planned to write since childhood."[5]

"After the war, my husband and I bought a house in the Berkeley Hills, and in the linen closet I found several reams of typing paper. 'Now I'll have to write a book,' I remarked to my husband.

"'Why don't you?' he asked.

"'Because we never have any sharp pencils,' I answered.

"The next day he brought home a pencil sharpener and I realized that if I was ever going to write a book, this was the time to do it. I sat down at a table in our spare bedroom and began a story based on an incident that had once amused me about two children who had to take their dog home on a streetcar during a heavy rain. This turned into a story about a boy who would be allowed to keep a stray dog if he could manage to take him home on a bus. When I finished that chapter I found I had ideas for another chapter and at the end of two months I had a whole book about Henry Huggins and his dog Ribsy.

"I wasn't quite sure what to do with the manuscript; so I typed my name and address on the title page and mailed it to William Morrow and Company because I had heard that Elisabeth Hamilton, who was then editor, was one of the best and because I had once heard an author remark that Morrow was kind to authors. The book was promptly accepted and I was suddenly dismayed to find that I was the author of a book about a small boy. At that time I had no children. What *had* I done? I didn't know a thing about small boys. I went straight to the library and read up on small boys in Gesell and was enormously relieved to find that Henry Huggins was psychologically sound, and that I really did know quite a bit about boys.

"Other books followed, and I continued to have ideas about Henry Huggins. *Henry and Ribsy* sprang from a suggestion made by my father who thought it would make a funny story if Henry and his father took Ribsy salmon fishing and Ribsy was so frightened by a salmon flopping around in the boat that he jumped out and tried to swim away. The idea appealed to me because, as a child, vacations along the Oregon coast had meant so much to me. My husband and I took a trip up the Oregon coast during salmon-fishing season and I stood at the mouth of the Rogue River and watched salmon being caught. This reminded me of the time my cousin caught a salmon with his bare hands when he was about Henry's age and I knew I had the end of my story. Henry, I decided, wanted more than anything to catch a salmon, but his father would not agree to take him fishing unless there were no complaints from the neighbors about Ribsy for the whole summer.

"When I am working on a book, ideas have the most delightful way of popping up unexpectedly. We had our car lubricated and it occurred to me that Henry would like to ride up on the grease rack and a dilemma could easily develop if he was in a car on the grease rack and his dog on the ground. A neighbor remarked that her son disliked taking out the garbage and I was reminded that the dog next door always barked furiously when the garbage men came. Of course Ribsy would feel that the garbage men were trying to steal the garbage. A dog eating a small girl's ice cream cone was the inspiration for another chapter, *Henry and Ribsy* was an easy book to write and I had a good time writing it.

"Adults often ask if I try out my stories on children before submitting the manuscripts to my publisher. They also want to know how I go about grading my stories for a certain reading level and if I use a word list. These questions always surprise me because they make writing sound like such hard work."[6]

"As I wrote I discovered I had a collaborator, the child within myself—a rather odd, serious little girl, prone to colds, who sat in a child's rocking chair with her feet over the hot air outlet of the furnace, reading for hours, seeking laughter in the pages of books while her mother warned her she would ruin her eyes. That little girl, who has remained with me, prevents me from writing down to children, from poking fun at my characters, and from writing an adult reminiscence about childhood instead of a book to be enjoyed by children. And yet I do not write solely for that child; I am also writing for my adult self. We are collaborators who must agree. The feeling of being two ages at one time is delightful, one that surely must be a source of great pleasure to all writers of books enjoyed by children.

"Although for over forty years I have been absorbed in stories that spring from the humor of everyday life, I try not to think about humor while writing, because of the sound advice given me by my first editor Elisabeth Hamilton. . . .'Darlin,' she said, 'don't *ever* analyze it. Just do it.' I have followed her advice. While I am writing, if I find myself thinking about humor and what makes a story humorous, I am through for the day; and that chapter usually goes into the wastebasket, for spontaneity has drained out of my work. Although introspection is valuable to every writer, I find that analyzing my own work is harmful because it makes writing self-conscious rather than intuitive.

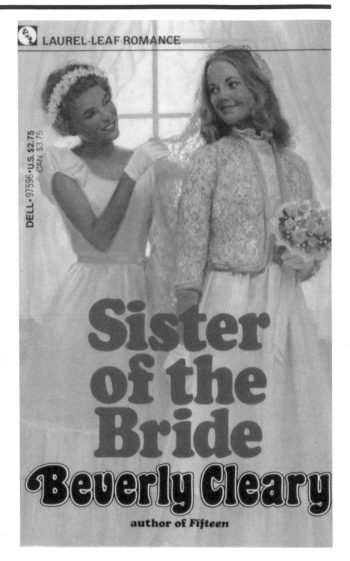

LAUREL-LEAF ROMANCE

DELL•97596•U.S. $2.75 CAN $3.75

Sister of the Bride

Beverly Cleary

author of *Fifteen*

Dell's 1981 paperback edition.

"By the time I had published five books, several things had happened which forced me to think about children and humor: I had children of my own, twins—a boy and a girl; reviews said my books were hilarious or genuinely funny; a textbook on children's literature said my books were to be read 'purely for amusement'; and enough children had written to me to give me some insight into their thoughts about my books.

"One phrase began to stand out in these letters from children. Letter after letter told me my books were 'funny and sad.'

"The insistence on the part of many children that my books were funny and sad, while adults and other children found them funny, made me wonder where the sadness left off and the laughter began. In seeking the answer I began to observe my own children. At seven months they delighted me by laughing when I recited 'The Three Little Kittens' and by making a gleeful game of refusing to open their mouths for the next bite until I spoke another line. As they grew I looked forward to the day when they would be ready for stories. What fun it was going to be—one active, outgoing boy and one quiet, imaginative girl—both full of laughter.

"I soon discovered that this pair, so full of fun but with such different personalities, were in complete agreement. *Books were serious.* No matter how funny I thought a book, no matter how lively my reading, they found nothing to laugh about....I read a rousing (I thought) rendition of Ruth Krauss's *A Very Special House* (Harper)—a funny book about a house in which children could do anything they pleased. 'Hooie, hooie, hooie,' shouted the children, interrupting to imitate the sounds of the story; but when I had finished reading, both were silent, thinking. Then my son spoke up. 'But Mommy,' he said, 'you aren't *supposed* to jump on chairs.' He had me there. I had failed my children. They were too well be-haved, and I was too good a housekeeper. They would never laugh at a story. They did laugh, however, at *Beady Bear* by Don Freeman. I was saved.

"*Ramona the Pest,* a book I thought about for fifteen years before writing, was the result of listening to children's requests, and it has proven to be one of my most popular books with children from kindergarten through junior high school. Many children tell me they laugh at Ramona because they used to act like her or because they have a little brother or sister exactly like her, implying that they are now much too grown-up to behave like that little brother or sister....I feel that books that help children laugh at their youn-ger selves are the books that help them survive."[7]

A prolific writer, Cleary produced a book almost every year. Critics and children alike have re-sponded enthusiastically to her work. She received the prestigious Laura Ingalls Award, as well as more than twenty-five state and regional child-selected awards. Her books have been translated in thirteen languages, and in Japan, an abridged English-language version of *Fifteen* is used in school to teach English. "My books are most popular in Germany and Japan and England.

"My Japanese translator had quite a struggle when she was translating *Runaway Ralph.* It takes place in a children's camp, and there are many nonsense songs. She was completely baffled. I finally said, 'There *isn't* any sense to the songs. They're just nonsense.' So she told me that she had to make up

her own, but she didn't think they were as good as mine. And in *Dear Mr. Henshaw* there's a reference to Angels Camp. She wrote...'Is this perhaps a reference to heaven?' I immediately had to look up Angels Camp; it's named after a man who discov-ered gold there."[8]

Cleary's overwhelming popularity as a writer for children is also attested by the number of letters she received from her readers—sometimes more than one hundred a day. For twenty-five years she answered all her mail, but gradually became more and more selective. "I look for letters that are genuinely childlike. Many of those *are* school letters. Many are exuberant, spontaneous, original, and a joy to answer.

"[But] if I catch the words *book report* or *project,* the letter usually goes into the wastebasket. I used to answer these long lists of questions, but, as my husband pointed out, why was I spending my time doing homework? I get so many letters that begin, 'I'm a gifted and talented child. We are studying authors. Please answer ——.' Then follows a list of twenty questions or so. If I answered all of those questions, I would have written an article that somebody would probably publish. I got a little testy once and said to one little girl that I thought a gifted and talented child should be able to use the reference books in the library. I think some teachers are teaching children to lean on other people rather than, as my mother used to say, 'stand on your own two feet.'

"And teachers more and more expect me to write letters convincing children that reading is worth-while. Oh dear, that dreadful article that appeared in *Teacher Magazine,* I believe it was, describing celebrity auctions where children were paid in play money for reading and at the end of the year bought at auction items donated by celebrities. I have received hundreds of identical letters copied from the magazine, and I feel this is teaching children to ask for free books and bracelets and tie clips. Certainly, since that letter, more children ask me for free books.

"I feel reading is its own reward, and I don't respond to those letters. Occasionally, if a teacher writes a very moving letter that comes with a batch of letters from her students, I will drop her a note and tell her why I don't participate.

"[Children] need adults to enjoy books and share books with them. That's the kind of guidance I had in mind. I feel children learn best by example. The happiest letters I get from schools say something like, 'The teacher read the book and she laughed, too,' or 'The teacher read *Dear Mr. Henshaw* and she cried on page 132.' I think children need to learn from adults that reading is important and worthwhile. The happy letters I get almost always tell of sharing books with somebody, sometimes reading with a best friend, which I used to do. We'd read the good parts to each other, or, when we got in high school, the 'juicy' parts.

"Many parents write to tell me that my books help them understand their children. Sometimes they're reading one of my books with a child, and the child will say, 'I felt that way,' and the mother had no idea. Some tell me how much my books meant in their own childhoods. These are lovely letters to receive. They are genuine communications from one human being to another."[8]

Much of what forms the backgrounds of Cleary's teen novels deals with incidents and problems common to the lives of most adolescents. Cleary has been criticized for not being entirely contemporary by the standards of some young readers. "Take the case of Mrs. Huggins," said Cleary. "When *Henry Huggins* was published in 1950, reviewers commented with approval that Henry's parents were supportive. Times and trends changed, and in 1978 there appeared in a reference book on children's writers a short critical essay which stated that 'Henry's mother is something of a stereotype, always cooking and keeping the house neat—though she did help Henry pick up nightcrawlers.' This critic overlooked the fact that Mrs. Huggins also delivered Henry's papers when Henry forgot and pitched in and helped when he was involved in a paper drive. Since Mrs. Huggins appears in the story only when she becomes involved in Henry's problems, there is no telling what she may be up to the rest of the time. Her activities, unless they concern Henry, have nothing to do with the story.

"Now let us consider the dilemma of the author who receives the first chapter of *Henry Huggins* with changes proposed for its inclusion in a textbook. When Henry telephones his mother to ask if he can keep the dog he has found, Mrs. Huggins must not say in one editor's reader, 'I don't know dear. You will have to ask your father,' a line I felt was funny because we have all heard a version of it so many times from both male and female parents. The editor informs the author that this line does not show Mrs. Huggins as a strong person. The author mulls this over. Must every female in fiction be a strong person? Fiction should mirror life. How dull fiction would be if all female characters were portrayed alike. And is poor Mrs. Huggins really

weak because she suggests her husband should be consulted, is she stalling a bit to give herself time to consider the situation, or is she considerate? Should not a father be consulted before a dog is added to the family? But wait. Farther down the page Mrs. Huggins relents and tells Henry he may keep the dog if he can bring it home on the bus. Here another thought occurs to the author but apparently not to the editor. Just possibly Mrs. Huggins is a weak person because she gives in to her son. Should the author point this out to the editor? No. Mrs. Huggins is a human being. She has both strengths and weaknesses.

"Still another textbook editor will not allow poor Mrs. Huggins to wipe her hands on her apron. It seems this simple act turns her into a stereotype. The author is chagrined, for she often wipes her own hands on her apron. Has she unknowingly become a stereotype, perhaps even a weak person? But what about her husband? At times he has not only worn an apron but wiped his hands on it. Does this mean she is a stereotype while he is an individual? The author tries to think of a male character in fiction who has been labelled a stereotype but cannot. She suspects that if Mrs. Huggins had wiped her hands on the seat of her jeans the editor would have been pleased. This somehow would make her a non-stereotyped strong person. Messy, perhaps, but strong in his eyes.

"When *Ramona and Her Father* was published, I was astonished to have several librarians remark that I had finally written about contemporary problems. I had? I feel I have been writing about small problems contemporary to children all along. And fifty years ago my father, like Ramona's father, lost his job through a merger, tried to give up smoking and became irritable, which made me fear he might not love me. A man's loss of livelihood, grimmer in those days before unemployment insurance, comes under the heading, not of contemporary problems, but of universal human experience which is the proper subject of a novel, adult or juvenile.

"All children, I feel, long to have their mothers say they love them, so this became the theme of *Ramona and Her Mother*. Mrs. Quimby's work as a doctor's receptionist brings about changes in the life of the family and some feelings of insecurity in Ramona. Women have told me they are glad Mrs. Quimby is working outside the home, and so am I, for she enjoys her work even though it was begun out of necessity, and I feel that every woman should have an interest outside her family. Whether Mrs. Quimby is liberated or enslaved remains to be seen and will probably depend upon whatever attitude is current, for these days children's books are pushed about by trends."[5]

"Fundamentally, I don't think children have changed through the years. Maybe they have acquired a certain sophistication from watching television, but it's only on the surface. Childhood is universal, and I write about childhood feelings as I knew them growing up."[4]

Footnote Sources:

[1] Beverly Cleary, *A Girl from Yamhill: A Memoir,* Morrow, 1988.
[2] B. Cleary, "Laura Ingalls Wilder Award Acceptance," *Horn Book,* August, 1975.
[3] B. Cleary, "Low Man in the Reading Circle; or, A Blackbird Takes Wings," *Horn Book,* June, 1969.
[4] B. Cleary, "Newbery Medal Acceptance," *Horn Book,* August, 1984.
[5] B. Cleary, "Regina Medal," *Catholic Library World,* July-August, 1981.
[6] B. Cleary, "Writing Books about Henry Huggins," *Top of the News,* December, 1957.
[7] B. Cleary, "The Laughter of Children," *Horn Book,* October, 1982.
[8] *Contemporary Authors New Revision Series,* Volume 19, Gale, 1987.

■ For More Information See

Books:

Charlotte Huck and D. A. Young, *Children's Literature in the Elementary School,* Holt, 1961.
Muriel Fuller, editor, *More Junior Authors,* H. W. Wilson, 1963.
May Hill Arbuthnot, *Children and Books,* 3rd edition, Scott, Foresman, 1964.
The Children's Bookshelf, Child Study Association of America, Bantam, 1965.
Nancy Larrick, *A Teacher's Guide to Children's Books,* Bobbs-Merrill, 1966.
Books for Children: 1960-1965, American Library Association, 1966.
G. Robert Carlsen, *Books and the Teen-Age Reader,* Harper, 1967.
Miriam Hoffman and Eva Samuels, *Authors and Illustrators of Children's Books,* Bowker, 1972.
Lee Bennet Hopkins, *More Books by More People,* Citation Press, 1974.
Children's Literature Review, Gale, Volume 2, 1976, Volume 8, 1985.
Lee Kingman, editor, *Newbery and Caldecott Medal Books: 1976-1985,* Horn Book, 1986.
D. L. Kirkpatrick, editor, *Twentieth-Century Children's Writers,* St. Martin's, 1978, third edition, 1989.

David Rees, *The Marble in the Water: Essays on Contemporary Writers of Fiction for Children and Young Adults,* Horn Book, 1980.
Glenn E. Estes, editor, *Dictionary of Literary Biography,* Volume 52, Gale, 1986.
Shirley Norby and Gregory Ryan, *Famous Children's Authors,* Denison, 1988.

Periodicals:

Top of the News, December, 1951 (p. 408), December, 1959 (p. 485), April, 1975, winter, 1977.
Pacific Northwest Library Association Quarterly, April, 1961.
Wilson Library Bulletin, October, 1961 (p. 179).
Elementary English, November, 1967 (p. 743ff).
Young Readers' Review, May, 1968.
Book World, September 8, 1968.
Southeastern Librarian, fall, 1968 (p. 194ff).
Horn Book, August, 1970 (p. 386), December, 1977 (p. 660), December, 1982 (p. 648), October, 1983 (p. 570), September-October, 1984 (p. 590).
Oklahoma Librarian, July, 1971 (p. 14ff).
Bulletin of the Center for Children's Books, July-August, 1975 (p. 175), December, 1977 (p. 58), September, 1982 (p. 5ff), September, 1984 (p. 2).
Growing Point, January, 1976, September, 1978, July, 1980 (p. 3736).
Publishers Weekly, February 23, 1976 (p. 54ff).
Washington Post Book World, October 9, 1977 (p. E6), July 12, 1981 (p. 6), September 12, 1982 (p. 7), August 14, 1983 (p. 7).
Times Literary Supplement, July 7, 1978, January 13, 1984, February 1, 1985.
Language Arts, January, 1979 (p. 55ff), October, 1987 (p. 619ff).
Catholic Library World, February, 1980 (p. 274ff).
New York Times Book Review, November 1, 1981 (p. 38), November 11, 1984 (p. 47), November 10, 1985 (p. 42).
Christian Science Monitor, May 14, 1982, June 6, 1983.
Early Years, August-September, 1982 (p. 24ff).
Writers Digest, January, 1983 (p. 20ff).
Washington Post, May 31, 1983, January 10, 1984.
Detroit News, August 10, 1983.
New York Times, January 11, 1984 (section III, p. 22).
St. Louis Globe-Democrat, February 13, 1984.
Instructor, November-December, 1985 (p. 22ff).
People Weekly, October 3, 1988 (p. 59ff).

Other:

"Meet the Newbery Author: Beverly Cleary" (filmstrip), Random House/Miller-Brody, n.d.

Collections:

Kerlan Collection at the University of Minnesota.

Wes Craven

(Spain), both for "The Hills Have Eyes"; Critic's Choice Award from the French Science Fiction and Horror Film Festival and Best Horror Film nomination from the Academy for Science Fiction, Fantasy, and Horror, both for "A Nightmare on Elm Street."

■ Writings

Films:

(Also director and editor) "Last House on the Left," Hallmark, 1972.

(Also director and editor) "The Hills Have Eyes," Castle Hill, 1977.

(Also director) "Deadly Blessing," United Artists, 1981.

(Also director) "Swamp Thing," AVCO-Embassy, 1981.

(Also director) "A Nightmare on Elm Street," New Line Cinema, 1984.

(Also director) "The Hills Have Eyes: Part II," Castle Hill, 1985.

(Also executive producer) "A Nightmare on Elm Street 3: Dream Warriors," New Line Cinema, 1986.

"Flowers in the Attic," New World, 1987.

Also author of film treatments and script rewrites. Writer for cabaret comedy.

Films; Director, Except As Indicated:

(Assistant producer) "Together" (also known as "Sensual Paradise"), New Line Cinema, 1971.

Born August 2, 1939, in Cleveland, Ohio; son of Paul and Caroline (Miller) Craven; married Bonnie Broecker (divorced); married second wife, 1985; children: (first marriage) Jonathan, Jessica. *Education:* Wheaton College, B.A.; Johns Hopkins University, M.A., 1964. *Agent:* Andrea Eastman, International Creative Management, 8899 Beverly Blvd., Los Angeles, Calif. 90048. *Office:* c/o Alive Films, 8271 Melrose Ave., Los Angeles, Calif. 90046.

■ Career

Westminster College, New Wilmington, Pa., instructor, beginning 1964; Clarkson University, Potsdam, N.Y., professor. Has also held positions as messenger, post-production assistant, synch-up assistant to filmmaker Sean Cunningham, director, producer, and screenwriter. *Member:* Writer's Guild of America, Director's Guild of America, Screen Actors Guild.

■ Awards, Honors

Best Director Award from the Madrid Film Festival, 1988; Best Picture Award from the London Film Festival and Sitges Film Festival Honors

(Editor) "It Happened in Hollywood," Screw Film, 1972.

(Editor) "You've Got to Walk It Like You Talk It or You'll Loose That Beat," JER Pictures, 1972.

"Deadly Friend," Warner Brothers, 1986.

"The Serpent and the Rainbow," Universal, 1988.

"Shocker," Universal, 1989.

Also co-director, "Tales to Tear Your Heart Out."

Television; Director:

"A Little Peace and Quiet," "Word Play," "Shatterday," "Chameleon," "The Road Not Taken," "Her Pilgrim Soul," and "Dealer's Choice," all "Twilight Zone," CBS-TV, 1985.

"A Stranger in Our House" (movie), NBC-TV, 1978.

"Invitation to Hell" (movie), ABC-TV, 1984.

"Chiller" (movie), CBS-TV, 1985.

Also directed "Casebusters," 1986.

■ Work in Progress

Directing films: "Artificial Intelligence" for Warner Bros., "Haunted" for Media Home Entertainment, and "Old Fears" for Highgate Productions.

■ Sidelights

With his first two films, "The Last House on the Left" and "The Hills Have Eyes," Wes Craven introduced himself as an engaging, often disturbing filmmaker. With his later films "Nightmare on Elm Street," "The Serpent and the Rainbow," and most recently "Shocker," Craven's name has become synonymous with horror. "I became 'The Guru of Gore' because that's what some writer decided to call me. I didn't set out to do that, and certainly don't think of myself in that way. I wince every time somebody calls me 'The Sultan of Slash' or 'The Maven of Mayhem,' because that's only a thin slice of me. It has become the world's entire perception because I'm very good, but it seems like an incredible waste of my spirit.

"I don't feel like I would ever want to move away from horror entirely, but there is a part of me which would like to show a little bit more of what's going on inside. (I laugh; people like me.) I would cite the career of Polansky, who has done some profoundly frightening films but, at the same time, could still do a comedy or a love story at which nobody would blink an eye."[1]

Craven's childhood experiences provided him with a foundation for his later works. He was born in Cleveland, Ohio, "a tough, fast, multi-ethnic urban center with lots of woods and streams. When I was born there, it was called 'the forest city,' a small, very beautiful, tree-lined place with decent neighborhoods and wonderful parks. But it became a bellwether city to pollution and environmental problems which would later affect the more protected places.

"By the time I was in junior high school, the lake was closed because it was polluted, infested with rats, and dead fish on its shores. The parks had also become too dangerous. There was a great influx of people from Kentucky and the southern parts of the United States who were looking for jobs. So while there was a very rich racial mixture of blacks, poor whites from the south, and Germans, Italians, and Slavs, there was also a lot of racial strife and very tough kids."[1]

When Craven was four, his father left the family. "My father was a bit of a mystery, rather scary in temperament. I still remember the day he left. There had been a lot of arguing around the house in the year or two before that, and things were stormy."[1]

Craven's father died the following year, leaving the responsibility of family in the very capable hands of his hard-working mother, a well-read woman who sought in her religion a source of strength. "It was hard for me. I was the youngest. I would go home for lunch to my best friend's family and return there after school until my mother came home from work at seven. That was my introduction to the reality of being a one-parent child. The loss of my father was profound.

"I remember the psychic tension of being without parents, mostly because my mother was working and my father wasn't there, and the sense of having to go into something that was very scary by myself. That was when I started to have nightmares. The sort of nightmare that came from the terror of being put into another family and growing up in a very tough neighborhood.

"There was one nightmare, in particular, that I've never forgotten. I was in the wrong neighborhood at the wrong time, pursued by a bully. He walked behind me, taunting me and kicking this flattened tin can. Suddenly the crushed can sailed through the air, like a little frisbee, and cut right through my Achilles tendon—a very 'Wes Craven' nightmare. Years later, I actually used it in 'The Hills

From "Last House on the Left," the first film that Craven wrote and directed.

Have Eyes,' when a dog bites through the character's Achilles tendon.

"I was introduced to the neighborhood on the new block by Bluzzy who told me to close my eyes, 'I'm gonna give you a big gift.' I was five years old—I closed my eyes. He beat me in the groin as hard as he could. Welcome to the neighborhood.

"Then there was the financial crunch. We didn't have a car until I was in high school and that was about the same for television. We were always the people with the least seniority in the apartment, and moved about seven times by the time I got into high school. We kept moving into different neighborhoods, so I was always getting to know new kids at school. But I think that's part of the reason why I became my own storyteller and learned how to think in extreme cases.

"Growing up poor and close to the bone kept my brother, sister, mother and me a tight family. It always made me grateful for whatever I was able to earn later, and also made me realize that the real foundation of strength is the family and the support you can give each other."[1]

"We were raised in the Baptist faith and our lives were very much circumscribed by the church. Our religion was very strict. The Bible was (I can still slip into their language) the holy creative word of God, was holy inspired, and should be taken word for word. There was no quibbling about whether this was a translation made by a bunch of old scholars five hundred years later or anything like that. They took everything very literally according to their interpretation, believing in the six-day creation and in the five cardinal 'No Nos': No drinking, No smoking, No dancing, No playing cards, and No movies. So that kept me a great deal out of the mainstream.

"But at that time, the church was full of its own life and we were very involved in that sort of prescribed world. It wasn't until later, when I got into high school and especially college, that I got into trouble.

"When I went to Wheaton College, a Liberal Arts fundamentalist school and *alma mater* of Billy Graham, I was in a group of young writers who were constantly in trouble. We had tried to update Christianity and make it something that made sense to us.

"I was becoming a pretty skilled writer and editor of the literary magazine. I published a beautifully

Based on DC Comics characters, Craven's fourth film, "Swamp Thing," starred Adrienne Barbeau.

written story by a gifted young writer about a white girl having a child by a black man. Then I published another story that concerned sex outside marriage. Well, I was denounced from the pulpit in Chapel, declared in dereliction of my duty, and the magazine was canceled for the rest of the year. I hold the distinction of being the only editor at Wheaton to have the literary magazine canceled."[1]

This was the first, but certainly not the last, major trouble Craven found himself in. "It was an interesting kind of trouble because it was one of ideas. You can expand that concept to realize what it would be like to live in a society like Russia where you'd be sent off to the Gulag for what you thought. Even America during Vietnam—I got in trouble for my anti-war demonstration."[1]

This sense of independence and rationality eventually caused Craven to separate from his faith. "We'd always gone to the same church, so my friendships within that church had lasted a long time. The wrenching thing was that when I left that church, the majority of those friendships died.

"My progression was an interesting one. As a graduate student at Johns Hopkins, I did a prodigious amount of intellectual work with about a dozen other young students who were struggling with the same issues. We were the literary outcasts on one hand and the literary lions on the other. We ran the magazines, wrote the yearbook, and did short stories and the like. My advisor, Elliot Coleman, was a Baltimore poet and ex-Episcopal priest who helped me a great deal in making my transition. He was our guru, a Joycean scholar, very erudite with a great sense of humor. He guided me into the writings of Baber and Tillich. I read my way through other great minds to make the transition from Christianity into a larger humanistic philosophy. I went through a period of psychedelic drugs, meditation, and eastern philosophy. I replaced those very rigid views for a broader view of consciousness and the holiness of life itself."[1]

After graduation from Johns Hopkins in 1964, Craven married and began teaching humanities at Westminster College. "Teaching was something that I did because I needed a job to support my family. My real interest was still in writing. But teaching had such great benefits as filling up at the college gas pump to having all summer off with pay. It was a great way to be around people, ideas, and books, and gave me a lot of time for reading and discussing ideas, keeping current in thought, and being challenged. So it was a very vital time.

Plus, I was around my family more at this time than I have since.

"The downside of teaching was that it was very formal and political. The basic push, and the thing that pushed me right out of teaching, was its focus on obtaining a Ph.D. A lot of people felt very entrapped by the protected lifestyle of tenure offered by the degree. Their ideas couldn't be challenged anymore.

"My interest in filmmaking really came out of left field. There was a sort of a buzz of *cinema verite*, filmmaking being written about a lot in things like *Evergreen Magazine* at the time when I found myself fascinated by it. Maybe it was due to my being disallowed films as a youngster, or the fact that my friend's father with whom I spent so much time while my mother worked was an avid filmmaker (home movies). I can't explain quite where it came from, but I basically decided to make a career move into films and left teaching."[1]

The transition from teacher to filmmaker was not quite as simple as that. Craven spent two summers looking for work before finding any, the strain of which broke his marriage. "Coming back between those two summers, I had to sort of bow my head with the realization that I couldn't go back into teaching college because I had quit my job. So I taught a year in a very poor high school and after that took a job as a messenger for a film post-production house. That was embarrassing and very, very scary because I didn't know whether I would ever get to make a film at all. In retrospect, it sounds very easy that I got a job as a messenger and then a year and a half later I was doing a film. But that was a year and a half of working all sorts of hours and going through a divorce. I was working all the time and didn't have enough money to live comfortably. I had to sell off cars and motorcycles, not pay banks, and all the while the wife was saying, 'What the hell are you doing to us!'"[1]

It was at this time that Craven met Sean Cunningham [who would later originate the "Friday the 13th" series]. "Sean was the first guy to hire me for something other than messenger. I kept the dailies for a little feature he was doing. We worked on that for about ten months and at the end of that time had a friendship. So when Sean got the offer to make a scary feature film, he said, 'Why don't we do it together?' and offered me the job of writing, directing, and cutting it.

"I was on the absolute ground floor of making a film. I had never gone to film school, never even read a book on making a film. I knew nothing about

"One, two, Freddy's comin' for you." From the 1984 movie "A Nightmare on Elm Street," starring Robert Englund as the terrifying Freddy Krueger.

coverage, screen directing, lenses and really just learned by doing."[1]

The 1972 film, "The Last House on the Left," an ultra-violent shocker about the brutal rape and torture of two teenage girls, was purportedly based on a true story. "The story outline was actually based on Bergman's 'The Virgin Spring.' We were total scam artists at the time. We even put our own rating on the film. After a continuous string of X-ratings, we finally got the negative for an R-rating and just put it on ourselves."[1]

It was tremendously successful for a low-budget film. In 1976, Cunningham and Craven followed this up with another violent thriller, "The Hills Have Eyes," which concerned a middle-class family harassed by crazies in the middle of the desert. This film received honors at the Sitges Film Festival in Spain and was named "Best Picture" at the London Film Fest.

With violence that set new standards for delighted audiences everywhere, Craven admitted that beneath the thin veneer of blood in his films, there lurked a great deal of thought. "The nuclear family has been under siege for at least the last twenty years, with profound effects. The sexual revolution and the subsequent backlash are factors, along with the Vietnam period and the destruction of the nice idea of 'the people next door,' the idea of fair play and all of it. I think the reality of the world is simply encroaching on American myth and that it must be redefined by that ragtag group of people that are not part of the Hollywood mainstream. They must at least play a part in reexamining this myth. I certainly felt this around the time of 'The Hills Have Eyes'; one phrase that kept coming up was that we were doing 'fairy tales for the apocalypse,' and this was before we were conscious of 'Apocalypse Now.'...*Heart of Darkness* [did] have some affect on my attitude toward the horror film. But more importantly, I think the horror film has become a specific way of digesting the horror that is really all around us; it's just never ending. You can't look at the annual issue of *Life* magazine without seeing piles of dead bodies, people being machine-gunned as a matter of course. It seems to be a time when people are being ground up in huge tectonic movements, these continental, psychic, cultural collisions. I don't think anybody buys the John Wayne image of how we confront violence, both collectively and in the individual.

"Before Vietnam, the image of war was the front line, which is the good guys vs. the bad guys myth that fell apart. There is no longer any such myth when you see civilians being killed all around you and this is being transmitted regularly by the media. The only way to survive this is by an enormous cynicism unless you are ready to confront the myth. I also wanted to confront the idea that the average citizen is incapable of violence, that he or she is supposed to turn the other cheek. In both my early films, much of the violence is carried out by the 'whitebread' types, the middle-American families. I *always* resented the way Hollywood glossed over this, although it's a more predominant theme today perhaps. Still, Hollywood's view of violence remains pretty unrealistic."[2]

"I'm interested in frightening people on a deep level, not just making them jump. My first two films blew away the cliches of handling violence. Before, screen violence had been neat and tidy; I made it painful and protracted and shocking and very human. And I made the people who were doing the killing human."[3]

Craven has also admitted that he hasn't made a film quite as nasty as his first two. His 1981 "Deadly Blessing," dealt more with the theme of religious repression then the agony and horror of death itself, and his other film of that year was actually the comic-book adventure, "Swamp Thing" a film rated PG in which Craven abandoned horror and shot for the comic-book look, "Lots of low angles, weird shadows, strange colors, and lots of fog."[4]

Nonetheless, Craven soon returned to his R-rated ways with the 1983 release of "The Hills Have Eyes: Part II," a film which he felt was released before it was finished, and is, therefore, not one of his favorites. The following year, one of his most popular films, "A Nightmare on Elm Street," was released. Craven had struggled for five years to have this movie, based largely on his childhood nightmares, made. With its unabashed mixture of fantasy and reality, a concept he had tinkered with in other films, "A Nightmare on Elm Street" opened up new realms in horror. The concept of consciousness intrigues Craven. "I've always had very vivid dreams. In college, I started writing

A practical joke backfires in the 1986 Warner Bros. film "Deadly Friend," directed by Wes Craven.

them down as part of a psychology course project and got very adept at it, a skill I've kept up. In fact, it's developed as a great creative aid.

"Steven LaBirge, a doctor of psychology, works in the Lucidity Institute at Stanford University studying lucid dreaming, a process in which you are consciously aware that you are dreaming and can learn to manipulate the dream for creative purposes. Suddenly you're in control and can say, 'This is me and I'm dreaming, so why don't I go over here, etc.?' This can become a valuable doorway into your subconscious creativity. I have been on the fringes of doing that, and in fact have had several lucid dreams on my own without even realizing that it was a named process.

"By the time I got to writing 'A Nightmare on Elm Street,' I was dealing very much with my philosophy of consciousness rather than any particular Christian belief, though that early religion did instill in me the idea of asking those kinds of spiritual questions and living a life according to principles that were beyond getting and spending.

"One of the great things to be said for horror is that it is not easily carried out by people who are part of the establishment. Therefore, they defer it to people who know how to do it, the ones whom they think are semi-crazy but still have a gift that can't be meddled with. So we're allowed to be very free, and that in turn gives us a great opportunity to explore our own philosophical beliefs and psyches. It also gives some the opportunity for exploiting the human experience—there has been that kind of horror film also. I'm not saying that the whole genre is a wonderful example of philosophical inquiry, but I don't represent the whole genre, and I've certainly known lots of people who are bright and quite motivated to think seriously. I've met Clive Barker [director of 'Hellraiser'] several times and he's no crazoid; he's thinking."[1]

Craven has received a substantial amount of criticism that his wise-cracking anti-hero, Freddy

Bill Pullman and Cathy Tyson starred in Craven's 1988 Universal film of voodoo and zombies, "The Serpent and the Rainbow."

Krueger, provided an unhealthy influence for young minds. "There was a period when that argument was going around, and I examined it very carefully. In England, there was a supposed 'Rambo' who killed people. It was followed by all sorts of legislation, but essentially, the guy dressed up in fatigues, so they called him Rambo. I'm very very skeptical of those reports. There was a case in the U.S. of a three- or five-year-old dressing up like Freddy and killing a younger kid. We investigated it and found it completely fabricated. There is a large disposition on the part of critics and people who want headlines to make up things like that.

"Statistically, if you look at the millions who go see these films, the chance that someone might use one of these characters as his calling card is remote. I think causes for these acts, insofar as they do exist, are quite outside the films themselves. If they did not choose the Freddy character, they would have chosen Jack the Ripper.

"I've found myself being censored not really for the gore in my films, but specifically (and they use these words) for the 'intensity.' They will say that something is simply too intense for the audience. That is always so ironic to me because when I see my films with the audience, usually young or underclass, I notice that they're having a fantastic time with it. There's a tremendous amount of energy in the theater. It's that energy, and the fact that the audience can celebrate mayhem, that scares the establishment. They're afraid that this underclass of young people—Blacks, Hispanics, and everybody else that goes to horror films—is ultimately going to get out of control. The feeling I really get is that they don't want to get 'anybody riled up down there on the plantation.'

"I think that there has always been a very careful regulation of ideas, as much as that's possible, by the people in the cat-bird seat. Anybody intelligent, which people who control things usually are, realizes that ideas are explosive and can upset the applecart very easily, usually to the detriment of the minority in control. So those people watch what is said and done very carefully. Even today, I find censorship in horror films because they express, on a deeply subconscious level, very psychologically powerful ideas, such as the idea of questioning authority. They display a great deal of autonomy because the parental and law figures are almost always inadequate when it comes to providing the needs of the people who are threatened (i.e. the phone doesn't work; the police don't come in time). The ultimate solution in a horror film almost always comes out of the individual, rather than the establishment. These films speak bluntly to the sort of madness at the core of things which the establishment would like to have us ignore. They'd prefer us to see a Disneyland, all under control with nice little animals dancing around. And that, to me, is the scary thing.

"The criticism comes from the threat that these films pose to people who are leading very restricted lives. It's like the old argument that Rock 'n' Roll will make everybody crazy. My feeling is, things are crazy already. We are only reflecting a world that's already there. It's the duty of the artist to remind the culture of what is really out there in the real world. the fact that there's this incredible network of atomic weapons aimed at all of our cities, right now, ready to go off and trigger a nuclear winter and the end of the species. Now we're talking serious; now we're talking about something that's really out there. Or we can talk about the amount of people that have been lost in warfare over our last several generations. Those are real deaths. Those are real traumas. And they've been perpetrated by God-fearing, Bible-quoting, cross-bearing adults that are our supposed leaders. Watergate, the assassinations, the corruption in high places, building billion-dollar bombers that will never be used—all of that madness is real. So I turn right around and say, 'You clean up all this and then I'll worry about my movie, buddy.'

"Besides, I have gotten years and years of fan mail, quite often from very young kids who have enjoyed the films and gotten a lot out of them. Now I get fan letters from people who used to be kids who grew up with 'Last House' and 'Hills Have Eyes' and are now young adults saying how much the films meant to them in some wacky way. So I've simply learned to listen to my fans, to look within myself and know that I'm doing things that have real validity and are done with care and a sense of responsibility, and also to find wiser critics."[1]

Though "A Nightmare on Elm Street" spawned a group of sequels that has grossed New Line Cinema about 171 million dollars to date, Craven's only other involvement with the series was as executive producer of "A Nightmare on Elm Street 3: Dream Warriors," mainly because he didn't have the time to write the sequels and felt that it wasn't in his interest to direct the scripts that were written.

Instead, Craven released his next film, "Deadly Friend," a general disappointment, and directed several episodes for the new "Twilight Zone" series, as well as directed several television movies. In his producing and directing for television, Craven has learned to make certain allowances. "Certainly the language and violence have to be toned down. I try to think more in terms of suspense and character rather than the complete 'Wes Craven' shocking violence. I can't bite somebody's lip off on TV. But it also forces me to be a little more traditional. In that sense, it's a bit more intellectually challenging and a little bit less viscerally challenging. The other thing about television is its very short schedules. Normally, I have four to five weeks of pre-production, around twenty days of shooting, and then four weeks of post-production. Television is three weeks of pre-production and one week of post. So we won't have time to build sets; it will all be shot at practical locations. I think somewhat differently as a producer than as director. As a producer, I'll try not to give myself as much night shooting as I normally would for something that's designed to be kind of scary and atmospheric, and I try to think of locations that already exist."[1]

Location played a large part in Craven's 1988 theatrical film, "The Serpent and the Rainbow," which was filmed in Haiti. Based on the book by Wade Davis, it took its name from the voodoo metaphors for earth and sky and dealt with an evil dictator and the existence of a real-life zombie potion that caused a pseudo-death in the person taking it, leaving that person in a zombie-like state of insanity. "I certainly did a fair share of research for that film. I read every book and saw every film I could get on the subject. Much of a film's look comes from hiring excellent production designers like Greg Fonseca ['A Nightmare on Elm Street'], Cynthia Shera ['Shocker'], or David Nichols ['The Serpent and the Rainbow']. Part of their job is to research the hell out of the subject matter. For instance, Greg Fonseca did very careful research on the interiors of mid-western houses for 'Nightmare,' and David Nichols lived in Haiti for six months for 'The Serpent and the Rainbow,' completely immersing himself in the culture, to the extent that he was married in a voodoo ceremony. We found out afterwards that he almost went native."[1]

The filming of "The Serpent and the Rainbow" was surrounded by many strange occurrences, from screenwriter Richard Maxwell becoming temporarily paralyzed and insane from voodoo experimentation to political unrest among the Haitian extras. "It wasn't safe to assemble large numbers of Haitians. They got very volatile when they were together. They saw all people from the outside as rich; they were full of grievances and suspicions. Finally, they struck for double the wages they were getting. They surrounded the equipment; the crew had to be evacuated to a mission. [Producer] David Ladd and I were nearly stoned.

"We agreed to the doubled wages, but for half the number of people—I think there were around 2000. They finally agreed, but demanded to be paid in cash. There was a mad scramble and people got trampled and we had to be barricaded in a police station. By 3 a.m., we no longer felt anything was under control. After we did the airport scenes at Port-au-Prince, we got on a plane we were using as a prop and got out. We shot the sacred waterfall scene later in the Dominican Republic."[5]

Craven returned to the United States and fashioned the movie from four hours of footage. It was released to favorable reviews, although some critics complained that Craven had tried to weave too much into the film's plot, while others admired his ambition.

Equally ambitious was Craven's latest film, "Shocker," a blend of video and film images which told the story of Horace Pinker, the world's most vicious serial-killer whose electrocution enabled him to reach his victims through the airwaves. "It was very ironic to me that in 'Shocker' I set out to use the very images from real life that the adult and so-called civilized world had presented to me. I used all these images from World War II, atomic testing from the government films, Vietnam, and I still was accused of making films with terrible images. I said, 'Wait a second! These images are coming right out of the news!' Then I'd get this blank look and they'd say, 'Yeah, but you put it in a movie.'

"With 'Shocker,' I wanted to see if I could do a highly technical film well, and do it on a very low budget. My work has become a bit more sophisticated, and I think the heart has moved it more. Certainly, even in the course of making 'Shocker,' I found myself going through the profound introduction of humor and hope into my film. It's strange that it anticipated the events in Europe before they happened. I started out to make a very scary, hard film, but by the end realized that the theme of the film was basically that the heart is stronger than the hand (or weapon). It made the film a lot lighter and fun towards the end. I've had a lot of people say, 'I don't usually like this kind of film, but in this film I was scared *and* had fun.'

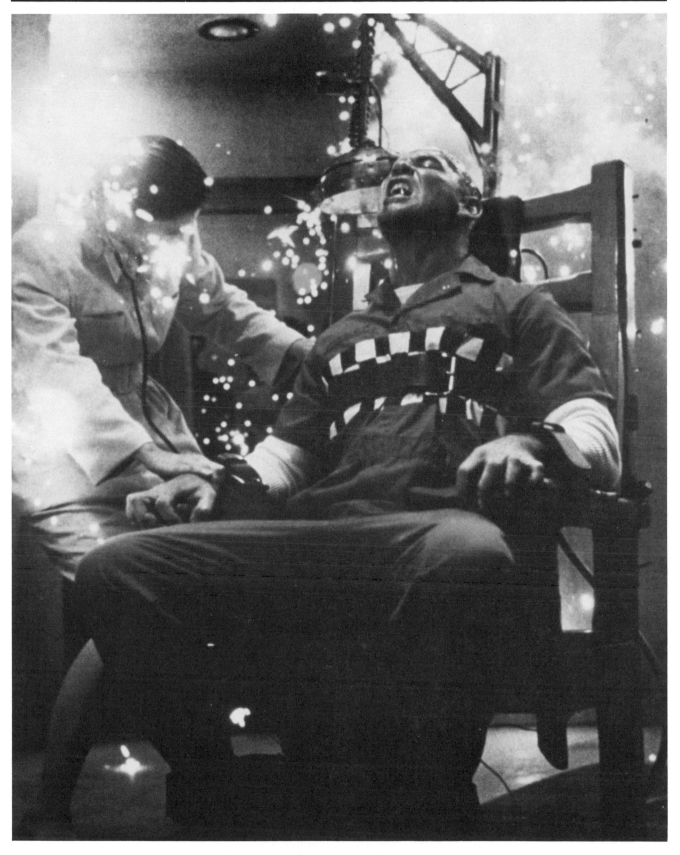

From the 1989 horror film "Shocker," starring Mitch Pileggi.

"I think that is part of a general trend in my career of moving away from just scaring people and getting more into character, taking a little bit more of a gentle or fun look at the human condition."[1]

Craven feels that he has also developed as a director. "I really started out in the business as a writer who became an editor. Then I realized that to have any control over a film, you had to be the director. 'The Last House on the Left' had been sort of a fluke, because it was done like a documentary. So I had to prove to myself and to a lot of other people that I really was a director. Many people who knew me never thought I could be one, because I was very quiet and wasn't the sort of person who would bark orders and scream on the set. A lot of people in the business think that is what a director should do. So I had to learn a lot of skills.

"The most profound change since 'Nightmare' is my sense of calm on the set. Directing is a process of inner-cover-demon navigation, and I've got a better handle on them after fifteen years. I tend to be extremely well organized on the set and have learned how to give myself an inner sense of calm with meditation and things like that. When you're calmer, ideas come a little bit easier because you're not so panicked about everything."[1]

Craven has needed that sense of calm for things other than filmmaking: in dealing with the break-up of his second marriage, and in dealing with the unpleasant processes of both defending himself in a law-suit and filing one. "There's been a lot of heavy things weighing on me in the last three years that have been suddenly lifted. Somebody had come out of the woodwork and sued me, saying that I had copied the idea of 'Nightmare' from a script of his that I had worked on. Even though I proved that I had written 'Nightmare' three years before, he kept suing. That was a very ticklish situation where New Line had left me liable not only for my own defense, but for their's as well, *and* for the defense of their media home entertainment. This guy sued all of them. But that's finally been resolved and taken off my shoulders."[1]

Craven filed suit against New Line Cinema himself. From the millions the "Nightmare" series had earned, including television and merchandising, he had received only five hundred thousand dollars for directing the first film. "Luckily, I found out that the Writer's Guild will, without charge, threaten to sue anybody who has not paid certain items that are guaranteed in the Writer's Guild basic contract. Had I not had anything contractual-

ly that would still give me a percentage of the merchandising. (There is a basic clause in the Writer's Guild that the creator of a character is guaranteed five percent of whatever the producing company gets from merchandising.) Neither I nor my agent had known that. A lawyer friend told me that a year and a half later, and so the Writer's Guild threatened to take New Line to court, and they decided to pay for things like the 'Freddy's Nightmares' television series."[1]

Because of new deals with NBC, Universal Studios, and Alive Films, Craven must maintain a steady hand to guide him through typically long days and an impressive amount of work. "A typical day is getting up around six-thirty, playing racquetball at eight o'clock with my stunt-coordinator friend at nearby Marina Del Ray, and then maybe having a fast breakfast and getting to the office. We are in a three week pre-production now for a two-hour movie-of-the-week, what they call a back-door pilot, which means that it's made as movie-of-the-week but it's also the pilot for a series. The story is a police drama about a burnt-out cop and a young girl who is almost schizophrenic—it turns out that her unconscious is using schizophrenia to deal with the trauma of being the sole survivor of a family murdered by a serial killer when she was just thirteen. It's a character piece with a lot of action. NBC picked it up, so we'll be going immediately into pre-production which means there will be a big scramble of making phone calls, viewing reels, interviewing people, going out for screenings, and things like that. Once we start shooting, I'll get up at six, shoot all day, and then look at the dailies and make the next day's shot list until one or two in the morning. Then I'll get up the next morning and do it again.

"We also have a second series idea that the network loves and wants us to write, called 'The Nightmare Cafe' [working title], which is basically a 'Twilight Zone'-type idea with week-to-week characters. That's based on an idea by my son and a friend of his. I'm writing a ten-minute blackout dramatic piece for a larger Broadway play called 'Granquinole,' which is inviting notoriously scary people like myself, David Lynch, and John Carpenter to do something for the stage. The script for 'Cold Eye,' based on the novel of the same name, is in the final stages of writing. I also have my Alive/Universal film clamoring to go next, which is called 'The People under the Stairs,' and am about eighty pages into that script. That's essentially what I've got on my plate for sure, besides a lot of other things that people say they would like to see me do. I'm sure if I did just those, it would take me the next two-and-a-half to three years.

"My one-line rule of thumb for filmmaking is, 'Would I like to go see it?' The other thing I usually ask myself is whether I've ever seen anything like this before, but that's really a corollary of 'Would I like to go see it?' I tend to go to things that I think will be totally different from anything I've seen and generally feel like I've wasted my time if I go to see a movie that's more of the same.

"A true idea grasps the perceiver on any of an infinite levels. The best stories deal with a simple and pure inner truth about the human condition. They could be studied for centuries by scholars, written about in reams of books, or be appreciated by the audience as a great yarn. An intellectual person can see 'Nightmare on Elm Street' as a study of consciousness and another can see it as a hell of a ride. They are both right. If there's one thing I'd like to see them come away with from my films it is the idea that there is hope. The world is what you imagine it to be. You imagine your own solutions, defenses, even attacks on the Freddy Kruegers of life.

"In my own films, I've found that there's been a progression from the capability of being just as violent, crazy, and aggressive as the characters are, to the capability of not playing their game, of turning away, attacking their violence and hate with an even higher force of light and love. It's hard to talk about these things without sounding like the sixties rehashed, but our culture has been haunted with these ideas of the Millennium and Revelations—sooner or later they're gonna drop the bomb, we are gonna exhaust the planet, the dictators will take over as in *1984*, the beast will come, etc.—all this really dark expectancy is in our culture. The most profound change I could imagine would be that human beings suddenly realize that they're not essentially bad, that life doesn't have to end in war, that marriage doesn't have to end in divorce, that there is possibility at least. Russia and America do not have to kill each other, and Eastern Europe doesn't have to stay under the lock and key of Russia.

"Some of that is now occurring on a planetary level, almost like the breaking of the ice that's choked a river all winter. Extraordinary events occur one after the other. I think at these times, the human spirit has a great opportunity to re-imagine itself and say, 'If all this was possible, why should we continue to be slaves? Why should we continue to screw up the environment? Maybe we *can* imagine a way to have a great consumer society and not devastate the planet for ourselves and our children.' That's the process that's going on right now, and it's very important for everybody, to the extent that we can do it honestly, to participate."[1]

In between his deadlines, directing, writing, and producing, Craven finds time to spend with his son and daughters, play classical guitar, and even take flying lessons. "I have a pretty good life; it just took me years to realize it. I'm a guy from Cleveland who grew up restricted enough to have a need to know everything. So I'm interested in a great many things. I've subscribed to about thirty-five magazines, ten newsletters, three newspapers and I go to plays, museums, and every film I can get myself to see. So, I think I'm pretty well informed. I'm also funny, probably work obsessed, but beyond that I don't know who the hell I am. I re-invent myself with every movie."[1]

Footnote Sources:

[1] Based on an interview by Dieter Miller for *Authors & Artists for Young Adults*.
[2] Christopher Sharrett, "Fairy Tales for the Apocalypse," *Literature/Film Quarterly*, Volume 13, number 3, 1985.
[3] Henri Bollinger Press Release.
[4] Embassy Press Release.
[5] Lloyd Sachs, "Wes Craven Crawls toward Respectability with 'The Serpent,'" *Chicago Sun Times*, February 14, 1988.

■ For More Information See

Fangoria, October 1984 (p. 38ff), number 51, February 1986.
Daily News, February 4, 1988 (p. 58).
Time, September 5, 1988 (p. 66ff).
Newsweek, September 12, 1988.
Rolling Stone, October 6, 1988 (p. 93ff).
Chicago Tribune, October 30, 1988 (p. 32ff).
Film Comment, September/October 1989 (p. 8).
Cinefantastique, November 1989 (p. 14ff).
People Weekly, November 13, 1989 (p. 161).

Len Deighton

Born February 18, 1929, in Marylebone, London, England; son of Leonard (a chauffeur) and Dorothy (a cook; maiden name, Fitzgerald) Deighton; married Shirley Thompson (an illustrator), 1960 (divorced); married Ysabele de Ranitz, February, 1970; children: (second marriage) Antoni, Alexander. *Education:* Attended St. Martin's School of Art, London, 1949-52; Royal College of Art, A.R.C.A., 1955. *Agent:* Jonathan Clowes, Iron Bridge House, Bridge Approach, London NW1 8BC, England.

■ Career

Author. Worked as a railway lengthman, an assistant pastry cook at the Royal Festival Hall, 1951, a manager of a gown factory in Aldgate, England, a waiter in Piccadilly, an advertising man in London and New York City, a teacher in Brittany, a co-proprietor of a glossy magazine, a magazine artist, and news photographer; steward, British Overseas Airways Corporation (BOAC), 1956-57; producer of films, including "Only When I Larf" (based on novel), and "Oh What a Lovely War!," both 1969. Founder, Continuum One Literary Agency, London, England. *Military service:* Royal Air Force, aircraftsman in special investigation branch, 1947-49.

■ Awards, Honors

SS-GB and *Airshipwreck* were each selected one of New York Public Library's Books for the Teen Age, 1980; Senior Fellow, Royal College of Art, 1987.

■ Writings

Only When I Larf (novel), M. Joseph, 1968, published as *Only When I Laugh,* Mysterious Press, 1987, large print edition, G. K. Hall, 1988.

Bomber: Events Relating to the Last Flight of an R.A.F. Bomber over Germany on the Night of June 31, 1943 (novel), Harper, 1970.

Declarations of War (story collection), J. Cape, 1971, published as *Eleven Declarations of War,* Harcourt, 1975.

Close-Up (novel), Atheneum, 1972.

SS-GB: Nazi-Occupied Britain, 1941 (novel), J. Cape, 1978, Knopf, 1979.

(Contributor) H. R. F. Keating, editor, *Whodunit? Guide to Crime, Suspense, and Spy Fiction,* Van Nostrand, 1982.

Goodbye, Mickey Mouse (novel), Knopf, 1982.

Winter: A Novel of a Berlin Family, Hutchinson, 1987, Knopf, 1988.

Espionage Novels:

The Ipcress File, Hodder & Stoughton, 1962, Simon & Schuster, 1963, reissued, Ballantine, 1982.

Horse under Water, J. Cape, 1963, Putnam, 1968.

Funeral in Berlin, J. Cape, 1964, Putnam, 1965.

Billion Dollar Brain, Putnam, 1966, large print edition, Ulverscroft, 1983.

An Expensive Place to Die, Putnam, 1967.

Spy Story, Harcourt, 1974.

Yesterday's Spy, Harcourt, 1975.

Twinkle, Twinkle, Little Spy, J. Cape, 1976, published as *Catch a Falling Spy,* Harcourt, 1976.

XPD, Knopf, 1981.

Berlin Game, Hutchinson, 1983, Knopf, 1984, large print edition, G. K. Hall, 1984.

Mexico Set, Hutchinson, 1984, Knopf, 1985.

London Match, Hutchinson, 1985, Knopf, 1986, large print edition, G. K. Hall, 1987.

Game, Set and Match (omnibus edition, includes *Berlin Game, Mexico Set,* and *London Match*), Hutchinson, 1986.

Spy Hook: A Novel, Knopf, 1988, large print edition, Thorndike Press, 1989.

Spy Line, Knopf, 1989.

Spy Sinker, Harper, 1990.

Nonfiction:

(Editor) *Drinks-man-ship: Town's Album of Fine Wines and High Spirits,* Haymarket Press, 1964.

Ou est le garlic: or, Len Deighton's French Cookbook, Penguin, 1965, revised edition published as *Basic French Cooking,* J. Cape, 1979, revised edition, Century-Random, 1990, published in the United States as *Ou est le garlic; or, French Cooking in Fifty Lessons,* Harper, 1979, also published as *Len Deighton's Basic French Cooking,* Creative Arts Books.

Action Cookbook: Len Deighton's Guide to Eating, J. Cape, 1965, published in the United States as *Len Deighton's Cookstrip Cook Book,* Bernard Geis Associates, 1966.

(Editor with Michael Rand and Howard Loxton) *The Assassination of President Kennedy,* J. Cape, 1967.

(Editor and contributor) *Len Deighton's London Dossier,* J. Cape, 1967.

Len Deighton's Continental Dossier: A Collection of Cultural, Culinary, Historical, Spooky, Grim and Preposterous Fact, compiled by Victor Pettitt and Margaret Pettitt, M. Joseph, 1968.

Fighter: The True Story of the Battle of Britain, J. Cape, 1977, Knopf, 1978.

(With Peter Mayle) *How to Be a Pregnant Father,* Lyle Stuart, 1977.

(With Arnold Schwartzman) *Airshipwreck,* J. Cape, 1978, Holt, 1979.

(Author of introduction) Simon Goodenough, *Tactical Genius in Battle,* Dutton, 1979.

Blitzkrieg: From the Rise of Hitler to the Fall of Dunkirk, J. Cape, 1979, Knopf, 1980.

Battle of Britain, Coward, 1980.

(Under name Cyril Deighton, with Fred F. Blau) *The Orient Flight L.Z. 127-Graf Zeppelin,* German Philatelic Society, 1980.

(Under name Cyril Deighton, with F. F. Blau) *The Egypt Flight: L.Z. 127-Graf Zeppelin,* German Philatelic Society, 1981.

ABC of French Food, Hutchinson, 1989, Bantam, 1990.

Screenplays:

"From Russia with Love," Eon Productions, 1963.

"Oh, What a Lovely War!" Paramount, 1969.

"Never Say Never Again," Taliafilm, 1983.

Also author of television script "Long Past Glory," ABC-TV, November 17, 1963. Contributor of articles to periodicals, including *Daily Express, Playboy, London Sunday Times, Elephanta,* and *Author.* Author of weekly strip on cooking, *Observer,* 1962—.

■ Adaptations

Motion Pictures:

"The Ipcress File," starring Michael Caine, Universal, 1965.

"Funeral in Berlin," starring M. Caine, Paramount, 1966.

"Billion Dollar Brain," starring M. Caine, United Artists, 1967.

"Only When I Larf," Paramount, 1968.

"Spy Story," Gala, 1976.

Television:

"Discipline" (based on *Declarations of War*), BBC, 1977.

"It Must Have Been Two Other Fellows" (based on *Declarations of War*), BBC, 1977.

"Game, Set, Match" (eleven one-hour episodes), PBS-TV, 1988.

■ Work in Progress

Untitled fiction about guerillas in Latin America; *The War before Pearl* about the political events and fighting prior to Pearl Harbor, 1941; a book about food and cooking around the world.

■ Sidelights

Len Deighton was born in London on February 18, 1929. "My father was a chauffeur in London, in Marylebone, and my mother was a cook—sort of upstairs-downstairs scene you know."[1]

"Even as a child I knew it was the last glimpse of a world that was about to vanish for ever."[2]

At the age of eleven Deighton passed the entrance exam for Marylebone Grammar School. "That was the last exam I passed. Then the war came along and I was a messenger at my father's first-aid [civil defense] post. School was knocked out, but then they continued it for a day a week in a vicar's front room, or somewhere. I stayed in school until I was 16, but I couldn't understand what they were talking about—chemistry, algebra, physics and that."[3] Deighton was to later regret the gaps in his education and worked hard to close them.

"My smartest days were when I played hookey and went to museums. You learn something ten times as fast when you are seeking knowledge rather than just receiving it. I also got absorbed in Shakespeare. There was a theater where you could go and see Olivier and Guinness and Richardson."[3]

"I still have nightmares about [playing truant]. I haven't been to school for like a month, and I'm thinking...they're going to find out, they're going to catch me!...I'd go to the British Museum or the Marylebone Public Library. I particularly liked the reference section—I think the seating was more comfortable—and I'd read all the magazines, and of course the encyclopaedias. I think in a funny sort of way that was very beneficial to me as a writer, and still today I read reference books for pleasure.

"I was a very poor scholar. I'd come home from the grammar school with these bad reports and my father, who didn't believe in corporal punishment, told me that he wouldn't punish me if he saw that I was regularly reading books. So whenever my father was around, I made sure I was reading, which wasn't very difficult because I quite enjoyed books....[I read] many of the same books I see my own children reading today: Conan Doyle, Jules Verne, *Treasure Island*, biographies, history and so on."[4]

While still in school Deighton looked forward to joining the service in the RAF. "I was much more interested in the idea of flying than the idea of

Softcover edition of Deighton's 1962 bestseller.

getting into fighting. I can't remember having any particular desire to sort of bomb anyone or shoot things down, but gradually I became more seriously interested in the problems of drawing, so that by the time I went into the air force, my ambitions had subtly changed, and I made every effort to be a photographer, which is what happened. I spent two-and-a-half years as an air force photographer, doing a certain amount of flying, as well."[1]

"I went into the Royal Air Force at 17...and learned to fly a plane, though I didn't qualify as a pilot. In two years I rose one rank, to the equivalent of Pfc. I heard an airman in the barracks use the words 'we intellectuals,' and that set me to thinking. If these characters were intellectuals, then I could be."[3]

After his discharge from the RAF, Deighton entered St. Martin's School of Art in London. "I think if you have working-class parents, probably you

Michael Caine as the anti-hero in Universal's 1965 film "The Ipcress File."

look forward to a life where you have a regular income of some sort. I think that taking on the life of a painter is an upper-middle-class ambition, certainly one that I didn't entertain. I did three years at art school and I was emboldened then to try for a scholarship at the Royal College of Art. After I'd done my time at the Royal College and become the world's oldest child protege, I felt that I ought to go and get a real job for a change."[1]

"When I left the Royal College of Art in 1955, I wanted to see something of the world, so I worked for a while as an airline steward [for BOAC]....I did drawings wherever I went."[4] After working for BOAC for a year, "I went to live in New York and began working as an illustrator and using the years and years of training that I'd had."[1]

Deighton recalled his gradual transition from images to words. "It would be neither wise nor true for any writer to declare that one picture is worth a thousand words. Perhaps that was something I believed when I was a photographer, or when I was a student at St. Martin's...because my whole life

was devoted to visual images. I enjoyed being an illustrator but could not resist the pleasures, of orchestrating visual ideas, that an art director's job provides. My sketchbooks reveal the same sort of direction. They begin with pages of drawings but as the years went past there was more and more description scribbled into the margins. By the time I graduated from the Royal College of Art I was convinced that a picture is only as good as the context in which it is displayed. A flattened Coca Cola tin in a Bond Street gutter is worthless garbage; moved into an art gallery and spotlit, it might fetch a thousand pounds."[5]

"I wasn't completely happy as an illustrator. Not that there's anything wrong with being one. In some ways there is more satisfaction to be gained from completing a picture than from writing a book. But some of the people you have to work for make life extremely depressing. When you're dealing with words, you never have to spend too much time taking advice and instructions from people who are totally illiterate: but when you're a commercial artist, almost all your instructions come from people who are unable to draw.''[4]

During the 1950s Deighton also did stints as assistant pastry chef, manager of a gown factory, waiter, teacher, news photographer, and co-proprietor of a glossy magazine. In 1960, he married illustrator Shirley Thompson. While the couple vacationed on an island near Toulon, France, Deighton began to write his first espionage novel, *The Ipcress File*. It revolved around the rescue of British biochemists from villains who intend to sell them to a foreign government. ''I just did it for a giggle. We returned to London for a time, but then found ourselves back in France relaxing in a cottage in Perigord. I finished the book there, but didn't know what to do with it. Months later, back in London, I found myself talking with a fellow at a party named Jonathan Clowes, who said he was a literary agent. I told him I had this thing. He said, 'Let me take it to some publishers.' The third publisher took it.''[3]

''After accepting it, Hodder & Stoughton suggested I could improve certain passages, and I made considerable changes, not only the ones on which they'd insisted. Their acceptance put me in a positive mood of wanting to improve it.''[4]

The Ipcress File sold about two million copies and was adapted into a film by Universal, starring Michael Caine as Harry Palmer, the name given to the anonymous narrator in the novel. ''[The success] was no part of a plan of mine—in fact, I had never read a James Bond book—but by an extraordinary coincidence, the month that *The Ipcress File* was published was the month in which the first James Bond film appeared in the West End. One of my friends came up to me and said: 'You're very lucky, Len, because you're a blunt instrument that the critics have used to smash Ian Fleming over the head with.' And this is really, I think, true, that a lot of people who perhaps liked the film, but didn't like the sort of success the film was having, were over-generous to me when I came along with

Michael Caine repeats his role as Harry Palmer in the 1966 Ipcress sequel, ''Funeral in Berlin.''

something which was a substantially different thing from the James Bond books.''[1]

Horse under Water, published in 1963, brings back the nameless middle-class spy in a plot involving a member of parliament and a narcotics ring. *Funeral in Berlin,* published in 1965, explored the Cold War and again featured the anonymous narrator who attempted to smuggle a disaffected East German biologist into the West. In *The Billion Dollar Brain* the same British agent set out to dismantle a computerized spy ring run by a reactionary Texas millionaire. Michael Caine returned as Harry Palmer in both movie adaptations. "In *Brain* I tried to make General Midwinter give a good cogent reason for his anti-Communism, his pressuring to double the arms budget in order to outdistance Russia. I think all this is very important in writing what might be called a 'political thriller.''[3]

"I think a book stands or falls on its construction, not necessarily its plot. When I began writing *Billion Dollar Brain* I decided to work out a system.

"I wanted the centre of the book to be very hot and each end of it very cold, so I designed a book with filing cards. A filing card represented each chapter, and on each one was written what was going to happen in that particular chapter.

"Then there was a card for each character and so on, until finally every chapter would have a dozen or two dozen cards, outlining the plot, characters, and physical descriptions, say, of New York or simply a room. When I sat down to writing the book, I always had the information pertinent to that particular chapter laid out in front of me on the filing cards.''[6]

Deighton himself produced the movie based on his 1968 novel *Only When I Larf,* in which three large-scale confidence tricksters took turns telling a part of the story. "I had no desire to make films of my own stories but I became obsessed with the idea of making a film version of Joan Littlewood's musical play 'Oh, What a Lovely War' and wanted to see if I could write a film version—something others had tried and failed to do for some years—and since I didn't want to run the risk of having someone else buy the film rights while I was working on it, I had to buy the film rights myself. Thus, almost by accident, I found myself in the film business. I hired [Richard] Attenborough as director because he'd never directed before and so was less likely to try changing my script, and soon found myself producing a big musical film. When I saw the schedule and what I was spending in overheads I

knew I had to fit in another film before it just to keep going. I couldn't afford to buy more screen rights so I made a film of *Only When I Larf* to keep solvent. When, after finishing the two films, I went back to writing, some people seemed very surprised, but I was only doing what I said I was going to do. Perhaps that can be surprising sometimes.''[2]

In 1970 Deighton published *Bomber.* "When finishing a book it is tempting to look back and try to remember the moment of its birth. Certainly this one goes back to an afternoon in 1944 when my boyhood friend Colin Smith—a flight engineer freshly returned from his first bombing raid—told me that during his briefing the crews had cheered when they heard that the more vulnerable Stirling bombers would be accompanying them.

"Although I have attempted to make its background as real as possible, this is entirely a work of fiction. As far as I know there were no Lancaster bombers named *Creaking Door, The Volkswagen* or *Joe for King.* There was no R.A.F. airfield named Warley Fen and no Luftwaffe base called Kroonsdijk. There was no Altgarten and there were no real people like those I have described. There was never a thirty-first day of June in 1943 or any other year.''[7]

"*Bomber. . .*took years of research and three trips to Germany—where much of the action takes place—as well as maps, charts, movies and recordings of interviews to get the material together. I had so many written notes—about half a million words—that I colour-coded the loose leaf notebook pages to help me find what I wanted.''[8]

"I was fascinated by the way in which a bombing raid on Berlin consisted of a lot of men going 20,000 feet into the air and then travelling a very, very long distance across the globe, and then travelling an enormous distance back and going home—coming so close to the cities, but then never visiting them. Then the idea that, on the German side, these aircraft were being contacted by means of radar beams, and that there were people who were going to be bombed—when I encountered this sort of information. I had the same sort of excitement which I sometimes find in people who are keen on science-fiction, and I think it was this unreal quality of electronic warfare which made me want to mix it with humans.''[1]

Declarations of War, published in 1971, dealt with fighting men from the Second Punic War to the Vietnam War. "*Declarations of War* was a book of short stories written over a period of a year during which my wife and I were living in hotels and

Michael Caine and Karl Malden as they appeared in the 1967 United Artists film "The Billion Dollar Brain."

temporary accommodation. We were looking for a house and in such conditions I could not have produced a long complete story but the travelling and talking provided material for the tales and *Declarations of War* turned out to be one of my favourite books."[8]

Two of the stories, "Discipline" and "It Must Have Been Two Other Fellows," were adapted for television by the BBC. "War, or the threat of it, has been with us all our lives and remains our greatest problem. Strange, then, that the serious study of war and its causes is still regarded as a rather perverse and not-to-be-encouraged pursuit. My own interest in the subject began after graduation from the Royal College of Art. . . .[When I was an air steward] my off-duty hours were devoted to a self-inflicted reading programme of geography and history, designed to help me understand the world through which I was flying at such a hectic rate.

"At the end of the year I concluded that the history of warfare was the 'cement' of which the walls of history were built. Wars evidenced the social changes that preceded them and marked the technological skills that so often decided them. . . .

"Liddell Hart's theories of war, expressed carefully in his many books, began with the thought that wars are linked to economics. He went on to modify these ideas and link war with psychology. Eventually he concluded that war was 'personal' in the sense that it was an expression of the attitudes of men in power. My study of military history supports that theory.

"War seems to be a reflection of those societies that engage in it. One sees, too, a curious interchange that affects both combatants. Prolonged warfare causes each nation to resemble its enemy."[9]

Close-Up, published in 1972, was not ". . .about lots of people, it was about just one person, an actor. Its dialogue was not that of wartime Britain but of contemporary show-biz. I'd spent a couple of years producing films and I wanted to use the knowledge I'd acquired. It was a safety valve;

something I did instead of murdering certain movie people. Although writers are notoriously unreliable accessors of their own work, I believe that *Close-Up* remains one of the best books I've ever written."[8]

In *Spy Story*, published in 1974 and adapted for the screen, U.S. nuclear submarines eavesdropped on the Soviet Union in the Arctic. "It's a fact of life that most espionage useful to the great nations is culled from clipping agencies, and from people monitoring radio broadcasts. The amount of useful espionage information gained from operatives with false beards, working in foreign countries, is minimal, if not to say microscopic."[10]

"I hadn't planned it as another spy story. The rough outline was concerned with computer-backed war games and it was to be written in the third person. But I realised that I was actually trying to prevent the book becoming a spy story in the style of *Ipcress File* and so on, and I thought, if that's the kind of book it wants to be, why fight it? I

changed to a first-person writing style and started all over again."[2]

In *Spy Story*, *Yesterday's Spy*, and *Twinkle, Twinkle, Little Spy* Deighton introduced two main characters, a British agent and an American boss. "I wish I'd thought of the idea before. The hero needs a Dr. Watson to sneer at and shout at. My only change was to reverse roles and make my 'Dr. Watson' the hero's boss."[2]

Fighter was published in 1977. "I decided that, for my own amusement, I would write what was going at first to be a 12-chapter book describing the Second World War in terms of the technical accomplishment. But I realised that I wouldn't be able to do it as a 12-chapter book. I would have to do it as a 12-volume series of books, so this really simply provided me with a chance to make a reading list, and to study what I consider to be 12 important battles of the world, choosing them so that each one would have an area of technology, such as submarines or aircraft carriers. Finally, I took the Battle of Britain, as an area in which I'd

From the 1969 Paramount release "Only When I Larf," starring David Hemmings.

done a lot of research, to be the first one published. The book is really five different books, which I've sort of threaded together, but to tell the story of the Battle of Britain in tactical terms, not as one damn thing after another, but to show it as cause and effect, and to show how each side responded to what the other side did in the way that one might describe a game of chess."[1]

"[Some RAF notables] told me that it was a sort of *folie de grandeur* that fiction writers succumb to, and that any history book I wrote would be torn to pieces by professional historians. Luckily those people were proved wrong, reviewers including military historians—were extremely generous and [international historian] A. J. P. Taylor even wrote a foreword for the book."[2]

Deighton returned to the subject in the illustrated *Battle of Britain*. "This book is an attempt to look at the Battle within the context of history, separated from the high-powered propaganda from both sides much of which still distorts current beliefs about what actually happened.

"Very small in scale, the Battle of Britain was the last of the gentlemen's wars. After this the air forces of both sides resorted to the area bombing of civilians in town centres. The war in the Pacific was a portent of wars to come. Hitler sent his armies into the Russian wastelands.

"And yet the more I study the Battle of Britain the more convinced I become that it was a pivotal point of the history of this century. To anyone who says that it was not one of the most important battles of the Second World War I ask, without it what other battles would there have been?"[5]

Published in 1978, *SS-GB* was set in Nazi-occupied Britain. "I think *SS-GB* was the only time a whole book has been suggested to me. I was sitting with Tony Colwell and Ray Hawkey in Cape's offices, and we were going over promotional material for *Fighter*. Tony asked what I thought might have happened had Hitler actually invaded Britain. I said I'd seen quite a lot of the German planning, and outlined what probably would have happened. Ray immediately suggested the subject would make a marvellous novel—what he called an 'Alternative World' book. I'd never heard the expression before. Anyway, I went home without too much enthusiasm for it, but the idea kept coming back to me, and the more I thought about it the more attractive it became. But then I thought, the readers aren't going to buy a central character who's a highly placed collaborator, and I didn't want someone who was sweeping the floor at the

German High Command and listening at the keyhole. The hero had to be English, I wanted him at the centre of affairs, but I just couldn't crack the problem of finding a sympathetic role for him. Then one night in bed I suddenly had an idea. He could be a policeman, doing something like crowd control, nothing controversial...then I thought murder! He's going to be investigating a murder— no one is going to mind him co-operating with the enemy if he's doing such a socially okay job. It was the key to making Ray's idea work, and without it *SS-GB* would probably never have been written."[4]

Airshipwreck, an illustrated history for which Deighton wrote the text, was published in the same year. It revealed another of his interests. "Hydrogen is the lightest gas and the invention of lightweight alloys made it possible to construct an airship. It was only just possible. The margins were tiny and getting these flying cathedrals into the air was a great achievement."

Deighton returned to Germany in his nonfiction book *Blitzkrieg*. "*Blitzkrieg* which dealt with the beginnings of the Nazi party and Hitler's control of the army was particularly demanding as I decided that I must go and sort out the material with people in Germany. I am most fortunate in having a wife who is a most gifted linguist; otherwise I would probably still be there."[9]

XPD, published in 1981, concerns an alleged clandestine meeting between Churchill and Hitler in 1940 to discuss the surrender of Britain.

Goodbye, Mickey Mouse was a story about American fighter pilots in England in World War II. Following its publication, Deighton received letters from American Air Force veterans convinced he had been a pilot during the war. "The achievement was that an Englishman had written so convincingly about Americans. So often such attempts fail; as do American writers who set their stories in British society. It was a reckless thing to attempt but I think I brought it off."[2]

Published in 1983, *Berlin Game* was the first installment of the trilogy *Game, Set and Match*, which chronicled Bernard Samson's efforts to expose a Soviet agent high up in British intelligence. *Mexico Set* and *London Match* completed the trilogy, which was adapted for television by Granada. "After *SS-GB*, *XPD* and *Goodbye, Mickey Mouse* I wanted to write a novel in the first person again. Normally everything I write is pared right down, so it's as cryptic and right as I can make it. But this time I deliberately wanted to allow the central character to talk more. I thought, I'm going to let

Novel cited as one of the New York Public Library's Books for the Teen Age in 1980.

him anticipate some of what's coming along and let him comment on everything."[4]

Asked whether Bernard Samson is Harry Palmer grown older, Deighton replied: "Yes, it is the same figure. In my first book, *Ipcress File*, I couldn't think of a name for the hero. When I got to the end, I found that I didn't seem to need a name, so I didn't get around to using one—it wasn't a contrivance. In later books I used a similar figure and I gave him names and there were inconsistencies in that I would, for the sake of the plot, have him born in different places or he would have background knowledge or training of a certain sort that was perhaps incompatible with a central figure in a previous book. But they are all variations on the same person. Although I've used myself as the figure, it's not really me.

"[But like me he is] terribly sarcastic, I suppose, and he knows that discretion is the better part of valour on occasions and he constantly complains about the people he's working for or who he feels are inconveniencing him. I suppose there are all

characteristics in myself. I think probably, there's an element of self-mockery in him—making him a comic figure is a defence mechanism that I use. It's my way of distancing myself from him. However, I would like him to be less funny than in some of the earlier books—I didn't want him to be wise-cracking because I think that is very often an impediment to the flow of the story. I would rather his humour be the black humour of the voyeur.

"I think I do [feel an identification with that character]–I'm a working class boy with a technical education and he is a working class boy with a technical education. London is full of such people. Oddly enough, Berlin is a very class-oriented city—it used to be much more so in the old days, but it sill exists. So I think it's fitting that I've had him growing up in Berlin and expressing a lot of ideas which Berliners share with Londoners."[11]

"I try to give raw information about the characters, without pronouncing judgement—that's part of the reader's enjoyment. There is nothing that I like more than having somebody tell me that he likes one character very much and another saying that he hates him. That is one of the most enjoyable things about writing books—smart aleck, wise-cracky books—they're making a lot of enemies for you in really good places. In the same way, I like irritating people I don't like, and then I like the fact that my hero has irritated people that I'm sure I wouldn't like."[3]

Winter, published in 1987, chronicled the life of a Berlin family from 1899 to 1945. In an interview published in 1987 Deighton explained his abiding fascination with Germany. "First of all there is the enigma about the nature of the German. No less importantly there is the geography. Germany's Elbe has long been a place where East meets West. If I may quote from *Mexico Set* 'Lombard from Slav, Frank from Avar, Christian from barbarian, Catholic from Protestant and Communist from Capitalist' to say nothing of being the place where the two greatest military powers, and vastly different political systems, face each other. As if that wasn't difficult enough to comprehend, we had Germany split into two: one committed to the East, the other to the West. There is even a town, a rather wonderful old town, split into two like a living virus dabbed onto a slide under a microscope. I find it quite irresistible."[4]

Deighton's next trilogy *Spy Hook, Spy Line* and *Spy Sinker* completed the story and bound the events in *Winter* to it, to make a seven-book saga. "It was a considerable commitment to outline seven books in advance, but I have always planned ahead. Because I do a lot of research, and like to meet experts or people with special experience, I have to have some idea of what I'm going to do for the next five books. I suppose about half my books have been spy stories. But such stories provide a chance for many different types of plot and varied locations."

Deighton explained how he became a writer of spy novels: "I didn't know enough about police procedure, for instance, to write those kinds of books. So I wrote my first books the way people would write science fiction, because they gave me much more latitude to invent situations."[11]

"There's a style of writing that's known as a 'Police Procedural,' which I find very good and sound, and certainly works well against what we read in the newspapers. It has an authenticity, and you believe the author knows exactly how, for instance, the New York police operate, right down to the paperwork. It's probably true to say that I had an instinctive desire to write a 'Spy Procedural,' and I think that's probably what I still write today.

"I think in England we are probably masters of telling people not quite what we want them to know. This is why we like a language every word of which must have at least a hundred meanings, and preferably none of the meanings the Englishman understands will be listed in the dictionary, thus preventing a foreigner ever communicating successfully in the English language. So when I began toying with the idea of writing, you can see that a spy story provided an ideal arena in which all this could be exaggerated and used."[4]

Yet Deighton is not entirely happy with the label "spy story." "I think it's very beneficial for books to have a label if it's going to give them more chance of reaching the right public. It's one of the functions of the jacket, the blurb and advertising to prevent readers who *won't* like your book from buying it. That's even more important than attracting people who will like it. But it can sometimes work against you. According to my mail, a lot of women read and enjoyed *Goodbye, Mickey Mouse*. They were surprised, because its 'war novel' label suggested it would be full of swearing marines storming the beaches and so on.

"Once I start writing I'm obsessed. I work almost without stopping because I have to. I can't truly say I like writing, but once I start on a book it's difficult to stop even for a day.

"I do the mail and that's by far the worst distraction for a writer. The door to my workroom is always open, so I can hear the sounds of the house, and the children don't hesitate to wander in and start talking. If I had to isolate myself from my family to write, I would find some other job."[4]

"Writers become very good at communicating information, and because of this skill, many people think that the information is of itself good. Writers have a very protected sort of life. We are well looked after, we work in a warm, sheltered environment and tap out our messages. We have to beware of sitting in judgement on the people who actually get things done. It's tempting to do so, when writing fiction, and even more when writing history. I think a writer should destroy cliches and make people rethink assumptions, but few writers, if any, are clever enough to tell people what to think.

"If we accept that all art is the imposing of order upon the chaos of nature, it's extremely tempting to inflict on this chaos a totalitarian pattern. All artists are inclined to be fascistic because they are, by the very nature of what they do, imposing by force of will an artificial arrangement of elements. Now one of the kinds of arrangement that I don't like is the meeting of force with brutal counter-force, because it doesn't lead to anything except the acceptance of force as benign. I think what we do have to promote as writers is the benefit of people using their brains."[4]

Deighton mused over what he would have liked to have done had he not become a writer: "I would like to have written the music, and anything else I could get my hands on, right down to designing the programme, for a big stage musical, such as 'Guys and Dolls' or 'Oklahoma.' I find it fascinating how such a thing comes together. The production and staging of it, the excitement of the last moment changes, the pacing and construction of the music and the plot interest me immensely. But I just haven't got the musical instinct or sympathy—it's a pipe-dream really, but it's one that I relive every time that I'm in a theatre and the curtain goes up, or even if I put a cassette on the tape-machine."[11]

Footnote Sources:

[1] Melvyn Bragg, "Len Deighton: 'The Most Hard-Working Writer I've Met,'" *Listener*, December 22-29, 1977.
[2] "Len Deighton, A Biographical Note," *Book News from Hutchinson*.
[3] Hugh Moffett, "Hot Spy Writer on the Lam," *Life*, March 25, 1966.
[4] Edward Milward-Oliver, *The Len Deighton Companion*, Grafton Books, 1987.
[5] Len Deighton, "Foreword," *Battle of Britain*, J. Cape, 1980.

[6] Rita Grosvenor, "Up in the Ops Room Len Deighton Talks by Telex and Plans Another Blockbuster," *Argosy*, July, 1969.

[7] L. Deighton, *Bomber*, Harper, 1970.

[8] L. Deighton, "Even on Christmas Day," *Whodunit? Guide to Crime, Suspense, and Spy Fiction*, edited by H. R. F. Keating, Van Nostrand, 1982.

[9] L. Deighton, "Introduction," *Tactical Genius in Battle*, Phaidon Press, 1979.

[10] Barbara A. Bannon, "Len Deighton Returns to the Spy Game Via Harcourt Brace Jovanovich," *Publishers Weekly*, July 8, 1974.

[11] "Len Deighton Interview," *Book News from Hutchinson*.

[12] Edwin McDowell, "Behind the Best Sellers," *New York Times Book Review*, June 21, 1981.

■ For More Information See

Ark, issue 10, 1954 (p. 40), issue 13, 1955 (p. 33).

New Statesman, December 7, 1962, September 18, 1964 (p. 406), May 12, 1967, June 18, 1976 (p. 822), August 25, 1978 (p. 249).

Newsweek, December 24, 1962 (p. 47), January 18, 1965, January 31, 1966 (p. 89), June 26, 1972, October 14, 1974 (p. 127ff), February 19, 1979, December 27, 1982, December 19, 1983, February 11, 1985, January 13, 1986.

Times Literary Supplement, February 8, 1963 (p. 92), June 1, 1967 (p. 491), June 22, 1967, September 25, 1970, June 16, 1972 (p. 67ff), May 3, 1974 (p. 465), October 28, 1977, September 15, 1978 (p. 1011), March 13, 1981 (p. 279), October 21, 1983 (p. 1170), December 14, 1989 (p. 1457).

New York Times Book Review, November 10, 1963 (p. 44), January 17, 1965 (p. 48), May 21, 1967 (p. 42ff), January 14, 1968, October 4, 1970, April 13, 1975 (p. 5ff), July 9, 1978, February 25, 1979, May 20, 1979 (p. 13ff), May 3, 1981 (p. 12ff), June 21, 1981 (p. 34), November 14, 1982 (p. 15), January 8, 1984 (p. 24), March 10, 1985, December 1, 1985 (p. 22), December 25, 1988 (p. 6).

New York Times, January 12, 1965, January 24, 1965, October 17, 1970, October 16, 1976, September 20, 1977, May 13, 1981 (p. 17), December 7, 1982 (section 3, p. 14), December 12, 1983 (section 3, p. 16).

Variety, March 24, 1965, March 12, 1975 (p. 4).

Vogue, July, 1965 (p. 94ff).

Morning Telegraph (New York), August 3, 1965, December 23, 1967.

New Yorker, August 14, 1965, February 3, 1968, September 23, 1974 (p. 147), May 7, 1979, February 6, 1984.

Playboy, May, 1966 (p. 103), August, 1968 (p. 103).

Saturday Review, January 30, 1965, December 31, 1966, June 10, 1978.

London Sunday Times Magazine, September 17, 1967 (p. 36ff), September 24, 1967 (p. 42ff).

Films and Filming, January, 1968, October, 1968.

London Sunday Times, November 16, 1969 (p. 77), September 11, 1977 (p. 14), September 18, 1977 (p. 12), September 25, 1977 (p. 14), March 1, 1981 (p. 39), October 30, 1988 (p. 67).

Washington Post, October 9, 1970.

Spectator, April 8, 1972 (p. 546), September 24, 1977, September 2, 1978 (p. 22), April 18, 1981.

Listener, May 9, 1974 (p. 606).

Washington Post Book World, September 29, 1974 (p. 3), September 12, 1976 (p. H3), June 4, 1978, March 20, 1979, April 14, 1981 (p. B1), November 7, 1982 (p. B1), January 8, 1984 (p. A1), January 27, 1985 (p. A1ff), December 15, 1985 (p. C1ff).

New Republic, December 13, 1975 (p. 32).

New Leader, January 19, 1976 (p. 16).

Chris Steinbrunner and Otto Penzler, editors, *Encyclopedia of Mystery and Detection*, McGraw, 1976.

London Times, March 15, 1977 (p. 16), September 11, 1977 (p. 14), August 3, 1984 (p. 11), June 6, 1987 (p. 21), November 12, 1988 (p. 37).

Armchair Detective, April, 1977 (p. 101ff), winter, 1986.

Village Voice, February 19, 1979 (p. 81ff).

Time, March 12, 1979, April 27, 1981, January 13, 1986.

Chicago Tribune Book World, March 18, 1979 (section 7, p. 4), January 19, 1986 (section 14, p. 33).

Wall Street Journal, May 21, 1980 (p. 22).

British Book News, December, 1980 (p. 764ff).

LeRoy L. Panek, *The Special Branch: The British Spy Novel, 1890-1980*, Bowling Green University Popular Press, 1981.

Sunday Times, March 1, 1981, October 30, 1988 (p. 67).

Harper's, November, 1982.

Los Angeles Times, November 26, 1982 (section 5, p. 19), February 16, 1986.

Christopher Lehmann-Haupt, "Books of The Times," *New York Times*, December 7, 1982.

New Society, December 22-29, 1983 (p. 493ff).

Globe & Mail (Toronto), December 1, 1984, December 14, 1985.

Lars Ole Sauerberg, *Secret Agents in Fiction*, St. Martin's, 1984.

Detroit News, February 3, 1985 (section H, p. 2), February 9, 1986 (section F, p. 2).

Chicago Tribune, February 24, 1985 (section 14, p. 39).

Los Angeles Times Book Review, March 17, 1985, February 16, 1986.

Current Biography 1984, H. W. Wilson, 1985.

John M. Reilly, editor, *Twentieth-Century Crime and Mystery Writers*, St. Martin's, 1985.

Edward Milward-Oliver, *Len Deighton: An Annotated Bibliography 1954-1985*, Sammler (London), 1985.

Donna Olendorf, editor, *Bestsellers 89: Books and Authors in the News*, Gale, 1989.

New York, March 27, 1989 (p. 80ff).

Judy Delton

Born May 6, 1931, in St. Paul, Minn.; daughter of A. F. (a plant engineer) and Alice (a homemaker; maiden name, Walsdorf) Jaschke; married Jeff J. Delton (a school psychologist), June 14, 1958; children: Julie, Jina, Jennifer, Jamie. *Education:* Attended School of Associated Arts, 1950, and College of St. Catherine, 1954-57. *Home:* St. Paul, Minn.

■ Career

Elementary school teacher in parochial schools of St. Paul, Minn., 1957-64; free-lance writer, 1971—. Teacher of writing classes. *Member:* Authors Guild, Authors League of America.

■ Awards, Honors

Two Good Friends was selected one of Child Study Association of America's Children's Books of the Year, 1974, and *Brimhall Turns to Magic* and *On a Picnic,* both 1979; Outstanding Teacher Award from Metropolitan State University, 1976; Picture Book runner-up from the Council of Wisconsin Writers, 1979, for *Brimhall Comes to Stay;* Children's Choice from the International Reading Association and the Children's Book Council, for

The New Girl at School; New Jersey Institute of Technology Authors Award, 1980, for *On a Picnic;* North Dakota Children's Choice Award from the North Dakota Library Association, 1980, for *My Mom Hates Me in January;* Parents' Choice Award in Literature from the Parents' Choice Foundation, 1986, for *Angel's Mother's Boyfriend.*

■ Writings

Fiction:

Two Good Friends (ALA Notable Book; Junior Literary Guild selection; illustrated by Guilio Maestro), Crown, 1974.

Rabbit Finds a Way (illustrated by Joe Lasker), Crown, 1975.

Two Is Company (illustrated by G. Maestro), Crown, 1976.

My Mom Hates Me in January (illustrated by John Faulkner), A. Whitman, 1977.

Three Friends Find Spring (Junior Literary Guild selection; illustrated by G. Maestro), Crown, 1977.

Brimhall Comes to Stay (illustrated by Cyndy Szekeres), Lothrop, 1978.

It Happened on Thursday (illustrated by June Goldsborough), A. Whitman, 1978.

Mariko Goes to Camp, Scott, Foresman, 1978.

Penny-Wise, Fun-Foolish (illustrated by G. Maestro), Crown, 1978.

(With Elaine Knox-Wagner) *The Best Mom in the World* (illustrated by J. Faulkner), A. Whitman, 1979.

40064-3 •U.S. $2.50
CAN. $2.95

A DELL YOUNG YEARLING

PEE WEE SCOUTS

BLUE SKIES, FRENCH FRIES

JUDY DELTON
ILLUSTRATED BY ALAN TIEGREEN

Fourth book in the "Pee Wee Scouts" series.

chicken memories. But when my grandma decided we would have chicken for dinner (chicken was a treat in those days, reserved for Sundays), it meant that Aunt Katie would get her ax out instead of the feed pail. I would go out with her while she fixed her eye on one fowl in the yard that looked the best for dinner, then leapt after him as feathers flew and squawking and screaming took place.

"Today I can't imagine letting a four-year-old child be witness to this bloody murder, but no one thought a thing of it then. At least in Norwood, I was also an accomplice to murder at that early age, when I accompanied Aunt Katie to the pond with a sack full of mewing baby kittens to be drowned. Life was crude then and we lived close to the earth. Amenities lacked and self-preservation seemed the only thing. Life was filled with more natural beauty it seems, but also with more natural horror."[2]

Growing up in such a strongly German-Catholic area instilled in Delton the rigors of religion. "In the house in Norwood, there was a neighbor girl...called Betsy. She was a Lutheran, and it was not acceptable to play with Lutherans or to go to

their homes. But Betsy and I played together despite objections. I remember mostly playing Mass on Aunt Katie's abandoned chicken coop. Betsy and I would dress up in long, flowing vestments, hold a cracker over our head for a host and a dirty cup for a chalice, and say profoundly, 'Domine Non sum Dignus,' and give each other communion. I taught her all of the Latin—the Kyrie, the Creed, the Tantum Ergo—and, at the end of Mass, the 'Ete Missa Est!' I was a Catholic twenty-four hours a day, and I was out to save souls.

"Since my aunt [Katie] worked in the church, I was privy to all kinds of holy things that regular children in my school in St. Paul never were. I remember what a celebrity I became in second grade when I was able to bring communion hosts to school, albeit unconsecrated. On the playground I could trade them for almost anything I wanted, and in the classroom Sister was impressed with this booty, useful in first communion practise. We were the only room that practised with real hosts."[2]

"Being a Catholic was certainly a full-time job. Our world was very narrow. We lived by the Legion of Decency. The Church was the only one who rated movies in those days, and we were terrified that if we saw any of those 'B' movies, we would go to hell. I don't think I ever consciously went to one. I'm sure that a lot of them were mild by today's standards and have since ended up on TV. Anything with Judy Garland, Mickey Rooney, or Shirley Temple was usually safe.

"We had no connection with the outside world and thought that 'public school' was a dirty word. We called those kids the Randolph Rats. You only went to public school because you were expelled from a Catholic one."[3]

Though Delton was German, her family experienced no trouble during the years of World War II. "We never had any huge traumas over that because the whole town of Norwood was German-American. All I remember about the war is just that whole way of thinking. For so many years, we never lived without war and accepted it as a permanent part of life. I never realized that rationing could be over, or that rubber, nylon, sugar, and meat could be plentiful. Just like Catholicism, you cast yourself into that way of thinking and never assumed it could be different. War only touched me in the fact that we had to buy ration stamps, and in school we prayed for it to be over."[3]

Delton graduated in 1949, but was tired of school. "I didn't want to keep going, so I just decided that I'd work forever. But I became dissatisfied with all my jobs and wanted something else. At the time, Catholic Schools had a hard time finding teachers because they didn't pay very well. So they offered a two-year scholarship course in teaching at the College of St. Catherine. In return, you had to sign a commitment to teach three years in a Catholic school. I liked children, so at the age of twenty four, I decided to go back to school to do that."[3]

Graduating in 1957, Delton spent the next few years as a parochial school teacher. "There was a real need; I always had over fifty children in a class. I loved teaching—for about five years. (Usually, I grow tired of anything I've done for five years.) During that time, I met my husband through one of those pen-pal clubs at a Catholic church. He was a school psychologist. We married in 1958 and had four children.

"In those days, you stayed home to take care of your children, and I did that a good part of the time."[3]

While at home, Delton's desire to write slowly blossomed. "I was always a very verbal child, always talked a lot and made up stories, but I'd never cared about writing at all. I read a lot, but I think never extraordinarily more than other children. But when we lived in Tomah in the seventies, I began to have trouble. My husband never seemed to hold a job very long, which left me very frustrated. So I started to write these feelings down in poetry, simply out of the need to verbalize on paper. Knowing now what I do about writing, I realize that those things were just the soul-searching that most kids do in high school, only I was doing it at age thirty-nine. But at the time, I read back over what I'd written and thought, 'My God, this is really great!'

"The local papers didn't know any more about writing than I did, so I actually started selling this awful poetry. I wrote about big generalities like Truth and Justice. But they published it all and paid me, which of course went right to my head. I figured if they're paying me for it, I'll persist. Over the years I branched out from poetry to essays. Then a friend suggested that if I could write two children's books a year, I could support my family, so I decided to try."[3]

Having awakened that small spark within herself, Delton knew that to succeed, she had to make the commitment. "It's difficult, or maybe impossible, to have two major priorities. It's like going into the candy store with one quarter—you have to choose! I don't believe that this means you have to entirely give up, say, your family. There are many things you do every day that would never be missed if you gave them up.

"Once I had chosen my priorities, it was clear sailing. I gave up the cooking, cleaning, mending, and gardening that I had done with such zest. I channeled all of that effort into my writing. Till then I had picked and frozen strawberries, canned vegetables, and cared for my children. I decided it was time for a change. I remember the day I told the kids I was going to write for the rest of my life and earn enough money to support us (instead of going to work in a bank, as my mother had suggested). I told them they would have to keep house. And they have, ever since.

"That was the end of my procrastination and the beginning of my writing career. I set up the card table in the living room and acted as a hub in the traffic around me. I was still at home. I knew what was going on. But my main occupation was now a writer.

One of Delton's 1989 softcovers.

"Virginia Woolf's 'a room of one's own' is a nice thing to have, but it is not essential.

"In the history of the greatest authors of the greatest books ever written, almost none of them had ideal working conditions. Most of them were poverty stricken and were lucky to have a pencil. Yet, with what they had, they eked out some of the strongest prose ever written.

"The essays and articles I wrote on my card table by hand and typed on my old manual Royal sold for the same amount of money they would have had they been written in an oak-paneled study. And I could oversee the children and the entire household from my vantage point. It was only when I got an oak desk years later, in fact, that I got writer's block with it. When conditions get too good, there is a real pressure to 'write as good' as your conditions are. At my card table, set up hastily every morning after breakfast, I felt spontaneous and prolific and free to concentrate on my words, not on the ring my teacup might make on the wood, or the spent batteries in the automatic pencil sharpener."[1]

Delton's first book, a picture book published in 1974 entitled *Two Good Friends*, was named an ALA Notable Book. "That was a book about a Bear and a Duck: the Duck was my mother and I was the Bear. And it may have sold the most of all my books."[3]

"Animals in a fantasy story are not animals and the story is not an animal story. It is a people story. The animals have all the characteristics and foibles of very specific persons. Duck is the same kind of perfectionist, the same kind of fanatical housekeeper, that my mother was. My mother swept and cleaned and polished just as Duck polishes furniture and puts paper under Bear's feet when he eats Brownies, and watches for falling crumbs. Bear is more myself, a better cook than housekeeper. The story evolves around the way Duck and Bear exchange their strengths and help each other out."[1]

"I don't believe that writing for children is any easier than writing for adults. In fact, a picture book has to have very few words with much imagery in them—a lot like poetry. Writing a longer book is easier because you don't have to have that kind of compression. But at least the same effort goes into it. If you don't consider children people, the work will certainly be patronizing. I don't write *for* children, I just write.

"As far as my writing is concerned, I think I had talent, but I'm fortunate to have met some editors along the way who taught me a lot of the skills. I got the attention of so many newspaper, magazine, and book editors who set me on the right path. This was in the Seventies, before everyone was a 'writer.'"[3]

"Why is it that everyone thinks writers are rich? The word *writer* gives the man on the street the impression of wealth—eccentricity perhaps as well, but first of all, a lot of money. Turn *writer* to *author,* and he expects you to dress like Barbara Cartland, drive a Mercedes, and live on the Riviera. The truth is, B. Cartland is one of a very few. More writers live below the poverty zone than people in any other profession. Most have to supplement their below average incomes in ways that are probably detrimental to the creative spirit they hope to nurture."[1]

Despite the odds, Delton has managed to profit from her craft. In addition to writing a number of children's picture books, Delton has written sever-

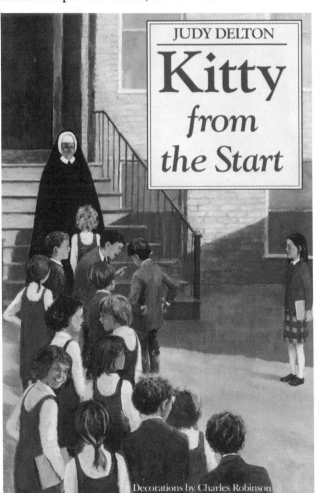

Jacket painting by Charles Robinson.

Kitty
in
High School

Judy Delton

The 1984 Houghton Mifflin hardcover.

al series of books for juvenile readers. *Kitty in the Middle,* published in 1979 was the first of her "Kitty" books. Delton based much of this series on her experiences growing up. "In the Seventies, there was a lot of popular interest in tracing people's origins, so I decided to write about growing up Catholic in the Forties."[3]

Much of *Kitty in the Middle,* as well as *Kitty in the Summer,* was based on Delton's memories of Norwood, "especially the summer [Aunt Katie] went out in the country to keep house for the German family when their new baby arrived. I went with her, and experienced a terrific culture shock. The family did not speak English. The nightmare was just as I had described it in the book. I felt alienated and, the worst part, I experienced my first bout of intense homesickness. I can conjure up the feeling just remembering it. I knew I'd never see my family again. Like Kitty, I ran away, back to my grandfather who did not know that I should not be there. As in the Kitty book, he worried about his dinner and who would cook it while Aunt Katie was

gone, and we crossed the alley to a cousin's house where she fed us both.

"Shortly after dinner Aunt Katie must have missed me because she came dashing home, hot and upset with me. In the book, Kitty went back to the farm. My editor said she had to face her problem. But in real life it didn't work out so neatly. I cried and pleaded and said 'I want to go home!'"[2]

Delton admitted basing the two other characters in the series on friends. "One of them is still a good friend of mine who I see frequently. I lost track of Margaret Mary. Of course, the characters are not exactly the same. I exaggerated. I'm sure my friend doesn't recognize herself. But I think the characters are very strong and each is well developed. You get lost in a book because of it's characters. I think kids will generally relate to the characters if they're portrayed honestly."[3]

For Delton, veracity is an important issue in fiction. "Honesty is not the same as truth. A person can be an honest writer and not always tell the truth. In my novels some of the things are 'made up' or exaggerated—the incidents. Perhaps they come out of someone else's life. Maybe a dress I remember was red and I turn it into blue. Maybe the main character was an only child and I give her a brother or a sister. These are simply 'facts.' They can be played with and turned upside down and rearranged and added and subtracted. Who you are as a writer cannot be manipulated so readily. Your value system, your culture and background, your emotions, your education, your experiences—none of these can be changed from red to blue with a snap of the fingers."[1]

"What I mean by dishonest is by writing something, usually an opinion, with which you have no experience. To write honestly, you must be inside the characters, know them, and believe in them. I can spot dishonesty in fiction and it makes me very angry. My first reaction is generally to throw the book.

"Woody Allen is my favorite writer for this reason. He takes the biggest disasters in his life and turns them into something that's beneficial. It's marvelous to be paid for your neurosis and psychosis. That's why he's so successful. He may be afraid of everything, but he's incredibly honest about it.

"You can't expect to hide much if you're a writer. People have told me that they can't write their life story because their parents, or a sister, is still alive. You can't write with those kind of inhibitions. Your blood and guts really have to be all over the

Jacket from the second book in the "Angel" series.

sidewalk. I don't know how to write any other way than using my own life. I'm in every one of my books.''[3]

"Discovery is what happens when you are honest. Writing *Kitty in the Summer* I discovered that my grandfather did not like me. I found that he always looked over my head when he spoke to me, never at me. I didn't know that before. And I found out that my aunt Katie liked me better than I thought she did at the time. Honest writing is full of surprises.''[1]

Delton based the title character of *Back Yard Angel*, the first book of her "Angel" series, partly on herself and her daughter. The books dealt a lot with the changing nature of modern families. "Though Angel really is me, my daughter gave me the idea because she used to pout a lot when she was little. She didn't smile for five years. All of my friends would try to cheer her up but nothing worked. After seeing her sitting there on the back steps for so many days, I said 'I'll start with that' and kept the picture in my mind. The book really grew out of that character. Angel hates change, just like me. I incorporated my mentality into her.

Because my characters are mostly me, emotionally, they usually go through what I do.''[3]

In 1984, Delton published her first young adult novel, titled, *Near Occasion of Sin*, whose critical view of the Catholicism in which Delton grew up pricked the ire of many reviewers. One decried the book as a subjective, obnoxious attack on the church. Delton viewed the book more as a reflection on former beliefs. "That book came out of an autobiographical urge to purge myself of that part of my life. Being raised Catholic in the Forties, when it was so prominent in your life, stays with you for a long time and it's hard to break old habits. I outgrew the church, have found a lot of it to be damaging. I suppose any book like that makes people nervous if they're still Catholic. But it was historical and something I thought should be recorded.''[3]

Nonetheless, Delton agrees with critics that the book probably should have been for an older audience. "That should never have been a YA book, but that's what the editors I knew were asking for at the time. The people who love it seem to be over fifty. They've remembered things and said, 'Oh yes, that's just how it was.' I realized that the book wasn't the kind that interests young adults. They want more contemporary things. *Near Occasion of Sin* is the only book of mine that hasn't paid off its advance.''[3]

For the moment, Delton is content to write her series books. "The contracts I have keep me busy. My editor asked me if I wanted to be remembered just for my 'Pee Wee Scout' books and when was I going to do something broader, with more impact. I do have a real guilt about not pursuing that, but in a series I can develop the characters and use them so many different ways. It just becomes a matter of talking with my friends to get new ideas of what kids do. Plotting isn't really a problem because the books are short. I enjoy that so much that I really neglect other areas of my writing. I like the 'Condo Kid' series, I just finished a lot because there was plenty of room to develop my characters and I think they are hysterically funny.''[3]

Actually, Delton prefers not to deal with heavy subjects in her work for young people. "My one pet peeve is writing that tries to change or instruct children. I hate books about rape, murder, and incest—all the problems with which they try to get kids to identify. If I were a kid with any of these problems, I would want to read something as far away from that as I could get.

"Of course, there are issues in my work, but they are secondary. Most of it comes out of character, looking at a situation and deciding whether it's something that Kitty would do.

"I think two things draw children to my books. The first is that I tap into real people for my characters, and secondly, I find that my books are funnier than most."[3]

Delton has often advised writers that ideas for them lie everywhere. "Writers look and listen, they see relationships. They know that overheard conversation on a bus could wind up in a picture book. The awareness that such relationships exist means ideas for your books and articles.

"The idea for *My Mom Hates Me in January* was just a title. I was working on an article at the typewriter and my small son (small at the time) kept asking questions. Impatiently I said, 'Go away, I'm working.' His response was, 'Boy, you're sure crabby in the winter.'

"Now many people (nonwriters) could hear this and ignore it; or hear it and feel guilty. But a writer thinks, 'with some changes, that would be a good title for a picture book—a picture book about a mother who is waiting for spring....' I let one word follow another and discovered that the crabby mother was not the little boy's fault at all. It was simply that winter was too long.

"I only had to go back a few years to spot my mother for a character in *Penny-Wise, Fun-Foolish*. She became the ostrich who collected coupons for money-off items in stores. I used to take my coupon-collecting mother grocery shopping and there was always a bit of confusion at the check-out counter while she tried to find the right coupon for the right store. One day I thought to myself, my mother could be a character who collects coupons.

"There is, by the way, no significance in the fact that my mother is portrayed as a duck, or an ostrich. Any animal is suitable; using an animal instead of a person gives an author more freedom. One can do funnier things with fantasy, crazy, bizarre things that might be offensive if one used real people. A fussy person-housekeeper is not funny, but a fussy duck is."[1]

Delton's children also began writing. Jina published her first novel, *Two Blocks Down*, in 1981, and Julie published her first picture book, *My Uncle Nikos*, in 1983. "I think of them seeing their mother writing all the time and imitating that. Plus, they all had a lot of talent. Jina used to write volumes of journals; one day I asked why she didn't

Dust jacket from the 1986 hardcover.

write a book. She said that she had and wanted me to sell it for her, and we sold her book when she was fifteen. But I think part of it was the fact that they always saw me writing."[3]

In 1985, Delton published *The Twenty-nine Most Common Writing Mistakes and How to Avoid Them*. "As I wrote in the beginning of that book, all of my students used to ask me about my lectures, 'When are you going to write all this stuff down?' In teaching so long, I'd evolved a set of guidelines that I used and decided that doing a book would be easy. I really wrote a different book and sent it to Writer's Digest Books. A year later they called me and said they liked one paragraph of it and asked me to rewrite the book. They wanted me to change the book around to say 'Don't' instead of 'Do.' Their marketing department wanted a negative angle: 'Don't do this' and 'Don't do that.' So I rewrote the book, threw most of it out, and then structured it differently."[3]

A main theme of that book stressed the value of persistence. "In the end, the difference between a published writer and an unpublished one comes down to one thing: The unpublished writer gave up, and the published writer didn't."[1]

Delton has since modified that belief. "I used to scoff and tell my students that success was five percent talent and ninety-five percent persistence, but now I've come full circle and think that it's the other way around. In teaching, I received hundreds of manuscripts in the mail to critique, and in reading them I realized that all the persistence in the world wasn't going to help these people. So I'm beginning to give talent more credit than ever. Skill alone won't do you any good. I've seen a lot of skilled, boring writers.

"I don't think I was putting myself down by saying that writing didn't take much talent, I really believed that. I was always very confident and knew that I could do anything I wanted. But in the years of teaching and critiquing so many manuscripts, I got to see the other side. Persistence will still help, there are a lot of poor magazines out there. I've always said that the better you write, the less you sell. You won't make much money writing for literary magazines, so it's nice to find a balance between the two."[3]

Anyway, persistence never *hurt* Delton. "I was gathering old manuscripts and correspondence together yesterday at the request of a university library (which keeps all of my old notes, paper napkins with cryptic jottings, and even my misplaced grocery list in climate controlled vaults) and I glanced at one of the carbons on which I had listed the places that manuscript had been peddled. They were scribbled on the margins, on the back, even right on top of the text when room had run out. Long gone dates jumped out at me, and I began to count how many places the manuscript had been before it sold and ended up in a university collection. The one I looked at by chance had been to *thirty-four* publishers, rejected, and returned!"[1]

Footnote Sources:

[1] Judy Delton, *The Twenty-nine Most Common Writing Mistakes and How to Avoid Them,* Writer's Digest, 1985. Amended by J. Delton.
[2] Joyce Nakamura, *Something about the Author Autobiography Series,* Volume 9, Gale, 1990.
[3] Based on an interview with Marc Caplan for *Authors and Artists for Young Adults.*

■ For More Information See

Periodicals:

Hudson Star-Observer, June 20, 1974, April, 1977.
St. Paul Dispatch, April 2, 1977.
St. Paul Pioneer Press, August 11, 1974, May 31, 1981.
School Library Journal, December, 1984 (p. 46).
Writers Digest, June, 1985 (pg. 39ff).

Collections:

Kerlan Collection at the University of Minnesota.

Annie Dillard

B orn April 30, 1945, in Pittsburgh, Pa.; daughter of Frank (an advertising executive) and Pam (Lambert) Doak; married Richard Henry Wilde Dillard (a poet and novelist), June 5, 1965 (divorced, 1975); married Gary Clevidence (a novelist), April 12, 1980 (divorced, 1987); married Robert D. Richardson (a scholar-biographer), December 10, 1988; children: (second marriage) Rosie. *Education:* Hollins College, B.A., 1967, M.A., 1968. *Politics:* Democrat. *Home:* (winter) Middletown, Conn.; (summer) South Wellfleet, Mass. *Agent:* Blanche Gregory, 2 Tudor City Place, New York, N.Y. 10017.

■ Career

Writer. Hollins College, Roanoke, Va., lecturer, 1975; Fairhaven College and Western Washington State University, Bellingham, teacher of poetry and creative writing, 1975-79, 1981-82; Wesleyan University, visiting professor, 1980-81, adjunct professor (full), 1983—, Writer-in-Residence, 1987—. Member of board of advisors: Wesleyan Writer's Conference, 1984—, Western States Arts Foundation, 1985—, the Milton Center, Friends University, Wichita, Kansas, 1988—; member of the United States State Department's cultural delegation to China, 1982. *Member:* Authors Guild, P.E.N., Poetry Society of America, Phi Beta Kappa.

■ Awards, Honors

Pulitzer Prize for General Nonfiction, 1974, for *Pilgrim at Tinker Creek;* New York Presswomen's Award for Excellence for "Innocence in the Galapagos," 1975; Washington State Governor's Award for Literature, 1978; National Endowment for the Arts/Literature Grant, 1982-83; Phi Beta Kappa Orator, Harvard Commencement Exercises, 1983; Literary Lions Award from the New York Public Library, 1984; John Simon Guggenheim Foundation grant, 1985-86; Doctor of Humane Letters, Boston College, 1986; Middletown Commission in the Arts Award, 1987; *American Childhood* nominated for National Book Critic's Circle Award, 1987; St. Botolph's Club Foundation Award for the Arts, 1989; Appalachian Gold Medallion from University of Charleston (West Virginia), 1989.

■ Writings

Tickets for a Prayer Wheel (poems), University of Missouri Press, 1974.
Pilgrim at Tinker Creek, Harper's Magazine Press, 1974.
Holy the Firm, Harper, 1977.
The Weasel (limited edition), Rara Avis Press, 1981.
Living by Fiction, Harper, 1982.
Teaching a Stone to Talk: Expeditions and Encounters, Harper, 1982.

Encounters with Chinese Writers, Wesleyan University Press, 1984.

(Contributor) *Inventing the Truth: The Art and Craft of Memoir*, edited by William Zinsser, Houghton, 1987.

An American Childhood, Harper, 1988.

(Editor) *The Best American Essays*, Ticknor & Fields, 1989.

The Writing Life, Harper, 1989.

Columnist, *Living Wilderness*, 1973-75. Contributing editor, *Harper's*, 1974-81. Contributor to periodicals, including *Atlantic Monthly*, *Tri-Quarterly*, *Kenyon Review*, *New York Times Magazine*, *Prose*, *American Scholar*, *Poetry*, *Harper's*, *Chicago Review*, and *Antaeus*.

■ Adaptations

"The Tree with Lights in It" (symphony by Sir Arthur Tippett; based on *Pilgrim at Tinker Creek*), first performed at the Centennial of the Boston Symphony Orchestra, summer, 1981.

■ Work in Progress

Frontier fiction.

■ Sidelights

Annie Dillard—the eldest of three daughters of Frank and Pam Doak—grew up in a world of country clubs, debutante parties, and private girls' schools in Pittsburgh, Pennsylvania. Her father was an executive in the old family firm, American Standard, before he switched to advertising. "I had been born at the end of April 1945, on the day Hitler died; Roosevelt had died eighteen days before. My father had been 4-F in the war, because of a collapsing lung—despite his repeated and chagrined efforts to enlist. Now—five years after V-J Day—he still went out one night a week as a volunteer to the Civil Air Patrol; he searched the Pittsburgh skies for new enemy bombers. By day he worked downtown for American Standard.

"Every woman stayed alone in her house in those days, like a coin in a safe. Amy and I lived alone with our mother most of the day. Amy was three years younger than I. Mother and Amy and I went out separate ways in peace."[1]

It hadn't always been that way. "I had made several attempts to snuff baby Amy in her cradle. Mother had repeatedly discovered me pouring glasses of water carefully into her face. So when

Dust jacket from Dillard's 1974 Pulitzer Prize winner.

Molly had appeared, Mother led me to believe the new baby was a kind of present for me."[1]

When she was ten, "The great outer world hove into view and began to fill with things that had apparently been there all along: mineralogy, detective work, lepidopterology, ponds and streams, flying, society. My younger sister Amy and I were to start at private school that year: the Ellis School, on Fifth Avenue. I would start dancing school."[1]

Managing to get a card to the adult section at her library, she came upon a "small blue-bound book printed in fine type on thin paper, like the *Book of Common Prayer*." Ann Haven Morgan's *The Field Book of Ponds and Streams*. "When you checked out a book from the Homewood Library, the librarian wrote your number on the book's card and stamped the due date on a sheet glued to the book's last page. When I checked out the book for the second time, I noticed the card. It was almost full. There were numbers on both sides. Morgan and I were not entirely alone in the world. With us, and sharing our secret lives, were many others.

"Annie Dillard is a poet."—Loren Eiseley, *Washington Post Book World*

TICKETS FOR A PRAYER WHEEL

ANNIE DILLARD

―――――――― AUTHOR OF ――――――――

Pilgrim at Tinker Creek & An American Childhood

Paperbound cover for Dillard's 1974 book of poems.

"Who were these people? Had they, in Pittsburgh's Homewood section, found ponds? Had they found streams? Every year, I reread that book. Often, when I was in the library, I simply visited it. I sat on the marble floor and studied the book's card. There we all were. There was my number. There was the number of someone else who had checked it out more than once. Might I contact this person, and cheer him up? Homewood was apparently full of dreamers."[2]

In her early explorations in natural science, one memory stands out. "I have no intention of inflicting all my childhood memories on anyone. Far less do I want to excoriate my old teachers who, in their bungling, unforgettable way, exposed me to the natural world....[But] once, when I was ten or eleven years old, my friend Judy brought in a Polyphemus moth cocoon. It was January; there were doily snowflakes taped to the schoolroom pane. The teacher kept the cocoon in her desk all morning and brought it out when we were getting restless before recess. In a book we found what the

adult moth would look like; it would be beautiful. With a wingspread of up to six inches, the Polyphemus is one of the few huge American silk moths, much larger than, say, a giant or tiger swallowtail butterfly. The moth's enormous wings are velveted in a rich, warm brown, and edged in bands of blue and pink delicate as a water-color wash.... This was the giant moth packed in the faded cocoon. We closed the book and turned to the cocoon. It was an oak leaf sewn into a plump oval bundle; Judy had found it loose in a pile of frozen leaves.

"We passed the cocoon around; it was heavy. As we held it in our hands, the creature within warmed and squirmed. We were delighted, and wrapped it tighter in our fists. The pupa began to jerk violently, in heart-stopping knocks. Who's there? I can still feel those thumps, urgent through a muffling of spun silk and leaf, urgent through the swaddling of many years, against the curve of my palm. We kept passing it around. When it came to me again it was hot as a bun; it jumped half out of my hand. The teacher intervened. She put it, still heaving and banging, in the ubiquitous Mason jar.

"It was coming. There was no stopping it now, January or not. One end of the cocoon dampened and gradually frayed in a furious battle. The whole cocoon twisted and slapped around in the bottom of the jar. The teacher fades, the classmates fade, I fade: I don't remember anything but that thing's struggle to be a moth or die trying. It emerged at last, a sodden crumple. It was a male; his long antennae were thickly plumed, as wide as his fat abdomen. His body was very thick, over an inch long, and deeply furred. A gray, furlike plush covered his head; a long, tan furlike hair hung from his wide thorax over his brown-furred, segmented abdomen. His multijointed legs, pale and powerful, were shaggy as a bear's. He stood still, but he breathed.

"He couldn't spread his wings. There was no room. The chemical that coated his wings like varnish, stiffening them permanently, dried, and hardened his wings as they were. He was a monster in a Mason jar. Those huge wings stuck on his back in a torture of random pleats and folds, wrinkled as a dirty tissue, rigid as leather. They made a single nightmare clump still wracked with useless, frantic convulsions.

"The next thing I remember, it was recess. The school was in Shadyside, a busy residential part of Pittsburgh. Everyone was playing dodgeball in the fenced playground or racing around the concrete schoolyard by the swings. Next to the playground a long delivery drive sloped downhill to the sidewalk and street. Someone—it must have been the teacher—had let the moth out. I was standing in the driveway, alone, stock-still, but shivering. Someone had given the Polyphemus moth his freedom, and he was walking away.

"He heaved himself down the asphalt driveway by infinite degrees, unwavering. His hideous crumpled wings lay glued and rucked on his back, perfectly still now, like a collapsed tent. The bell rang twice; I had to go. The moth was receding down the driveway, dragging on. I went; I ran inside. The Polyphemus moth is still crawling down the driveway, crawling down the driveway hunched, crawling down the driveway on six furred feet, forever."[3]

Insects weren't the only thing dissected. Her parents loved jokes and would tear "a still-kicking joke apart, so we could see how it worked....

"Telling a good joke well—successfully, perfectly—was the highest art. It was an art because it was up to you: if you did not get the laugh, you had told it wrong. Work on it, and do better next time." They worked on narrative structure, analyzed pacing. "We admired with Father the leisurely meanders of the shaggy-dog story. 'A young couple moved to the Swiss Alps,' one story of his began, 'with their grand piano'; and ended, to a blizzard of thrown napkins, 'oppernockity tunes but once.' 'Frog went into a bank,' another story began, to my enduring pleasure. The joke was not great, but with what a sweet light splash you could launch it!....

"Father was also very fond of stories set in bars that starred zoo animals or insects. These creatures apparently came into bars all over America, either accompanied or alone, and sat down to face incredulous, sarcastic bartenders.... Our mother favored a staccato, stand-up style; if our father could perorate, she could condense. Fellow goes to a psychiatrist. 'You're crazy.' 'I want a second opinion!' 'You're ugly.' 'How do you get an elephant out of the theatre? You can't; it's in his blood.'

"My parents favored practical jokes of the sort you set up and then retire from.... When I visited friends, I was well advised to rise when their parents entered the room. When my friends visited me, they were well advised to duck.

"Central in the orders of merit, and the very bread and butter of everyday life, was the crack. Our mother excelled at the crack. We learned early to feed her lines just to watch her speed to the draw....

"She regarded the instructions on bureaucratic forms as straight lines. 'Do you advocate the overthrow of the United States government by force or violence?' After some thought she wrote, 'Force.'"[1]

"She was interested in language. Once my father and I were in the kitchen listening to a ballgame—the Pirates playing the New York Giants. The Giants had a utility infielder named Wayne Terwilliger. Just as Mother walked through the kitchen, the announcer said, 'Terwilliger bunts one.' Mother stopped dead and said, 'What was that? Was that English?' Father said, 'The man's name is Terwilliger. He bunted.' Mother thought that was terrific. For the next ten or twelve years she made this surprising string of syllables her own. If she was testing a microphone, or if she was pretending to whisper a secret in my ear, she said, 'Terwilliger bunts one.'"[4]

Dillard was baseball crazy. "On Tuesday summer evenings I rode my bike a mile down Braddock Avenue to a park where I watched Little League teams play ball. Little League teams did not accept girls, a ruling I looked into for several years in succession. I parked my bike and hung outside the chain-link fence and watched and rooted and got mad and hollered, 'Idiot, catch the ball!' 'Play's at first!' Maybe some coach would say, 'Okay, sweetheart, if you know it all, you go in there....' At school we played softball. No bunting, no stealing. I had settled on second base, a spot Bill Mazeroski would later sanctify: lots of action, lots of talk, and especially a chance to turn the double play.... I was playing with twenty-five girls, some of whom did not, on the face of it, care overly about the game at hand. I waited out by second and hoped for a play to the plate."[1]

Her discoveries, however, were not exclusive to science, jokes, and baseball. While stretched out in her bedroom, she got hooked on the French and Indian war. "A whole continent was at stake, and it was hard to know whom to root for as I read. The Indians were the sentimental favorites, but they were visibly cruel. The French excelled at Indian skills and had the endearing habit of singing in boats. But if they won, we would all speak French, which seemed affected in the woods....

"I saw Indian braves behind every tree and parked car.... I had taught myself to walk in the woods silently: without snapping a twig, which was easy, or stepping on a loud leaf, which was hard.... I

Dillard stands before a silk-cotton tree.

practiced traveling through the woods in Pittsburgh's Frick Park without leaving footprints. I practiced tracking people and animals, such as some pedigreed dachshunds that lived nearby, by following signs. I knew the mark of my boy hero's blunt heel and the mark of my younger sister's sharp one. I practiced sneaking up on Mother as she repotted a philodendron, Father as he waxed the car, saying, as I hoped but doubted the Indians said, 'Boo.'"[5]

Always a reader, she began to focus in on books of war in her early teens. "We read Leon Uris's popular novels, *Exodus*, and, better *Mila 18*, about the Warsaw ghetto. We read Hersey's *The Wall*— again, the Warsaw ghetto. We read *Time* magazine, and *Life*, and *Look*. It was in the air, that there had been these things. We read, above all, and over and over, for we were young, Anne Frank's *The Diary of a Young Girl*. This was where we belonged; here we were at home.

"I say 'we,' but in fact I did not know anyone else who read these things. Perhaps my parents did, for they brought the books home. What were my friends reading? We did not then talk about books; our reading was private, and constant, like the interior life itself. Still, I say, there must have been millions of us. The theaters of war—the lands, the multiple seas, the very corridors of air—and the death camps in Europe, with their lines of starved bald people. . .these combined were the settings in which our imagination were first deeply stirred."[1]

Adolescence hit with a vengeance. "When I was fifteen, I felt it coming; now I was sixteen, and it hit. . . .

"I was growing and thinning, as if pulled. I was getting angry, as if pushed. I morally disapproved most things in North America, and blamed my innocent parents for them. My feelings deepened and lingered. The swift moods of early childhood—each formed by and suited to its occasion— vanished. Now feelings lasted so long they left stains. They arose from nowhere, like winds or waves, and battered at me or engulfed me.

"When I was angry, I felt myself coiled and longing to kill someone or bomb something big. Trying to appease myself, during one winter I whipped my bed every afternoon with my uniform belt. . .trying to rid myself and the innocent world of my wildness. It was like trying to beat back the ocean.

"Sometimes in class I couldn't stop laughing; things were too funny to be borne. I began then, my surprise that no one else saw what was so funny. . . .

"'Calm yourself,' people had been saying to me all my life. Since early childhood I had tried one thing and then another to calm myself, on those few occasions when I truly wanted to. Eating helped; singing helped. Now sometimes I truly wanted to calm myself. I couldn't lower my shoulders; they seemed to wrap around my ears. I couldn't lower my voice although I could see the people around me flinch. I waved my arm in class till the very teachers wanted to kill me.

"I was what they called a live wire. . . . For as long as I could remember, I had been transparent to myself, unselfconscious, learning, doing, most of every day. Now I was in my own way; I myself was a dark object I could not ignore. I couldn't remember how to forget myself. I didn't want to think about myself, to reckon myself in, to deal with myself every livelong minute on top of everything else—but swerve as I might, I couldn't avoid it."[1]

She rebelled against religion. "I was raised Presbyterian. . .[but] for four consecutive summers I had gone to a fundamentalist church camp in the country. We sang Baptist songs and had a great time—it gave me a taste for abstract thought. But I grew sick of people 'going to church just to show off their clothes,' so I quit the church. Instead of quietly dropping away, I wanted to make a big statement, so I marched into the assistant minister's office. I gave him my spiel about how much hyprocrisy there was in the church. This kind man replied, 'You're right, honey, there is.' Before

Indian children of the Napo River enjoy braiding Dillard's hair.

leaving, I said, 'By the way, I have to write a senior paper for the school—do you have any C. S. Lewis books?' He gave me an armful and I started a long paper on C. S. Lewis. By the time I finished I was right back in the arms of Christianity. My rebellion lasted a month."[6]

Things got worse. "I'd been in a drag race, of all things, the previous September, and in the subsequent collision, and in the hospital; my parents saw my name in the newspapers, and their own names in the newspapers. Some boys I barely knew had cruised by that hot night and said to a clump of us girls on the sidewalk, 'Anybody want to come along for a drag race?' I did, absolutely. I loved fast driving."[1]

At a loss, her mother asked the age-old question, "Dear God, what are we going to do with you?" "My heart went out to them. We all seemed to have exhausted our options. They asked me for fresh ideas, but I had none. I racked my brain, but couldn't come up with anything. The U.S. Marines didn't take sixteen-year-old girls."[1]

In 1963, Dillard went to Hollins College near Roanoke, in southwestern Virginia—partly because of its literary reputation (William Golding had been writer-in-residence), partly because her parents thought the Southern gentry would calm her down. She studied English literature. At the end of her sophomore year, she married her creative writing teacher, Richard H. W. Dillard, a poet nine years her senior who was also a film critic.

Elected to Phi Beta Kappa, she got her B.A. in 1967, then wrote on Thoreau's *Walden* for her master thesis in literature, 1968. "It was unusual to do a critical thesis for Hollin's master's degree. But I had this notion writing was immoral because it made you feel so good. I really wanted to be a writer, but I didn't have the nerve to do it."[7]

After graduation, she continued living in Roanoke in a house near Tinker Creek in a valley of Virginia's Blue Ridge Mountains. "I proceeded to lead a completely enviable life. I would lie down and read—every day. Go to lunch at the Hollins College snack bar, play softball, take a long walk. I was having a wonderful time."[8] It was a purely intellectual life, a life of books.

Then, in 1971, a slow convalescence from a near-fatal case of lobar pneumonia required her to do something with the life she'd been given back. She started to keep journals; she continued writing poetry. Her poems began to appear in *American*

"Annie Dillard...archingly transcends all other writers of our day."
—R. Buckminster Fuller

TEACHING A
STONE TO TALK

► EXPEDITIONS AND ENCOUNTERS ◄

ANNIE
DILLARD

———AUTHOR OF———

Pilgrim at Tinker Creek & An American Childhood

Cover for the paperback edition of the 1982 book.

Scholar, New York Quarterly, and *Southern Poetry Review.* In 1974, twenty-one of her poems were collected in *Tickets for a Prayer Wheel.*

She stopped smoking. Needing something to do with her hands, she got a spiral notebook, filled it with passages from books, and information from her reading. After a camping trip in Maine, where she read a "bad" nature book and thought she could do better, she began to copy the journals onto index cards, accumulating 1,100. Then, in 1973, she worked for eight months, seven days a week, up to fifteen hours a day, incorporating some of those facts from the notebooks into *Pilgrim at Tinker Creek,* while her houseplants died from neglect. Contrary to the myth, she did not write in the shade of a weeping willow on the banks of Tinker Creek but in a library carrel surrounded by cinder blocks so dull to look at, she took to changing the color of her pen.

She roamed the woods, combed the banks—looking, observing, living. She froze to watch an unobservant muskrat. "He never knew I was there.

I never knew I was there either. For that forty minutes...I was as purely sensitive and mute as a photographic plate; I received impressions, but I did not print out captions. My own self-awareness had disappeared; it seems now almost as though, had I been wired with electrodes, my EEG would have been flat. I have done this sort of thing so often that I have lost self-consciousness about moving slowly and halting suddenly; it is second nature to me now. And I have often noticed that even a few minutes of this self-forgetfulness is tremendously invigorating. I wonder if we do not waste most of our energy just by spending every waking minute saying hello to ourselves."[3]

Her intellectual concerns in *Pilgrim at Tinker Creek* were "all that providence implies: the uncertainty of vision, the horror of the fixed, the dissolution of the present, the intricacy of beauty, the pressure of fecundity, the elusiveness of the free, and the flawed nature of perfection.... We wake, if we ever wake at all, to mystery, rumors of death, beauty, violence.... 'Seem like we're just set down here,' a woman said to me recently, 'and don't nobody know why.'"[3]

"Like the bear who went over the mountain, I went out to see what I could see. And...like the bear, all that I could see was the other side of the mountain: more of same. On a good day I might catch a glimpse of another wooded ridge rolling under the sun like water, another bivouac." She proposed to keep what Thoreau called "a meteorological journal of the mind," "telling some tales and describing some of the sights of this rather tamed valley, and exploring, in fear and trembling some of the unmapped dim reaches and unholy fastnesses to which those tales and sights so dizzyingly lead.

"I am no scientist. I explore the neighborhood. An infant who has just learned to hold his head up has a frank and forthright way of gazing about him in bewilderment. He hasn't the faintest clue where he is, and he aims to learn. In a couple of years, what he will have learned instead is how to fake it; he'll have the cocksure air of a squatter who has come to feel he owns the place. Some unwonted, taught pride diverts us from our original intent, which is to explore the neighborhood, view the landscape, to discover at least *where* it is that we have been so startingly set down, if we can't learn why."[3] She asks, "Have we rowed out to the thick darkness, or are we all playing pinochle in the bottom of the boat?"[3]

1974. Dillard was unprepared for the books' enormous success and the deluge of fan letters. Reader's reactions were personal. Helped along by Harper's publicity department, they thought Dillard lived alone through all of those Tinker Creek musings. Readers felt they knew her; she was bombarded by letters. "I lived in that house for twelve years with my husband. And when I was writing the essays, I asked my husband, 'How am I going to deal with you?' And he said, 'Leave me out.' And so I did, and everybody thinks I was up there alone."[2]

"People want to make you into a cult figure because of what they fancy to be your 'lifestyle,' when the truth is your life is literature. You're writing consciously, off of hundreds of index cards, often distorting the literal truth.... It's all hard, conscious, terribly frustrating work. But this never occurs to people. They think it happens in a dream, that you just sit on a tree stump and take dictation from some little chipmunk."[9]

Cover of the 1988 paperbound edition.

"A lot of successful first-novelists commit suicide, and I think I understand why. You feel guilty; you don't go so far as to say what you write is no good; I can't say 'Pilgrim' was a lousy book. But people write to you and say they think you're so good that you're as pure as the earth, but it's not true.... My success has nothing to do with me; it's not remarkable that I could write, and write well; I was trained as a writer. But success is absolutely random; the race is not to the swift."[10]

Pilgrim at Tinker Creek was awarded the Pulitzer Prize, sold over half a million copies, and is still selling steadily here and abroad. "I thought maybe forty monks would read this book. In fact, those forty monks did read the book. And so did everybody else."[2]

Divorced in 1975 and uncomfortable with all the attention, she fled—becoming scholar-in-residence at Western Washington University in the coastal town of Bellingham, Washington; a post she held from 1975 to 1979 and again from 1981-82. Living alone on a northern Puget Sound island with a cat named Small and a spider of "uncertain lineage," she went there to "study hard things— rock mountain and salt sea—and to temper my spirit on their edges."[11]

For periods of time she lived in a log cabin on an even more remote island in Puget Sound reachable only by mail boat twice weekly. "When I came to the Northwest, I knew absolutely nobody in the state of Washington.... [F]ew people realized that a stranger is a stranger in a strange place."[10]

For two years, she questioned time, reality, sacrifice, death and the will of God. "I am drinking boiled coffee and watching the bay from the window. Almost all of the people who reef net have hauled their gears for the winter; the salmon runs are over, days are short. Still, boats come and go on the water—tankers, tugs and barges, rowboats and sails. There are killer whales if you're lucky, rafts of harlequin ducks if you're lucky, and every day the scoter and the solitary grebes. How many tons of sky can I see from the window? It is morning: morning! and the water clobbered with light. Yes, in fact, we do. We do need reminding, not of what God can do, but of what he cannot do, or will not, which is to catch time in its free fall and stick a nickel's worth of sense into our days. And we need reminding of what time can do, must only do; churn out enormity at random and beat it, with God's blessing, into our heads: that we are created, *created,* sojourners in a land we did not make, a land with no meaning of itself and no meaning we

can make for it alone. Who are we to demand explanations of God? (And what monsters of perfection should we be if we did not?).... We are most deeply asleep at the switch when we fancy we control any switches at all."[11]

Out of this came *Holy the Firm,* a spare recollection of three days on an island in Puget Sound—in a wooden room with "one enormous window, one cat, one spider and one person.... I decided to write about whatever happened in the next three days. The literary possibilities of that structure intrigued me. On the second day an airplane crashed nearby, and I was back where I had been in *Pilgrim*—grappling with the problem of pain and dying.... I kept getting stuck. Those forty-three manuscript pages took me fifteen months to write...."

"I simply needed a certain amount of events— whatever might happen—to make a minor point: that days are lived in the mind *and* in the spirit.... Every day has its own particular brand of holiness to discover and worship appropriately. The only way to deal with that was to discover the relationship between time and eternity. That single question interests me artistically more than any other."[6]

On April 12, 1980, Dillard married Gary Clevidence, a novelist and anthropology professor at Fairhaven College. The couple had moved to Middletown, Connecticut where she had been appointed Visiting Professor at Wesleyan University. She has almost always lived within a college community. "I came to Connecticut because, in the course of my wanderings, it was time to come back east—back to that hardwood forest where the multiple trees and soft plants have their distinctive seasons and their places in sun and shade.... So why, if I came for the forest, don't I live in the forest? I live on a residential street, smack dab on the Wesleyan University campus...."

"Many of the people I know who live as hermits among other hermits far from cities honestly find the self an object worthy of study. They are more interesting than I am. When I study myself, I fall asleep. I am a social animal, alive in a gang, like a walrus, or a howler monkey, or a bee.

"I can imagine, after my death, looking down, as it were, on this planet where I had lived, and on those I had loved who were still alive, and remembering our days in the light. I can imagine this, but I cannot imagine thinking, from such a vantage, 'I wish I'd spent more time alone.'"[12]

In 1984, their daughter, Rosie, was born.

An American Childhood was published in 1988. The book is about two things: "a child's interior life—vivid, superstitious and timeless—and a child's growing awareness of the world."[4]

"The world around me while I was growing up consisted of people who believed in Pittsburgh society per se, and I didn't. Reading showed me an enormous number of worlds that were alternatives to that. I spent much of my childhood and now much of my adult life reading. I often reread books. In the process, some fall from favor. I don't read Dostoevsky any more. Tolstoy, on the other hand, gets better and better. I read *Anna Karenina* when I was twenty and thought 'What's the fuss?' But you do a little suffering and see some marriages come and go, and it means a lot more. There are some great books you can't appreciate when you are younger. There are a lot of people who are always rereading the canons, going back every ten years to Dickens, to Henry James, to *Moby Dick*, which is the best novel in English, if not in any language. Everything I want to do as a writer is in that book—the use of information metaphorically, the insistence on reading every event and every object for meaning. Melville is my man.

"Many of the writers I feel closest to—Melville, Emerson, Dickinson, Thoreau, Whitman—are from the 19th century. Perhaps, in some sense, I have a 19th-century sensibility. But I have much more irony in my prose than they did. The possibilities for prose in this century are more interesting. And if I'd lived then, I would have died of pneumonia by now.

"I'm terrified that I will. . .read through all I want to, and be forced to learn wildflowers at last, to keep awake."[3]

"I believe in trying to stay out of the limelight. I want enough sanity to keep on writing because it's literature that I love—and that means not being too famous. I once saw Billie Jean King rush through the lobby of the Plaza Hotel in New York. I thought to myself: "Jeez, I'd rather look around at everything than have to go places with my head down.""[13]

She loves games: "Any game of skill that's competitive—pinochle, anagrams, chess, ping-pong. . . . I live for the double play. It's one of the things that keeps me alive and gets me out of bed in the morning, the possibility that there's going to be a double play and I'll be in the middle of it." And life: "I wake up, look out the window and say, 'Good! Wonderful! Be right out.'"[14]

Footnote Sources:

[1] Annie Dillard, *An American Childhood*, Harper, 1988.
[2] Harper Barnes, "Millions of Friends Share the Secret of Annie Dillard," *St. Louis Post Dispatch*, May 1, 1983.
[3] A. Dillard, *Pilgrim at Tinker Creek*, Harper's Magazine Press, 1974.
[4] William Zinsser, editor, *Inventing the Truth: The Art and Craft of Memoir*, Houghton, 1987.
[5] A. Dillard, "The French and Indian War in Pittsburgh: A Memoir," *American Heritage*, July/August, 1987.
[6] "A Face of Flame: An Interview with Annie Dillard," *Christianity Today*, May 5, 1978.
[7] Jeannette Smyth, "Annie Dillard: Southern Sibyl," *Washington Post*, May 19, 1974.
[8] "Young, Successful, and First," *Saturday Evening Post*, October, 1974. [Amended by Dillard.]
[9] Mike Major, "Annie Dillard, Pilgrim of the Absolute," *America*, May 6, 1978.
[10] Robert Lindsey, "Annie Dillard, Far from Tinker Creek," *New York Times Biographical Service*, November, 1977.
[11] A. Dillard, *Holy the Firm*, Harper, 1977.
[12] "Why I Live Where I Live: by Annie Dillard of Middletown, Connecticut," *Esquire*, March, 1984.
[13] Alvin P. Sanoff, "Remembrances of Things Past," *U.S. News & World Report*, November 16, 1987.
[14] William McPherson, "A Conversation with Annie Dillard," *Book-of-the-Month Club News*, April, 1974.

■ For More Information See

Publishers Weekly, December 10, 1973 (p. 22), March 18, 1974 (p. 28), July 14, 1989 (p. 62), September 1, 1989 (p. 67ff).
Time, March 18, 1974, October 10, 1977.
New York Times Book Review, March 24, 1974 (p. 4ff), September 25, 1977 (p. 12ff), May 28, 1989 (p. 1ff).
New Republic, April 6, 1974.
America, April 20, 1974, February 11, 1978, May 6, 1978.
New York Times, May 12, 1974, September 21, 1977, November 9, 1977 (p. C1).
Washington Post, May 19, 1974 (p. G1ff).
New Leader, June 24, 1974.
Ms., August, 1974.
Virginia Quarterly Review, autumn, 1974 (p. 637ff).
Living Wilderness, autumn, 1974 (p. 2ff), winter, 1974-75 (p. 62ff), spring, 1975 (p. 46ff).
Horn Book, October, 1974.
Commentary, October, 1974.
Harper's, May, 1975 (p. 74ff), January, 1976 (p. 58), November, 1978 (p. 45ff), August, 1980 (p. 61ff).
Holiday, September/October, 1975 (p. 24ff).
Commonweal, October 24, 1975 (p. 495ff), February 3, 1978.
Washington Post Book World, October 16, 1977.
Best Sellers, December, 1977.
Michael Bennett, "An Interview with Annie Dillard," *Fairhaven Review*, Fairhaven College Publications, 1978.

Comtemporary Literary Criticism, Volume IX, Gale, 1978.

Atlantic Monthly, February, 1978 (p. 74ff), February, 1981 (p. 36ff).

North American Review, spring, 1978 (p. 50ff).

Christianity Today, May 5, 1978 (p. 30ff), July 15, 1983 (p. 50ff).

A. Dillard, "Is There *Really* Such a Thing as Talent?," *Seventeen,* June, 1979.

Glynne Robinson Betts, *Writers in Residence: American Authors at Home,* Viking, 1981.

Book World, April 4, 1982.

Christian Science Monitor, April 8, 1982 (p.20).

New York Times Magazine, May 16, 1982 (p. 47ff).

Progressive, June, 1982.

Chicago Tribune, July 5, 1982 (section 2, p. 1ff).

Christian Century, May 18, 1983 (p. 483ff), November 14, 1984 (p. 1062ff).

Yale Review, January, 1985 (p. 312ff).

Esquire, August, 1985 (p. 123ff).

Saturday Review, May/June, 1986 (p. 23).

People Weekly, October 19, 1987 (p. 99ff).

Stephen Trimble, editor, *Words from the Land: Encounters with Natural History Writing,* Gibbs M. Smith, 1988.

Annie Dillard, "A Writer's Landscapes," *Wesleyan,* spring, 1989 (p. 28ff).

Ken Follett

B orn June 5, 1949, in Cardiff, Wales; son of Martin D. (a lecturer and a clerk in the Inland Revenue) and Lavinia C. (Evans) Follett; married Mary Emma Ruth Elson, January 5, 1968 (divorced, 1985); married Barbara Broer (a student), November 8, 1985; children: Emanuele, Marie-Claire. *Education:* University College, London, B.A., 1970. *Politics:* Labour Party. *Religion:* Atheist. *Residence:* Chelsea, London, England. *Agent:* Writers House, Inc., 21 West 26th St., New York, N.Y. 10010.

■ Career

South Wales Echo, Cardiff, Wales, reporter and rock music columnist, 1970-73; *Evening News,* London, England, reporter, 1973-74; Everest Books Ltd., London, editorial director, 1974-76, deputy managing director, 1976-77; full-time writer, 1977—. *Member:* Mystery Writers of America, Authors Guild, Society of Authors (Great Britain), National Union of Journalists (Great Britain).

■ Awards, Honors

Edgar Allan Poe Award from the Mystery Writers of America, 1978, for *Eye of the Needle.*

■ Writings

Novels, Except As Indicated:

(Under pseudonym Simon Myles) *The Big Needle,* Everest Books, 1974, published as *The Big Apple,* Kensington, 1975.

(Under pseudonym Simon Myles) *The Big Black,* Everest Books, 1974.

(Under pseudonym Simon Myles) *The Big Hit,* Everest Books, 1975.

The Shakeout, Harwood-Smart, 1975, reissued, Armchair Detective, 1990.

(Under pseudonym Martin Martinsen) *The Power Twins and the Worm Puzzle,* Abelard, 1976, published in America as *Power Twins,* Greenwillow, 1990.

The Bear Raid, Harwood-Smart, 1976.

The Secret of Kellerman's Studio (juvenile), Abelard (London), 1976, published in America as *The Mystery Hideout,* Morrow, 1990.

(Under pseudonym Bernard L. Ross) *Amok: King of Legend,* Futura, 1976.

(Under pseudonym Zachary Stone) *The Modigliani Scandal,* Collins, 1976, reissued, Morrow, 1985, large print edition, G. K. Hall, 1986.

(Under pseudonym Zachary Stone) *Paper Money,* Collins, 1977, 2nd edition, Morrow, 1987.

(Under pseudonym Bernard L. Ross) *Capricorn One,* Futura, 1978.

Eye of the Needle, Arbor House, 1978, movie edition, New American Library, 1981 (published in England as *Storm Island,* Macdonald & Jane's, 1978).

(With Rene Louis Maurice) *The Heist of the Century* (nonfiction), Fontana Books, 1978, published as *The Gentlemen of 16 July,* Arbor House, 1980, published as *Under the Streets of Nice,* Knightsbridge, 1990.

Triple, Arbor House, 1979.

The Key to Rebecca, Morrow, 1980.

The Man from St. Petersburg, Morrow, 1982.

On Wings of Eagles (nonfiction), Morrow, 1983, large print edition, G. K. Hall, 1984.

Lie Down with Lions, Morrow, 1986, large print edition, G. K. Hall, 1986.

Pillars of the Earth, Morrow, 1989.

Film Scripts:

"Fringe Banking," British Broadcasting Corp., 1978.

(With John Sealey) "A Football Star," 1979.

Contributor to periodicals, including *Writer.*

■ Adaptations

"Eye of the Needle" (motion picture), adapted by Stanley Mann, directed by Richard Marquand and starring Donald Sutherland and Kate Nelligan, United Artists, 1981.

"The Key to Rebecca" (television miniseries), starring Cliff Robertson and David Soul, Operation Prime Time Productions, April, 1985.

"On Wings of Eagles" (television miniseries), starring Burt Lancaster and Richard Crenna, 1986.

Recordings:

"The Key to Rebecca" (cassette; abridged edition), Listen for Pleasure, 1982, Books in Motion, 1985.

"The Eye of the Needle" (cassette; abridged edition), Listen for Pleasure, 1983, Brilliance, 1989.

"On Wings of Eagles" (cassette), Brilliance, 1984.

"The Man from St. Petersburg" (cassette), Warner Audio, 1985, Random House, 1988.

"Lie Down with Lions" (cassette), Brilliance, 1986.

"Triple" (cassette), Books on Tape.

"Under the Streets of Nice" (cassette), Recorded Books.

"Paper Money" (cassette), Dove Books on Tape, 1988.

"The Modigliani Scandal" (cassette), Dove Books on Tape, 1989.

"Pillars of the Earth" (cassette), Brilliance, 1989.

■ Work in Progress

Night over Water, a novel set almost entirely on board a Pan American flying boat during a single transatlantic flight in September, 1939.

■ Sidelights

Ken Follett was born in Wales, "in a little terrace house in Cardiff in 1949. It was very much a petit-bourgeois background. My dad was a clerk in the Inland Revenue [English equivalent of the IRS], and I went to state schools.

"At that time I wanted to be a captain of industry, then later I thought I'd be a great reporter."[1]

Even so, Follett was fascinated with thrillers and spy novels from an early age. Before reaching adolescence, he had devoured all of H. G. Wells' science-fiction work and Ian Fleming's entire James Bond oeuvre.

In 1967, while a student at the University of London, the eighteen-year-old Follett married twenty-one-year-old Mary Emma Ruth Elson. Their son Emanuele was born later that year. While her husband continued his schooling and watched after their son, Mary Follett supported the family by working as a bookkeeper.

In 1968, Follett graduated with an honours degree in philosophy, and went to work as a reporter and rock music columnist for the *South Wales Echo* in Cardiff. In 1973 he moved back to London to become a crime reporter for the *Evening News,* a sensationalistic tabloid. "It was a rotten newspaper. I mean it really stank.... I used to do everything. I covered a lot of crime, but quite often I got sent on trials because my shorthand was very fast."[2]

But the pay was not quite adequate for his needs, so while working for the *Evening News,* Follett felt compelled to try his hand at fiction. A fellow reporter had just gotten a sizeable advance for his first mystery novel, and when Follett incurred various expenses, including the birth of his daughter, the purchase of a new house and major repairs on his car, he took the pseudonym Symon Myles to write *The Big Needle,* a mystery about a heroin dealer. It had "a lot of sex and a hero with fancy cars, but it wasn't all that bad. I'm not ashamed of it." The book didn't sell particularly well, but well enough for him to pay his debts and whet his interest in writing commercial fiction. "I read Forsyth's *Day of the Jackal* to see why it had sold so many copies, and I realized I was writing with the wrong attitude. What was in the book didn't *matter* enough to me. I had to know more, be more attentive to detail."[1]

Soon after he abandoned journalism to join a small London publishing house, Everest Books Limited—"to learn how and why books become best sellers." At Everest, Follett continued to write in his spare time, producing nine more novels—mysteries, thrillers, and two children's mysteries—using pseudonyms for six of them because his agent was convinced that he would write better books in the future. None of these books became very well known, but each made about $5000, and provided Follett with a literary apprenticeship. Follett later acknowledged that he learned how to write good books "by writing mediocre ones and wondering what was wrong with them." In 1977, by then a deputy managing director at Everest, Follett resigned to become a full-time writer.

"In a modern thriller the hero generally saves the world. Traditional adventure stories are more modest: The central character merely saves his own life, and perhaps the life of a faithful friend or a plucky girl. In less sensational novels—the middlebrow, well-told narratives that have been the staple diet of readers for more than a century—there is less at stake, but still a character's efforts, struggles and choices determine his destiny in a dramatic fashion.

"I don't actually believe that life is like that. In reality, circumstances quite beyond our control usually determine whether we live or die, become happy or miserable, strike it rich or lose everything. For example: Most rich people inherit their money. Most well-fed people simply had the luck to be born in an affluent country. Most happy people were born into loving families, and most miserable people had crazy parents.

"I'm not a fatalist, nor do I believe that everything in life is blind chance. We do not control our lives the way a chess player controls his pieces, but life is not roulette either. As usual, the truth is complicated. Mechanisms beyond our control—and sometimes beyond our understanding—determine a person's fate, yet the choices he makes have

Softcover edition of the 1978 award-winning novel.

consequences, if not the consequences he anticipated.

"In *The Modigliani Scandal* I tried to write a new kind of novel, one that would reflect the subtle subordination of individual freedom to more powerful machinery. In this immodest project I failed. It may be that such a novel cannot be written: Even if Life is not about individual choice, perhaps Literature is.

"What I wrote, in the end, was a lighthearted crime story in which an assortment of people, mostly young, get up to a variety of capers, none of which turns out quite as expected. The critics praised it as sprightly, ebulient, light, bright, cheery, light (again), fizzy. I was disappointed that they had not noted my serious intentions.

"Now I no longer look on the book as a thriller. It *is* fizzy, and none the worse for that. The fact that it is so different from the book I intended to write, should not have surprised me. After all, it rather proves my point."[3]

In 1978 Follett's eleventh book, *Eye of the Needle*, fulfilled his long-standing desire for a bestseller. The novel, which took only three months to write, resulted from his attendance at a sales conference held by Futura Publications, Everest Books' distributor. Anthony Cheetham, Futura's managing editor, asked him to write an adventure having to do with World War II. Follett liked the idea and the following morning wrote a plot synopsis which he described as follows: "Early in 1944 German Intelligence was piecing together evidence of a huge army in south-eastern England. Reconnaissance planes brought back photographs of barracks and airfields and fleets of ships in the Wash; General George S. Patton was seen in his unmistakable pink jodhpurs walking his white bulldog; there were bursts of wireless activity, signals between regiments in the area; confirming signs were reported by German spies in Britain.

"There was no army, of course. The ships were rubber and timber fakes, the barracks no more real than a movie set; Patton did not have a single man under his command; the radio signals were meaningless; the spies were double agents. The object was to fool the enemy into preparing for an invasion via the Pas de Calais, so that on D-Day, the Normandy assault would have the advantage of surprise.

"It was a huge, near-impossible deception. Literally thousands of people were involved in perpetrating the trick. It would have been a miracle if none of Hitler's spies ever got to know about it.

"Were there any spies? At the time, people thought they were surrounded by what were then called Fifth Columnists. After the war, a myth grew up that M15 had rounded up the lot by Christmas 1939. The truth seems to be that there were very few: M15 did capture nearly all of them.

"But it only needs one spy!"[4]

The *Eye of the Needle*, which was accompanied by a major marketing campaign became an instant international success, selling more than five million copies in twenty languages and earning Follett $525,000. The same year United Artists acquired the movie rights and the film version starring Donald Sutherland and Kate Nelligan was released in 1981, similarly to commercial success.

Triple, published the following year, was Follett's second bestseller, and earned him more than a million dollars. On the strength of the sales of his two previous works, he signed a three-book, three million dollar deal with New American Library to become, according to his publishers, one of the world's youngest millionaire authors. "I was a great liver in fantasy worlds from an early age. I wanted to write best sellers, yes. And if I had made a reasonable—oh, I don't mean reasonable, I mean realistic—guess about seven years ago, before I happened, as to what my chances were, I would have said, 'Well, you're a No. 10 best seller, not a No. 1.' But then being a daydreamer and a fantasist, I thought of the various things I could do with that million."[5]

Oddly enough, Follett's books didn't sell well in England. "Some rather better writers than me have had that experience—such as D. M. Thomas. I kind of am amused by that. I mean, Don Thomas is the man who may turn out to be the most outstanding writer of his generation. The English had him right in their midst, and they didn't even know it."[5]

Morrow published *The Key to Rebecca* in 1980, a fictionalized historical incident about the mission of a German spy operating in the Middle East during the Rommel campaigns of 1942. The protagonist, Alexander Wolff, was modeled after the real Nazi spy John Eppler who, from Cairo, transmitted intelligence reports in a code based on Daphne du Maurier's 1938 novel *Rebecca*. A suit was brought against Follett by Leonard Mosley, who claimed that characters and events in *The Key to Rebecca* were largely copied from his 1958 book *The Cat and the Mouse*—a nonfiction account of John Eppler's exploits. The judge dismissed the case on the ground that as Mosley's was a work of nonfiction, he could not prevent others from using the information presented.

The same year Follett fought a legal battle of his own against Arbor House. "Arbor House announced publication of *The Gentlemen of 16 July* [Follett had edited the English translation from the French] with myself as principal author and listed the book as a 'non-fiction novel.' I sought to prevent their using my name on the book. The judge's verdict was a compromise: Arbor House was obliged to name the original authors first, in letters no smaller than those used for my name, and to list the book as nonfiction. Although this was not the verdict I had hoped for, it was, in the event, almost as good: because of the stir caused by the trial, the book when published had a bad smell, and it did not become a bestseller either in hardcover or paperback."

Donald Sutherland played a ruthless Nazi spy in the 1981 United Artists movie "Eye of the Needle."

Like his other books, *The Man from St. Petersburg* Follett's fourth thriller [1982], immediately made the bestseller lists. "I suppose that I'm continually looking over my shoulder and wondering if what I'm doing is as good as *Eye of the Needle.* [But] the main task in my life is still to write good books."[6]

"I'm not under the illusion that the world is waiting for my thoughts to appear in print. People want to be told a story, and that's what I'm up to. I think of myself as a craftsman more than an artist.

"I don't kid myself that I write as well as Le Carre, though I may get that good one of these days, but my stories are better than his and I certainly write a hell of a lot better than Forsyth does."[7]

"I do constantly compare myself to great classical writers. Why compare yourself to John Le Carre when you might just as well compare yourself to, say, Jane Austen? I compare myself all the time with great English writers like Dickens and Thomas

Hardy and George Eliot—and wonder why I can't do better."[5]

Follett plans each work carefully. Before starting the actual writing of a novel, he researches all aspects of the plot and setting through a wide variety of sources, including magazines, books and newspapers. The next step is the preparation of a detailed outline. Only after all is set does he commence the actual writing of the novel. He often revises with the help of his agent and his editor feeling that collaboration can be helpful for a writer whose object is the widest possible audience. "I rewrite [the outline] many times, trying to solve the problems at that stage. Most authors, I think, try to solve them as they go along. Then, although I may later rewrite many big scenes, I do two drafts.

"Fast is my normal speed. I just got into the habit of putting my thoughts down at 40 words per minute—and right the first time. I never rewrite anything more than once."[7]

In addition to spy thrillers, Follett wrote *On Wings of Eagles*, a nonfiction account of the rescue of two American businessmen from an Iranian prison during the revolution of 1979. "I was approached by the PR director at Electronic Data Systems in Dallas, who wanted to do a book on how his boss, the multimillionaire H. Ross Perot, had rescued some of his key men from Iran at the time of the revolution. They wanted an authorized book because they were afraid someone would do an unauthorized one. It seems that Perot's wife, Margot, recommended me because she liked my stuff, but she didn't realize I wasn't an American. I was interested because I'd just done three novels in quick succession, and I was tired of it and looking for something different.

"The real problem in doing the book was in how to explain all the preliminary negotiations without boring the reader. In the end, I did it by having people make phone calls to Perot reporting on developments and did it all in dialogue, with him asking the right questions. I learned a whole new way of writing for *Eagles,* and I could easily imagine doing another nonfiction book, in order to acquire new skills I could use again."[1]

"The bloody book went through four drafts. Now a book of Ken Follett's that goes through four drafts doesn't get intensely suspenseful by accident. I mean!

"I was sort of in the care of Perot down there [in Texas] and you get the feeling the man can arrange anything. One day I mentioned how it was rather ironic that, here I write all these shoot-bang thrillers, and I've never fired a gun. So the next day I found myself on a firing range with some Uzi submachine gun and an AK-17 and I think what you call a Walther PPK.

"In the beginning Perot and I had the advantage of considering ourselves total aliens. I think we were both surprised at how well we got along. Texas just reeks of prosperity, doesn't it? And that's very intriguing, certainly these day, and kind of nice, too.

"I have to admit, I like him a lot. I think he's a great man. I don't think I saw him through rose-colored glasses. The striking thing about him is his sense of humor. He's very short, you know. And not very handsome. We asked him who was going to play him in the movie and he said immediately, 'Mickey Rooney.' A-ha ha-ha."[4]

In 1986, Follett returned to fiction with *Lie Down with Lions*. Like all his thrillers, the book is set against the backdrop of war and features an off-beat romantic angle. Being one of the best-selling novelists of his generation, Follett often has to deal with the label "popular writer"—a term he doesn't object to. In his own words, he chose the thriller format because the readers keep turning the pages. "Why are good books so boring? We wondered about this as students, plodding through Henry James or Virginia Woolf while we longed to get back to *My Gun Is Quick*. Perhaps we were afraid to ask, for fear of seeming naive. As writers I think we should be asking the question still. It could turn out to be the most important question around.

"Literature wasn't always so dull: this is a truism. *Oliver Twist* was a magazine serial. I read somewhere that one episode ended as Bill Sikes began to beat up Nancy; and when the ship carrying the next issue of the magazine arrived in New York, there was a crowd on the quay waiting to find out if Nancy died. The story may be apocryphal, but it makes a point: the greatest novelist in the English language used melodrama as liberally as any writer of soap opera.

"Nowadays melodrama is unfashionable. Or is it? The literary phenomenon of the decade is the romantic-historical blockbuster—the kind of book my English agent calls a Sweet Savage Hysterical. There's melodrama—but it doesn't get reviewed in the *New York Times*. All right, I know—Kathleen Woodiwiss isn't in the Dickens class. Actually, that's the point. Nobody that good writes melodra-

From the 1986 television mini-series "On Wings of Eagles," starring Burt Lancaster and Richard Crenna.

ma any more. Nobody that good writes mass-market fiction any more. This is a catastrophe. How did it happen?

"First, character became the only permissible subject for a serious novel. (This was new: *Robinson Crusoe* was no more about *character* than *Raise the Titanic*.) Second, after the publication in 1922 of James Joyce's *Ulysses*, introspection became the paramount literary technique.... Although occasionally capable of touching an exposed nerve—as did *Fear of Flying*, for example–the light-comic approach of intellectual fiction today generally can't cope with much more than the trivia of middle-class life. Revolution, tragedy, passion, power, death: Thomas Hardy and Emily Bronte could write about these, but Kingsley Amis and John Updike can't; and when Gore Vidal writes about the end of the world he does it as a comedy.

"I realise all this is not too terrifically scholarly; I'm just saying how it looks to me as a working storyteller.

"While the intellectuals were plodding through Evelyn Waugh the rest of us were gasping with Mickey Spillane and swooning with Daphne du Maurier. And, just as they had to eat an awful lot of pudding to get at the plums, so we found—didn't we?—that cotton candy may be sweet but it nourishes not at all.

"What went wrong (stick with it, now, I'm getting to the point) was that both fiction markets set themselves low standards. So long as they gave us thrilling tales the great mass-market writers, from Edgar Rice Burroughs to Dennis Wheatley, were permitted cardboard characters, sloppy writing, and texture as bland as Formica. The elite, who could get away with none of that, were allowed to dispense with plot, story, excitement, sensation, and the world outside the mind, so long as they were deep.

"Well, what's to be done? I hope it's clear by now that this isn't going to be another plea for thrillers to be treated with critical seriousness: most of them, mine included, don't merit it because they aren't good enough (and it's small consolation that most serious novels aren't either). But our profession won't produce too many great writers while we continue to opt either for exciting trash or thoughtful tedium.

"Will the intellectuals learn to enchant as well as enlighten us? It *can* be done. *One Flew Over the Cuckoo's Nest* satisfies the intellect without boring the pants off us. There are a few others: *The Grapes of Wrath*, *1984*, *Lord of the Flies*. They're all mavericks, though: freaks, off-shoots from the literary mainstream; each of them is about something more than character, and none of the authors produced a body of mass-market hits.

"But let's learn other things from the intellectuals. Watch how Faulkner creates a rural community, and forget *Peyton Place*. We know how Agatha Christie creates suspense on stage, but what is Harold Pinter's trick? If there's an adolescent in the story, compare him with the boy in *Catcher in the Rye*, not the girl in *The Exorcist*.

"I know, it's a depressing experience. It tells us how shallow our work is. But it also tells us how good fiction *can* be. Writing successful fiction is a matter of getting lots of different things right (which is why there's no formula for a best seller) and the way to get better, I suspect, is to discover new things to get right.

"Writers have something of a responsibility. People get an awful lot of their ideas about life from fiction. Like it or not, one or two of us will probably change the way our contemporaries

The 1990 Morrow hardcover.

Follett's 1990 novel for school-age readers.

think—and it's mass-market stuff that does that. My generation learned about Nazi Germany from the TV show 'Holocaust.' The popular view of life under communism comes from George Orwell's *1984*, not *The Gulag Archipelago.* British people never understood Watergate until we saw the movie 'All the President's Men.' And then there's *Roots.*

"It's often said that a romance or a mystery can't be well characterised, true to life and beautifully written because everything has to be subordinate to the plot. I think that's like saying verse will never have the impact of prose because the choice of words is constrained by metre and rhyme. In fact the rules of formal poetry give the words *more* impact. Plot ought to do the same for character.

"'When the spymaster's everyday life begins to make the plot implausible, which do you sacrifice—story or realism?'

"Sorry, you don't get off the hook that easily. The object is to have a plot and a character that fit together like ball and socket. It is terribly difficult to write beautiful rhyming verse, because the rules

are so restricting. Similarly, the need for a happy ending, a violent climax, a ludicrously ambitious theft, or a love interest for the hero—all of these make it harder to write real people and credible events and sensitive prose. Anyone can write: it's writing *well* that is so tough.

"But then, who told you it was easy?"[8]

Follett's latest achievement, *The Pillars of the Earth*, a 1,100-page historical novel that chronicles the building of a cathedral in twelfth-century England, was published in 1989. His interest in cathedrals dated his years as a reporter for the London *English News.* While on assignment in Peterborough, East Anglia Follett visited the local cathedral and started wondering about the religious, political, and social forces able to engender such monumental creations. "The medieval cathedrals of Europe are the most beautiful buildings in the world. They are technically brilliant and artistically breathtaking. They have stood for hundreds of years, almost a millennium. Yet they were designed by men who had virtually no mathematics, built with the simplest of tools, and financed by people who were dirt poor. *Why?*"[9]

"The Church itself is not something I'm interested in. What does interest me is the struggle to create a more decent society, a more civilized world. At that moment in history, the Church served that function. I was also concerned to show that not everything the Church did was good."[10]

For a year and a half Follett immersed himself in medieval literature, learning about church architecture and the history of the period. "It's quite a formidable feeling to work for a year and a half on a book before you have written a *word.*

"I half expected [my publishers] to say, 'Terrific, but it gives us a marketing problem.' But they didn't. And actually, if the thing is good enough, you never have a marketing problem. It used to be said that you can't sell novels about the Middle Ages. But along came *The Name of the Rose*, which toppled that theory on its ear."

After completion of *The Pillars of the Earth*, Follett felt that he would probably not go back to writing thrillers. "I don't think I'll ever go back to that type of suspense novel. An historical novel is a much more difficult type of book to write than a thriller. In fact, it's hard as hell, but it's also much more satisfying."[11]

Follet now lives with his second wife, Barbara, in an eighteenth-century house overlooking the Thames River in the Chelsea district of London.

When he is not writing, he likes to play bass guitar in his twenty-one-year-old son's rock band. He no longer reads quantities of thrillers, preferring instead the Victorian novelists, especially Jane Austen and Thomas Hardy.

Footnote Sources:

[1] John F. Baker, "PW Interviews: Ken Follett," *Publishers Weekly*, January 17, 1986.

[2] *Chicago Tribune*, October 15, 1983.

[3] Ken Follett, *The Modigliani Scandal*, New American Library, 1985.

[4] Production notes from United Artist, 1981.

[5] Paul Hendrickson, "Ken Follett's Winging Ways," *Washington Post*, September 21, 1983.

[6] Barbara Isenberg, "No Cheap Thrillers from Follett Pen," *Los Angeles Times*, October 1, 1980.

[7] Fred Hauptfuhrer, "When It Comes to Cliff-Hanging, Ken Follett Has, at 29, Clawed into Competition with LeCarre," *People Weekly*, September 25, 1978.

[8] K. Follett, "Books that Enchant and Enlighten," *Writer*, June, 1979.

[9] Morrow publicity for *The Pillars of the Earth*.

[10] Sybil Steinberg, "The 'Pillars' of a New Success from Ken Follett and Morrow," *Publishers Weekly*, July 21, 1989.

[11] *Globe & Mail* (Toronto), September 12, 1989.

■ For More Information See

Donald McCormick, *Who's Who in Spy Fiction*, Elm Tree Books/Hamilton, 1977.

New York Times, May 12, 1978 (p. C26), July 16, 1978 (p. 24), October 3, 1979, September 21, 1980, April 29, 1985 (p. C16).

Washington Post Book World, July 2, 1978 (p. F1ff), April 25, 1982, August 20, 1989.

New York Times Book Review, July 16, 1978, September 21, 1980 (p. 9), May 9, 1982.

Saturday Review, August, 1978 (p. 51).

Newsweek, August 7, 1978, September 29, 1980.

New Yorker, August 21, 1978 (p. 96), August 16, 1982.

Time, October 30, 1978, November 5, 1979, September 29, 1980, May 3, 1982.

Los Angeles Times Book Review, October 7, 1979, September 28, 1980, May 30, 1982, September 11, 1983.

Washington Post, October 11, 1979, September 15, 1980, September 7, 1983.

Chicago Tribune Book World, October 5, 1980.

Times Literary Supplement, December 20, 1980 (p. 1458), June 4, 1982, June 20, 1986.

San Francisco Chronicle, July 24, 1981 (p. 49).

Contemporary Literary Criticism, Volume XVIII, Gale, 1981.

Dictionary of Literary Biography Yearbook: 1981, Gale, 1982.

Women's Wear Daily, April 24, 1985 (p. 23).

Times (London), January 14, 1988 (p. 12).

Daily News (New York), September 17, 1989 (section II, p. 3).

Donna Olendorf, editor, *Bestsellers 89: Books and Authors in the News*, Gale, 1990.

Current Biography, January, 1990.

Rumer Godden

B orn December 10, 1907, in Sussex, England; daughter of Arthur Leigh (a steamship agent) and Katherine (Hingley) Godden; married Laurence S. Foster, 1934 (deceased); married James Haynes-Dixon, November 11, 1949 (died, 1973); children: (first marriage) Jane, Paula. *Education:* Attended Moira House, Eastbourne; studied dancing privately. *Religion:* Roman Catholic. *Home:* Ardnacloich, Dumfriesshire, Moniaive, Scotland. *Agent:* Curtis Brown Ltd., 10 Astor Place, New York, N.Y. 10003. *Office:* c/o Macmillan & Co., 4 Little Essex St., London WC2R 3LF, England.

■ Career

Novelist, poet, and author of books for children. Founded and operated a children's dancing school in Calcutta, India. *Member:* Imperial Society of Teachers of Dancing.

■ Awards, Honors

New York Herald Tribune's Children's Spring Book Festival Award Honor Book, 1951, for *The Mousewife*, 1960, for *Candy Floss*, and 1961, for *Miss Happiness and Miss Flower;* Carnegie Medal Commendation from the British Library Association, 1956, for *The Fairy Doll*, and 1962, for *Miss Happiness and Miss Flower;* International Board on Books for Young People Honor List, 1958, for *The Fairy Doll; Operation Sippacik* was selected one of Child Study Association of America's Children's Books of the Year, 1969, *The Diddakoi*, and *The Old Woman Who Lived in a Vinegar Bottle*, both 1972, and *Mr. McFadden's Hallowe'en*, 1975; Whitbread Children's Book Award from the Booksellers Association of Great Britain and Ireland, 1973, and Silver Pen Award for Children's Book of the Year (Holland), both for *The Diddakoi;* Parents' Choice Award for Literature from the Parents' Choice Foundation, 1984, for *Thursday's Children; The Story of Holly and Ivy* was selected a Notable Children's Trade Book in the Field of Social Studies by the National Council for Social Studies and the Children's Book Council, 1986.

■ Writings

Novels:

Chinese Puzzle, P. Davies, 1936.
The Lady and the Unicorn, P. Davies, 1938, reissued, 1969.
Black Narcissus, Little, Brown, 1939, reissued, New American Library, 1968.
Gypsy, Gypsy, Little, Brown, 1940, reissued, Macmillan (London), 1965.
Breakfast with the Nikolides, Little, Brown, 1942.

Rungli-Rungliot, (Thus Far and No Further), P. Davies, 1944, published as *Rungli-Rungliot Means in Parharia, "Thus Far and No Further"*, Little, Brown, 1946, 2nd edition, published as *Thus Far and No Further*, Macmillan (London), 1961.

Take Three Tenses: A Fugue in Time, Little, Brown, 1945 (published in England as *A Fugue in Time*, M. Joseph, 1945, reissued, Macmillan, 1976).

The River, Little, Brown, 1946, reissued, Macmillan, 1967.

A Candle for St. Jude, Viking, 1948.

A Breath of Air, M. Joseph, 1950, Viking, 1951.

Kingfishers Catch Fire, Viking, 1953.

An Episode of Sparrows, Viking, 1955, large print edition, 1968.

The Greengage Summer, Viking, 1958, large print edition, Ulverscroft, 1986.

China Court: The Hours of a Country House, Viking, 1961.

The Battle of Villa Fiorita, Viking, 1963.

In This House of Brede, Viking, 1969.

The Peacock Spring: A Western Progress, Macmillan, 1975, Viking, 1976, large print edition, Ulverscroft, 1980.

Five for Sorrow, Ten for Joy, Viking, 1979.

The Dark Horse, Viking, 1981.

Thursday's Children, Viking, 1984, large print edition, G. K. Hall, 1985.

Juvenile:

The Doll's House (ALA Notable Book; illustrated by Dana Saintsbury), M. Joseph, 1947, Viking, 1948, new edition (illustrated by Tasha Tudor), Viking, 1962.

In Noah's Ark (narrative poem), Viking, 1949.

The Mousewife (ALA Notable Book; illustrated by William Pene du Bois), Viking, 1951, new edition (illustrated by Heidi Holder), Viking, 1982.

Impunity Jane: The Story of a Pocket Doll (ALA Notable Book; illustrated by Adrienne Adams), Viking, 1954.

The Fairy Doll (ALA Notable Book; illustrated by A. Adams), Viking, 1956.

Mouse House (illustrated by A. Adams), Viking, 1957.

The Story of Holly and Ivy (illustrated by A. Adams), Viking, 1958, new edition (illustrated by Barbara Cooney), 1985.

Candy Floss (illustrated by A. Adams), Viking, 1960.

St. Jerome and the Lion (poems; illustrated by Jean Primrose), Viking, 1961.

Miss Happiness and Miss Flower (ALA Notable Book; *Horn Book* honor list; illustrated by J. Primrose), Viking, 1961.

Little Plum (*Horn Book* honor list; illustrated by J. Primrose), Viking, 1963.

Home Is the Sailor (*Horn Book* honor list; illustrated by J. Primrose), Viking, 1964.

(Adapter) Hans Christian Andersen, *The Feather Duster: A Fairy-Tale Musical*, music by Kai Normann Anderson, Dramatic Publishing, 1964.

The Kitchen Maddona (ALA Notable Book; *Horn Book* honor list; illustrated by Carol Barker), Viking, 1967.

Operation Sippacik (Junior Literary Guild selection; illustrated by James Bryan), Viking, 1969.

The Diddakoi (illustrated by Creina Glegg), Viking, 1972.

(Reteller) *The Old Woman Who Lived in a Vinegar Bottle* (ALA Notable Book; *Horn Book* honor list; illustrated by Mairi Hedderwick), Viking, 1972.

Mr. McFadden's Hallowe'en (illustrated by Ann Strugnell), Viking, 1975.

The Rocking Horse Secret (illustrated by Juliet S. Smith), Macmillan, 1977, Viking, 1978.

A Kindle of Kittens (ALA Notable Book; illustrated by Lynne Byrnes), Macmillan, 1978, Viking, 1979.

The Dragon of Og (ALA Notable Book; illustrated by Pauline Baynes), Viking, 1981.

The Valiant Chatti-Maker (illustrated by Jeroo Roy), Viking, 1983.

Four Dolls (includes *Impunity Jane*, *The Fairy Doll*, *The Story of Holly and Ivy*, and *Candy Floss*; illustrated by Pauline Baynes), Greenwillow, 1983.

Fu Dog, Macmillan, 1989, Viking, 1990.

Other:

Bengal Journey: A Story of the Part Played by Women in the Province, 1939-1945, Longmans, Green, 1945.

Hans Christian Andersen: A Great Life in Brief, Knopf, 1954.

Mooltiki: Stories and Poems from India, Viking, 1957 (published in England as *Mooltiki and Other Stories and Poems from India*, Macmillan, 1957).

(Translator) Carmen B. de Gasztold, *Prayers from the Ark* (poems), Viking, 1962.

(Translator) C. B. de Gasztold, *The Creatures'
Choir* (poems), Macmillan, 1962, Viking,
1965, new edition published as *The Beasts'
Choir*, Macmillan (London), 1967.

(With sister, Jon Godden) *Two under the Indian
Sun* (reminiscences), Knopf/Viking, 1966,
large print edition, ABC-CLIO, 1987.

Gone: A Thread of Stories, Viking, 1968
(published in England as *Swans and Turtles:
Stories*, Macmillan, 1968).

The Tale of the Tales: The Beatrix Potter Ballet,
Warne, 1971.

(With J. Godden) *Shiva's Pigeons: An Experience
of India* (documentary), Viking, 1972.

*The Butterfly Lions: The Story of the Pekingese
in History, Legend and Art*, Macmillan, 1978.

*Gulbadan: Portrait of a Rose Princess at the
Mughal Court* (biography), Macmillan, 1980,
Viking, 1981.

A Time to Dance, No Time to Weep: A Memoir
(autobiography), Morrow, 1987.

A House with Four Rooms (autobiography),
Morrow, 1989.

Editor:

(With Margaret Bell) *Round the Day: Poetry
Programmes for the Classroom or Library*,
Macmillan, 1966.

(With M. Bell) *Round the Year: Poetry
Programmes for the Classroom or Library*,
Macmillan, 1966.

(With M. Bell) *The World Around: Poetry
Programs for the Classroom or Library*,
Macmillan, 1966.

Emily Dickinson, *A Letter to the World: Poems
for Young People* (illustrated by Prudence
Seward), Bodley Head, 1969.

Olga Sarah Manders, *Mrs. Mander's Cookbook*,
Viking Macmillan, 1968.

The Raphael Bible, Viking Macmillan, 1970.

Godden's works have been translated into fourteen
languages.

■ Adaptations

Motion Pictures:

"Black Narcissus," Universal, 1947.

"Enchantment" (based on *Take Three Tenses: A
Fugue in Time*), RKO, 1948.

(Adapter with Jean Renoir and author of
screenplay) "The River," United Artists,
1951.

(Also author of screenplay with Neil Patterson)
"Innocent Sinners" (based on *An Episode of
Sparrows*), Rank Organisation Film
Productions Ltd., 1957.

"Loss of Innocence" (based on *Greengage
Summer*), Columbia, 1961.

"The Battle of Villa Fiorita," Warner Bros.,
1965.

Television:

"In This House of Brede," CBS-TV, 1975.

"The Diddakoi" (series).

"Tottie" (series; based on *The Doll's House*).

Cassettes:

"The Doll's House," Listening Library, 1978.

"Kingfishers Catch Fire," Recorded Books,
1981.

"The Battle of Villa Fiorita," Recorded Books,
1982.

"Black Narcissus," Recorded Books, 1982.

"The Greengage Summer," G. K. Hall, 1983.

■ Sidelights

Godden's early years were spent in India. "Our
father, 'Fa,' worked for one of the oldest of the
Indian Inland Navigation Steamer Companies
which, between them, were responsible for the
navigation of the great rivers of Assam and Bengal.
This meant that we had not lived in cities...but in
remote small towns always on the bank of a great
river, most of the time in Narayangunj, a jute
station in Bengal on the river Megna which, in
places, was two miles wide; yet it was only a
tributary of the Brahmaputra, which itself mingles
with the Ganges....Our Megna flowed between
banks of mud and white sand from which fields
stretched flat to the horizon under a giant bowl of
sky; if we children grew up with any sense of space
it was from that sky.

"As an extremely small girl I took my airings not in
a pram but with my ayah on an elephant inappro-
priately called Birdie; when we came back and
Birdie obediently knelt to let us get down, I always
picked her a bunch of grass and she would take the
infinitesimal offering with the end of her trunk and
stuff it in her mouth."[1]

It was the custom for parents living abroad to send
their children home to be educated. When Godden
was five and her sister, Jon, six, the pair were
shipped to England to stay with their grandmother
and four maiden aunts in a tall dark house in west
London. The way of life they encountered came as
a tremendous shock. "For the first time we had to

live by rules, strict rules. To begin with we were banished to certain rooms, a night nursery at the top of the house and by day, to what had been the morning room in the basement. I remember the extraordinary silence in the house between, a silence which quelled us—not always: Jon was once driven to dance like a dervish on the morning room table, breaking Aunt Mabel's magnifying glass which had been left in the drawer. 'Why dance, dear?' asked the puzzled Aunts. Only the kitchen was lively but we were not allowed in the kitchen except now and then, invited by Polly the cook who had been Fa's old nurse and had a soft spot for us.

"Our own nurse took us for an afternoon walk in the park where we were forbidden to speak to other children; every day we took it in turns to have luncheon in the dining room, where we were not allowed to speak at all, and if our knife or fork or spoon made the slightest clink of noise on our plate Grandmother's and the Aunts' eyebrows were raised....At five o'clock we were 'changed' into velvet dresses—white muslin in the summer—and sent down to the drawing room where the Aunts devoted a children's hour to us with music, duets on the piano, readings aloud by us...and learning embroidery. We did play spillikins and sometimes cards, 'Beggar my Neighbour' and, suitably, 'Old Maid,' but on Sundays all toys were put away and, worse, books. We went to church twice and had to learn the collect of the Sunday to say to Aunt Evelyn, who was in charge of our spiritual state and much grieved by it....The Aunts were so truly good, noble and dedicated..., but never in all that house was there a gleam of laughter, fun or enterprise."[1]

Godden's stay with the Aunts coincided with the outbreak of the First World War and, after eighteen months, her mother, fearful of the zeppelins, brought the two children back to India where they remained for another five years. It is these years which Godden and Jon later recalled in their joint book, *Two under the Indian Sun.*

"I have always thanked God we did not have sensible parents; it was the custom then for women and children...to leave the plains in hot weather, March to October, and go up to the cool of the hills; sensible parents would have chosen a hill station near us, rented a house and sent us every year to the same school; though schools in India had drawbacks, they at least provided a steady education. Mam chose instead to take us to a different hill station every year so that we travelled the length and breadth of India, from Kashmir in the far north-west, four day's journey by train and road, to Coonoor and Ootacamund in the Nilghiri hills to the south....

"We had travelled through the scorched aridness of the Scinde desert, lived in the Himalayas facing the peaks of the snows, seen cities and mud-walled villages. We had picked gentians and edelweiss in Kashmir and hibiscus, amaryllis lilies and bougainvillacea in our own garden....Our house was a mingling of religions: Hannah, the ayah, was a Thomist Catholic: the table servants Mohammedan: Fa's personal bearer, Jetta, was a Buddhist from Sikkim. The gardeners were Hindu Brahmins of the highest caste: the sweeper, Hindu too, an Untouchable. They all lived and worked together in contentment."[1]

Although family life was, on the whole, stable, a chance remark of her father's made a deep impression on Godden and shook her confidence. "One day at luncheon Fa came back from the office for 'tiffin,' as it was called, and we all had it together—he looked down the table at me and said, or rather murmured, 'Where did that child get that face?' I know now he was only thinking aloud but I had heard and when we were allowed to get down from our chairs, I went out and wept among the canna lilies in the side garden; the cannas were higher than my head and, as I knelt, their brilliant colours seemed to mock me. With my instinct for drama I could have said, had I known the words, that iron had entered my soul, but it was not funny....What was saddest was that for a time, after his remark, I hated Fa."[1]

A special relationship existed between Godden and her sister Jon, but it was not without difficulty. "Fourteen months apart, Jon and I were so close that we might have been Siamese twins, I then in her shadow, which was natural.

"Jon was not only the family beauty, she had unmistakable talent and, too, an almost uncanny power over the rest of us....Part of Jon's power was that by contrast she made almost everyone else seem dull; no-one could have a more vivid imagination, often of a strangely macabre kind, which was to be her greatest asset when she became a novelist. It could, too, be sadistic.

"My eyes were green—and not for nothing; I was wildly jealous....Mam said often, 'Jealousy hurts no-one but yourself, don't be jealous,' but if you are, how can you help it? I do not remember who told me it was not wrong to be jealous, 'It's what you do with jealousy that can be wrong,' and that has comforted me."[1]

In March, 1920, when Jon and Rumer were thirteen and twelve, respectively, they were again taken to England for schooling. This time there was no reprieve. They were sent first to St. Monica's, a High Anglican Convent. Holidays were spent in rented houses at Eastbourne, where their mother was based. Unused to the conventions of a British boarding school, the pair were unable, and unwilling, to settle down.

"Perhaps our greatest shock was that Mam seemed to take it for granted that we should be unhappy. 'School is always like that at first,' wrote Mam. 'You will get used to it, then you will like it,' wrote Fa. 'Like it!' said Jon as if she had been stung. 'I shall never forgive them for this. Never!' It was the first time we had known that a father and mother could be against their children; indeed, with great love and tenderness, they made things worse....Mam wrote to Sister Gertrude asking for us to be excused from chapel. For the nuns this was the last straw; offended and shocked they shut us out. Now we really were outcast, horribly and conspicuously alone...and we burned in our heathen shame.

"Jon and I did not stay at St. Monica's, not even to the end of term....We went to five schools in the next two years....It was altogether an unsettled time. Fa had refused to buy a house in England as he would have had to pay English tax; in consequence we moved from rented furnished house to rented furnished house, taken only for six months, at most nine, because Mam was always on the point of going back to India and Fa—and did not go....The houses had to be cheap and they were small with shabby furniture....We would not ask any of our school friends to those shoddy houses....Eastbourne, too, seemed to me the epitome of mediocrity. I liked extremes....'Eastbourne's all middle, middle, middle,' I used to moan....I pined for London..., for adventure. No-one, I was sure could have adventures in Eastbourne. In adolescence things, good or bad, seem as if they could go on forever; good or bad would at least have been

Deborah Kerr and Jean Simmons starred in the 1947 Universal film "Black Narcissus."

From the movie "The River," directed by Jean Renoir. Copyright 1951 by United Artists Corp.

interesting—for us Eastbourne was simply dull, and I despaired of ever getting away from it."[1]

In the summer of 1924 the children's boredom was relieved when their mother took them on holiday to Chateau Thierry, a town on the river Marne in France. During these months the gap between Godden and Jon widened as the latter moved towards adulthood, leaving her sister behind. The adventures of this summer were to form the basis of Godden's *The Greengage Summer,* published in 1958 and filmed in 1961.

"Chateau Thierry was set in champagne country, a luxury town to which the buyers came for the vintage. It was, too, famous for its liqueur chocolates—Jon was to be given boxes of them....We gorged ourselves, and on the delectable food, especially the ripe fruit in the orchard. Perhaps part of the feeling of being in a dream was because we ate so much; we were, too, out of ourselves from being so suddenly immersed in France....Chateau Thierry was altogether a poet's town or a painter's, with its houses, spaced along

the river and crowded in the streets, showing the faint variations of shabby plaster, and the pink and grey-green of the paint that had blistered on doors and shutters.

"The weeks passed, the vintage began, and everything, the hotel, the whole town was filled with bubbling life;...Jon and I saw men and women drunk; I remember a gutter running with wine from a broken cask and children scooping it up to drink. The young men were rowdy and no longer stared at us but sometimes would not let us pass. I knew enough now to know they would not have given even a wolf whistle for me—it was Jon....That summer I was not jealous; Jon was Jon and I was only I, but I was sad, a contained sadness because she had gone beyond me."[1]

When the family returned to England, Godden was sent to Moira House and for the first time enjoyed her education. "To begin with the teaching at Moira House was utterly different, much of it centering round history, and not only of British as in all other schools I had been to; Moira House taught history of the world, from the most ancient of civilizations to the present day, a cycle that took two years. Each period transformed the school so that, for instance, in the Egyptian term we were steeped in Egypt, for the Greek term in things Grecian, history, literature, art, architecture and philosophy, even to the pictures on the walls and the school play....I discovered that I loved to learn, which was a revelation as was the ordering of this school's life; we were respected as people, not children; when the teachers had taught us, they left us for their own world of the staff room and their own concerns. We governed ourselves, the older girls supervising and keeping order. I would not have believed I could like any school, but this was different."[1]

The vice-principal of the school, Mona Swann, recognized Godden's talent as a writer and suggested that she be excused the bulk of the curriculum, taking only literature, history, French and music, in order to work privately on her writing. The discipline Swann imposed on Godden taught her the foundations of her skill, and with this came a sense of herself as a separate entity from her family. "In the two years I worked with Mona I did not write a single story. I spent the first term reducing the leader in the *Times* to fourteen lines; anyone who has tried precis will know what gruelling work that is. Another term went in comparing the consonants in *Il Penseroso* and *L'Allegro* to show how Milton achieved the melancholy of one poem, the gaiety and lightness of the other....I had to write articles without using an adjective, others without adverbs: reviews in which she rationed the use of 'I'...I did write poems but always in some straight-jacket form: sonnets, rondels, triolets, even haiku. I studied and wrote Anglo-Saxon riddles.

"Long ago, Jon and I had discovered what we called 'truthful writing' which does not mean the stories or studies had to be true, only that credibility was not distorted or manipulated, even in fantasies. A master of this was Hans Andersen; in his *Tales*, a tin soldier can speak but he must speak and act as would a soldier: a daisy like a daisy;...it often seems that writers do not see things as they are but as they would like them to be; a daisy is not just the wee modest crimson-tipped flower of Burn's poem but a tough strongly rooted plant...and it has a pungent smell. Now, for the first time, I was made to look honestly at what I wrote and it was Mona who gave me the confidence to do it. 'If you don't respect your work,' she said, 'no-one else will.'

"She told me, long afterwards, she sometimes wondered how much more I would take but, rebellious and opinionated as I was, by some marvel I had the wit to understand what she was doing for me. No-one can teach anyone else how to write but one can teach them basic technique, give them a firm grounding; that is what she gave me.

"I had six terms with Mona....Best of all about that time, for me, was that it was private; no-one could enter into it—not even Jon–particularly not Jon. Perhaps I had to lose Jon in order to find her and also to stand equal with her in the way that mattered most to us, our work."[1]

In October, 1925, turning down an invitation to go to college in France, Godden returned to Narayangunj in India with her mother and Jon. Having harboured romantic childhood memories, the reality was an anti-climax. She became engaged to a man thirteen years her senior, whom she had known since childhood, but quickly realized that the marriage wouldn't work and broke off her engagement. "In those two years...as I paced our flat and parapeted roof, it seemed, as it had seemed in Eastbourne, that nothing could ever happen, that I should never find myself; as eighteen turned to nineteen, nineteen to twenty, I was sure my life was over."[1]

Godden became increasingly aware, partly through reading E. M. Forster's *A Passage to India*, of how little the English in India understood the country and its peoples. She attempted to learn Hindi and, sensing that she was unhappy, her father invited her to work with him on one of his projects connected with the Agricultural College and Farm outside Dacca. "I drove to Dacca with him in the mornings. Sometimes he left me in the College all day, keeping records, making charts, diagrams, testing. I knew it was important work and Mona had taught me to be thorough and careful. I met and worked with the students....Soon I was accepted....I learnt the precious anonymity of work in which there are no distinctions except that of merit, though I was sometimes chagrined when they lapsed into Bengali or even Hindi, so rapid that I could not follow.

"I rode out with Fa among villages to which there were no roads, only small built-up paths of earth between the fields; sometimes I rode alone, which is astonishing when I think of how women or girls in India now are rash if they adventure unprotected into the countryside....Riding, as part of my work...made me look with different eyes as I went cross country among the humble fields, walled

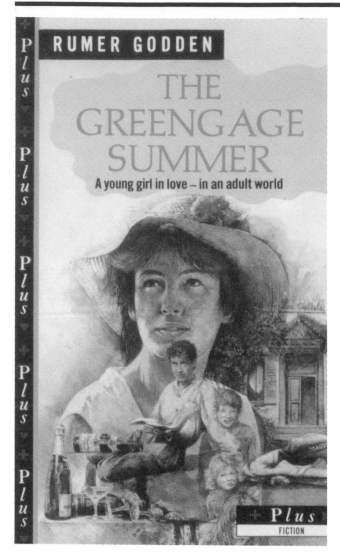

RUMER GODDEN

THE GREENGAGE SUMMER

A young girl in love – in an adult world

Plus

FICTION

Softbound edition of Godden's 1958 book.

with mud to hold water necessary for rice and which was ladled, from field to field, by clumsy wooden scoops worked by hand. There were bigger fields, yellow with mustard and, always, jute growing high. In the villages I saw small intimate scenes that in the mysterious way of sights and sounds were to come back later in my books.

"It was only for one cold-weather season. Fa was due for long leave and we all went back to England in April, but it was an indelible time and has stayed woven into my work."[1]

When Godden was twenty she inherited a legacy from her godfather which she used to obtain training at a London school to enable her to teach dancing to children. To do so was a challenge since, due to a childhood accident, she had a damaged spine and would never be able to demonstrate many of the steps and techniques to her pupils. It was the first time she had lived in London and

away from her family. "Most writers want to do, or have to do, something quite different in their early days; most are wise and refrain from things for which they are quite unsuited, as I with dancing and yet, for ten years or more, I lived for it, and from it; it has haunted my books.

"The work did not cease to be hard, but, slowly, I also discovered that I...was an innate teacher. I have always been good at telling people what to do, equally bad at doing most things myself. Teaching needs authority and that, mysteriously, I had....I also discovered that I was a ballroom dancer; in six months I passed the examination and became what I had not thought possible, a qualified teacher and member of the Imperial Society of Teachers of Dancing, the only examination I have ever taken. I have to say, too, that if I had nothing else I had initiative. In my second summer season I rented a studio in Mayfair's Hertford Street for a few hours a week—it was inordinately expensive—and taught Court curtseys to debutantes."[1]

In 1929 Godden had her first poems published (apart from an edition of poems printed by a vanity publisher when she was fifteen). *In the Realms of Fantasy* appeared in the Christmas edition of the *Illustrated London News* of 1929 alongside illustrations by her sister, Jon. The "poems and illustrations were mannered chinoiserie—it was the day of art nouveau and chinoiserie was in the air....The poems had a certain crispness and wit; the illustrations were sharp, in clear colours—and both had charm, than which to a serious artist nothing could be more deadly."[1]

Following her training in England, Godden returned to India with the aim of setting up a dancing school in Calcutta. She encountered difficulties with the social conventions which prevented well-born Europeans from engaging in paid work of any kind, and also prejudice when she sought to teach local children rather than those of wealthy expatriot families.

"I started my teaching in a modest and safe way in Darjeeling, safe because it had few of the barriers I was presently to encounter in Calcutta....It was a successful season for me and when, in October, I braved Calcutta I had a nucleus of pupils with whom to start and, more importantly, the beginning of a reputation that had gone before me....For the first time too I was independent with my own flat—a sitting room, bedroom and bathroom.

"In those first years Fa had nobly underwritten me, more than nobly when he strongly disapproved of what I was doing. . . .Fa had warned me of what would happen and he was right.

"In Calcutta's then almost closed society, 'nice girls' did not work or try to earn their living. There were women doctors, school inspectors, matrons of hospitals, missionaries, but they did not rank as 'society,' whose girls should stay at home, perhaps do some charity work or amateur acting or painting, strictly unpaid; anything else was taboo, a taboo into which I blithely stepped. . . .For a while, invitations ceased; most of Calcutta's ladies, if we met by chance, pretended not to see me, their daughters were kept away; even some of the young men with whom I had ridden and danced did not ask me now. I pretended, of course, not to care but it stung when I innocently dropped in at a house where we had always been welcome to be told the family were 'not at home.'"[1]

While Godden was running her dance school she met Laurence Sinclair Foster, whom she was later to marry. "I cannot imagine why Laurence chose me; perhaps it was because he had not met a girl like me and it piqued him but, when other young men fell away, he was still there and was unfailingly kind, which I have been told is my favourite epithet. In all our years and in all our troubles, I never knew Laurence to lose his temper—perhaps he did not care enough—but through those hard-working years he faithfully came, especially in the evenings, coaxing me away from the practising and accounts I should have been doing—and how pleasant it is to be coaxed—to have a drink, to go out to dinner, or for a drive and soon it was more than that. . . .Then I found out I was going to have a child.

"It was not legal then to take a baby away but to Laurence every Indian had his price. 'No!' the whole of me cried out against it. 'It's our child.' I should have had the courage to have the baby on my own and face the consequences. . . .'You'll have to marry me,' said Laurence, and added with a percipience I had not given him credit for, 'and pretend you like it. . . .'

"Laurence and I were married in March, 1934. If I felt a sham in my white satin dress and veil nobody knew it, not even Jon, but there is a moment in the Church of England marriage service when the priest, as the bride and groom kneel before him, takes the end of his stole and symbolically binds their two hands together; in that moment I had the first real inkling of what we had done."[1]

Godden's novel, *Chinese Puzzle*, was accepted for publication on the day of daughter Jane's birth.

This had been written during her pregnancy while she stayed with Laurence's parents in England, using her father-in-law's surgery when he was out on his rounds in the evenings. It was Godden's third attempt at a novel and the hero of the book was a Pekingese dog. She had owned her first Pekingese as a child and her second, Chini—a gift from Jon—was at her feet as she wrote *Chinese Puzzle*.

"I wrote with the small original of my chinaman asleep in his basket at my feet—always over the years at least one pekingese, sometimes three or four, have borne me company while I write."[1]

"Pekes are not really dogs, they're spirit dogs, the sacred dogs of China where no-one was allowed to own one except members of the Imperial Family. They're very, very hardy—I took four over the Zoji La, the pass across the Himalayas in the

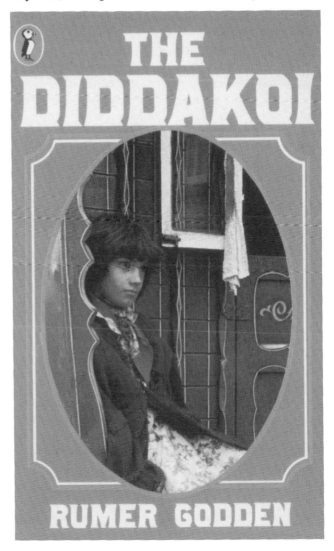

Paperback cover of the 1972 award-winning novel.

Ladakh district of Kashmir, into Tibet and they did twenty-one mile marches with no difficulty."[2]

"*Chinese Puzzle* bought me an advance of twenty-five pounds, normal for a first novel then, and almost the best reviews I have had. . . .Looking at it now, I know it is a piece of whimsy chinoiserie, the whimsy made worse by my having used capitals for all the nouns and adjectives in a mannered affectation; they had not been too noticeable when hand-written—in those days publishers would accept a hand-written manuscript—but as soon as I saw them in proof there was a sickening recoil and I realized I had spoilt the book. It was too late; *Chinese Puzzle* was printed."[1]

Returning to India to resume her teaching at the dancing school, Godden began her next novel, *The Lady and the Unicorn*. This time she wrote at her desk on the school's verandah, a space which acted also as her office and the room where mothers, nurses and ayahs waited for the pupils to finish their classes.

"*The Lady and the Unicorn* is a sad book—perhaps poignant is a better word because it is the story of Rosa, a young Eurasian girl—she could have been one of the cabaret girls I had come to know so well—who, when they fall in love with an Englishman, are almost inexorably doomed to unhappiness. I have a tenderness for this book; it belongs to a poignant time."[1]

It was Godden's third published novel, *Black Narcissus*, that was to bring her wide recognition and financial rewards—a book which has not been out of print since it was first issued in 1938. This time, the body of the book was written on board ship, on her journey to England for the birth of her second daughter, Paula, in September, 1938. Godden was still resident in England, staying at her parents' Cornish home, when the book was published.

"On the voyage home, not feeling able to cope with ship-board life. . .when Jane went to bed at half-past six, I went to bed as well. A kind steward brought me dinner and, as she slept in the lower bunk, I, sitting up in the top one so that my head almost touched the ceiling, wrote in cheap little Indian exercise books, filling one after the other, until ten or eleven at night. Bombay to Tilbury then took eighteen days and when we landed at Tilbury I had almost the full draft of a book. The book was *Black Narcissus*.

"When I was, I think, eighteen years old and we were in Shillong, we went on a picnic to nearby Cherrapunji, a deserted cantonment on a plateau, high above the surrounding gorges. I wandered away from the others and going down a steep little path came upon a grave; it was marked only by a small headstone in the shape of a cross with a name, 'Sister. . .' and two dates; she had died when she was only twenty-three.

"No-one could tell me anything about her; no other graves were near, no sign of any mission, but the villagers had made her grave a shrine; it was daubed with whitewash and there were offerings: a saucer of rice, an egg—in India eggs are thought particularly valuable—a string of marigolds.

"I never saw that grave again, for all I know it may have disappeared but, twelve years later in that bunk on board the *Orion* I began: 'The Sisters left Darjeeling in the last week in October. They had come to settle in the General's palace at Mopu which was now to be known as the Convent of St. Faith.'

"All imaginative writing starts the same way, from some note of sight or sound, heard, read or seen—once, for me, it was a painting—that does not pass away, leaving only a memory but which lodges in the mind like a seed. Why one thing more than another I do not know, nobody knows but, like a seed, it germinates, occasionally at once but, usually, years later. When it does quicken, it begins, like grit in an oyster, to use another metaphor, to secrete things round it—'secretes' because this should be an intensely secretive time. This—can it be called a process?—goes on until the grit grows into a whole. The result, of course, is seldom a pearl but it is a whole book, novel, short story, children's book or poem.

"*Black Narcissus* was published in January, 1939. By some oversight nobody told me—probably Spencer Curtis Brown, [Godden's agent] and Peter [Davies, her publisher] were too dismayed by what was happening in Europe; the lull after Munich was more than uneasy. . . .In February Fa suggested I should go with Mam to London for a few days. . . .As I meant to devote myself to Mam and we had our plans, there seemed no particular reason to break them to see either the Davies brothers or Spencer. . .but the day before we were due to go back to Cornwall, I was travelling along Charing Cross Road on a bus, which was held up for a moment or two opposite Foyle's twin bookshops which were divided by a narrow street, Sutton Row. There, stretched between them, hung a banner: '*BLACK NARCISSUS* by RUMER GOD-

From the 1965 Warner Bros. film "The Battle of the Villa Fiorita."

DEN.' I was nearly run over as I flung myself off the bus; I went into Foyle's, and stood there dazed.

"Perhaps there were not really as many people milling around as there seemed to my amazed eyes; most of the people were round a table in the centre of the shop which was piled high with *Black Narcissus* in its striped green and grey jacket....People were queuing as two salesmen tried to deal with them....I stood and watched trying to believe this was really happening."[1]

The success of *Black Narcissus* was a boost to Godden's confidence. "A writer's life is, necessarily, such a lonely one, so uncertain that we flourish on praise and I was now on firm ground, acknowledged in the literary world and confirmed in the belief that I had cherished so long in secret, that I was born to be a writer. This almost did away with two miseries that had beset me—and, I know, have diminished me all my life—jealousy and fear. I hope I was a nicer person. Some people are improved with success, as long as it does not

become a habit; with writers there is little chance of that, there is always the next book to write."[1]

The dramatic rights of *Black Narcissus* were sold within a month of its publication. Godden disliked the script which was adapted by another writer and she later wrote her own. By now her sister, Jon, had published a novel, and the two maintained a close working relationship, often by correspondence since they were frequently based in different countries.

"Jon was, and always had been, more talented than I, though she was to have critical acclaim—her first novel to be published in Britain was a Book Society Choice—she did not have the same measure of what is called 'success.' Yet she rejoiced if anything good came my way and not once was in any way envious. She wanted me to tell her everything.

"Jon and I sent each other everything we wrote, this almost until the day of her death."[1]

By the time *Black Narcissus* was published, Godden was already working on *Gypsy, Gypsy*. It was not

RUMER GODDEN

THE PEACOCK SPRING

'I won't like anything or anyone in India . . .'

Plus

FICTION

Penguin paperback of the 1975 novel.

"I suppose *Gypsy, Gypsy* had a measure of success. It seems it was a Book Society Recommendation, was published on both sides of the Atlantic, had foreign sales, paperbacks, dramatization, but I had gone into the melee of war and such trouble that...for the first time in my life books and writing did not seem to matter."[1]

In June, 1940 when England seemed in danger of invasion, Godden took her two children and their nanny, Giovanna, aboard the *Strathallan,* and they set sail for India. After a gruelling journey the four arrived at Howrah, where Laurence met them, and for a while family life seemed to go smoothly. During this time Godden began to write again.

"The book was *Breakfast with the Nikolides* which, of all my novels, though I know it is faulty, comes nearest to our 'truthful writing' and nearest to the India I love so deeply. Set in a juxtaposition of Narayangunj and the Agricultural College near Dacca where I had worked on the jute seed with Fa, some of those small intimate glimpses of Indian life I had seen on my lonely rides came back....Scene after scene came; I seemed to know exactly how to write them; the people's voices were in my head. How strange, in the midst of war I was able to write that book held in such peace and I finished it before the bubble burst."[1]

Godden abruptly had to face that all was not as it seemed as far as their family life was concerned. Laurence gave four days notice that he was leaving for the Army. She soon discovered that he had borrowed money from his firm in Calcutta and yet left enormous debts behind him. It took nearly all her earnings from *Black Narcissus,* and the sale of many personal belongings, to settle the amounts owed. Godden then took her children and Giovanna to stay in an 'out' bungalow at a tea-garden at Rungli-Rungliot, to give herself time to decide what to do next, and it was there that she regained peace of mind.

"By providence, before Laurence left, we had decided I was to take the children and Giovanna out of the heat to the hills....It had all been arranged, our fares mercifully had been paid. I had even sent a few things in advance, in particular the children's desks, a few pictures and vases...; especially precious, three little bowls of Cantonese pink enamel in three sizes with which the children loved to play the story of the 'Three Bears' and in particular my first extravagance in what perhaps I love best, a Persian carpet. It was a Tabriz hunting carpet, 'hunting' because horses, deer, hares and dogs were woven into its pattern. These few things

until her agent, Spencer Curtis Brown pointed it out, that Godden realized she had been influenced by a D. H. Lawrence novel.

"The most difficult feat of a writer's career is to write the next book after a success. Perhaps it is a mistake even to try—because there is a great difference between a book written when you are looking for something to write, searching for a theme, and one that seems to arise of itself, demanding to be written. It is better to wait, and I should have waited because that eventually came—was vouchsafed, as it were—with my fifth novel, *Breakfast with the Nickolides* but, at least, with *Gypsy, Gypsy* I had broken away....I had not known it, but it was true; my *Gypsy, Gypsy,* though its theme was completely different, was strongly influenced by D. H. Lawrence's *The Virgin and the Gypsy.* Which shows what the unconscious can do.

were saved as they had already gone. We lost everything else.

"Rungli-Rungliot means in Paharia 'thus far and no further'....It is a real place on the spur of the Himalayas...where we stayed for eight months, unique in beauty, humour and joy. This was surprising as I had no expectation of anything, certainly not of joy, but...I was made whole again.

"When we had gone, Jon put together the pages of a diary I had kept....Edited them and sent them to London....In 1943 they were published as a wartime edition, poor paper and paper cover, and called *Rungli-Rungliot*; they have been published twice again as *Thus Far and No Further*. It has brought me more letters than anything else I have written."[1]

When they had to leave the tea-garden, Godden moved with her daughters and Giovanna to Kashmir. "We came to Kashmir as an 'abandoned family' which is not as tragic as it seems, meaning in wartime simply an army wife and her family whose husband, normally based in India, was serving overseas. The army was responsible for us and we were told, as there was no possibility of repatriation, to choose one place in which to stay for the duration under the protection of a Provost Marshall. I chose Kashmir because of the better climate—though I had not realized how frozen the winters would be—because there were possible schools there and because, in the high north-west corner of India, it seemed comparatively safe."[1]

Paula developed a bad illness and the family was forced to move into a houseboat for purposes of isolation. Gradually it became clear that Godden's marriage was over and that she could expect no support whatsoever from her husband. Godden herself developed par-typhoid and pneumonia and the family was taken in by the missionaries at the nearby Mission Hospital. On her recovery she investigated a building she had glimpsed up a mountainside and, on discovering that it was free, set about renting Dove House. The isolated spot was outside the jurisdiction of the Provost Marshall and Godden knew she was taking a risk in settling her household there.

"I have always loved houses and have written books round them. Fa's and Mam's house in Cornwall was, in part, *China Court*; my grandmother's in London, though not as large, was the house in *A Fugue in Time*. I have had several cherished houses; always, by circumstance not by desire, I have had to leave them but never have I loved a house as I loved Dove House.

"It was a rarely beautiful little house; in spring, all round it were flowering trees, peach, apricot, cherry, almond, acacia; in summer it was hung with vines and honeysuckle and scented white roses, while along its terraced orchards white iris grew wild. In the courtyard the stream splashed to a small waterfall and, high above, the mountain cut off the sky....

"The whole house was dilapidated but the wood was sound, the earth floors dirty but not damp. There was no glass in the windows, only brown paper, no electricity, no means of heating, no water except the stream and, as I discovered later, a spring on the mountain; except for a two-roomed hut in the courtyard, meant for a kitchen and a servants' room, no other house was near. No road went to Dove House, only that steep rocky path. 'Every possible drawback,' everyone was to say. I took it for five years."[1]

Godden had three hundred pounds with which to make Dove House habitable for herself and the children. They moved in on New Year's Day 1943. It was at Dove House that Godden completed *A Fugue in Time*, its title and structure inspired by Bach's music. Also she had become fascinated with Dunne's *Theory of Time*. "In which time is all one, not divided into past, present and future....Dunne explains it simply: 'If you are in a boat on the river and round a bend you cannot see what is behind you, nor until you have rounded another, what is before you but, were you in an aeroplane, you would see the whole.' My story is written from the point of view of the aeroplane and covers three generations of a family living in the same house in London, not told consecutively but mingled together.

"When the book was published in America it was called *Take Three Tenses* which, though not as subtle, was exactly what I did. I must have written that book eight times, often in despair, before I found the key: by putting the past into the present, the present into the past it worked—and more remarkably no-one, not even the critics noticed the shifts; the whole had miraculously blended."[1]

Instead of remaining at Dove House for five years, Godden was forced to leave after twenty months when she discovered that one of her servants was trying to poison the family, using a mixture of ground glass, marijuana and belladonna.

In July, 1945, two months after the end of the war, the family's repatriation papers came through and Godden and the two children set sail for England. One of the only assets Godden possessed when she arrived in Britain was the completed manuscript of her novel, *The River*.

"We landed in Liverpool and must have looked a disconsolate trio in our dirzee-made clothes, I still thin and pale—I weighed only six stone—while Paula was a thread. Though we were going to Darrynane [the home of Godden's parents]—I had told the children much about it—we still felt disconsolate, mingled with apprehension, the same apprehension Jon and I had felt on the quay at Plymouth those twenty-five years ago. I could see it in Jane's face. Paula was too young but she, too, pressed closely to me.

"To be trusted can be terrible. I had had everything for them and had lost everything. Even the pekingese had to be left behind—a troop ship does not allow dogs—and there had been another blow of that time: the few things I had packed from Dove House had been sent to Lloyd's warehouse in Bombay for shipment and the warehouse had been sabotaged and burnt....We should have to start all over again."[1]

From Liverpool, Godden and the children travelled to her parent's house in Cornwall. Despite the security offered to her there, Godden left to set up house in London and make a new life for the family.

"I found that my dear parents had made plans. They had a little lodge at the gate of the house and they proposed that they make it over to me without, of course, any rent and that I could do with it as I liked. I knew if I stayed there I would never do anything because life would be so protected and cosseted—that had happened to my younger sisters. Much as I was touched by the idea, I felt I must go away and begin to do new work.

"When my father heard I was going to London he said, 'Well, if you go to London, you're on your own.' Which I was. Completely. But I had very good friends...."[3]

In 1949 Godden married her second husband, James Hayes Dixon, "after long, long times of refusals. I...didn't want to get married again, but as it turned out my second marriage balanced the first. James had been married before too, but he knew nothing of family life. I'd previously bought a little house in Buckinghamshire for me and the children, the first home that we really owned, and they bitterly resented their stepfather at first. I hadn't been prepared for his natural feeling that he was responsible for us and that we were under his authority. Jane and Paula weren't used to being under anybody's authority except mine and the first two years were fairly rough.

"Then it settled down. When I came to write the second volume of my autobiography I said I was going to skip the fifteen years from about 1951 because those were years of contentment, and contentment is not interesting to read about. We lived in Buckinghamshire, London and Sussex—including a period at Lamb House in which Henry James had lived in Rye—and I was writing during all that time."[3]

Shortly after her second wedding, Godden went to Hollywood to work on the screenplay of *The River* with the film director, Jean Renoir. Prior to this two of Godden's novels had been translated onto the screen, *A Fugue in Time* and *Black Narcissus* (which starred Jean Simmons), neither of which had met with her approval.

"[Producer Samuel] Goldwyn bought *A Fugue in Time* but his film bore no relation to the book at all. The house looked rather the sort of house I had described and the characters had the names of the characters in my book, but apart from that I recognized nothing. I don't know why he bothered to buy it. It's like buying a bottle of wine and taking a desert spoon out and filling it up with lemonade.

"Everybody writes to me and says 'what a beautiful film "Black Narcissus" is,' but I simply hate it. It's phoney from beginning to end. Michael Powell, the director, has told me since that he saw it as a fairy tale, whereas to me it was absolutely true. I was so angry, because I knew what it could have been."[3]

"I'll always remember Jean Simmons coming to audition when she was sixteen and I've never seen anything so beautiful—she was really like a basket of [ripe] fruit.

"It was made in Pinewood [Studios] on the cheap, the Himalayan peaks were faked out of draped muslin, the Indians were caricatures. After that I said nothing would persuade me to have any more films made. When Jean Renoir wanted to make 'The River' I said, 'no.' then when I heard that before coming to see me he had gone to India, visited our house and slept in our old nursery, I relented."[2]

"Renoir and his Brazilian wife came to dinner at my little cottage in Buckinghamshire. I didn't know how to cook, but I did know that French people like wine. The children waited on us at table and Renoir was utterly congenial and insisted on washing up with them afterwards and then tipped them. Paula came out with her eyes bulging and said, 'He's given us a pound!' After dinner we went into my tiny sitting room and talked and talked. The chairs were too small for Renoir so eventually he lay down on the floor. He created his own atmosphere.

"I went out to his house in Beverly Hills to write the script. The house was an absolute revelation, full of Renoirs, Cezannes, Manets and Pisarros. Life with the Renoirs wasn't the slightest bit like the Hollywood you hear described; they had their own private circle with Charles Laughton, Stravinsky and his wife, Vera, and Charlie Chaplin and his wife, Oona.

"The first thing Jean said to me when I arrived in Beverly Hills was, 'We'll put the book on the shelf. I don't want you to think about it. We've got to recreate it in visual terms.' When I came to write the script he made me do it all in shots; longshots, middleshots, close-ups. It was quite difficult to begin with. Jean was a perfectionist and I was worried that I wasn't going to be able to reach his standard. But he was marvellous to work with and I was soon as at home working with him as I would have been in my own study. He had a flaring temper, but never once did he use it on me.

"We went to India to shoot 'The River.' At the time it was made no films for the western market had been made there. Renoir was a great pioneer and all the beautiful Indian films we now have owe a great, great deal to him. The producers did everything they could to make it difficult for him. He worked under terribly difficult conditions and a lot of the time he had to operate through an interpreter. Normally the director, the designer and the cameraman are able to see the rushes on the day that they were shot, but because there were no facilities in India, Jean had to wait until they were flown to Technicolor in London, printed and sent back again. They were continually held up at customs.

"'The River' was financed on condition that seventy-five percent of the crew had to be Indian; these young men had never even seen a colour camera before and Renoir's working methods were a revelation to them, though some people thought him completely mad! When, for instance, we shot the scene when the coolies carry jute back and forth, it took all day because Claude Renoir, Jean's nephew and our cameraman, was shooting from all angles. The Indians said, 'These Americans are mad! Here they are, paying us to go backwards and

forwards with the same load and never getting anywhere!'

"Jean was a great detailist. An example is one tiny shot, the scene during the siesta time when the youngest child has rolled off her cot and stays asleep on the floor. The family pet rabbit has to come to the edge of the bed and look down at the child as if to say, 'What's happened? Why am I up here and you down there?' It was just a detail, but it took us three days to get that shot. I made dialogue changes virtually every day while we were shooting because Jean insisted on having more. He was carrying his vision in his head as the film developed, which must have been very difficult.

"The house Jean used was similar to the one we had lived in, because the real one was too far away to use. The river wasn't as big as my Megna, which was a pity. My nephew, Richard—my sister Nan-

The 1984 Dell paperback.

cy's son—played the little boy. The character in the book was based on Nancy—I don't know why I made her a boy—and there was a grain of truth in the story because my mother once found her playing in a flowerbed with a cobra. Both Nancy and Richard had an uncanny power over animals. What Harriet goes through in the book was similar to what I went through with Jon (my parents nearly called me Harriet, thank God they chose Rumer—which is a family name—it's a perfect name for a writer and I've never met another). Harriet is in love, she's overwhelmed. The man she's in love with, Captain John, who has only one leg, was based on someone we knew."[3]

In 1961 *The Greengage Summer* was also filmed. Although not so closely involved as with "The River," Godden was pleased with the result.

"Susannah York as Joss—Jon—seemed utterly unlike her yet was Jon to the life. The film ends after the tragedy with Joss coming out on the road between the slopes of vineyards in sun—the film was all green and gold. As she walks, tears still on her face, she deliberately kicks a little stone, sending it rolling down the hill; it has all gone—out of her way—and she lifts her face to the sun."[1]

In 1966 Godden collaborated with Jon on *Two under the Indian Sun*. They were later to work together on *Shiva's Pigeons*.

"When Jon and I did *Two under the Indian Sun* we decided roughly what each chapter would say and then each went away and wrote one. Then we exchanged our chapters and over-wrote and afterwards met and discussed them. There was a lot of antagonism and we collaborated with difficulty. It was more difficult with *Shiva's Pigeons* because we had to be actually together when we assembled it. My sisters have always challenged what I wrote, because everybody's memory differs."[3]

"I became a Catholic after a long time; not until I really understood what catholicism was—nobody can judge the Catholic church from the outside, you've got to be in it to know. By chance I met a wonderful man, Archbishop Roberts, who was Archbishop of Bombay. He taught me his concept of catholicism which was totally different from, for instance, an Irish priest's concept of it which might be rules and regulations and superstitions."[3]

Through her daughter, Jane, Godden got to know the nuns at Stanbrook Abbey well, particularly Dame Felicitas Corrigan. "I was talking to [her] one day and she said she wished someone would write about nuns as they really were and not as the author would like them to be. I thought it was a challenge and that I should try. I was allowed lodgings near to the Abbey and spent whole days with the nuns. The Abbess gave me permission to ask questions, but I promised never to ask a personal question. I wanted to know about the ritual and the kind of life that the nuns led. My great difficulty was not betraying what one nun had told me to another. The more I was with them the more I understood and learnt. I didn't have a sign of a vocation myself and I wouldn't have lasted a fortnight as a novice. The result was a novel *In This House of Brede*, published in 1969.

"When I had finished the book the Abbess appointed three people to act as devil's advocates to try to fault it. They were all wearing wimples and habits—they've never modernized them except to make them lighter and shorter—and I sat in my trousers and jersey and defended what I'd written. They couldn't imagine anyone being interested in their daily life and what their cells and the chapter house were like. They wanted me to leave out all the descriptions. They couldn't understand how fascinating 'shop' is for other people and that it is exactly what the public wants to read; being so familiar with it themselves they couldn't see why it would be interesting to outsiders."[3]

Godden now lives in Scotland, on the edge of the quiet village of Moniaive in Dumfriesshire, where she completed her autobiographies, *A Time to Dance, No Time to Weep* and *A House with Four Rooms*. "After my husband died I had continued to live in Rye, which I love, but when you are getting old you can be a nuisance to your family but you can't be a nuisance to your friends; both my daughters were living in Scotland and I hardly ever saw them, so in 1978 I moved up to be near them. I miss Sussex but living here is an ideal solution because we've converted what was really an outhouse at my daughter's into somewhere for me to live."[3]

"It's a very good place to work. My life is governed by my work and when you are working you don't need many people. I write longhand. I like to write in the morning and work again in the evening because the evenings are very lonely. I will not do anything in the afternoons because, to me, that's siesta time and I like to tend my animals and garden. I've still got a Pekingese, Silk and an exquisite Persian cat called Whisper.

"I believe that writing should have an inner rhythm. Almost inevitably it will be read aloud in the media, so a writer must consider the rhythm and make it balance. I always read my work aloud, not to find out the opinion of the other person, but for my own benefit. Fortunately, I have a very dear friend who is a book person. She lives near to me and loves listening as I read.

"I try to do a children's book in between novels but the second volume of my autobiography, which I have just completed, was heavier than usual so I feel written out at the moment, which is not usual. Normally I have another pot boiling before I've finished."[3]

"I am a story-teller. Well, if I were asked which of two great writers I would choose to be, Proust or Robert Louis Stevenson, much as I honour and enjoy Proust, I would unhesitatingly choose Stevenson but, of course, there is no choice; storytellers are born not made.

"A short while ago I was sent one of those publisher's publicity questionnaires. It ran to several pages, wanting to know every fact about me from the day I was born—everything that has little or nothing to do with writing. I am afraid my answers were mostly negative. Education?—in my case almost nil. Qualifications?—none except for dancing. Politics?—none. Hobbies?—none—but the last question temporarily floored me, 'What makes you think your books are different from anyone else's?'

"At first I decided not to answer it; it seemed impertinent, besides I had never thought that. Then, slowly, I began to see it is a vital question–and absolutely relevant; in fact there is only one answer. 'What makes you think your books are different from anyone else's?' The only answer is, 'Because they were written by me.'

"That sounds conceited but it is not; all authors should be able to say it, whether they are a lion or just one of many sparrows. Fulfilment can be all sizes."[4]

Footnote Sources:

[1] Rumer Godden, *A Time to Dance, No Time to Weep*, Macmillan (London), 1987.
[2] Ena Kendall, "A Room of My Own," *Observer*, February 9, 1986.
[3] Based on an interview with Cathy Courtney for *Authors & Artists for Young Adults*, 1988.
[4] R. Godden, *A House with Four Rooms*, Morrow, 1989.

■ For More Information See

Newsweek, September 30, 1963, April 4, 1976.
Time, October 11, 1963, April 19, 1976.
Muriel Fuller, *More Junior Authors*, H. W. Wilson, 1963.
May Hill Arbuthnot, *Children and Books*, 3rd edition, Scott, Foresman, 1964.
Life, August 5, 1966.
Brian Doyle, *The Who's Who of Children's Literature*, Schocken, 1968.
Horn Book, December, 1969, August, 1976.
Calendar, September/December, 1972.
Hassell A. Simpson, *Rumer Godden*, Twayne, 1973.
Publishers Weekly, February 3, 1975.
Justin Wintle and Emma Fisher, *The Pied Pipers*, Paddington Press, 1975.
Writer, July, 1977, May, 1985 (p. 13ff).
New Yorker, March 23, 1981.
Spectator, October 17, 1981.

Eileen Goudge

Born July 4, 1950, in San Mateo, Calif.; daughter of Robert James (an insurance executive) and Mary Louise (a housewife; maiden name, Woodruff) Goudge; married second husband, Roy Bailey, August 4, 1974 (divorced); married Albert J. Zuckerman (a literary agent), April 28, 1985; children: (first marriage) Michael James; (second marriage) Mary Rose. *Education:* Attended San Diego State College (now University). *Politics:* Democrat. *Religion:* Jewish. *Home and office:* 234 West 22nd St., New York, N.Y. 10011. *Agent:* Albert J. Zuckerman, Writers House, 21 West 26th St., New York, N.Y. 10016.

■ Career

Worked as a secretary; Spin Physics, San Diego, Calif., micro-electronics assembler, 1971; writer, 1973—.

■ Writings

Young Adult Romance Novels:

(Under pseudonym Marian Woodruff) *It Must Be Magic*, Bantam, 1982.

(Under pseudonym Marian Woodruff) *Forbidden Love*, Bantam, 1983.

(Under pseudonym Marian Woodruff) *The Perfect Match*, Bantam, 1983.

(Under pseudonym Marian Woodruff) *Dial L for Love*, Bantam, 1983.

(Under pseudonym Marian Woodruff) *Kiss Me, Creep*, Bantam, 1984.

(Under pseudonym Elizabeth Merrit) *'Till We Meet Again*, Silhouette, 1984.

Winner All the Way, Dell, 1984.

Smart Enough to Know, Dell, 1984.

Too Much Too Soon, Dell, 1984.

Afraid to Love, Dell, 1984.

Too Hot to Handle, Dell, 1985.

Bad Girl, Dell, 1985.

Before It's Too Late, Dell, 1985.

Don't Say Goodbye, Dell, 1985.

Forbidden Kisses, Dell, 1985.

Hands Off, He's Mine, Dell, 1985.

Presenting Superhunk, Dell, 1985.

A Touch of Ginger, Dell, 1985.

Against the Rules, Dell, 1986.

Gone with the Wish, Avon, 1986.

Hawaiian Christmas, Dell, 1986.

Heart for Sale, Dell, 1986.

Kiss and Make Up, Dell, 1986.

Life of the Party, Dell, 1986.

Looking for Love, Dell, 1986.

Night after Night, Dell, 1986.

Old Enough: Super Seniors Number One, Dell, 1986.

Sweet Talk, Dell, 1986.

Treat Me Right, Dell, 1986.

(With Fran Lantz) *Woodstock Magic*, Avon, 1986.

Something Borrowed, Something Blue, Dell, 1988.

Deep-Sea Summer, Dell, 1988.

Adult:

Garden of Lies (novel), Viking, 1989.

Contributor of stories and articles to periodicals, including *McCall's*, *Highlights for Children*, and *Good Housekeeping*.

■ Work in Progress

A novel for Viking, *Such Devoted Sisters*, about two generations of sisters and their love/hate relationships, set in the world of gourmet chocolate.

■ Sidelights

Little in Eileen Goudge's childhood would seem to prepare her for the dramatic course of events her life later took. "I was born in San Mateo, California, the second of six children, and was raised in Woodside, which, after the freeway, became a suburb of San Francisco. I went to a neighborhood elementary school, and from there a little high school, and I don't think the first seventeen years of my life were in any way remarkable. But after that, I felt like Dorothy caught up in the cyclone.

"When I was active in writing young adult novels, I kept my high school yearbook by my desk so I could summon memories from that period. I had the great advantage of being unpopular back then, and I think every unpopular kid has a secret yearning to reinvent his high school years—not for revenge, but just to be more accepted by others. In the young adult books, I could be part of the cool crowd, a cheerleader or class president; in truth, I was just a shy bookworm, and though I had my little circle of friends, none of us even approached the popular kids in school.

"A lot of the kids who read my books are also in the same predicament. Most of them aren't in the cool crowd, and the novels give them a chance to live that life vicariously. The crucial difference is my characters' sense of compassion—the cool crowd at my school weren't particularly sympathetic people. They weren't very open to society at large, nor did they care about the rest of us in school. My characters have a more understanding view of mankind, and in this respect I've succeeded as a writer because many of the kids who've written me say that these characters are their best friends. And that feels nice."[1]

For as long as she could remember, Goudge was interested in writing. A distant cousin of Elizabeth Goudge, the author of *Green Dolphin Street* and *Dean's Watch*, she grew up on stories of her literary heritage. "I never actually met Elizabeth, though I once came pretty close. On my first trip to England, I called her, but she was too ill to see me. She passed away shortly after that, but other members of my family had visited her, and one of my aunts had sent her an article I had published, so she was aware that I would be 'carrying the torch' for her after she died.

"Beyond family lore, my most important influences growing up were *The Wizard of Oz* and good ol' Nancy Drew—my first feminist heroine. Though I nearly went blind from reading her books under the covers with a flashlight, you'll never hear me knock any of them. I was also a very precocious reader; in seventh grade I read *The House of the Seven Gables*. I was enchanted by books that were slightly beyond my grasp, and I was less inclined to throw a book down if I had to look words up than if the vocabulary was too simple. I'm still a voluminous reader, and my tastes continue to run toward the gothic side of literature.

"The most beneficial aspect of high school for me was one of my English teachers who really believed in my writing. She sent one of my poems to a national contest for high school students sponsored by *Atlantic Monthly* in which I won Honorable Mention. That really spurred me on because until then I didn't believe my name could appear in print, and once that was proven to me, it really lit my fire."[1]

The author's quiet, suburban lifestyle was radically upset in 1968 when she left San Diego College with her graduate-student fiance after her first year. "I met my first husband at an Eldridge Cleaver lecture. Actually, I was more a rebel without a cause than a student activist, but we ended up spending a couple of years in Vancouver when he opted to leave the country rather than serve in Vietnam.

"In British Columbia, there's very little to do—it mostly rains–and that's when I started to think seriously about becoming a writer. But it was just a pipe dream then; I had an image of myself as Laura Ingalls in *Little House on the Prairie*, staying in this little country cottage, making jam and babies, and surviving. All that was just inside my head. We did live in a fairly isolated area just outside of the city, but we were also part of an expatriate community that had come to Canada for the same reason we did. It was an odd feeling being cut off from my own country, especially when I could go back, but my husband and friends couldn't.

"Today, people look back nostalgically at the sixties the way my generation looked back on the fifties, as a magical, idyllic time. You glorify the preceding generation when your own times become difficult, but whatever era you grow up in will be a struggle because growing up itself is a painful experience. My generation was shaped to a great degree by Vietnam–people I went to school with were killed in the war, my first husband and I lived with the fear of waiting for his draft notice to arrive. . . .It was a scary time, and that's hard to appreciate these days when the worst thing to arrive in the mail is a jury notice or an American Express bill."[1]

Nonetheless, the emotional burdens which the couple assumed proved very taxing for two people barely out of adolescence. "It was like running away from home—I guess that's what I was doing. . . .We were so young. I was eighteen and he was twenty-one. How could it work?"[2] In fact, the marriage began to fall apart after the birth of their son.

Later describing her husband as "very talented but not terribly parental,"[2] Goudge separated from him after only two years of marriage. "He's still living in Canada today. I keep in touch with him because, of course, you try to remain in contact with the father of your children; he would probably know what became of me anyway, though, because after my story appeared in so many newspapers, there's been nothing very secret about my life.

"After my divorce, I went back to California with my one-year-old son. There, I discovered that a college dropout with no marketable skills, no child support and various other hindrances couldn't do much of anything. I tried to work, but I couldn't earn any money, and although my parents were fairly well-to-do, we mutually took the position that they wouldn't offer and I wouldn't ask for help. Once you're an adult, you have to make your own bed and lie in it. I was still fairly close to my family back then—one of my sisters lived with me for a few months during that time—but aside from birthday presents and a little help babysitting, I was very much on my own."[1]

The author's most pressing concern, at this point, was making ends meet with an inadequate income. ". . .So I found a job as a clerk in a dress shop and moved into a small, shabby apartment. . . .A co-

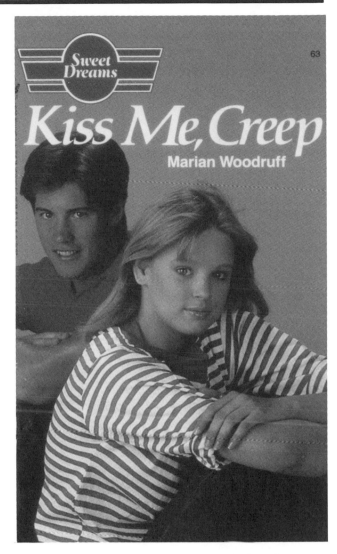

The 1984 Bantam edition published under Goudge's pseudonym, Marian Woodruff.

worker suggested welfare. I was outraged. I wanted to *earn* my living. But when I realized that having two jobs meant that Michael would have to be raised by day-care workers and baby-sitters, I changed my mind. My son needed me, and that was more important.

"Swallowing my pride, I applied for Aid to Families with Dependent Children. Once a month I received a check for $197.50. That had to cover rent, utilities, food, clothing and transportation. I always made sure Michael had enough to eat, but often I went hungry.

"To society I was a sponger. The day I went in to court when my divorce became final, the judge glowered at me from the bench. 'I don't see why an able-bodied woman can't work for a living like the rest of us,' he bellowed. I felt as if I'd been found guilty of a terrible crime.

"The judge's disgust, I found, was shared—by grocery clerks, bank tellers, even men I dated. The pride I'd once felt in myself was being whittled down to nothing."[3] Because of her status as a welfare recipient, Goudge was required to report to the welfare department so that a social worker could evaluate her case. "There I was, a ward of the state. My child was a ward of the state. I had to deal with social workers and the bureaucracy and the shame. It's a terrible stigma in our society. And people would make the most godawful comments, like: 'Well, if you can't take care of your child, why don't you put him up for adoption?' Things like that.

"Today, if you said to me, 'You have [$1.15] in your pocket. You have a choice. You can spend that [money] on a scrub brush and be a freelance scrub woman for the rest of your life. Or you can use it on a bus token to get down to the welfare office,' I would be a scrub woman. I would spend the rest of my life on my hands and knees before I'd ever do that again."[2] Goudge learned quickly that one of the hindrances to establishing a better life was a paradox within the welfare system. "I discovered I was actually making less money working at the dress shop—between maintaining my car and paying for babysitting—than I would have made staying at home collecting checks.

"This was one of the failings of the Welfare System which is now changing; people in the system I've talked to since say that despite its problems there is finally more awareness of the 'Catch-22,' and more emphasis on job training and self-sufficiency. But at the time, I didn't feel like I had a lot of choices, or any means of improving myself."[1] The author's first step toward rebuilding her life was her second marriage, in 1974.

"It was not the land of milk and honey....My poverty stretched on another nine years. Oh, God, we were so poor. I never bought a new dress in those nine years. My mother every birthday got me a new dress. The children [a daughter, Mary Rose, was born in 1976] wore hand-me-downs or clothes from the Salvation Army. I had $20 a week for groceries for all of us. Orange juice was a big luxury. I used four cans of water instead of three to make it last longer. I used to wish the dog wouldn't eat so much."[2]

"My second husband was a gardener who had spent about a year in the Navy. He was on his way to be shipped out to the fighting when something went wrong and he ended up staying in the States. By the time we were married he was suffering from a lot of health problems, which kept him chronically unemployed. I basically supported the family—a fact I'm sure he wasn't crazy about—and that's when I began finding work as a magazine writer.

"I wanted a job in which I could stay home with my children, but beyond that, this was something I'd always wanted to try. It was very difficult in the beginning because I didn't even have a typewriter that worked and I had to set up a makeshift desk in my kitchen. I wasn't very good at first, but I eventually sold articles at the rate of one acceptance for every fifteen submissions. The secret is if you pump out enough volume, if you throw enough stuff at the wall, one or two will stick."[1]

"I'll never forget the day I sold my first article. The *National Star* bought a short piece I'd written titled 'An Egg in Your Car Will Save You Money.' I'd gotten the idea from a race-car driver on TV, who'd said one way to save on gas was to drive as though there were an imaginary egg between your foot and the gas pedal. I was so thrilled I wanted to frame the check, but I needed the twenty dollars for food.

"Gradually other publications began accepting my work. I also enrolled in a free night-school course called Writing to Sell. My teacher had published several novels, and she encouraged me to try my hand at a gothic romance. I was excited and nervous. Suppose I was no good? When I completed a few chapters, I gave them to her. After the next class she took me aside. My heart was in my throat. Alice smiled. 'I'm saving a shelf in my book case for all the books you're going to write someday....'"[3]

After a few years of magazine work, Goudge herself was teaching a writing class. "I had earned a vocational degree to teach and was instructing night classes. What was frustrating about the job wasn't the students who brought in writing that was bad or had a lot of problems, it was the people who brought in nothing. If someone came to class with a load of excuses, I assumed that they didn't want to do the work; hopefully they found something they did want to do. Whether it's writing or anything else you choose to do, the key is to dig in your heels and really do it. If you can only write one page a day, or even one sentence a day, it may take you ten years to write a book, but at least at the end of ten years you'll have something. The only way I kept hope alive during the lean years was through sheer grit and a belief in myself.

"For nine years, though, all I knew was struggle. We had to scrape by on what my husband made, and what I earned writing, which didn't amount to a small hill of beans. During that time we never earned more than ten thousand dollars a year; for a family of four that's way below the poverty line. But it's amazing how little you can live on when you have to ride your bike everywhere, when you go to the grocery store to pick up the stale produce they give away. And it's great now, because I can write about people in desperate situations with a certain amount of veracity!"[1]

The stress of those years, however, eventually took its toll. "It wasn't just the poverty....My ex-husband was a very abusive man. This was another trap. I was very unhappy, very miserable. I finally just said enough one day. Who knows when you reach that point? One day, you think you can stand it; the next day you can't handle it anymore."[2]

By 1982, when the couple separated, Goudge was working on the Young Adult novels which eventually brought her sustained popularity as a writer. "The first books I wrote, in California, were for the 'Sweet Dreams' series. With the money I made from those books, I financed my move to New York. Soon thereafter, I arrived deep in the heart of Brooklyn with the dream of finding fame and fortune. It was the same story as every other starving artist from the sticks, and although it worked out for me, I wouldn't call it a realistic expectation."[1]

After answering an ad for an apartment, the author found herself living in a neighborhood of Hasidic Jews, the most devoutly observant and traditional sect of the religion. Despite her own unfamiliarity with the culture, and her neighbors' suspicion of outsiders, the move was a harmonious one.

"I don't think I'd ever seen the inside of a synagogue before....I didn't know anything about it. I was raised a Catholic....So I was living in this empty place....It was like a barn. I had a desk and a typewriter and a few kitchen utensils and that was it. I got my son [then twelve]...to do the laundry. He'd take it down to the laundromat and he'd bring it back and it would be beautiful— neatly folded and every sock matched and the whites were with the whites and the colors separate. And I thought he'd learned this incredible system. It turned out these nice Jewish ladies felt so sorry for him. 'What kind of mother would send her boy to do the laundry?' I think he'd been telling them he was an orphan. He had his ways. We managed."[2]

Thus established in New York, the author quickly renewed her contacts in the Young Adult book market, and with a salary of $5,000 per book was finally supporting her family as a writer. "I wrote five of the first twelve 'Sweet Valley High' novels. Francine Pascal had created the series, and her name appeared on each volume, but other writers were hired to complete the individual titles. It was like Carolyn Keene for the Nancy Drew series— her name was used as a collective pseudonym for the entire staff.

"Next, I began working with a book packager who came up with an idea for a series about four girls who were seniors in high school. That's how the 'Seniors' series came to be; I took his suggestion and created the characters, outlined a few plots and completed the first eight books. In all, there were twenty-four volumes, and although I turned the rest of the novels over to other writers, I still devised plots and supervised the project—I directed the series from start to finish. It was hard to let

The 1986 Dell paperback.

go of the books after I began because I had gotten very close to my characters, and they seemed like real people to me.

"I also made a lot of terrific fans because of those books. In general, most of these series are good because they get kids to read. I used to get letters from kids in Mississippi, for example, in which every other word was misspelled, but they would tell me that this was the first book they'd ever read, and ask if I could recommend any others to them. That's very heartwarming. There are also kids who read for entertainment. You learn to spread the net as wide as possible and catch as many different types as you can, for whatever reason they are reading."[1]

Goudge credits these books with teaching her many valuable lessons about appealing to an audience. "Writing for children has been the greatest 'university' for me in terms of seasoning my craft. I never write down to my teen audience, because they are the most discriminating of all readers. If a book doesn't grab their interest by page three, they'll put it down (unless it is assigned reading in school, in which case they'll either suffer through till the end or try to sneak by on Cliff Notes). But if the magic clicks, they'll devour the book, and everything else the author has written, inside a matter of weeks—sometimes days. Teens are passionate in their appetites. An author must be unstinting when it comes to filling their hunger for pathos, romance, fun."[4]

"I like hearing from kids about the books and have always made my address accessible so they can write. I don't always have time, but I try to write back at least once. The ones that keep at it, I generally turn over to my daughter, who's real big with pen pals. Once a little girl from Tazmania wrote me about one of the 'Seniors' novels in which the main character has a brother who dies of Cystic Fibrosis. This girl has the disease, and she was very impressed that I knew exactly how it felt, so we ended up corresponding. Being that isolated, she hasn't always been able to find books, and I have sent her a few. We developed a nice friendship over the years, and now my daughter has been writing her, as well.

"My kids, and now my stepdaughter, have sometimes helped me find plots. They would say something that sparked a story in my head, then I would fill in the details from my own experiences and take it from there. Both my daughter and my stepdaughter were of 'Sweet Valley High' age when I was working in the Young Adult field, and

they not only read my books, but also kept me up to date with what was on the minds of teenagers. Mostly I realized from them that no matter what the generation, kids will always have the same concerns, the same feelings and questions: 'Will I be popular?' 'Will he ask me to dance?' None of that stuff ever changes."[1]

With the economic security these books brought her, the author made improvements in her personal life, as well. The most important of these changes was her third marriage to Albert "Al" Zuckerman, president of Writer's House and one of New York's top literary agents. The couple had met at a convention in California a few years earlier, but because they were both married at the time, no romance developed until after the author moved to New York and became one of Zuckerman's clients. By then, they were both divorced, and quickly fell in love. "He's a terrific agent and a wonderful husband. He's everything. I got it right the third time."[2]

Once engaged, Goudge decided to convert to Judaism. "I'd always had a lot of problems with Catholic dogma, yet I still got a good feeling from worship, and I found in Judaism a more personal, individual involvement with religion, apart from the Pope and the Vatican. I take it very seriously; my conversion was a Conservative procedure that took nine months. There are quicker versions, but I wanted to know and understand what I was doing. My daughter also converted, though my son, who's a little older, chose not to. I felt that both of them were old enough to make their own decision.

"Fortunately my husband's family has been very accepting of us. I've never really discussed the issue with my family, as I've grown more distant from them in the past few years. The publicity my success has incurred, with the scrutiny that's been given to my past, has been difficult on them. Although they're pleased my writing has become so popular, we haven't had much contact lately."[1]

Following these sweeping changes, Goudge felt ready to take stock of her experiences and use them as the basis for a full-length novel. "One year on my birthday, the fourth of July, I began pondering the fact that the day you are born is the most important time in your life because it's the moment when you have no control over your own fate. You can't ask to be born into a certain kind of family, and you can't change who your parents are. So I created these characters who were exchanged at birth, then conceived a story through which their lives became intwined. Their situations reflect my own experiences, and I could draw upon the contrast between my life in Brooklyn and in Manhattan to give their reactions a certain amount of gut feeling."[1]

The author turned to the lessons of her Young Adult books to create a work her readers would be unable to resist. "Kids don't read for the same reasons as adults. Writers can get an adult to plow through a hundred pages of background information just to get to the good part because a hardback book costs $22.95 and they want to get their money's worth, or because they want to know what their friends are talking about at parties. A book for teenagers has to grab their attention and never let go of it.

"Kids also have a tendency to say, 'I'll read up to the next chapter then I'll stop'—we all do—so the trick I learned was to always end a chapter in such a way that you have to turn the next page to find out what happens. After the novel was published, I heard a lot of people say, 'Oh God! I was up all night with your book,' or 'I didn't get dinner ready for my husband and he was furious with you!' That's when I knew I'd achieved something."[1]

This achievement was in fact a nearly 600-page novel titled *Garden of Lies*. The story begins in 1943, when during a hospital fire a wealthy socialite exchanges the baby she has had by her lover for a lighter-skinned baby who better resembles her husband. From there, the book traces the growth of the two children—Rachel, the fair one in upper class Manhattan; Rose, the darker one in lower-class Brooklyn—through medical school and law school, respectively. After the two women become involved with the same Vietnam veteran, Rose becomes attorney for Rachel in a malpractice case, and then the secrets of their lives become untangled.

The book's publication history is nearly as dramatic as the plot itself. In October, 1986 Goudge completed the original outline of the story and gave it to her husband, who was on his way to Frankfurt, Germany. There, Zuckerman sold the British rights to Bantam Corgi; upon his return to the States, he also secured an agreement with Susan Ginsburg, then editor at Atheneum, whom the author credits as "the book's godmother."[5] However, by the time the novel was completed, Ginsburg had left Atheneum, giving Goudge the option to buy back her rights to the manuscript. Shortly thereafter, in January, 1988, Zuckerman arranged an auction of the rights in New York City. With five bidders at the outset, the competition

quickly came down to Bantam Books and Viking Penguin/New American Library, who ultimately won with a bid of $900,000 for *Garden of Lies* and Goudge's next novel.

In Zuckerman's submission letter, the novel was described as "conceived to be a best seller,"[5] and soon after publication it proved to be just that. "I was somewhat mystified when I read that, but I suppose every writer hopes her book will do well, and in that sense *Garden of Lies* was conceived on a broad enough scope to appeal to the popular imagination, as opposed to a specific audience or a scholarly element."[1]

Goudge attributes the success of her writing to meticulous research and hard work. "I try as hard as I can to make the details of my story precise, to be as authentic as possible when describing my characters. Fortunately I'm within walking distance of the world's biggest book store and one of

Goudge's 1988 softcover.

the best research libraries, so I've managed to collect a fair amount of information that way.

"I found the most helpful research about the Vietnam War came from a conversation I had with the veteran who installed my computer. One of my husband's clients, Paul Wilson, is a medical doctor who writes horror novels in his spare time—a hobby I'm sure his patients find reassuring—and he was kind enough to check my manuscript for medical inaccuracies. The story's courtroom scenes were the most difficult facet to research; I had to wade through a lot of Latin books, and I enlisted a brother-in-law, who is a lawyer, to read over those chapters.

"My conversion to Judaism also enabled me to write convincingly about both religions. People would ask me how a Jewish woman could know what it's like inside a confessional, and I would say, 'I know all too well what it's like, and I hope I never have to see another confessional for the rest of my life!' In fact, however, I begin the book with quotes from the Catholic Act of Contrition and the Jewish Yom Kippur service; pairing them together demonstrates how much the two faiths have in common.

"The only way to gather all this information, though, and turn it into an entertaining story, is through hard work, revisions and outlines. Craft is just as important as talent in writing successfully; I'm a firm believer in outlines and rewrites. I also depend on constructive criticism from an editor or an agent, but even if a writer doesn't have that team behind him, it's still important to solicit someone else's opinion on the work.

"Too many writers have an image of themselves holed up in a garrett working on a sacred mission. In truth, writing isn't much different from building a house; just as you need blueprints and a strong foundation for a house, you also need a good outline and an interesting story to write a novel. In the process, of course, you usually discover a spiritual aspect to what you're doing, but without a clear idea of what you set out to achieve, you can find yourself on some mystical tangent, completely divorced from the story itself.

"The other important key to success is discipline. I'm usually at the IBM by nine every morning, sometimes even earlier. I am fortunate to have an assistant now who takes calls and handles annoying paperwork, so I can concentrate fully on my work. Some days I find myself at the computer until midnight, but I usually stop around five or six in the evening—after sitting at a keyboard all day, I like to spend some time keeping my body in shape. Following my workout and dinner, I usually keep my evenings free for reading. Al brings books home by the truckload, so he often asks me to look over a manuscript, and I always have work of my own that needs copy editing–it's really an endless task, but one that I enjoy."[1]

Looking back on the completion of her first full-length novel, the author sees a continuous line of development from her teen books to *Garden of Lies*. "My writing hasn't really changed, it's just expanded. In the YA novels, I had to keep my stories smaller and more compressed, whereas with *Garden of Lies*, I could let it all hang out. As much as I enjoyed writing for kids, it felt like graduating from high school again. I think I will return at some point to the books for teens because I love that audience. I might try my hand at another series; maybe this time I would focus on the 'uncool crowd.'

"Right now, however, I'm completing another novel along the lines of *Garden of Lies*. It's called *Such Devoted Sisters* and has some of the same themes recur—family angst, thwarted love, the love/hate relationship between sisters—only this time without the mixed babies. In general, a lot of writers find themselves dealing with the same issues in more than one book; it's like a refrain that keeps going even though the melody changes. This novel is also about the same length as the previous one—I seem unable to work in miniature anymore."[1]

Though the range of Goudge's experiences has been immense, she sees her life as only beginning. "I have some interesting stories to tell about myself now, but hopefully I'll have more by the time I'm sixty. Maybe at that point if people are still interested I'd consider writing them all down, but right now it's a little premature to think about an autobiography because I've only lived up to about chapter three.

"Of all the rewards I've reaped in the past few years, none of the material luxuries compares with the opportunity to write full time without having to worry about my family's well-being. Losing that would be the worst hardship of my life; I feel as though I would give up eating before I would give up writing. If someone were to say to me, 'OK, you've made enough money; you don't need to write anymore. Put away your computer,' I would whither up and die. I enjoy my current lifestyle, but it was my writing that got me this far, and it continues to be my first priority. There's security in knowing that, because I wasn't born with a silver spoon in my mouth—I've been through hard times and I've learned how to get by without help from anyone. I could do it again if I had to.

"Realistically, my financial position will probably stay secure as long as there's an audience for my work. But sometimes I wake up in a cold sweat, and I have a hard time believing all this is real. In a way, that's good because it gives me compassion for people who aren't as fortunate. I can't walk by a hungry person on the street and say, 'Get out of my way.' I feel more in touch with that side of life, and I believe firmly in sharing my wealth. My principal charity is run by a cousin, an ex-priest, who works as a missionary in the Philippines. He's out in one of the rural areas trying to educate, feed and give medical care for people who have absolutely nothing. Of course, there are people in the same predicament living right on my doorstep—I can't ignore them either.

"Life hasn't necessarily gotten easier because of my accomplishments. Each event presents as many challenges as the previous one, each book requires just as much work as the last one. It's nice to have a little extra help nowadays, and of course I'm not struggling with basic concerns like feeding my babies or paying rent, but it's hard to devote myself 100% to my writing, my husband and my children. Finding a balance between the three is a struggle I undertake on a daily basis.

"I'm lucky, though, to have a family that supports me. My kids are my best promoters; my son works part time as a checker in a supermarket where my books are sold, and he always tries to sneak a copy in and get people to buy it. So he's made a few bucks for me—which he asks for in return quite frequently. He has Tom Sawyer's gift for getting people to do things for him, but he's wonderful, as are my daughter and stepchildren.

"When people ask me if I ever imagined I would achieve this kind of life, I always reply, 'Yes.' I believe very firmly in not only working hard toward a goal, but setting that goal concretely in your mind. I've always had a talent for fantasy and visualization, so I could picture what I wanted, then go out and capture it. And the image I had in mind was a beautiful old house on a city street, with a curving staircase and enough money, as Scarlett O'Hara said, to never go hungry again."[1]

Footnote Sources:

[1] Based on an interview by Marc Caplan for *Authors and Artists for Young Adults.*

[2] Michael Kilian, "Gutter to Glitter," *Chicago Tribune,* May 12, 1989.

[3] Eileen Goudge, "From Welfare Mom to Millionaire," *Ladies' Home Journal,* August, 1989.

[4] Susan Trosky, editor, *Contemporary Authors,* Volume 126, Gale, 1989.

[5] Leonore Fleischer, "Talk of the Trade," *Publishers Weekly,* February 19, 1988.

■ For More Information See

Marilyn Kirby, "Novel Bound for Best-Sellerdom," *Monterey Herald,* May 24, 1989.
Publishers Weekly, September 23, 1988.

Tony Hillerman

Born May 27, 1925, in Sacred Heart, Okla.; son of August Alfred (a farmer) and Lucy (a nurse; maiden name Grove) Hillerman; married Marie Unzner, August 16, 1948; children: Anne, Janet, Anthony, Monica, Stephen, Daniel. *Education:* Attended Oklahoma State University, 1943; University of Oklahoma, B.A., 1948; University of Mexico, M.A., 1965. *Politics:* Democrat. *Religion:* Roman Catholic. *Home:* 2729 Texas N.E., Albuquerque, N.M. 87110. *Agent:* Curtis Brown Ltd., 575 Madison Ave., New York, N.Y. 10022.

■ Career

News Herald, Borger, Tex., reporter, 1948; *Morning Press-Constitution,* Lawton, Okla., city editor, 1948-50; United Press International, political reporter in Oklahoma City, Okla., 1950-52, bureau manager in Santa Fe, N.M., 1952-54; *New Mexican,* Santa Fe, political reporter, later editor, 1954-62; University of New Mexico, Albuquerque, assistant to the president, 1963-66, 1976-81, associate professor, 1965-66; professor of journalism, 1966-85; chairman of the department of journalism, 1966-73; writer. Lecturer. *Military service:* U.S. Army, 1943-45; received Silver Star, Bronze Star, and Purple Heart. *Member:* Mystery Writers of America (president, 1988), Albuquerque Press Club, Sigma Delta Chi, Phi Kappa Phi.

■ Awards, Honors

Shaffer Award from the New Mexico Press Association, 1952, for reporting; Burrows Award from the New Mexico Press Association, 1960, for editorial writing; *The Blessing Way* was selected one of American Library Association's Best Books for Young Adults, 1970, and *A Thief of Time,* 1988; Edgar Allan Poe Award from the Mystery Writers of America, 1974, for *Dance Hall of the Dead;* Navajo Special Friend Award, 1986, for "authentically depicting the strength and dignity of the Navajo culture in his books"; Western Writers of America Honor for Children's Literature, 1986, for *The Boy Who Made Dragonfly;* Grand Prix de Litterature Policiere (France), and Golden Spur Award from the Western Writers of America for Best Novel of the Year, both 1987, both for *Skinwalkers.*

■ Writings

The Blessing Way (ALA Notable Book), Harper, 1970.
The Great Taos Bank Robbery: And Other Affairs of Indian Country (essays), University of New Mexico Press, 1970.
The Fly on the Wall, Harper, 1971, reissued, Garland, 1985.

The Boy Who Made Dragonfly: A Zuni Myth (juvenile; illustrated by Laszlo Kubinyi), Harper, 1972, new edition (illustrated by Janet Grado), University of New Mexico Press, 1986.

Dance Hall of the Dead, Harper, 1973.

New Mexico, Graphic Arts Center Press (Portland, Ore.), 1975.

Rio Grande (juvenile), Graphic Arts Center Press, 1975.

(Editor) *The Spell of New Mexico,* University of New Mexico Press, 1976.

The Listening Woman, Harper, 1978.

People of Darkness, Harper, 1980.

The Dark Wind, Harper, 1982, large print edition, Thorndike, 1984.

The Ghostway, Harper, 1984.

Skinwalkers, Harper, 1986, large print edition, Thorndike, 1987.

Indian Country: America's Sacred Land (illustrated with photographs by Bela Kalman), Northland Press, 1987.

A Thief of Time, Harper, 1988, large print edition, G. K. Hall, 1989.

Talking God, Harper, 1989.

Coyote Waits, Harper, 1990, large print edition, 1990.

Hillerman's books have been published in thirteen languages. Contributor to periodicals, including *True, New Mexico Quarterly, National Geographic, Popular Psychology, Reader's Digest, Audubon, Elle, Arizona Highways, Native People, Writer, New York Times,* and *Book World.*

■ Adaptations

"Dance Hall of the Dead" (cassette), Simon & Schuster, 1985.

"A Thief of Time" (cassette), Caedmon, 1988.

"Fly on the Wall" (cassette), Caedmon, 1989.

"Talking God" (cassette), Caedmon, 1990.

■ Work in Progress

A book set in Southeast Asia; a mystery, *Hillerman Country,* photographs and essay with photographer Barney Hillerman; consultant to movie "Dark Wind," based on *The Dark Wind,* scheduled for release in 1991.

■ Sidelights

Tony Hillerman grew up during the Depression in the small, farming community of Sacred Heart, in Potawatomie, Oklahoma. His father's farm came without indoor plumbing, tractor, or electricity. The nearest library was thirty-five miles away and the once-a-week movie in the nearest town was too expensive to attend. The battery radio was, therefore, "a big deal when it was operating. Growing up where I did, high value and respect were attached to being able to tell a story, to interest, or entertain people."[1]

"My father, who hated the Nazis and who was very sensitive about being a German in America during Hitler's rise to power, often made it a point to tell us kids that people are all basically alike. Once you know that, then you start finding out the differences. It was true for us. Our neighbors were Seminoles and Blackfeet, all of them just like us, trying without success to make a living on a worn-out landscape. And like all kids we played cowboys and Indians a lot, only we had to bribe the Indian kids to *play* Indians because they wanted to be cowboys, too."[2]

The local two-room schoolhouse was so bad that for the first eight grades Hillerman attended St. Mary's Academy, a boarding-school for Indian girls run by the Sisters of Mercy. He was one in a handful of boys admitted. "The nuns forgave us for not being Potawatomies, but they never forgave us for not being girls."[3]

Hillerman was a motivated student. "If you grow up surrounded by poverty, everyone shares one ambition: get the hell out."[1]

On Christmas day in 1941, his father died at home after suffering for years with a bad heart. The next year it was decided that Hillerman, the youngest of three, would attend college. He enrolled at Oklahoma State in Stillwater, but after the first semester returned to run the farm when his brother enlisted in the military. America had entered World War II, and in 1943 Hillerman also enlisted. "It was a way to get some adventure and see the world."[1]

Within the year he saw action in France as a member of a rifle company in the 410th Infantry. In 1945 he sustained leg injuries, burns and was blinded for several months when he was hit by a grenade behind German lines in Alsace.

Returning home with a Silver Star, Hillerman got a job delivering drilling equipment in New Mexico. One day, he found himself on a Navajo Reservation watching "Twelve or thirteen men in ceremonial attire, the horses all duded up."[1] It was a Navajo Enemy Way ceremony, a curing ritual for a marine just back from the war. "To see people with a living culture still affecting how they live—that interested me. I'm drawn to people who believe in something enough that their lives are affected by it."[1]

Hillerman began reading about Navajo culture and visited the reservation regularly. "I'm kind of a garrulous fellow and after a while, they recognized me as another country boy."[4]

About the same time, he met a reporter from the *Daily Oklahoman.* "She had read the letters I sent home to my mother for an article she wrote about my Silver Star and she told me she thought I was a good writer."[4] He had never considered becoming a writer "because it didn't dawn on me that real human beings wrote books."[5]

With her encouragement, Hillerman enrolled at the University of Oklahoma where he earned a B.A. in journalism, edited their humor magazine and met Maria Unzner, a Phi Beta Kappa bacteriology major, whom he married after graduation.

His first job was writing Purina Pig Chow radio commercials for an advertising agency in Oklahoma City. "It was the most taxing writing assignment I have ever had. I had to write three commercials for the 6 A.M. broadcast every day. Each one had to have a unique angle and none of them could be even remotely similar to the other. I lasted about four weeks."[2]

His next job was police reporter for the *News-Herald* of Borger, Texas. "I think it had to be the worst newspaper in Christendom, and Borger, which is in the Panhandle north of Amarillo, was the carbon-black capital of the world—it manufactured smog and soot. My beat was crime and violence, and this was a boom town, so it was a great place to be a police reporter. And no one stayed long, so in a couple of months I was the senior member of the staff."[3]

The town was such a high-crime area that "within six months I covered every offense listed in the Old Testament and several mentioned only in Krafft-Ebing. Of course I had to record such things as incest and sodomy in vague, ambiguous sentences because the *News-Herald* was a family newspaper."[2]

Next came a stint with the *Morning News,* UPI bureaus in Oklahoma City and Santa Fe, and then Santa Fe's daily the *New Mexican* as political reporter. There he rose to the position of city editor, managing editor and, finally, executive editor. "But it wasn't really enough. I had to find out once and for all if I could tell stories; and if it

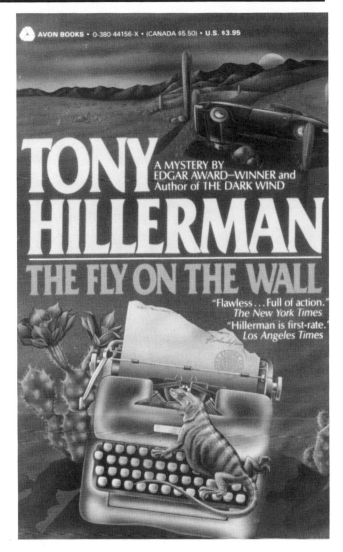

Paperback edition of Hillerman's second novel.

hadn't been for the encouragement of my wife, Marie—we had five kids, you see, and had adopted a sixth [five of the six have been adopted]—I never would have risked it."[2]

In 1962, he resigned and enrolled in the graduate program in English literature at the University of New Mexico. He worked as a free-lance writer and as a part-time assistant to the University's president to earn some money.

Hillerman received his master's degree in 1965. His thesis, *The Great Taos Bank Robbery,* was published in 1970 along with other nonfiction essays about life in New Mexico. At the university's request, Hillerman stayed on to teach journalism. This gave him time to write. "I'd always wanted to write fiction, to turn up a notch, and I had the feeling that if I didn't do something about it, all of a sudden I was going to be too old."[3] "[Nonfiction has] the strength of credibility, but you have to dig out the truth. It's inflexible material. I thought: Wouldn't it be wonderful to work in plastic instead of flint; make your own imagination drive the writing."[1]

His fascination with Native American life deepened and his research continued. In the late 60s he decided to incorporate Indian culture within the context of detective fiction. "[It's] a shorter form that has shape and flexibility, a story line with a lot of narrative."[1]

Immersing himself in the mystery writings of Eric Ambler, Graham Greene, Raymond Chandler, and G. K. Chesterton, he spent three years writing his first novel, *The Blessing Way.* But his agent at the time suggested he "get rid of all that Indian stuff," which comprised seventy percent of the book. "I thought the hell with that. I've got three years' work in this. I was either going to publish the book or feel like a failure."[1]

He then sent it to Joan Kahn at Harper who published it in 1970. "Fundamentally, of course, *The Blessing Way* is an effort to tell a story of suspense, to command the attention of the reader quickly and to hold it to the end. My theory about how this can be done evolved gradually. It is based on the methods of writers who always managed to hold my attention. . .and it is based on seventeen years of writing and editing nonfiction for United Press, various newspapers, and magazines.

"It's a simple theory and nothing new. You must win that 'willing suspension of disbelief' on the part of the reader—and to win it you must accomplish two things. You must first make your characters seem to be real human beings. And then all of their actions must be the logical outgrowths of the personalities you have given them.

"My purpose in *The Blessing Way* was to tell a suspense yarn against the background of the Navajo Reservation. I wanted to contrast the value system of the Navajos—to whom greed is the ultimate evil—with our own materialistic values. Having known Indians as playmates, classmates, and friends, I have no patience with the 'Noble Redman' stereotype. To understand how Indians are different, to appreciate the beliefs stemming from the Navajo Origin Myth and the values represented in the rituals of The People, it is necessary first to realize that they are basically not different at all.

"I hope first that *The Blessing Way* will entertain. But I also hope that it leaves the reader with a better understanding of the Dinee, of The People who occupy and rule, through their Tribal Council, a piece of America as large as New England."[6]

The book introduces his character Joe Leaphorn, a Navajo Reservation police lieutenant with a degree in anthropology and a penchant for skepticism. "I said to myself, 'Here's a Navajo who's a very intelligent fellow, and he's not going to be a fundamentalist in terms of his religion. He may well be a religious man, but he's going to see mythology in a more abstract, poetic sense.'"[3]

Continuing with the mystery form and Leaphorn as the protagonist in *Dance Hall of the Dead*, Hillerman incorporated riveting descriptions of Zuni religious rites. He based his next book, *The Listening Woman*, on the Navajo origin story which describes the Hero Twins, mythological figures who represent man's intellect and his aggressiveness. The novel concerns two Navajo brothers who have parted ways, and it is Leaphorn who must deal with the criminal intent of one of them. "I wanted to explore the dichotomy of human nature that the Hero Twins represent by closely examining the personalities of these two brothers. It was a grandiose notion, and I'm not sure that I accomplished what I wanted to accomplish, at least on the metaphysical level."[3]

In his fourth novel, *People of Darkness*, Hillerman introduced Jim Chee, an Indian detective, also college educated, who adheres strongly to Navajo values, even studying to be a shaman in order to perform tribal ceremonies. Hillerman created him, in part, to counter Leaphorn's cynicism. "At first, I thought I would be maligning the Navajos by making them more witch-craft-ridden than they were. But the further I got into it, the more I felt there was something not quite right. Finally, an Indian fellow I've known for years—he's from the Streams Come Together clan, has a master's degree in fine arts, lives on the reservation—told me, 'The one thing that bothers me about your books, and I think is false to the culture, is that Leaphorn is so skeptical about witches. I've never known a Navajo, educated or not, who was skeptical about witches.'"[3]

So far, Hillerman has written nine detective novels with Leaphorn and/or Chee as the protagonists. The books not only deal with the spiritual aspects of Navajo culture, but with the more painful elements of alcoholism and unemployment.

His series has brought him several awards and a large, enthusiastic audience. "It's always troubled me that the American people are so ignorant of these rich Indian cultures. For me, studying them has been absolutely fascinating, and I think it's important to show how aspects of ancient Indian ways are still very much alive and are highly germane even to our ways."[2]

"[The Navajo] have a fascinating religious philosophy and a lot of good values. They're the very bottom of the pecking order among Indian tribes out here. They're the country bumpkins. And I've always identified with that. We were the kids that wore bib overalls and carried lunch in a sack."[5]

Hillerman continues to do extensive research on Navajo and other Native American cultures, a research that takes him from library stacks to reservations, where he spends a good deal of time. "People say to me, 'How do you get acquainted with a Navajo? They're so distant and aloof.' It's like getting acquainted with a country boy, a hillbilly. He's got a little thin shell of defense. He sees someone from the city and he thinks, 'This guy's got wax on his car, he's going to look down his nose at me, think I'm inferior.' But as soon as you get through that, you're just another human being, and since they don't see too many strange human beings, you're suddenly new and different and interesting.

"Growing up around rednecks, hell, being one myself, I didn't know very many people who ever talked about natural beauty. They seemed really unconscious of it. But I find it remarkable how many Navajos will talk frankly and almost emotionally about the beauty around them."[3]

In 1972 the students at Zuni High School voted to have Hillerman as their commencement speaker, an event he regards as a high honor. "They study *Dance Hall of the Dead*, which takes place on a Zuni reservation, in their classes there—the Navajos study my other books in their schools as well—and yes, that means a great deal to me. I believe they feel that I understand their culture or at least try to, and that I will always treat them with respect."[2] "Lots of Navajo kids bring me raggedy books to sign—that's the ideal kind. I've had dozens [of them] look surprised and say, 'I thought you were a Navajo.'"[1]

In 1986 he was made "an honorary redskin" by the Navajo Window Rock tribal council. It is an honor Hillerman considers to be his "Academy Award." "[I] had no missionary impulse when I started, now I do, a little, when I become aware of the possibilities."[1]

"Novels of mystery and suspense seem to be an ideal way to engage readers in a subject of life-long interest to me—the religions, cultures, and value systems of Navajo and Pueblo Indians. To play the game as it should be played, I think the setting must be genuine—the reader must be shown the Indian reservation as it is today. More important, my Navajo tribal policeman's knowledge of his people, their customs, and their values must be germane to the plot. More than that, the details must be exactly accurate—from the way a hogan is built, to the way a sweat bath is taken, to the way it looks, and sounds, and smells at an Enemy Way Ceremonial at 2:00 A.M. on a wintry morning.

"It has been a great source of pleasure to me that both Navajos and Zunis have recognized themselves and their society in my books. They are heavily used in schools on both reservations and—for that matter—throughout the Indian world by other tribes. In fact, the authenticity of ceremonial details in *Dance Hall of the Dead* caused Zuni

Softcover edition of the 1973 award-winning novel.

Cover from the 1978 Avon paperback.

elders to cross-examine me about whether members of their kiva societies had revealed secrets to me.

"The background must be authentic. *But,* the name of the game is mystery and suspense. What's really important is the narration which moves against the authentic background. I feel strongly that in our genre, the reader must be caught up quickly and moved rapidly along. I like to keep my novels in a very tight time frame."[7]

"In [my many] years of writing, I have accumulated two bits of wisdom which may be worth passing along.

"First, I no longer waste two months perfecting that first chapter before getting on with the book. No matter how carefully you have the project planned, first chapters tend to demand rewriting. Things happen. New ideas suggest themselves,

new possibilities intrude. Slow to catch on, I collected a manila folder full of perfect, polished, exactly right, pear-shaped first chapters before I learned this lesson. Their only flaw is that they don't fit the book I finally wrote. The only book they will ever fit will be one entitled *Perfect First Chapters* which would be hard to sell. Thus Hillerman's First Law: NEVER POLISH THE FIRST CHAPTER UNTIL THE LAST CHAPTER IS WRITTEN.

"[The second law is] SOME PEOPLE, SOMETIMES, CAN WRITE A MYSTERY NOVEL WITHOUT AN OUTLINE.

"Or, put more honestly: If you lack the patience (or brains) to outline the plot, maybe you can grope your way through it anyway, and sometimes it's for the best."[8]

"As many writers do, I imagine myself into scenes—seeing, hearing, smelling everything I am describing.

"I have gradually learned that this sort of creative thinking happens for me only when I am at very close quarters with what I am writing—only when I am in the scene, in the mind of the viewpoint character, experiencing the chapter and sharing the thinking of the people in it. From the abstract distance of an outline, with the characters no more than names, nothing seems real to me. At this distance, the details which make a plot come to life always elude me.

"I have learned, slowly, that outlining a plot in advance is neither possible, nor useful, for me. I can get a novel written to my satisfaction only by using a much freer form and having faith that—given a few simple ingredients—my imagination will come up with the necessary answers.

"Those ingredients—not in any order of importance:

"*A setting with which I am intimately familiar.* Although I have been nosing around the Navajo Reservation and its borderlands for more than thirty years, I still revisit the landscape I am using before I start a new book—and often revisit it again while I am writing it. And then I work with a detailed, large scale map beside my word processor.

"*A general idea of the nature of the mystery* which needs to be solved, and a good idea of the motive for the crime, or crimes.

"*A theme.* For example, *The Dark Wind* exposes my Navajo cop to a crime motivated by revenge—

to which Navajos attach no value and find difficult to understand.

"*One or two important characters,* in addition to the policeman-protagonist. However, even these characters tend to be foggy at first. In *Dance Hall of the Dead,* the young anthropology graduate student I had earmarked as the murderer turned out to be too much of a weakling for the job. Another fellow took on the role."[8]

"Every writer is engaged in a joint venture every time he writes. He looks at what's behind his own forehead and translates it into words. At the other end of the crosscut saw, the reader drinks in those words and tries to transmute them back into images.

"It's a partnership. We work at it. So does the reader.

"I always write with some clear notions about those for whom I write. They are, for example, a little more intelligent than I am and have a bit better education. They have good imaginations. They enjoy suspense. They are important. They are middle-aged. They are busy. They know very little about the specific subject I'm writing about. They are interested in it only if I can provoke that interest.

"For example, as far as I can remember, I have never given more than the vaguest descriptions of either Joe Leaphorn or Jim Chee. . . .Yet, scores of readers have described them to me. Tall and short, big and little, plump and lean, handsome and homely. The reader's imagination creates the character from his or her own experience, making the policeman look exactly the way he should look. Why should the writer argue with that? Why should the person who is investing money and time in reading my story be denied his role in the creative process?

"Minor characters, I think, need more description. The reader is likely to see them only briefly through the eyes of the protagonist. He should be as curious about minor characters as is the viewpoint character—looking for the spot of gravy on the necktie, the nervous twitch at the corner of the eye, the dark roots of the bleached blonde hair, the scar tissue on the left cheek. Our reader won't see this minor actor enough to fit him into any personal mold.

"I have been doing this for years: stripping down people and places, dissecting their looks and their mannerisms, filling the storage bins of imagination with useful parts; doing the same with street

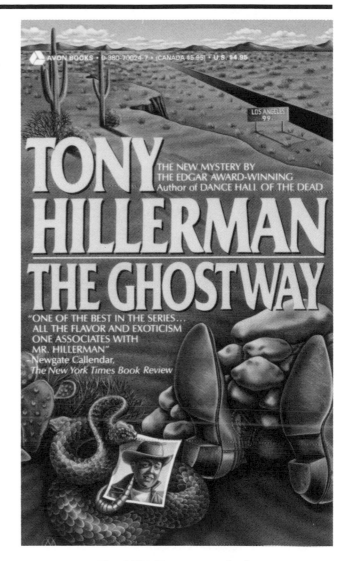

The 1984 Harper paperback.

scenes, with landscapes, with the weather. When I wrote only nonfiction, such stuff was jotted in my notebook—the telltale details I trained my mind to isolate and collect. The anthropologist squatted on a grassy slope beside an anthill, his calloused fingers sifting through those tiny grains ants bring to the surface, frowning in his fierce hope of finding a chip from a Stone Age artifact. The same fingers sorting through the residue left on the sifter-frame over his wheelbarrow, eliminating the gravel, roots, and rabbit droppings, saving the tiny chips flaked from a flint lance point; finding a twig to fish out the angry scorpion and return him to the grass. And that final detail, I hope my reader will agree, does more than put him on the scene with me. It gives him insight into the character of the man who owns the calloused fingers."[9]

"Writing (or at least writing tolerably well) is difficult for me. It requires intense concentration and it's helped by a particular mood. That's true of several other writers I know, and I suspect it's also true of almost everyone engaged in forcing the reluctant imagination to produce.

"New Mexico is rich in locales where this mood, this excitement, this urge to write seems to come. Those places that stir me have features in common. All are empty and lonely. They invoke a sense of both space and strangeness, and all have about them a sort of fierce inhospitality."[10]

The land surrounding his home in Albuquerque, and the rest of New Mexico and the Southwest, has a profound effect on Hillerman. He has written several essays, articles, and accompanying texts to photography books, about this environment and its culture. "Viewed objectively, it is a harsh and hostile landscape. In fact, none of this vast territory which Easterners once called 'The Great American Desert' offers much to the pragmatic person with

BREAKOUT BESTSELLER

TONY HILLERMAN

SKINWALKERS

"...full of mystery, intrigue and dangerous magic. SKINWALKERS is a treat."
Ross Thomas, author of *BRIARPATCH*

Harper & Row's 1986 paperback.

materialistic values. Westward from the New Mexico-Texas border, all across the southern Rockies, the Colorado Plateau and the dry and eroded high country which finally slopes away toward California, there is little to appeal to man's yearnings for a fruitful land of milk and honey. Our Genesis, the Judeo-Christian story of creation, teaches that God said that man should have 'dominion over all this earth.' But this country is hard to dominate. It is built too big for human convenience. It lacks the fertility that man values and the moderation that makes him comfortable. Something primal in even the most urbane citizen warns him of hunger and thirst out there beyond that train window, of merciless sun in the summer, cold in the winter, of a two-day walk to the nearest neighbor, of places where a person could die as easily as a field mouse. It puts man on a scale in which he is not comfortable—a tiny insignificant creature surrounded by emptiness.

"The Hopis' legends tell them that they are tied to their high corner of desert by destiny; they are living out supernatural prophecies. God told them to make migrations to the ends of the earth, to find the Center of the Universe, and to live there until this Fourth World ends. They found this center, this 'Tuwanasavi,' at the south end of Black Mesa. There they will live into eternity. The same is true in varying ways of the other tribes who found their sacred places and built their Pueblo societies up and down the Rio Grande, and at Acoma, Zuni, Laguna and elsewhere. In different ways it is true of the Navajos. . .and of the Apaches, held by their Mountain Spirits, and for the Utes, the Papagos, the Havasupais and all the others. For all of them, these first comers, this is the Holy Land."[11]

Although Hillerman's success has brought him recognition and large financial rewards, he remains an unpretentious man. He and his wife have lived in the same house for over twenty-seven years. He drives a secondhand car, rarely reads his royalty statements and does not know his gross income. "I don't particularly like or understand those people who measure success by numbers.

"The worst thing you can be called in Navajo is a ghost or a coyote. The worst insult is 'He acts like he doesn't have any relatives.' There's this sense that what counts first is the human being, not money."[1]

His books are published in thirteen languages, and in 1989 Robert Redford bought the movie options on all of his Navajo books. The filming of the first, *The Dark Wind*, began in June 1990 with Hiller-

Cover for the 1988 paperback.

man serving as consultant, intended for release as "Dark Wind" in 1991. Errol Morris is the director.

In the past Hillerman had not wanted to have his books adapted to the screen, since he felt that all previous filmscripts, including one by him, were less than satisfactory. "I used to pray that nobody would ever make a movie. [I didn't want to] spend the rest of my life explaining that I didn't have a damn thing to do with it."[1] But with Redford, Hillerman was pleased. "Having a guy like Redford, with his track record of being sensitive to the people—that's different."[1]

In 1985, Hillerman retired from teaching at the University of New Mexico and now spends his time writing at his computer, researching at the library and driving through the countryside, visiting reservations. "[I wouldn't write] if I didn't think of them as moral books. But you can sell the moral only if you give the reader his money's worth of entertainment.

"[And I] wouldn't write if it wasn't fun. I really do think each book reflects what I've learned, and is technically better. Otherwise I'd quit, because writing is really hard to do, and it doesn't get any easier."[1]

Footnote Sources:

[1] Catherine Breslin, "PW Interviews: Tony Hillerman," *Publishers Weekly*, June 10, 1988.
[2] Patricia Holt, "PW Interviews: Tony Hillerman," *Publishers Weekly*, October 24, 1980.
[3] Alex Ward, "Navajo Cops on the Case," *New York Times Magazine*, May 14, 1989.
[4] Deborah Stead, "Tony Hillerman's Cross-Cultural Mystery Novels," *New York Times*, August 16, 1988.
[5] Katrine Ames, "In the Heart of Navajo Country," *Newsweek*, June 19, 1989.
[6] "Tony Hillerman: *The Blessing Way*," *Library Journal*, February 1, 1970.
[7] John M. Reilly, editor, *Twentieth-Century Crime and Mystery Writers*, Macmillan, 1980.
[8] T. Hillerman, "Building without Blueprints," *Writer*, February, 1986.
[9] T. Hillerman, "The Reader as Partner," *Writer*, October, 1987.
[10] T. Hillerman, editor, *The Spell of New Mexico*, University of New Mexico Press, 1976.
[11] T. Hillerman, *Indian Country: America's Sacred Land*, Northland Press, 1987.

■ For More Information See

New Yorker, May 23, 1970.
Library Journal, June 15, 1970.
Variety, August 19, 1970.
Los Angeles Times, November 5, 1980, January 12, 1981, May 27, 1982, July 2, 1989 (section V, p. 4).
American West, June, 1987 (p. 22ff).
New York Times Book Review, July 3, 1988 (p. 6).
People Weekly, July 18, 1988, August 14, 1989.
Harper's, September, 1988 (p. 45ff).
Wayne Chatterton and James H. Maguire, editors, *Tony Hillerman* (pamphlet), Western Writers Series, number 87, Boise State University, 1989.
Time, June 19, 1989 (p. E8).
Audubon, July, 1989 (p. 30ff).

Ann Martin

Missing Since Monday; Children's Choice, 1985, for *Bummer Summer; Inside Out* was selected one of Child Study Association of America's Children's Books of the Year, 1986, and *Stage Fright, With You and Without You,* and *Missing since Monday,* all 1987.

Born August 12, 1955, in Princeton, N.J.; daughter of Henry Read (a cartoonist) and Edith (a teacher; maiden name, Matthews) Martin. *Education:* Smith College, A.B. (cum laude), 1977. *Politics:* Democrat. *Residence:* New York, N.Y. *Agent:* Amy Berkower, Writers House, Inc., 21 West 26th St., New York, N.Y. 10010. *Office:* c/o Scholastic, Inc., 730 Broadway, New York, N.Y. 10003.

■ Career

Plumfield School, Noroton, Conn., teacher, 1977-78; Pocket Books, Inc., New York City, editorial assistant for Archway Paperbacks, 1978-80; Scholastic Book Services, Teen Age Book Club, New York City, copywriter, 1980-81, associate editor, 1981-83, editor, 1983; Bantam Books, Inc., Books for Young Readers, New York City, senior editor, 1983-85; writer and free-lance editor, 1985—. *Member:* Authors Guild, Society of Children's Book Writers, PEN American.

■ Awards, Honors

New Jersey Institute of Technology Authors Award, 1983, for *Bummer Summer,* and 1987, for

■ Writings

Bummer Summer (young adult novel), Holiday House, 1983.

Just You and Me (young adult romance novel), Scholastic, 1983.

(With Betsy Ryan) *My Puppy Scrapbook: Featuring Fenwick* (illustrated by father, Henry Martin), Scholastic, 1983.

Inside Out (young adult novel), Holiday House, 1984.

Stage Fright (illustrated by Blanche Sims), Holiday House, 1984.

Me and Katie (the Pest) (illustrated by B. Sims), Holiday House, 1985.

With You and Without You, Holiday House, 1986.

Missing since Monday, Holiday House, 1986.

Just a Summer Romance, Holiday House, 1987.

Slam Book, Holiday House, 1987.

Fancy Dance in Feather Town (illustrated by H. Martin), Western, 1988.

Ten Kids, No Pets, (Junior Literary Guild selection), Holiday House, 1988.

Yours Turly, Shirley, Holiday House, 1988.

Moving Day in Feather Town (illustrated by H. Martin), Western, 1989.

Ma and Pa Dracula (illustrated by Dirk Zimmer), Holiday House, 1989.

"Baby-Sitters Club" Series:

Kristy's Great Idea, Scholastic, 1986.
Claudia and the Phantom Phone Calls, Scholastic, 1986.
The Truth about Stacey, Scholastic, 1986.
Mary Anne Saves the Day, Scholastic, 1987.
Dawn and the Impossible Three, Scholastic, 1987.
Kristy's Big Day, Scholasic, 1987.
Claudia and Mean Janine, Scholastic, 1987.
Boy-Crazy Stacey, Scholastic, 1987.
The Ghost at Dawn's House, Scholastic, 1988.
Logan Likes Mary Anne!, Scholastic, 1988.
Kristy and the Snobs, Scholastic, 1988.
Claudia and the New Girl, Scholastic, 1988.
Little Miss Stoneybrook and Dawn, Scholastic, 1988.
Stacey's Mistake, Scholastic, 1988.
Hello, Mallory, Scholastic, 1988.
Jessi's Secret Language, Scholastic, 1988.
Mary Anne's Bad-Luck Mystery, Scholastic, 1988.
Claudia and the Bad Joke, Scholastic, 1988.
Baby-Sitters on Board!, Scholastic, 1988.
Good-bye Stacey, Good-bye, Scholastic, 1988.
Kristy and the Walking Disaster, Scholastic, 1989.
Mallory and the Trouble with Twins, Scholastic, 1989.
Baby-Sitters' Summer Vacation, Scholastic, 1989.
Baby-Sitters' Winter Vacation, Scholastic, 1989.
Kristy and the Mother's Day Surprise, Scholastic, 1989.
Jessi Ramsey, Pet-Sitter, Scholastic, 1989.
Mary Anne and the Search for Tigger, Scholastic, 1989.
Dawn on the Coast, Scholastic, 1989.
Claudia and the Sad Good-Bye, Scholastic, 1989.
Jessi and the Superbrat, Scholastic, 1989.
Welcome Back, Stacey!, Scholastic, 1989.
Mallory and the Mystery Diary, Scholastic, 1989.
Mary Anne and the Great Romance, Scholastic, 1990.
Dawn's Wicked Stepsister, Scholastic, 1990.
Kristy and the Secret of Susan, Scholastic, 1990.
Claudia and the Great Search, Scholastic, 1990.
Mary Anne and Too Many Boys, Scholastic, 1990.
Stacey and the Mystery of Stoneybrook, Scholastic, 1990.

Jessi's Baby Sitter, Scholastic, 1990.
Dawn and the Older Boy, Scholastic, 1990.
Kristy's Mystery Admirer, Scholastic, 1990.
Baby-sitter's Island Adventure, Scholastic, 1990.

"Baby-Sitters Little Sister" Series:

Karen's Witch, Scholastic, 1988.
Karen's Roller Skates, Scholastic, 1988.
Karen's Worst Day, Scholastic, 1989.
Karen's Kittycat Club, Scholastic, 1989.
Karen's School Picture, Scholastic, 1989.
Karen's Little Sister, Scholastic, 1989.
Karen's Birthday, Scholastic, 1990.
Karen's Haircut, Scholastic, 1990.
Karen's Sleepover, Scholastic, 1990.
Karen's Grandmothers, Scholastic, 1990.
Karen's Prize, Scholastic, 1990.
Karen's Ghost, Scholastic, 1990.
Karen's Surprise, Scholastic, 1990.

Martin's works have been published in Sweden, Spain, France, Germany, Holland, Belgium, Japan, and Norway.

■ Work in Progress

Enchanted Attic for Bantam; *Eleven Kids, One Summer,* a sequel to *Ten Kids, No Pets,* for Holiday House; continuation of "Baby-sitters Club" and "Baby-sitters Little Sister" series for Scholastic.

■ Sidelights

Ann M. Martin has found success in writing two series of books for young readers, "The Baby-sitters Club" and "The Baby-sitters Little Sister," and writes practically every book in each series herself, at the rate of one a month. "Since I've become a full-time writer, I can accommodate the schedules set up by Scholastic, but I've certainly had to speed up the writing process to do so. In addition, I'm still writing a hardcover every one or two years. There's no way I could write a new hardcover every month. With the series books, I know the characters and the kind of situations they can get themselves into, and can predict the kind of conversations they will have. So, although writing two books a month sounds impossible, it's easier with a series. However, I still have to be incredibly disciplined."[1]

To keep up with this gruelling schedule, Martin rises each workday at 5:30 A.M., and spends the morning writing. "I can't just get up and write in my pajamas. I have to make my bed, get the apartment in shape and feed Mouse [her tabby cat] before I start."[2] Her afternoons are spent editing

Cover of one of Martin's 1987 books.

manuscripts and reading fan mail, of which she receives as many as 12,000 letters a year. During quiet evenings, the author is fond of reading and sewing clothes for the children of friends.

"I modeled Mary Anne of 'The Baby-sitters Club' after my character—very shy and not always able to speak her mind. Since the series has become more successful, however, I think I've changed."[1] The club leader, Kristy, was modeled after Martin's childhood friend, Beth Perkins. According to Perkins, "There is a lot of Ann in her books.... She really cares about the words she writes and who she writes them for. She listens to kids and understands their sensitivity, like how it feels to wear the wrong-colored sneakers or be snubbed in the lunch line."[2]

Martin was born in Princeton, New Jersey on August 12, 1955. "I grew up in a very imaginative family. My mother was a preschool teacher and my father, an artist. Both liked fantasy and children's literature, so my world was one of circuses, animals, Beatrix Potter, *Winnie-the-Pooh*, . . . elves and

gnomes and fairies. It was a lot of fun, and it stayed with me...."[3]

"My parents are the two people who most influenced me to become a writer by ... [encouraging] me ... when I was a child. Thanks to them, my sister and I grew up in a house filled with books, and Mom and Dad made reading fun. For instance, they read *The Wizard of Oz* with us, and we watched the movie on TV, and then one day as a surprise my father helped my sister and me make papier-mache puppets of Dorothy, the Scarecrow, the Tin Woodsman and the Cowardly Lion. Later my mother helped us make clothes for the puppets."[4]

"I was moody and temperamental, but those were very happy years ... because I had parents who would ... teach us magic tricks and roast marshmallows in the woods with us. They never cared if we made a mess. My mother called our playroom 'toy soup.'"[2] Martin's mother also recalls, Ann "always had projects.... One summer she organized a lending library of her books for the

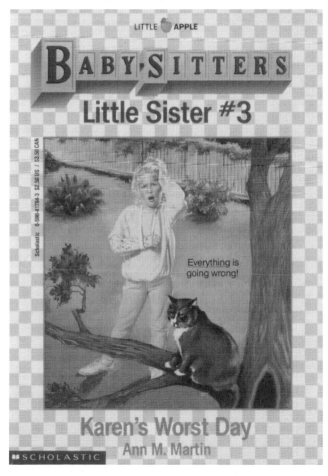

From the "Baby-Sitters Little Sister" series by Ann M. Martin.

neighborhood children, and I remember one irate mother complaining because Ann had insisted that her child pay for an overdue book."[2] Martin was herself a baby-sitter, and her most unusual experience on the job was the weekend supervision of a friend's pet snake which ended, inexplicably, with the reptile's demise.

"One of the most important tools I use in my writing is my memory.... I can remember what the first day of kindergarten was like—the way the room looked, the children, how I felt when my mother left. And I remember my senior prom and my tenth birthday and vacations at the shore and junior high graduation just as clearly. Little things, too—making a bulletin board display in sixth grade and making doll clothes and playing statue after dinner on hot summer nights. It's just as important to be able to transport oneself back to childhood as

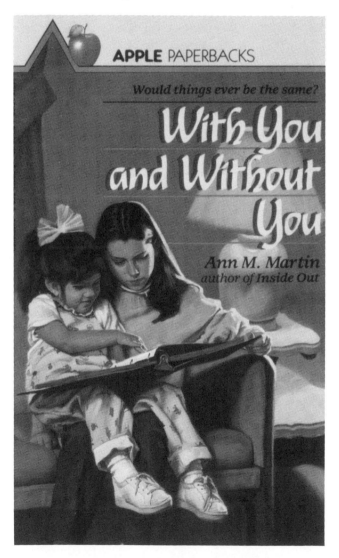

APPLE PAPERBACKS

Would things ever be the same?

With You and Without You

Ann M. Martin
author of Inside Out

Scholastic paperbound edition of the 1986 novel.

it is to have a vivid imagination, in order to write believable children's books.

"When I speak through my young characters, I am remembering and reliving: redoing all those things one is never supposed to be able to redo, having a chance to play out the 'if onlys.'"[3]

Martin's academic background, her double major in psychology and early childhood education, as well as her subsequent work as a teacher, have also contributed to her writing. "All the children I taught were special in one way or another. Some were dyslexic and some were physically handicapped. The school at which I taught after graduation drew mostly special children of one kind or another. So, working with kids who had special problems or needs, plus seeing the natural way they got along with each other in school—the groups and rivalries that form among children—has all influenced me."[1]

"[One] 'Baby-sitters Club' book, *Kristy and the Secret of Susan*, is about Kristy's sitting job with an autistic savant, a little girl who can not communicate and is mentally handicapped, yet who can memorize and play piano pieces and calculate in a flash the day of the week on which any date fell.... There's no real Susan; she's a mix of many children I worked with and became fascinated by."[4]

In 1978, Martin moved from teaching into publishing, eventually becoming Senior Editor of Bantam's Books for Young Readers in 1983—the same year she published her first novel, *Bummer Summer*. "Some of my books are based on actual experiences; others are based more on imagination, and memories of feelings.... *Me and Katie (the Pest)* is loosely based on riding lessons I took in the third grade. On the other hand, *Bummer Summer* is about a first overnight camp experience, and I never went to camp. (I was afraid to go.) *With You, Without You* is about the death of a parent, and my parents are still living."[3]

"[Another] of the 'Baby-sitters Club' books, *Claudia and the Sad Good-bye*, about the death of Claudia's grandmother, is based on the death of my own grandmother, which had happened less than a year earlier.... I tried to remember how I felt when my grandmother was sick, what her last words were to me, and the events on the day of the funeral—I used all of those things in the story."[4]

It was Jean Feiwel, editor-in-chief of the Book Group at Scholastic, who first suggested that Martin write a book about baby-sitting. "'Why don't you create characters and plots for four books?' was Jean's suggestion. So I did. The idea was really to entertain, and to present a group of girls who were friends and who ran a successful business. They're bright, funny, outgoing, and have a lot of adventures, but not light adventures. The more popular books in the series are the ones that deal with more serious issues, like *Kristy and the Snobs* about the death of Kristy's pet, or *Jessi's Secret Language* in which Jessi baby-sits for a deaf boy who communicates using only American Sign Language.

"A lot of the problems that occur in the series are the sort of problems that kids nowadays have to deal with. I don't remember seeing the faces of missing children on milk cartons when I was a kid. I grew up in the fifties and sixties, and things were much more simple. But the books also deal with the problems that any child encounters—being snubbed at school, having misunderstandings with teachers, getting into fights with siblings and friends. Those problems are ageless.

"Jean Feiwel and I thought that 'The Baby-sitters Club' was going to be a nice, four-book mini-series, but the first four did well enough for Jean to say, 'Let's try two more.' Suddenly, we were signing up for six and twelve books at a time."[1]

The success of her series about the girls who form a baby-sitting cooperative surprised Martin. "I think it surprised everybody, including the publisher. Scholastic decided the books were doing exceptionally well when the sixth book of the series hit number one on the B. Dalton Juvenile Bestseller list, sometime in 1987. That was when we decided that we really had something. We stepped up the schedule to one book every other month and eventually one every month."[1] Despite the financial rewards of such popularity, the author's personal life has changed little. She prefers to spend her money on others, sponsoring a Princeton student, supporting a dance program at an elementary school, donating toys to needy children at Christmas, co-founding the Lisa Novak Community Libraries, and founding the Ann M. Martin Foundation to benefit children, education and literacy programs, and the homeless.

Creating the books remains a collaborative process. "Whenever we have a contract for either series, 'The Baby-sitters Club,' or 'Baby-sitters Little Sister,' Jean Feiwel, Bethany Buck (my other editor), and I sit down together and brainstorm. At first, we don't come up with much more than a sentence for what's going to happen in each book, just enough for us to know where the series is

Jacket illustration by Stephen Mancusi.

going. When it comes time to write the individual book, I'll call Bethany or Jean to work out the plot in more detail.

"We work extremely well together. My editors have good ideas which I usually like. We've all had so much fun working on the books that we really haven't had any conflicts. 'The Baby-sitters Club' books are aimed at readers who are about eight to twelve, but I get letters from some as young as six and as old as fifteen. And 'The Baby-sitters Little Sister' books are for an audience of about seven- to nine-year-olds, but I hear of parents reading the books to kids as young as four. So, although we have target audiences, the kids read each series at whatever age they feel comfortable. My editors and I have established a few limits and guidelines for my writing. I don't use four-letter words in either series. I guess the books are pretty 'safe,' though we have touched on subjects that may seem a bit scary. I suppose that, somewhere in the back of my mind, I'm always thinking of the audience for whom I'm writing, but I don't talk down to kids, and I don't work with a controlled vocabulary. I

Cover of the Scholastic paperback.

holidays or summer vacations, which is a little bit unfair and confusing to the readers, but it's the only way to do it. Otherwise, the characters would soon be thirty-five.

"I also try not to allude to anything which would set the books in any particular time. I don't quote the prices of things or use the name of current rock groups. If I need to refer to a rock group, I'll either use an old standby or make one up. I hope by keeping it timeless, the series will keep going.

"My editors and I intend to publish the series for as long as sales hold up. I'm contracted to write sixty-something books, more than half of which have already been written. I suppose when sales start to drop off we'll sit back and consider what to do with the series, but for now...."[1]

"My role models are Paula Danziger, Judy Blume, and Paul Zindel. I like the fact that they are contemporary, funny, and issue-oriented. Each has a voice that I find very appealing."[1]

Martin attributes the success of her work to, among other qualities, humor. "Kids respond to humor

Jacket of the 1987 hardcover.

just seem to fall into a younger voice for Karen, the narrator of 'The Baby-sitters Little Sister' series, and into older voices for the girls who narrate 'The Baby-sitters Club' books."[1]

"Also, Jean, Bethany, and I have decided, although this isn't in writing anywhere, that while we'll touch on subjects such as death, racism, divorce and family, and school problems, we will not deal with child abuse in any form, alcohol or drug abuse, or the death of a parent or sibling because, while reading about those subjects might be helpful for older children, I know that there are six-year-olds out there who are precocious enough to read the 'Baby-sitters Club' books."[1]

The baby-sitters will also remain their respective ages for eternity. "Two of them are permanently in the sixth grade, and the rest are permanently in the eighth grade. I can't let them grow up because the books come out too fast. I try not to allude to and appreciate it. Secondly, I think the kids find characteristics they can relate to in all the main characters or the topic we've chosen. Whether I'm writing about a handicapped child or divorce, I believe in keeping it down-to-earth. I've received letters from children who have said that the characters in the books are their friends. So something in there makes these books seem real. Some kids have written me, asking for phone numbers because they want to call the characters in the books. Then I sort of sadly explain that they are not real, so they can't get in touch with them.

Occasionally, Martin receives help writing the series. "I finally decided that I did need some time off, so two months each year, one author writes a 'Little Sister' book and another writes a 'Baby-sitters Club' book. So now I'm writing twenty of the twenty-four books a year.

"But I still have input. I outline those books chapter by chapter the same way I would outline a book that I would write. Then I edit the galleys. Jean and Bethany have told me that it it's no longer necessary to outline my own books in such detail, but I insist on doing it anyway. It tends to head off problems later. For instance, if I resolve a plot twist a certain way in the outline, and Jean and Bethany don't think it's working, we can catch it before I've started to write the book.

"Thankfully, I don't seem to suffer from writer's block. The outline helps because I always know where the story is going. The outline sets up the problem at the beginning, works it through, and resolves it by the end of the story."[1]

Martin follows basically the same process for her hardcover novels. "Those outlines tend to be more detailed because I need to describe the characters, which I don't do any more for the series books.

"Both of my series are formulaic in that they include the same number of chapters in each book. In the 'Little Sister' books, Karen is always the narrator. In the older books, the seven main characters take turns telling the stories. My other books, however, can be for any age level and almost any length. I've used different devices. One book took the characters through the months of the school year.

"The ideas for books come from all over the place. Several years ago I heard a story on the news which I thought was very funny. The parents of two kids bet them five hundred dollars that they couldn't go for an entire year without watching any television. The kids took their parents up on the bet; they really did go for a year without watching TV and at the end of the year their parents kept up their end of the bargain. They gave each of the children two hundred and fifty dollars—and each one went out and bought a TV set for his bedroom. I haven't turned that into a story yet, but I plan to one day."[4]

"I'm always writing two and sometimes three books at once. Shifting back and forth is a little tough, but I enjoy it. 'The Baby-sitters Club' and the 'Little Sister' books have reached the point where they are almost easy to write, but I still love them. My hardcover novels are more of a challenge—new characters, new situations, new plots—and I like them for that reason. But for the time being, I hope that the series of books will maintain their popularity. Of course, as demographics and tastes change, kids do, too, and maybe in a few years they will find that they want pure fantasy and escape, like the C. S. Lewis books. That might signal the end of the 'Baby-sitters Club'; I can't really imagine them travelling to an imaginary kingdom or another planet."[1]

Footnote Sources:

[1] Based on an interview by Marc Caplan for *Authors and Artists for Young Adults*.
[2] Kristin McMurran, "Ann Martin Stirs Up a Tiny Tempest in Preteen Land with Her Bestselling 'Baby-Sitters Club,'" *People Weekly*, August 21, 1989.
[3] Anne Commire, editor, *Something about the Author*, Volume 44, Gale, 1986.
[4] "Author Talks" (cassette), Children's Book Council, 1990.

■ For More Information See

Periodicals:

Publishers Weekly, July 26, 1985 (p. 108ff), February 21, 1986 (p. 94ff), July 25, 1986 (p. 164ff), November 25, 1988 (p. 27).
New York Times Book Review, April 30, 1989 (p. 42).

Peter Matthiessen

Military service: U.S. Navy, 1945-47. *Member:* American Academy and Institute of Arts and Letters, New York Zoological Society (trustee, 1965-78).

■ Awards, Honors

Atlantic "First" Award, 1950, for short story "Sadie"; *Wildlife in America* is in the permanent library at the White House; National Institute and American Academy of Arts and Letters Grant, 1963, for *The Cloud Forest* and *Under the Mountain Wall;* National Book Award nomination, 1966, for *At Play in the Fields of the Lord;* Christopher Award, 1971, for *Sal si puedes;* National Book Award nomination, 1972, for *The Tree Where Man Was Born;* "Editor's Choice" citation from the *New York Times Book Review,* 1975, for *Far Tortuga;* National Book Award for Contemporary Thought, 1979, for *The Snow Leopard;* first recipient of David Marc Belkin Memorial Lectureship at John Muir College, University of California, San Diego, 1979; American Book Award, 1980, for paperback edition of *The Snow Leopard;* John Burroughs Medal from the John Burroughs Association, and African Wildlife Leadership Foundation Award, both 1982, both for *Sand Rivers;* Literary Lion from the New York Public Library, 1983; Gold Medal for Distinction in Natural History from the Academy of Natural Sciences, 1985.

■ Writings

Fiction:

Race Rock, Harper, 1954.

S urname is pronounced *Math*-e-son; born May 22, 1927, in New York, N.Y.; son of Erard A. (an architect) and Elizabeth Bleecker (Carey) Matthiessen; married Patricia Southgate, February 8, 1951 (divorced, 1957); married Deborah Love, May 16, 1963 (deceased, 1972); married Maria Eckhart, November 28, 1980; children: (first marriage) Lucas, Sara; (second marriage) Ruc, Alexander. *Education:* Attended Sorbonne, University of Paris, 1948-49; Yale University, B.A., 1950. *Politics:* Independent. *Religion:* Buddhist. *Home and office:* Bridge Lane, Sagaponack, Long Island, N.Y. 11962. *Agent:* Candida Donadio Associates, Inc., 231 West 22nd St., New York, N.Y. 10011.

■ Career

Writer, 1950—; Yale University, New Haven, Conn., assistant instructor, 1950-51; *Paris Review,* New York City (originally Paris, France), co-founder, 1951, editor, 1951—. Former commercial fisherman; captain of deep-sea charter fishing boat, Montauk, Long Island, N.Y., 1954-56; member of expeditions to Alaska, Canadian Northwest Territories, Peru, Nepal, Central Africa and East Africa, and of Harvard-Peabody Expedition to New Guinea, 1961; National Book Awards judge, 1970.

Partisans, Viking, 1955, published as *The Passionate Seekers*, Avon, 1957.
Raditzer, Viking, 1961.
At Play in the Fields of the Lord, Random House, 1965.
Far Tortuga, Random House, 1975.
On the River Styx and Other Stories, Random House, 1989.
Killing Mister Watson, Random House, 1990.

Nonfiction:

Wildlife in America, Viking, 1959, reissued, Penguin Books, 1987.
The Cloud Forest: A Chronicle of the South American Wilderness, Viking, 1961.
Under the Mountain Wall: A Chronicle of Two Seasons in the Stone Age, Viking, 1962.
Oomingmak: The Expedition to the Musk Ox Island in the Bering Sea, Hastings House, 1967.
(With Ralph S. Palmer and artist Robert Verity Clem) *The Shorebirds of North America*, Viking, 1967, published as *The Wind Birds* (illustrated by Robert Gillmor), Viking, 1973.
Sal si Puedes: Cesar Chavez and the New American Revolution, Random House, 1970.
Blue Meridian: The Search for the Great White Shark, Random House, 1971.
Everglades: With Selections from the Writings of Peter Matthiessen, edited by Paul Brooks, Sierra Club-Ballantine, 1971.
(Contributor) Alvin M. Josephy, editor, *The American Heritage Book of Natural Wonders*, American Heritage Press, 1972.
(With photographer Eliot Porter) *The Tree Where Man Was Born/The African Experience*, Dutton, 1972.
The Snow Leopard, Viking, 1978.
Sand Rivers (illustrated with photographs by Hugo van Lawick), Viking, 1981.
In the Spirit of Crazy Horse, Viking, 1983.
Indian Country, Viking, 1984.
Men's Lives: Surfmen and Baymen of the South Fork, Random House, 1986.
Nine-Headed Dragon River: Zen Journals 1969-1985, Shambhala, 1986.

Juvenile:

Seal Pool (illustrated by William Pene Du Bois), Doubleday, 1972 (published in England as *The Great Auk Escape*, Angus & Robertson, 1974).

Contributor of numerous short stories, articles, and essays to periodicals, including *Atlantic*, *Esquire*, *Harper's*, *New Yorker*, *Saturday Evening Post*, *Audubon*, *Newsweek*, and *New York Review of Books*.

■ Adaptations

"Peter Matthiessen" (cassette), American Audio Prose, 1988.
"At Play in the Fields of the Lord" (motion picture), starring Tom Berenger, John Lithgow, Daryl Hannah, Aidan Quinn, Tom Waits, and Kathy Bates, Saul Zaentz (producer), in production.

■ Work in Progress

A sequel to *Killing Mister Wilson*.

■ Sidelights

Peter Matthiessen was born on May 22, 1927, in New York City to Elizabeth Carey and Erard Matthiessen. "I am a New Yorker by birth, not inclination; I have never remained there very long.

"My formative years left me unformed; despite kind family, superior schooling, and all the orderly advantages, I remained disorderly. By the time I was sixteen, I had determined that I would write. Strange callow pieces with my byline were already appearing in the school publications."[1]

After a year in the U.S. Navy, Matthiessen attended Yale University in 1947, spending his junior year in Sorbonne, Paris. At this time, some of his short stories were published in various magazines. After earning a B.A. in English, Matthiessen taught creative writing at Yale, and in 1951 married Patsy Southgate whom he had met in Paris.

Returning to the United States with their son, Lucas Conrad, in 1953, they settled in the Springs, East Hampton, New York. For the next few years Matthiessen worked as a commercial fisherman, scalloping and clamming during the spring and fall. "I don't think I could have done my writing without the fishing. I needed something physical, something non-intellectual."[2]

In 1954, his first novel, *Race Rock*, was published. Written in the Conradian tradition, it traced the coming of age of upper-middle-class Americans on the New England coast. The five characters struggle with the tension between primitive vitality and the burden of tradition. The following year, Viking published *Partisans*, an adventure story about an American journalist's encounter with Parisian working-class life. The novel reflected liberal disillusion with Communism.

By 1957 Matthiessen was single again and for the next five years wandered about the world, traveling the backwoods of the Americas from Point Barrow to Tierra del Fuego.

His first nonfiction work, *Wildlife in America*, is an exhaustive survey of the white man's effect on the wildlife of North America. It garnered high critical acclaim and established Matthiessen as a gifted naturalist-writer. "I have always been a student of natural history and wild animal behavior, and the anatomy of the universe. My interest is pragmatic on the one hand ... but I wish also to identify a sense of man's fate on earth and instill it in both fiction and nonfiction. The nonfiction is more or less spare and objective, but my fiction is realistic only in the most superficial sense; someone has called it *surreal*, in the sense of intensely, or *wildly* real, and I think this is correct. At least, the idea attracts me, because in the intensity of true reality—as opposed to 'realism'—lie the greatest mysteries of all."[1]

Raditzer, his next novel, was set in the Pacific area at the end of World War II. "[It] is a little bit too tight. I don't like to read ... [it] much, but there's some good stuff in it, I think, and it was very clearly a transition from my first two books to my most recent novels."[3]

After traveling throughout the Sudan, East Africa, Nepal, and South-East Asia, an account of his experiences with the Harvard-Peabody expedition to New Guinea was published as *Under the Mountain Wall: A Chronicle of Two Seasons in the Stone Age*. "I am frequently described as a 'naturalist' and 'anthropologist': Actually, I am only an informed amateur in both fields."[4]

He married writer Deborah Love in 1963. Two years later, *At Play in the Fields of the Lord* was published—a novel nominated for the National Book Award and optioned by Metro-Goldwyn-Mayer. Set in the Amazonian jungle, this adventure story tells of the confrontation between the primitive Niaruna and a group of missionaries intent on "civilizing" the Indian tribe they all but destroy. "I became fascinated by a certain kind of guy, and the hero, Lewis Moon, ... as far as I can piece it together, is kind of an amalgam of three people. First, a young Navajo guy. When I was doing the research for *Wildlife in America*, traveling through the West, I picked up this young Navajo kid, who was so hostile ... any attempt to be friendly was just rebuffed. We eat and we drive and we don't talk. And then somewhere in the middle of the desert, 600 miles later, he bangs on the side of the

window and I let him out. Now I know Indian people an awful lot better.... At the time I saw alienation, tremendous alienation from white culture and I probably romanticized it.

"Second was a guy I ran into in Belem, Brazil, at the mouth of the Amazon River. Absolutely strange lonely loner of a man, pursuing some dream of exploration. He had a little kit of maps and one spare shirt and one spare set of underpants. Everything was cut down, so he had a little packet, he carried his whole life in a little packet like a big envelope, no more. He told me he'd had an interesting life.... Oh, he had a successful business in Canada, he got sick of it, ran out on his wife and children and then he became a merchant seaman, was washed off the deck of a cargo and was miraculously picked up by another ship ... and that gave him real pause about his life. He wanted to see everything, didn't want inhibitions or anything to stop him.... And in that guy I found certain aspects of me, all three came together as Lewis Moon."[3]

In 1967 both *Oomingmak: The Expedition to the Musk Ox Island in the Bering Sea*, and *The Shorebirds of North America* were published. In an article for *Audubon* magazine, Matthiessen recorded his keen and passionate observations of bird life. "This story begins, as stories should, with a mysterious track on the beach. The beach, moreover, is located on an island without permanent inhabitants. The island, called Tuckernuck, lies off the west end of Nantucket and before the Atlantic intervened was the western point of the main island.

"Before daybreak and at evening I go surf-casting for bluefish and striped bass; in the days we swim and explore the island. For fun, I am compiling a bird list, which already includes such uncommon species as the upland sandpiper, peregrine, and Ipswich sparrow; having walked the island for a week without seeing any sign of grouse or pheasant, I am surprised on the last day to come upon the track of a large gallinaceous bird on the ocean beach.

"Conceivably, three native species of wildfowl might occur here, but of these, the quail, or bobwhite, is too small to have made the track, and the ruffed grouse is a woodland form, rarely seen in open country. The one species that belongs on the moors of Tuckernuck is the eastern race of the prairie chicken or pennated grouse, known as the heath hen, which thirty years ago was declared extinct.

"Having collected a few feathers, I scatter a small bag of bird seed, after which we build a blind in a waist-high clump of oak. I choose a clump inland from the dancing ground, toward the high ground in the northeast, so that tomorrow the rising sun will be behind us. Just before the blind is finished, a bird rises from the dune grass and flies east. When alarmed, the grouse fly strongly and steadily for some distance, but this one flies slowly, with long glides, and lands in plain view against a grassy bank a half-mile away; landing, it spreads its tail feathers, which in the full sunlight show a lot of white. The heath hen has light tips on these feathers, but this much white is bothersome; unlike the prairie chicken, the sharptail has white outer feathers on its tail. I hope it is the light. The bird stands upright in the sunshine for a while before subsiding in the blowing grass. In other years, out west, I have seen both species, but I am not familiar enough with either one to make a positive identification at this distance."[5]

Then, in the summer of 1969, Matthiessen had his first encounter with Zen Buddhism, which was to become an important force in his life. "On an August day of 1969, returning home to Sagaponack, Long Island, after a seven-month absence in Africa, I was astonished by the presence in my driveway of three inscrutable small men who turned out to be Japanese Zen masters. Hakuun Yasutani-roshi, eighty-four years old, was a light, gaunt figure with hollowed eyes and round, prominent ears; as I was to learn, he had spent much of that morning upside down, standing on his head. Beside him, Nakagawa Soen-roshi, slit-eyed, elfin, and merry, entirely at ease and entirely aware at the same time, like a paused swallow, gave off emanations of lightly contained energy that made him seem much larger than he was. The roshis were attended by Tai-san (now Shimano Eido-roshi), a compact young monk with a confident, thick-featured face and samurai bearing. Though lacking the strange 'transparent' presence of his teachers, Tai-san conveyed the same impression of contained power.

"The teachers were guests of my wife, Deborah . . . a new student of Zen, but I was ignorant of this as of much else on that long-ago summer day. Because of my long absence and my unannounced return, the atmosphere between Deborah and me was guarded, and my first meeting with Zen masters was even less auspicious than an encounter that almost certainly took place in the 1890s between the first Zen master in America, Soyen Shaku, and the senior partner in his host's manu-

Jacket from the reissue of Matthiessen's 1959 book.

facturing firm who, as karma would have it—and the Dharma, too—was none other than my forebear, Frederick Matthiessen. (This problematical meeting was at best unpromising, since it passed unrecorded in the annals of either side.) No doubt I revealed what I presume was my great-grandfather's wary attitude toward unanticipated orientals in outlandish garb. For years thereafter, Tai-san would relate how Soen and Yasutani, perceiving my unenlightened condition at a glance, had shaken their shining heads and sighed, 'Poor Debbolah.'

"For the next few years, I was often away on expeditions. Even when I was at home, my wife kept me well away from her Zen practice, not wishing to contaminate the zendo atmosphere with our dissension. Yet a seed had sprouted all the same, those men in my driveway knew something that I wished to know. I poked about in the Zen literature and pestered her for inside information.

"In December of 1970—perhaps hoping to nip that bad seed in the bud—Deborah took me along to a weekend *sesshin*, or silent retreat, at the New

York Zendo. I had had no experience or training in *zazen*—literally, 'sitting Zen'—and suffered dreadful pain in the cross-legged posture, which I maintained, with the stubbornness of rage, for twelve hours daily for two days, weeping in pure shock during the rest periods. Though I won high praise from the zendo masochist, Monk D., I swore that this barbaric experience would never be repeated; in addition to all that pain, it had been so *boring!* A week later I departed gladly for Italy, Africa, and Australia, where I accompanied a more prudent group of human beings underwater in quest of the first film of the great white shark.

"That winter, to my own astonishment, I found myself doing zazen every day, not only in my Australian hotel room but on shipboard. The following summer I was working for a while in California, and in a vague impulse toward pilgrimage, I went on foot over the mountains from Carmel Valley to the San Francisco Zen Center's retreat at Tassajara.

"I have often tried to isolate that quality of 'Zen' which attracted me so powerfully to its literature and later to the practice of zazen. But since the essence of Zen might well be what one teacher called 'the moment-by-moment awakening of mind,' there is little that may sensibly be said about it without succumbing to that breathless, mystery-ridden prose that drives so many sincere aspirants in the other direction. In zazen, one may hope to penetrate the ringing stillness of universal mind, and this 'intimation of immortality,' as Wordsworth called it, also shines forth from the brief, cryptic Zen texts, which refer obliquely to that absolute reality beyond the grasp of our linear vocabulary, yet right here in this moment, in this ink and paper, in the sound of this hand turning the page.

"Later that summer, all but inexplicably, my wife and I at last embraced each other's failings. Happily she invited me to join a reconnaissance led by Soen-roshi and Tai-san of a tract of mountain land at Beecher Lake, in the headwaters of the Beaverkill River in the Catskills. This beautiful place would be chosen as the site of Dai Bosatsu (Great Bodhisattva), the first Zen monastery ever constructed in America. What struck me most forcibly during our visit was the quiet precision, power, and wild humor of Soen-roshi, who became my Zen teacher even before I realized that I was a student."[6]

In 1971 Deborah became critically ill. A year later she died. "In mid-November of 1971, Deborah and I attended a weekend sesshin at the New York Zendo. For two months Deborah had been suffering from pains that seemed to resist all diagnosis, and she decided to limit herself to the Sunday sittings. On Saturday evening, meeting me at the door of our apartment, she stood there, smiling, in a new brown dress, but it was not the strange, transparent beauty in her face that took my breath away. I had been in zazen since before daybreak, and my mind was clear, and I saw Death gazing out at me from those wide, dark eyes. There was no mistaking it, and the certainty was so immediate and shocking that I could not greet her. In what she took as observance of sesshin silence, I pushed past quietly into the bathroom, to collect myself in order that I might speak.

"On Sunday, Deborah chanced to sit directly opposite my own place in the two long lines of buddha figures that faced each other. During morning service, still resisting what I had perceived the night before, and upset that this day might exhaust her, I chanted for her with such intensity that I 'lost' myself, obliterated my *self*—a

Softcover of the 1961 book.

Softcover edition of the 1962 award winner.

function of the ten-line *Kannon Sutra*, dedicated to the bodhisattva Avalokiteshvara, which is chanted hard, over and over, thirty-three times, with wood gong and bells, in mounting volume and intensity. At the end, the chanters give one mounting volume and intensity. At the end, the chanters give one mighty shout of *MU!*—a mantric word corresponding to *Om*, which symbolizes the Absolute, eternity—this followed instantly by a great hush of sudden, ringing silence, as if the universe had stopped to listen. But on this morning, in the near darkness—the altar candle was the only light in the long room—this immense hush swelled and swelled and kept on swelling, as if this 'I' were opening out into infinity, in eternal amplification of my buddha being. There was no hallucination, only awe, 'I' had vanished and also 'I' was everywhere.

"Then I let my breath go, gave myself up to immersion in all things, to a joyous *belonging* so overwhelming that tears of relief poured from my eyes. For the first time since unremembered childhood, I was not alone, there was no separate 'I.' Wounds, anger, ragged edges, hollow places were all gone, all had been healed; my heart was the heart of all creation. *Nothing was needed*, nothing missing, all was already, always, and forever present and forever known. Even Deborah's dying, if that had to be, was perfectly in place. All that day I wept and laughed.

"Two weeks later, describing to Tai-san what had happened, I astonished myself (though not my teacher, who merely nodded, making a small bow) by a spontaneous burst of tears and laughter, the tears falling light and free as rain in sunlight.

"The state of grace that began that November morning in the New York Zendo prevailed throughout the winter of my wife's dying, an inner calm in which I knew at once what must be done, wasting no energy in indecision or regrets. When I told Tai-san about this readiness and strength, and confessed to a kind of crazy exaltation, he said quietly, 'You have transcended.' I supposed he meant 'transcended the ego,' and with it all horror and remorse. As if awakened from a bad dream of the past, I found myself forgiven, not only by Deborah but by myself.

"Deborah never spoke again, but neither did she return to the wild fear and distress of earlier days. She seemed to be in a blessed state, and Tai-san wondered if she had not had a spontaneous kensho [enlightenment experiment]. That afternoon she returned into the coma, and she died peacefully three nights later, with Tai-san and I holding her cooling hands. After three suspended pauses between breaths, my beautiful wife—how incredible!—made no effort to inhale again. We sat with her for two more hours until her body was removed for autopsy."[6]

Two years later Matthiessen wrote: "In the bright snow outside the kitchen [of the Dai Bosatsu Zendo, in the Catskill Mountains] crisp jays and chickadees share this first day of spring. Two years ago, in winter dusk, as I set out to dig Deborah's grave in the south meadow, a chickadee came from this tree to light on the handle of my pick, and afterward, in stone-filled earth that was locked in snow and ice, the pick sank without hindrance into the one soft place among the stones where her urn would lie.

"Across the wind, an early redwing sings, undaunted, though its forage lies beneath yesterday's snow. In the long sittings, I am having pain, and the fragile bird's acceptance of hard going gives me courage. 'Torn redwing, / blown to the white birch by the white lake, / sings / *blackbird!*'

"Each evening I go to Deborah's grave and listen to the wind in the dark pines; the voices of wild geese pass overhead, from south to north."[7]

In 1973 Matthiessen journeyed across the Himalayas with zoologist George Schaller. "A Himalayan pilgrimage undertaken ... that autumn ... had its inception on the path of Zen taken years earlier, as well as in a lifelong attraction to wild places. In the rigors of hard travel on foot, in the monumental landscapes, the calm of ancient peoples and wild creatures, lay a simplicity and silence which restored perspective to the death of my wife the year before. The journey exposed me to Tibetan Buddhism as practiced in a remote region of the Tibetan Plateau, and particular to an ancient 'Zenlike' sect, Karma-Kagyu, which is now well established in America.

"Despite the stern injunction of Zen teachers to seek nothing, to keep one's feet upon the ground, I was still stuck in that wide-eyed early stage of practice in which one yearns for 'miraculous' experience of the universal self, for so-called 'enlightenment.' ... The inevitable struggle to apply such insights as have been attained on the black cushion to the more rigorous Zen of everyday life."[5]

Far Tortuga was published in 1975. "*Far Tortuga* is based on a sea turtle fishing voyage off Nicaragua: *tortuga* is the Spanish word for sea turtle, and sometimes refers to a cay where green turtles are found. I started work on the book in 1966, and since then, it's been put aside many times, but I never tired of it. I was moved by the stark quality of that voyage, everything worn bare by wind and sea—the reefs, the faded schooner, the turtle men themselves—everything so pared down and so simple that metaphors, stream-of-consciousness, even such ordinary conventions of the novel as 'he said' or 'he thought,' seemed intrusive, even offensive, and a great impediment, besides. So from the start I was feeling my way toward a spare form, with more air around the words, more space: I wanted the descriptions to be very clear and flat, to find such poetry as they might attain in their very directness and simplicity. In fact, I can only recall one simile in the whole book. And eventually, I attempted using white space to achieve resonance, to make the reader receive things intuitively, hear the silence in the wind, for instance, that is a constant presence in the book."[8]

In *The Snow Leopard,* published in 1978, Matthiessen synthesized his 1973 journey across the Himalayas, during which he watched blue sheep and tracked down the snow leopard. "Having got here at last, I do not wish to leave the Crystal Mountain. I am in pain about it, truly, so much so that I have to smile, or I might weep. I think of D[eborah] and how she would smile, too. In another life—this isn't what I know, but how I feel—these mountains were my home; there is a rising of forgotten knowledge, like a spring from hidden aquifers under the earth. To glimpse one's own true nature is a kind of homegoing, to a place East of the Sun. West of the Moon—the homegoing that needs no home, like that waterfall on the upper Suli Gad that turns to mist before touching the earth and rises once again into the sky.

"High on the ridge above Tsakang, I see a blue spot where [George Schaller] is tracking; I come up

"One of the best novels in years"
—HERB CAEN, *San Francisco Chronicle*

"A flaming soul wringer, a marvelously exciting yarn"
—VIRGINIA KIRKUS

"Extraordinary"
—EMILE CAPOUYA, *The New York Times*

Peter Matthiessen

AT PLAY IN THE FIELDS OF THE LORD

Paperback edition of the 1965 novel.

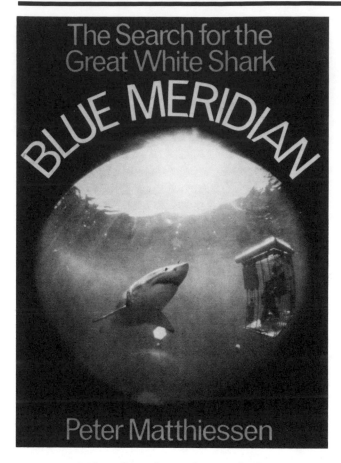

The Search for the
Great White Shark

BLUE MERIDIAN

Peter Matthiessen

Jacket of Matthiessen's 1971 book.

with him in the next hour. 'It fooled me,' he calls by way of greeting. 'Turned up the valley just below the trip line, then over the ridge, not one hundred yards from where I was lying, and down onto the path again—typical.' He shifts his binoculars to the Tsakang herd, which has now been joined by the smaller bands of the west slope. 'I've lost the trail now, but that leopard is right here right this minute, watching us.' His words are borne out by the sheep, which break into short skittish runs as the wind makes its midmorning shift, then flee the rock and thorn of this bare ridge, plunging across deep crusted snow with hollow booming blows, in flight to a point high up on the Crystal Mountain. Blue sheep do not run from man like that even when driven.

"The snow leopard is a strong presence; its vertical pupils and small stilled breaths are no more than a snow cock's glide away. GS murmurs, 'Unless it moves, we are not going to see it, not even on the snow—those creatures are really something.' With our binoculars, we study the barren ridge face, foot by foot. Then he says, 'You know something? We've seen so much, maybe it's better if there are some things that we *don't* see.' He seems startled

by his own remark, and I wonder if he means this as I take it—that we have been spared the desolation of success, the doubt: is this *really* what we came so far to see?"[9]

In his 1981 book, *Sand Rivers*, Matthiessen defended the threatened African rhino, for which he received the John Burroughs Medal and the African Wildlife Leadership Foundation Award.

The author's 1983 book, *In the Spirit of Crazy Horse*, focused on the shoot-out at the Pine Ridge Reservation near Wounded Knee, South Dakota between FBI agents and members of the American Indian Movement. One Indian and two FBI agents were killed. Matthiessen argued that Leonard Peltier, who was convicted of killing the FBI agents, was in fact railroaded into prison and deserved a new trial. Two libel suits were brought against author and publisher, one by FBI agent David Price, the other by former governor William J. Jankow of South Dakota. Eventually a federal judge dismissed the former and a circuit court the latter.

Indian Country, published in 1984, was a passionate defense of the rights of Indians and a plea for ecological balance. "Some of these chapters, in different form, appeared in *Audubon, Geo, The New York Review of Books, The Nation, Parabola, Rocky Mountain*, and the Sunday magazines of *The New York Times, The Washington Post*, and the Miami *Herald*, in an attempt to draw wider attention to transgressions on Indian land and life all over the country. Although history is drawn upon for background and perspective, *Indian Country* is essentially a journal of travels and encounters with Indian people over the past decade. My hope is that these Indian voices, eloquent and bitter, humorous and sad, will provide what history and statistics cannot, a sense of that profound 'life way' which could illuminate our own dispirited consumer culture. Hear these voices, listen carefully: the Indian spirit is the very breath of the Americas.

"We can no longer pretend—as we did for so long—that Indians are a primitive people: no, they are a traditional people, that is, a 'first' or 'original' people, a primal people, the inheritors of a profound and exquisite wisdom distilled by long ages on this earth. The Indian concept of earth and spirit has been patronizingly dismissed as simplehearted 'naturalism' of 'animism,' when in fact it derives from a holistic vision known to all mystics and great teachers of the most venerated religions of the world.

"The people who know this country best are Indians, many of them full bloods who speak their own language: not many such people are left in North America. Their culture has survived because of an ability and will to endure and fight and hide in an inhospitable and trackless reach of swamp and marsh where heat and humidity, deer flies and mosquitoes, and the tall, razor-edged sedge called sawgrass all become their formidable allies; it persists because of an unrelenting mistrust of the white man. In terms of men as well as money, the United States fought the longest and most costly of its Indian Wars before abandoning its efforts to clear the last Indian out of Florida, and for a century thereafter, the Everglades and the Big Cypress hid from the world the scattered fires of these people. Even when it was safe to reappear, the Indians preferred their isolation. But in recent years, they have been driven out into the open, not by soldiers but by bureaucrats and politicians; the white man had simply usurped the land that was theirs by right and by prior occupation. Never defeated but no longer acknowledged, they found themselves homeless in their own country."[10]

Men's Lives: The Surfmen and Baymen of the South Fork, about the difficulties of Long Island's fisherman today, was published in 1986. "[It] is a book I always knew I was going to do. I was pushed into it faster because these guys were in an emergency, these fishermen. They were pushed off the map by the tourist economy.... We wanted to get that book out in a hurry to help them out. It was too late. We should have started ten years ago."[3]

He then published *Nine-headed Dragon River: Zen Journals 1969-1985*. "The unwary reader has in hand a 'Zen book' composed against the best instincts of its author, who has no business writing upon a subject so incompletely understood—far less a subject such as Zen, which is fundamentally impossible to write *about*.

"Journals kept during fifteen years of practice provide a rickety armature for Zen poems, stories, and teachings, those luminous expressions of deep insight by Zen masters, past and present, which have delighted me and refreshed my life. This book will only justify itself if it transmits enough of that delight so that others may be drawn toward the path of Zen."[6]

Matthiessen prefers writing fiction. "I find it exhilarating. I've always thought of nonfiction as a livelihood, a way of making a living so I could write fiction. Nonfiction may be extremely skillful, it may be cabinetwork rather than carpentry, but it's still assembled from facts, from research, from observation; it comes from outside, not from within. It may be well made or badly made, but it's still an assemblage. If you're an honest journalist, you're inevitably confined by the facts; you can't use your imagination beyond a certain point."[9]

Matthiessen lives on Long Island and mourns its changes. "I live in a potato-farming country by the sea, on the south edge of a glacial outwash plain where rich loam from the far north extends to the very edge of the Atlantic dunes, and walking by the ocean in the spring, one feels exhilarated by strange smells, by the strong moist mix of sea and land coming to life in primordial regeneration. After a storm the ribs of dead ships may rise beckoning out of the surf.

"This broad shore of mist-silvered sand extends a hundred miles from east to west. When the wind is right and fish are running, I cast for blues and stripers. I swim in this surf, wander this shore, scan the restless sea on the lookout for whale spouts, shark fins, the bone-white flash of diving gannets.

"Behind the beach lies Sagaponack Pond, which winds south to the sea, and the white perch and whitebait, eels and blue crabs come and go. With its reeds and channels and broad tide flats, this pond behind the dunes is a favored resting place for migrant shore birds, storm-lost sea birds, herons, gulls and terns.

"Many years ago I began a book, 'The pond at Sagaponack, where I live....' I live here still and will be buried here because it is the country of my heart, my home. Yet in recent years these fields and dunes have filled with tricky houses; they erupt like popcorn, while the haul seiners, the farmers, too, are disappearing. Standing on the dunes, I know that the sea itself is changing, that like the fresh water and the land and air, it can no longer cleanse itself of our human progress."[11]

Footnote Sources:

[1] John Wakeman, editor, "Peter Matthiessen," *World Authors 1950-1970*, H. W. Wilson, 1975.
[2] "Peter Matthiessen," *Contemporary Authors: New Revision Series*, Volume 21, Gale, 1987.
[3] "Interview with Kay Bonetti," American Audio Prose Library, 1987. Amended by P. Matthiessen.
[4] Ruth Montgomery, "WLB Biography: Peter Matthiessen," *Wilson Library Bulletin*, March, 1964.
[5] P. Matthiessen, "A Track on the Beach," *Audubon*, March, 1977.
[6] P. Matthiessen, *Nine-Headed Dragon River, Zen Journals 1969-1985*, Shambhala, 1986.
[7] P. Matthiessen, "Common Miracles," *Search*, edited by Jean Sulzberger, Harper, 1979.

[8] P. Matthiessen, "The Craft of Fiction in *Far Tortuga*," *Paris Review*, winter, 1974.
[9] P. Matthiessen, "At Crystal Mountain," *Words from the Land*, edited by Stephen Trimble, Gibbs M. Smith, 1988.
[10] P. Matthiessen, *Indian Country*, Viking, 1984.
[11] P. Matthiessen, "Treasured Places," *Life*, Volume 10, number 7, 1987.

■ For More Information See

Books:

William Parker, editor, *Men of Courage: Stories of Present-Day Adventures in Danger and Death*, Playboy Press, 1972.

Charles Moritz, editor, *Current Biography Yearbook 1975*, H. W. Wilson, 1976.

Contemporary Literary Criticism, Gale, Volume VII, 1977, Volume XI, 1979, Volume XXXII, 1985.

D. Nicholas, *Peter Matthiessen: A Bibliography 1952-1979*, Orirana, 1980.

Dictionary of Literary Biography, Volume VI: *American Novelists since World War II*, Second Series, Gale, 1980.

William Styron, *This Quiet Dust and Other Writings*, Random House, 1982.

D. L. Kirkpatrick, editor, *Contemporary Novelists*, St. James, 1986.

Periodicals:

Bazaar, August, 1953 (p. 122ff).
Atlantic, June, 1954, March, 1971, November, 1972, June, 1975, September, 1978, March, 1983.
Library Journal, August, 1955.
Commonweal, October 28, 1955.

Nation, February 25, 1961, December 13, 1965, June 1, 1970, May 31, 1975, September 16, 1978, August 25-September 1, 1979 (p. 135ff).
Book World, December 10, 1967, April 18, 1971.
Natural History, January, 1968.
Critic, May-June, 1970.
Literary Quarterly, May 15, 1975.
Time, May 26, 1975 (p. 80ff), March 28, 1983 (p. 70).
New Republic, June 7, 1975, September 23, 1978, March 7, 1983, June 4, 1984.
New Leader, June 9, 1975.
People Weekly, August 4, 1975 (p. 36ff).
Audubon, November, 1975 (p. 64ff), September, 1981 (p. 82ff).
Hudson Review, winter, 1975-76, winter, 1981-82.
Antaeus, spring, 1978 (p. 7ff).
National Review, October 13, 1978.
Los Angeles Times, March 22, 1979.
Newsweek, December 17, 1979 (p. 21), February 1, 1988 (p. 47).
New York Review of Books, February 7, 1980 (p. 31ff).
Chicago Tribune Book World, April 5, 1981, March 13, 1983.
Los Angeles Times Book Review, May 10, 1981, March 6, 1983, May 18, 1986, August 24, 1986.
Georgia Review, winter, 1981.
Christian Science Monitor, March 11, 1983.
Globe and Mail (Toronto), July 28, 1984.
Publishers Weekly, February 15, 1985 (p. 25), November 1, 1985 (p. 20ff), January 29, 1988 (p. 314), September 1, 1989 (p. 8).
P. Matthiessen, "The Case for Burning," *New York Times Magazine*, December 11, 1988.

Anne McCaffrey

Born April 1, 1926, in Cambridge, Mass.; daughter of George Herbert (a city administrator and colonel, U.S. Army) and Anne Dorothy (a real estate agent; maiden name, McElroy) McCaffrey; married H. Wright Johnson (in public relations), January 14, 1950 (divorced, 1970); children: Alec, Todd, Georgeanne. *Education:* Radcliffe College, B.A. (cum laude), 1947; graduate study in meteorology, University of City of Dublin; also studied voice for nine years. *Politics:* Democrat. *Religion:* Presbyterian. *Home and office:* "Dragonhold," Kilquade, Greystones, County Wicklow, Ireland. *Agent:* Virginia Kidd, Box 278, Milford, Pa. 18337.

■ Career

Liberty Music Shops, New York City, copywriter, 1948-50; Helena Rubinstein, New York City, copywriter and secretary, 1950-52; writer, 1954—. Former professional stage director for several groups in Wilmington, Del. *Member:* Science Fiction Writers of America (secretary-treasurer, 1968-70), Authors Guild, Authors League of America, PEN (Ireland), Novelists, Inc.

■ Awards, Honors

Hugo Award for Best Novella from the World Science Fiction Society, 1967, for "Weyr Search"; Nebula Award for Best Novella from the Science Fiction Writers of America, 1968, for "Dragonrider"; E. E. Smith Award for Fantasy from Boskone, 1975, for imaginative fiction; Ditmar Award (Australia), Gandalf Award from Worldcon, and Eurocon/Streso Award from the European Science-Fiction Convention, all 1979, all for *The White Dragon;* Balrog Citation from Fools' Con (Kansas), 1980, for *Dragondrums;* Golden Pen Award, 1981, for young adult fiction; Science-Fiction Book Club Award, 1986, for *Killashandra,* and 1989, for *Dragonsdawn.*

■ Writings

Restoree, Ballantine, 1967.
Dragonflight, Ballantine, 1968, hardcover edition, Walker, 1969.
Decision at Doona, Ballantine, 1969.
The Ship Who Sang, Walker, 1969.
(Editor) *Alchemy and Academe,* Doubleday, 1970.
Dragonquest: Being the Further Adventures of the Dragonriders of Pern, Ballantine, 1971.
The Mark of Merlin, Dell, 1971.
Ring of Fear, Dell, 1971.
(Editor) *Cooking out of This World,* Ballantine, 1973.
To Ride Pegasus, Ballantine, 1973.

*A Time When: Being a Tale of Young Lord
    Jaxom, His White Dragon, Ruth, and Various
    Fire-Lizards,* NESFA Press, 1975.
The Kilternan Legacy, Dell, 1975.
Dragonsong (ALA Notable Book; *Horn Book*
    honor list; illustrated by Laura Lydecker),
    Atheneum, 1976.
Get Off the Unicorn, Ballantine, 1977.
Dragonsinger (ALA Notable Book; Junior
    Literary Guild selection), Atheneum, 1977.
Dinosaur Planet, Ballantine, 1978.
The White Dragon, Ballantine, 1978.
Dragondrums (illustrated by Fred Marcellino),
    Atheneum, 1979.
The Crystal Singer, Ballantine, 1981.
The Coelura, Underwood-Miller, 1983.
Moreta: Dragonlady of Pern, Ballantine, 1983.
Stitch in Snow, Ballantine, 1984.
Dinosaur Planet Survivors, Futura, 1984.
Killashandra, Ballantine, 1985.
Nerilka's Story, Ballantine, 1986.
The Lady, Ballantine, 1987.
(With Robin Wood) *The People of Pern,*
    Donning, 1988.
Dragonsdawn, Del Rey, 1988.
The Renegades of Pern, Del Rey, 1989.
(With Jody L. Nye) *The Dragonlover's Guide to
    Pern,* Del Rey, 1989.
*Three Gothic Novels—Omnibus: Ring of Fear,
    Mark of Merlin, The Kilternan Legacy,*
    Underwood-Miller, 1990.
(With Elizabeth Moon) *Sassinak,* Baen Books,
    1990.
Rowan, Putnam, 1990.
(With J. L. Nye) *The Death of Sleep,* Baen
    Books, 1990.
Pegasus in Flight, Del Rey, 1990.
Generation Warriors, Baen Books, 1991.

Contributor:

Crime Prevention in the 30th Century, Walker,
    1969.
The Disappearing Future, Panther Books, 1970.
Infinity One, Lancer, 1970.
The Many Worlds of Science Fiction, Dutton,
    1971.
Future Quest, Avon, 1973.
Ten Tomorrows, Fawcett, 1973.
Science Fiction Tales, Rand McNally, 1973.
Demon Kind, Avon, 1973.
Omega, Walker, 1973.
Continuum, Putnam, 1974.
Future Love, Bobbs-Merrill, 1977.
Cassandra Rising, Doubleday, 1978.
Visitors' Book, Poolbeg Press, 1980.

The Great Science Fiction Series, Harper, 1980.
The Best of Randall Garrett, Pocket, 1982.

Contributor of short stories to *Science Fiction,
Galaxy, Fantasy and Science Fiction, Analog,* and to
anthologies.

■ Adaptations

"The Dragon Riders of Pern: The White
    Dragon" (cassette), Caedmon, 1979.
"Moreta: Dragonlady of Pern" (cassette),
    Warner Audio, 1985.
"Dragonsongs" (cassette), Performing Arts,
    1986.
"Nerilka's Story" (cassette), Random House,
    1986.
"The Rowan" (cassette), Brilliance, 1990.

■ Work in Progress

All the Weyrs of Pern, third in the trilogy comprising *Dragonsdawn* and *The Renegades of Pern; Generation Warriors,* with Elizabeth Moon, third in the "Planet Pirates" trilogy; *Near the Twain* and *Border, Breed or Birth,* both with Jody-Lynn Nye.

■ Sidelights

"To be born, as I was, on April First imposes a certain responsibility on you to Be Someone. At nine I was convinced that being a writer was the easiest way to accomplish this goal. My first novel was entitled 'Flame, Chief of Herd and Track.' The second novel was completed in Latin class, and had I written 'Eleutheria the Dancing Slave Girl' in Latin, I might have come off better in my teacher's eyes."[1]

"If I were asked to choose which influence was the most important in my life, I'd have to answer that it was my parents. Neither fit the patterns of style and behavior in the 1920s, '30s, and '40s for our middle-class status.

"My dad was a Harvard graduate with an M.A. in city planning and management; in 1938, he received his doctorate. He also maintained his Reserve Army status as an Infantry lieutenant colonel, departing every summer to Camp Dix in the New Jersey hinterlands to do war games. I distinctly remember tactical maps spread out on the old deal table in his bedroom, along with his stamp albums. He trained all three of his children—I was the only girl—in close-order drills, and taught us how to run properly, a skill I have found nearly as useful as my older brother did when he was romping through the jungles of Cambodia and Laos.

"My mother, whose family had not been able to put her through college, took courses at our local teachers' college, studying, among other exotic subjects, Russian. She nursed my younger brother, Kevin, through seven years of osteomyelitis to health, with a little help from the innovation of penicillin.

"During World War II, with my father and older brother overseas and Kevin in and out of hospitals and surgery, she coped brilliantly while other women we knew wrung their hands and wept that they were so alone. Nor did Mother complain that she didn't see her husband for five years."[2]

Following the end of World War II, McCaffrey's father spent several years in occupied Japan consulting on the restructuring of the Japanese tax system. When war broke out in Korea, he volunteered as a finance officer with the United Nations Forces in Pusan. After his death from tuberculosis in 1954, McCaffrey's mother returned to selling real estate. "Is it any wonder I write about strong women? From very early on, I was expected to achieve at a high level, constantly exhorted to do so. More subtly, I was indoctrinated with 'Well, Anne, you're going to marry and have children and then what are you going to do with the rest of your life?'

"With such unorthodox parents, achieving in so many different occupations, I certainly had spectacular role models and was well conditioned to achieve. In fact, it never once occurred to me, during the restrictive years of childbearing, that I did not have the right to do so. I don't think any of us considered that it would be science fiction that I would be doing for the rest of my life. But I certainly don't complain.

"The early lessons I learned, generally the hard way, in standing up for myself and my egocentricities, being proud of being 'different,' doing my own thing, gave me the strength of purpose to continue doing so in later life. You have to learn how not to conform, how to avoid labels. But it isn't easy! It's lonely until you realize that you have inner resources that those of the herd mentality cannot enjoy. That's where the mind learns the freedom to think science-fictiony things, and where early lessons of tenacity, pure bullheadedness, can make a difference. Most people prefer to be accepted. I learned not to be.

"Helpful, too, was the fact that I was such an opinionated, asocial, extroverted, impossible, egregious brat that I was forced to books as companions; none of the children my age would play with me. I developed a tendency to talk with the family cats and, later, when Dad got me riding lessons at the South Orange Armory, horses. I was horse-hooked by the time I was nine. In my loneliness, I used to challenge myself to do great deeds and achieve impossible goals. I'd make them sorry they wouldn't play with me; they'd be sorry they'd ignored me and teased me. I'd be rich and famous.

"We were read to as children, my father declaiming Longfellow and Kipling's poems; Mother narrating the *Just-So Stories* and Mowgli, and offering me A. Merritt's *Ship of Ishtar*. My early conditioning to science fiction and fantasy undoubtedly sprang from those days."[2]

"And I discovered Edgar Rice Burroughs for myself. Tarzan and also the John Carter series, which I much preferred. To this day, when I reread Edgar Rice Burroughs, I think of oranges, because as a small girl I'd sit on my back porch with a plate of oranges all cut up into sections so that I could eat them while I was reading and go through what was available of the 'Martian' series.

"What I did not realize was that Edgar Rice Burroughs was a war correspondent in the Pacific Ocean at the time I was eating oranges and reading his books. It was with a great sense of shock that I realized later that he had died somewhere in between that point and my recognition of science fiction."[3]

"All readers have one or two—perhaps many more—books or stories that have affected them deeply in the course of their reading life.

"The science fictional story that has had the most influence on me personally and philosophically is Austin Tappan Wright's *Islandia*. An exceptional novel on every count, *Islandia* is surviving the test of time on sterling merits. The book was published first in 1942. I took my voyage to Islandia's shores at fourteen, and I've reread the abridged version of 1,032 pages roughly every two or three years."[4]

In 1947 McCaffrey received her B.A. from Radcliffe College, with a senior thesis on Yevgeny Zamyatin's *We*, and George Orwell's *Brave New World*. She then worked for several years in New York City as an executive secretary and copywriter for the Liberty Music Shops and for Helena Rubenstein. "Having decided that I would be a writer, I stopped writing at about seventeen and concentrated on learning anything and everything. I've always maintained that a college education teaches you how to find out, absorb, what you *don't* know. I majored in Slavonic languages and literatures and . . . also studied cartography, Celtic folk legends, Chinese philosophers, history, American foreign policy."[1]

Although McCaffrey had always been interested in music and theater, it was during these years that she began to study opera and drama. "I think I had in mind the ever-alluring notion of a screen career, as I was already 'acting' to get attention. My size, rather plain countenance (I've improved with the years as good wine does), and gift for acting led me more to character parts than the leads I would have preferred. Though I trained as a dramatic soprano and had both volume and range, like Killashandra, there was an unattractive burr in my voice, which was useful for singing character parts but unpleasant for Aida, for instance, or Princess Turandot. More suitable for the Old Lady in Bernstein's original 'Candide,' or an old witch in Carl Orff's Christmas pageant, or Queen Agravaine in 'Once

Jacket of the 1976 multi-award-winning novel.

Upon a Mattress,' Margot the Innkeeper in 'The Vagabond King,' and the Medium in Gian Carlo Menotti's opera—or singing descant above full choir and organ in the Presbyterian Church in Wilmington, Delaware."[2]

Before abandoning her professional ambitions in the theater in 1965, McCaffrey performed in and directed over thirty productions of the Wilmington Opera society and the Brecks Mill Cronies. The high point of her musical career came as director and performer of the American premiere of Carl Orff's "Ludus de Nato Infante Mirificus" at the Greenville Church in Wilmington. Frederick N. Robinson, a director-singer with whom she worked at Pennsylvania's Lancaster Opera Workshop, became the model for Master Robinson, the master musician of her "Pern" series.

McCaffrey married H. Wright Johnson in January, 1950. The couple had three children: Alec, Todd and Georgeanne. "I also learned that I had a right to marriage, children, and a later-life career. (Mind you, I lost the husband after twenty years, but as his second wife also divorced him, perhaps the faults were not all on my independent head.)"[2]

It was during the first year of her marriage that McCaffrey discovered science fiction which led to her return to writing. "I was sick with bronchitis, which is my usual winter sport. I started reading a lot of current science-fiction magazines and I came across Edmund Hamilton's *Star Kings*. I couldn't put the magazine down. That's what *I* wanted to write. Fantastic! Great! I had never read anything like this before. I wanted it!

"It was like a drug. I couldn't keep my hands off science fiction. And my husband, a Princeton English major, was having canaries about it. What was I doing reading this *trash?* Then I started to try to write science fiction.

"I had rejection slip after rejection slip. I could have papered a wall with them! It was a little discouraging.

"In 1953 I wrote a short story that Sam Moskowitz picked up for *Science Fiction Plus*. That was my first published story. What a thrill it was. I had a young baby at home, but *this* production was almost more important."[5]

"I think the field was waking up to the fact that women could write science fiction. There was no reason why not, or why they had to hide under another name. I wouldn't have done so. If they weren't going to put the story under the name of

Anne McCaffrey, I wouldn't have let them print it."[6]

In Wilmington, where she had moved in 1958 with her husband and children, McCaffrey continued to write stories in her spare time, but didn't sell her second novella, "Lady in the Tower" until five years later. "'Lady' is the story I prefer to acknowledge as my first; it appeared in the *Magazine of Fantasy and Science Fiction* in April 1959, in the distinguished company of Daniel Keyes' 'Flowers for Algernon.' Algis Budrys was a reader for Bob Mills at the time and he brought the story to Bob's notice. They both felt that it needed some reworking and asked my permission, which, needless to say, I immediately and ecstatically gave. (Someone wanted to *publish* a story of mine? Leap, grab, say YES!) I don't remember what changes Algis made, nor does he.

"Ten years later, 'A Meeting of Minds' [a sequel to 'Lady in the Tower'] was published by Ed Ferman, the new editor of *Fantasy and Science Fiction*. I have also done a good deal of rewriting on it, since that story had appeared so long after its parent story.

"'Lady in the Tower' and 'A Meeting of Minds' are really logical extensions of the concept found in *To Ride Pegasus*, in which parapsychic powers are combined with machines in a gestalt that gives the mind enough power to reach the stars. They both predate Dai op Owen and the Eastern Parapsychic Center.

"Both are unashamed love stories. That's what I do best: combining either science fact or fantasy with heterogenous inter-reaction."[7]

"And then in the sixties science fiction was improving. It was being carefully built, let us say, by the Milford Science Fiction Conference which Damon Knight, Judy Merril and Kate Wilhelm managed. They wanted us writers to improve the product, and we succeeded beyond their modest ambitions of the time.... Damon Knight always said that science fiction went in twelve-year cycles, and perhaps he's right. 'Star Trek' gave it a tremendous impetus in the mid-to-late sixties and then the men landing on the Moon in '69 made another tremendous impact."[3]

"The spin-off from that accomplishment has brought new methods of freeze-drying foods, cryogenic surgical tools that make organ transplants possible, the great surge in computer technology and the oil platforms in the North Sea and Irish coast. A whole gaggle of industries of which Mr.

John Average isn't aware are the direct result of the space programme ... and people who read science fiction.

"I once told a distinguished literary gathering, the PEN International Congress in 1971 at Dun Laoghaire, that the reason there have been so few accidents in space was because the science fiction writers of the 30s, 40s and early 50s had racked their brains for every possible problem and solved them well in advance of need. The Russians cornered me later and asked me, very seriously, what did I mean by that? What I'd said, was my prompt reply, and furthermore, most American science fiction had been translated into Russian so they had the benefit of 'our' experience as well. The Russians do not have much collective sense of humour."[8]

Following the publication of her second story, McCaffrey welcomed the interchange with other science fiction enthusiasts. She began to attend the Milford Science Fiction Conferences in 1959. "I was very pregnant with my daughter, Georgeanne. Judy Merril invited me up to Milford. And I went up, great with child, and met, to my eternal delight, Rosel George Brown and Kate Wilhelm. We were all, shall we say, freshmen at the same time. And you learn by observing, I think, as much as by hearing your stories criticized. I am not a critical writer. I'm not too good in a conference situation myself, because I'm not analytical enough. It was listening to what other people had to say that helped me, not so much the criticism of my story."[3]

"People were always very helpful in getting me over the rough spots. One day Bob Silverberg took me aside and said, 'Anne, will you cut it with the adverbs?' Jim Blish gave me advice too. 'Anne, there is a wonderful word in the English language. It is called *said*. You don't need to use any other one when you're describing a conversation.' Every once in a while I feel a tap on my shoulder when I'm writing. If it's on the left, it's Jim. If it's on the right, it's Robert. They keep me on the straight-and-narrow path."[5]

"Later I was asked to be chairperson of the English Milford conferences because I was a Hugo and Nebula winner and I was a well-known author. Jim Blish was physically not up to being chairperson, so I was asked to take over, which I did for four years. When I submitted a story which most of the conferees liked, I decided that's it, I'll quit while I'm ahead. Otherwise, most of my stories were ripped into tiny shreds. I must say they were better for dissection, because out of them came such things as *To Ride Pegasus* and *Crystal Singer*. And some of my other good ideas were expanded and assisted by the criticism I received at Milford conferences. It's a daunting experience, and I do not recommend it for just any young writer. It can be destroying to hear your own work criticized. You come out of the session in which your story is being work-shopped and you head for the nearest bottle of booze. After a while you do learn to be self-critical, but not self-destructive."[3]

In 1965, McCaffrey and her family moved to New York. It was only after her youngest child went off to school full-time that she was able to devote herself to writing. By 1969 she had published four novels. "It was like 'Who pulled out the plug?' I suddenly had a lot of time on my hands. I had written a story back in the fifties called 'Restoree,' which no one had liked a lot. I rewrote it. It became what I call my space gothic novel. And it was a parody. I was so tired of reading about the girl standing in the corner wringing her hands as the hero fought for her honor."[5]

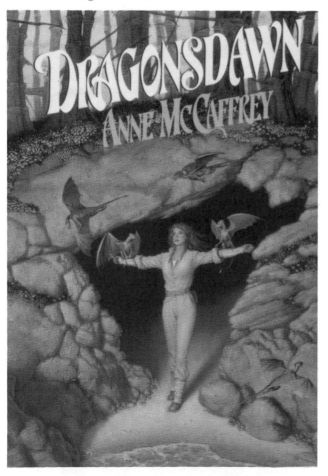

McCaffrey's sixth book in the "Dragon" series.

Most of McCaffrey's novels are characterized by their portrayals of powerful women protagonists with a strong emotional life. Her heroines are capable of love, art, work, and, if necessary, killing. They usually gain their independence through perseverance, courage and cleverness. Early in her career, McCaffrey established a reputation for bringing active women—a quality that had been lacking in much of the early science fiction—into predominance.

In 1969, *Decision at Doona* was published, McCaffrey's only novel directed toward adults that lacks a central heroine and a love story. "Generally speaking, I don't 'do' messages in my novels (except for *Decision at Doona*, written during the Vietnam War, wherein my male protagonist remarks, 'Mankind will be mature as a species when it no longer feels the need to impose its moral judgments on anybody or anything'). What I do do is practice what I preach and write what I practice. The example is there in the action of the stories, and the effect that the stories have unexpectedly wrought on their readers remains one of the most heartening aspects of being a writer."[2]

After her divorce in 1970, McCaffrey moved to the outskirts of Dublin, Ireland. "I moved to Ireland because I wanted some place safe for my kids and my aged mother, and New York wasn't it. There was a bad drug situation at the local high school, and one of the girls there had her face slashed to ribbons. I didn't want that for my lovely daughter. I also wanted a place to live that was fairly inexpensive. Ireland offered all of it. I had been there before, so I knew what I was getting into."[9]

Living in Ireland also allowed McCaffrey to fulfill a childhood dream: "Now I'd wanted to own a horse since I was a knee-high to a donkey. I'd ridden whenever possible as a child, less frequently when there were other demands on my purse as an adult. But there was always this unfulfilled yearning. Once bitten by the horse bug, you don't always get over it.

"Here I was in Ireland, the Home of Horses, and there was this enticing advert, just begging me to do something about it. My conscience reminded me that I had two children to consider, that they were doing rather well at Burton Hall, and what would I *do* with a heavy-weight hunter. I didn't belong to any Hunt!

"My mother, who had ... seen the ad, knew how frustrated I was riding school horses (let's face it, they do lose their enthusiasm and cultivate obstina-

CORANA

© Robin Wood 1988

From *The People of Pern* by Anne McCaffrey.

Detail from the 1985 novel *Killashandra.*

cy), so she suggested that it didn't hurt to phone and find out what the situation was.

"Little did I know, as they say in romantic fiction, that that phone call was to change the course of my life!

"Not only did I acquire the heavy-weight dapple grey hunter, Mr. Ed, for 'the rest of the season,' I acquired him for the rest of his life.

"He was exactly what I, as a middling horsewoman, needed: a well-schooled beastie, with a great deal of personality. He and I got on excellent terms immediately.

"I discovered the problems of horse-owning and keeping. Getting a blacksmith, finding good strong hay, and what to do with the endless quantity of manure which Ed regularly produced. My figure was never trimmer after those weeks of matinal mucking out and riding. I do admit to a certain sense of relief when Ed went out for a summer at grass."[10]

Although McCaffrey was making a basic living from writing, she was unable to support both her family and her horse on her earnings. Instead, she bartered Mr. Ed's room and board for part-time work in a riding school. "I began to work Saturday and Sunday at Brennanstown, first in general groomsmanship and then, as the need arose, as office staff in charge of the bookings.

"In many ways, this 'job' became more interesting than my writing. There was always something occurring at Brennanstown—whether a German film company was shooting in the Yard, or the Junior Event Team was training there, or the hunting season was on with all its earnest children, bit by the same horse bug that had infected me. The paramount consideration was that I could look down the line and see my beloved horseface. I used to convulse clients and staff alike by appearing in the Yard in the morning and roaring 'Horseface.' The noble white equine head turns, the small Connemara ears perk up, all attention, and the nostrils flutter with a whiffle of dignified welcome.

"Over the next three years, matters improved professionally for me.... My first thought was that I could buy enough land on which to keep my darling Ed. No, I did not buy a house for myself or my children—I bought it for my horse."[10]

"He was extremely intelligent for a horse, and he and I, like a dragon, had our own rapport. He would do things for me, and to me, that he would

not do to or for anyone else. He meant a great deal to me.

"Then I retired Ed. At twenty-one he was developing very serious arthritis in the pelvic area. The arthritis got to his jaw, and he even found it hard to chew. So I realized that I must do for him what humans can do for their animal friends. I arranged a date with the vet, and he came up, and Ed was put down in his own stable. It was one of the worst days of my life. I thought I would really never get through the day. Then, at 11:22, my oldest son phoned me from Boston, in the hospital delivery room, to say that his daughter, my granddaughter, had been born. And *that* is the last two chapters of *Moreta*.

"Somehow or other, if you are really feeling the emotion you are writing, it transfers through all the various stages it takes to get a book from the typewritten page, to the galley, to the printed page, to the distributor. It comes through. And I've used that ruthlessly as a tool of writing."[11]

When she wrote "Weyr Search" and "Dragonriders" in 1967, McCaffrey had no idea that her stories about the dragons of Pern would become science-fiction classics, nor that a cult would grow around the subsequent series of dragon novels she published over the next two decades. The series, composed of five adult novels and a young adult trilogy, is a tale of the telepathic bonding between humans and dragonlike aliens in a long-lost colony of Earth on the planet Pern. The major theme of all the volumes deals with how humans and the great dragons learn to cope with a planet-wide menace and survive!

"The true genesis of the Dragon series was a conversation I had with an underground film director, a young friend of Ed Emshwiller's, Dick Adams. We'd seen his excellent film on the tribulations of American teachers of English in a Polish university summer course. Dick mentioned that he wanted to do a film on the 'aloneness' of man. I suggested that that had been done to death, but had he ever considered filming those times when man/woman/child are united in a common emotion?

"This must have been at the back of my mind when I started casting about my brains for a story idea. That's why the dragons are telepathic: their riders are never alone. Further, the dragon never criticizes: he adores his rider no matter what he does or is. This is the facet of the dragon stories which, I feel, has captured the attention of readers. And so much of modern literature is keyed to the statement of aloneness or sharings the great togetherness urge."[12]

"I almost didn't write ['Weyr Search'] because I had gotten the first twenty-five to thirty pages done, and then I wasn't sure when I reread it whether it was any good at all. So I took it up to Virginia Kidd, my agent, and asked her to read it. She said, 'Oh, Anne, please finish it,' so I went back to the typewriter after a lapse of about two months and finished what became 'Weyr Search.' Now, it was an inconvenient length at 28,000 words, and John W. Campbell, the editor of *Analog* asked me to edit out about 8,000 words to fit it in one issue."[3]

Impressed by "Weyr Search," John Campbell encouraged McCaffrey to further explore the imaginary world of Pern she had created. "So at top speed I wrote the story *Dragonflight,* and he said, 'Anne, you haven't told me anything I didn't know. This is a good bridging material, but it's not telling the story.' Then I wrote 'Black Dust' and he said, 'Yes, but you haven't shown me the riders actually contending with Thread, and you haven't solved their problem. There are only 192 dragons, in one weyr, and you say there were six weyrs. What happened to the other five?'

"He was pointing out the weak links. So he made me write 'Dragonrider,' the two-parter in *Analog,* and pushed me on. I think I wrote the second 20,000 words in about a week, which is the biggest output I've ever done. With managing three kids and a husband at the same time it was a bit much. But I did it. He published that as 'Dragonrider,' then Betty Ballantine bought the four sections, including 'Dragonflight' which John had rejected, and that became the novel *Dragonflight.*"[3]

"The Dragons of Pern are unusual beasts, constructs if ever there were some: they get 'impressed' on hatching like ducklings, are telepaths, oviparous but their mating is comparable to bees rather than lizards (although I've never observed saurian habits); dragons are carnivorous but can last eight days, when full-grown, on one full meal, like a camel. They have two stomachs like cows, one for comestibles, one for combustibles.

"Actually, dragons don't fly; they only think they do which is how they do it. Even with a boron-crystalline exo-skeleton, dragons have too much mass for their wing-span. They levitate, using wings for guidance, braking and self-deception. True, the fire-lizards from which the Terran colonists developed the Pern dragon could fly: it was

their parapsychic abilities that the geneticists strengthened.

"Having more or less settled my dragonology, I forget it and build the plot structure around the humans. It followed logically, however, that men who could think to dragons would be regarded with considerable awe by their less talented peers. Ergo, an exclusive confraternity, self-immolating, self-sustaining. (I may well have been reading about the Knights Templar at that point, I've forgotten, but the social structure of Pern is decidedly feudal with occasional modern-child-rearing overtones.) F'lar was the epitome of the proper dragonman.

"Now introduce the outsider into the Weyr for observation and comparison. It's more fun to put the sexes together so enter Lessa, in Cinderella guise, with sufficient wit and courage not to need the cop-out of a fairy godmother. (I don't have one, don't see why she should.)

"There are several villains, 'cause half the fun of writing is the villain: Fax who is greedy, R'gul who is well-motivated but dense, and the Threads which couldn't care less and therefore are the best variety of menace. (I tend to develop outside menaces anyway: I've had enough in my lifetime of nation versus nation.)

"The last ingredient was the timing: the dragons were created (by me and Pern) for a necessity—remove that necessity from the memory of living man, and see what happens. We've all seen certain customs upended, debased, disregarded, yet at their inception, there were good reasons for them. Why do men customarily place women on their left side? So their sword/gun arm is free ... or so they can protect the woman from slops thrown out an upper story window. Swords (and guns, God willing) are no longer *de rigeur*, but the convention/tradition/custom continues: and modern plumbing takes care of the other hazard that initiated the custom. A simple instance, granted, but valid. ... Pern fascinates me utterly: the dragons are, in essence, mature concepts of the imaginary characters that bore me company in my youth. Or an itch which I can't leave alone."[13]

McCaffrey's Pern novels have been praised for their convincing use of scientific details. Having taken supplementary courses in physics, she also seeks the advice of specialists in order to create a credible science fiction. "[Regarding the planet Pern] Hal Clement helped me with the solar system. I have since heard from an astronomer in Australia who tells me the spectro-analysis of

Rukbat, the sun that I picked, proves it could not generate planets. However, when I was writing John Campbell told me, 'Oh, it doesn't matter. There's no way they can find out.' At the time, in the 1960s, they did not have the sophisticated spectroanalysis, so it was perfectly within my rights to choose Rukbat out of the *National Geographic* astronomy maps as my sun, so I did. It looked like a good name. And that the dragons could be genetically developed from the fire lizards is eminently plausible, but it cannot be stated at the time *Dragonflight* starts. Besides, I didn't think of it then.

"Since I'm writing the story from the point of view of the people who are contemporary with it, I cannot do a lot of things that I want to. I went into the subterfuge of saying 'Eureka!—my mycorrhizoid spores' for Thread, but mycorrhizoid spores are perfectly legitimate in Arrhenius's theory of space traveling, which is what I used from the back of my head. Also I very definitely state that the dragons have two stomachs, in one of which they digest the phosphine-bearing rock. Well, phosphine gas, when it hits oxygen, ignites. Now, okay, that's not Larry Niven-type science, it's soft-core science fiction."[9]

"Once Betty Ballantine had bought *Dragonflight*, I charged ahead with a sequel that was going to be my most ambitious novel to date. I took it up to my dear agent, and she handed it back to me and said, 'Anne, burn it.' So I burned it. I can't remember too much of it now, but it really was sick. This is what comes of having a swelled head!"[11]

"A basic theme in *Dragonflight* and *Dragonquest* is the symbiotic love relationship between humans and their dragon companions. Love in several facets is the main theme of both novels. Emotional content and personal involvement are *expected* in stories written by me. In fact, I've had stories returned to me by editors because they lacked these elements: a case of 'I'm damned if I do, and damned if I don't.'

"Prior to the '60s, stories with any sort of a love interest were very rare. True, it was implied in many stories of the '30s and '40s that the guy married the girl whom he had rescued/ encountered/discovered during the course of his adventure. But no real pulse-pounding, tender, gut-reacting scenes. The girl was still a 'thing,' to be 'used' to perpetuate the hero's magnificent chromosomes. Or perhaps, to prove that the guy wasn't 'queer.' I mean all those men locked away on a spaceship for months/years at a time. I mean. . .and

The 1987 Ballantine softcover.

you know what I mean even if I couldn't mention it in the sf of the '30s and '40s. Did you ever *see* Flash Gordon kiss Dale Arden or hold her hand loverly-like? And Tarzan only *admits* that Jane is his woman.

"Fortunately for the maturity of sf, newcomers wiggled into the pages of *Fantasy and Science Fiction, Analog, Galaxy,* and *If.* Keyes published a quiet story entitled 'Flowers for Algernon' which was later screened as 'Charley.' In 1952, in *F. and S. F.,* Zenna Henderson introduced the People: tender stories with a high emotional content about a race of parapsychic people who are forced to flee their world (the sun went nova), and their problems blending into the multitude on Earth. Her two books, *The Anything Box* and *The People, No Different Flesh,* compel the reader to share the tremendous sadness of the People for the loss of their beautiful homeworld; one appreciates the gallantry of their exodus and the sacrifice of the ones too old to make the terrible journey. The aura projected by Miss Henderson stays with the reader like a benediction.

"New lyrical writers started publishing and were acclaimed by the fans: Roger Zelazny and Samuel R. Delany were notable among the men. Carol Emshwiller paints her canvases with a delicate brush and an economy of word, delineating some portion of intensely experienced personal conflict: i.e., 'Pelt.' Sonya Dorman's wry sense of humor and the macabre lends her writing unusual color. The late Rosel George Brown humorously depicted Future Woman's domestic problems with aliens to baby-sit and she created the inimitable Sybil Sue Blue, galactic policewoman.

"Real humor in sf is at the highest premium. Humor is as much an emotional involvement as tragedy—but rarer. Jack Wodhams is a very funny man; so is Harry Harrison. And Avram Davidson, Randall Garrett, dear Grendel Briarton, and Damon Knight. But not often enough. Keith Laumer pokes fun at diplomacy in all of his Retief yarns, and David Gerrold in combination with Larry Niven is a good gag team. Theodore Cogswell once did an elaborate story, caricaturing (all in good fun) sf writers and editors. Personally, I think Carol Carr outdid them all in her absurd story—'Look, You Think You Got Problems?'—a Jewish (would you believe?) sf story. Feh!

"In passing I note that two of the most powerfully emotional scripts written for 'Star Trek' were 'Journey to Babel' by D(orothy) C. Fontana and 'The Empath' by Joyce Muskat. First-rate seat-clutching panic-watching was provided by Norman Spinrad's 'The Doomsday Machine,' and David Gerrold's 'The Trouble with Tribbles' bags the honors for the funniest episode of that much lamented series.

"These writers are modern, as far as sf goes. The oldest fans may beat their breasts for the good ol' days of thud and blunder and *real* science in *Astounding, Fantastic,* and *Amazing* magazines, but if sf were still driving the star trails with sawdust heroes and cardboard villains—more translated from westerns than integrated in the space age—sf would have been trapped in a Mobius Strip.

"With the injection of emotional involvement, a sexual jolt to the Romance and Glamour, science fiction rose out of pulp and into literature."[4]

In 1978, seven years after the publication of *Dragonquest, the White Dragon,* the last of the first

Dragonriders trilogy was published. "Andre Norton suggested it. She said if I was going to have blue, green, brown, and gold dragons, I could have a white one too."[11]

"Now, what happened after *Dragonquest* was that I was scared out of my tiny mind about writing *The White Dragon.* I'd done two books which were very successful. And things sort of hung there. Then in 1974 or 5 Beth Blish, who is Jim Blish and Virginia Kidd's daughter, was talking to Jean Karl at the U.S. Publishers, Atheneum. She said, 'I wish that Anne McCaffrey would do a juvenile female protagonist in a book, aimed at the teenage market, because we have tremendous requests for this.' So Beth organized the contract and queried whether I would be interested, and I was. The genesis of that was that Roger Elwood, the mad anthologist, had asked me to do another young protagonist in a book and I had tried to work with the Menolly theme for Roger. I couldn't push it very far, so I had written about The Smallest Dragonboy, and he published that. By the way, that is one of my most reprinted stories, 'The Smallest Dragonboy.' It's all over the world. It's been scaled down for poor readers and for second-language readers, so it's had a very good track record. At any rate, I went back to the original Menolly material, and suddenly it started to flow, and I wrote *Dragonsong* and delivered it. On the way back to Ireland, on the plane, I thought, you know, I've got Menolly where I want her, with the master harper. So what happens to her when she gets to the Harper Hall? So I wrote a letter to Jean Karl saying, 'Would you be interested in a contract?' and she was writing to me at the same time, 'Anne, would you possibly consider writing a sequel to *Dragonsong?*' So, anyway, that's the genesis of *Dragonsong/ Singer. . . .* Meanwhile, the pump has been primed for *The White Dragon* and I'm feeling more comfortable about it. And so I wrote *The White Dragon.*"[3]

". . . *Dragonsong* and *Dragonsinger* were extremely successful. Bantam bought the paperback rights for a figure that made me fall over in my chair."[11]

In 1981 *The Crystal Singer,* the story of the singer Killashandra who learns that because of a slight burr in her voice she will never be a top-rank solo singer was published. Disappointed, Killashandra enters the dangerous but prestigious profession of crystal singing to discover that fame and wealth are unsatisfactory by themselves. "Someone once said to me that he thought Killashandra was a beautiful name for a heroine and I agreed with him. And that night, contrary to my habit, I got up out of bed and went to my typewriter and typed out the first two

Anne McCaffrey (foreground) with her horse "Our Jack."

pages of 'Killashandra—Crystal Singer.' At the same time Roger Elwood, the mad anthologist, was looking for material and this was a fairly explicit sex relationship which Virginia didn't think that Roger would stand for, but he did.

"I'm always looking around for character names and I've learned to keep long lists of typos and odd place names. At that point in time I was very deeply into Ireland and I was surrounded by all these marvelous alien names like Ballybran and Ballybrack and Shankill and Shanganagh and all the rest. They seemed easy to use. After all, people with certain ethnic backgrounds are going to name alien planets after things that are familiar to them, simply to give themselves a feeling of home. So the Irish background is there."[3]

In addition to her science fiction work that made her a legend to million of readers, McCaffrey edited *Cooking out of Their World*, a collection of recipes by sixty-two science fiction authors. She has contributed stories to many science fiction magazines, and produced several romantic novels including *Mark of Merlin*, *Ring of Fear*, and *The Kilternan Legacy*. Although of a different genre, these novels explore many common themes and images found in McCaffrey science fiction work.

"Personally, I devote a great deal of time to the physical act of writing, i.e. sitting at that typewriter and slogging it out. I have worked up to 12 hours a day when a story was going well, but I've learned not to 'write' at night, just copy edit or worry about plot ramifications. I don't outline, I don't take notes, except when I'm talking to Jack Cohen or to John Campbell, God rest him. I revise and rewrite extensively, sometimes a whole 'nother novel's worth. I generally work in the mornings because if I can get going, I can last the whole day at it. And have, and do. Then there are other days when Word One won't be followed by Word Two and like forget it man, go ride a horse or shop or take your mother to the library.

"Anyway, that's the way—the only way—it's done.

"The process must be intuitive for I never consciously shape a novel. It 'tells' itself one way, bogs down hopelessly if I try to 'force' it another.

"In my lexicon, a short story differs from a novel by the wealth of detail. In a short story you must stick to the facts-man-just-the-facts-lady required to tell the minor incidents/major happenings and eliminate all others. In a novel, you have more leisure to describe, to work in development of character, atmosphere, to 'clothe' the superstructure.

"I do not *plan* a novel. I take a situation and people logically involved in that situation. If the situation is a valid one in terms of human reactions and inter-reactions, if the characters are living, the plot develops from that inter-relationships and interactions. When the story line bogs down, I've made someone do something inherently incorrect, and I go back to the place where I, the author, am bored by re-reading and try to ring in another switch or another facet of conflict.

"I'm the sort of person people confide in and I've learned some of the complexities and involvements possible in human relationships. I've been told some beauts—not all of which wind up in my stories, but from which I constantly borrow this grief, that joy, a snatch of history or background; and work out a different story/ending/problem. Tis all grist to the writer's mill, my friend."[11]

Footnote Sources:

[1] *Junior Literary Guild,* March, 1977.

[2] Denise Du Pont, editor, *Women of Vision,* St. Martin's, 1988.

[3] Chris Morgan, "Interview: Anne McCaffrey," *Science Fiction Review,* fall, 1982. Amended by A. McCaffrey.

[4] Reginald Bretnor, editor, *Science Fiction Today and Tomorrow,* Penguin, 1974. Amended by A. McCaffrey.

[5] Ed Naha, "Living with the Dragons: Anne McCaffrey," *Future,* November, 1978. Amended by A. McCaffrey.

[6] Richard Wolinsky and Lawrence Davidson, "Anne McCaffrey," *Rigel Science Fiction,* winter, 1982.

[7] Anne McCaffrey, *Get Off the Unicorn,* Ballantine, 1977. Amended by A. McCaffrey.

[8] A. McCaffrey, "A Chance of Hobbit," *Ireland of the Welcom,* July/August, 1977.

[9] Joseph McLellan, "For Love of Dragons," *Washington Post,* April 4, 1978.

[10] A. McCaffrey, "My Bold Irish Boy," *Ireland of the Welcom,* November/December, 1978.

[11] "Anne McCaffrey: Dragonwriter of Pern," *Leading Edge,* fall, 1985. Amended by A. McCaffrey.

[12] R. Bretnor, *Science Fiction and Fantasy Literature,* Volume 2.

[13] A. McCaffrey, "On Pernography," *Algol,* fall, 1968. Amended by A. McCaffrey.

■ For More Information See

Lloyd Biggle, Jr., *The Double: Bill Symposium,* D. B. Press, 1969.
Locus, January 12, 1970, February, 1982 (p. 1ff), December, 1984, September, 1988.
Luna Monthly, April, 1970 (p. 6), November, 1974 (p. 33ff), winter, 1976 (p. 12ff).
Marilyn Gardner, "Anne McCaffrey," *Milwaukee Journal,* March 13, 1975.
Times Literary Supplement, March 14, 1975 (p. 284).
Mary Brinkerhoff, "Anne McCaffrey: Saturated Sponge Isn't All Wet," *Dallas News,* March 25, 1976.
Authors in the News, Volume 2, Gale, 1976.
Damon Knight, *Turning Point: Essays on the Art of Science Fiction,* Harper, 1977.
Paul Walker, *Speaking of Science Fiction: The Paul Walker Interviews,* Luna, 1978.
A. E. Zeek and others, *Pern Portfolio,* Isis/Yggdrisil Press, 1978.
Crawdaddy, June, 1978 (p. 51).
Washington Post, June 26, 1978.
Donna Joy Newman, "'Dragonlady' Author Loves Her Fire-Eaters," *Chicago Tribune,* July 4, 1978.
Susan Wood, "Women and Science Fiction," *Algol/Starship,* winter, 1978/1979.
Frank N. Magill, editor, *Survey of Science Fiction Literature,* Salem Press, 1979.
Publishers Weekly, March 12, 1979 (p. 40), September 18, 1987, October 30, 1987, September 16, 1988.
Steve Pinder, "Dragondame: An Interview with Anne McCaffrey," *Fantasy Media,* June/July, 1979.
Rhoda Katerinsky, "What to Read This Summer," *Ms.* July, 1979.
Martin Morse Wooster, "The White Dragon," *Science Fiction Review,* August, 1979.
Contemporary Literary Criticism, Volume XVII, Gale, 1981.
Dictionary of Literary Biography: Twentieth-Century American Science-Fiction Writers, Volume VIII, Gale, 1981.
Curtis C. Smith, *Twentieth-Century Science-Fiction Writers,* St. Martin's, 1981.
Patricia Mathews, "Dragons and Daughters," *The Stone and the Stars,* March, 1981.
Lina Mainiero, editor, *American Women Writers,* Volume 3, Ungar, 1982.
Rosemarie Arbur, *Leigh Brackett, Marion Zimmer Bradley, Anne McCaffrey: A Primary and Secondary Bibliography,* G. K. Hall, 1982.
E. F. Bleiler, *Science Fiction Writers: Critical Studies of the Major Authors from the Early Nineteenth Century to the Present Day,* Scribner, 1982.
Extrapolation, spring, 1982 (p. 70ff).
New York Times Book Review, August 29, 1982, May 2, 1982, January 8, 1984 (p. 18).
Donald M. Hassler, editor, *Patterns of the Fantastic,* Starmont House, 1983.
Vector, Volume 123, 1984.
Karen Wynn Fonstad, *The Atlas of Pern,* Ballantine, 1984.

Starlog, March, 1984, November, 1985 (p. 22).

People Weekly, March 12, 1984 (p. 82ff).

Analog, August, 1984 (p. 168ff), August, 1986 (p. 177ff), December, 1986 (p. 181ff).

English Journal, November, 1984 (p. 89).

"Anne McCaffrey to the Rescue," *Locus,* December, 1984.

Chris Henderson, "Anne McCaffrey," *Starlog,* November, 1985.

Mary T. Brizzi, *Anne McCaffrey,* Starmont House, 1986.

Wilson Library Bulletin, February, 1989 (p. 94ff).

Bestellers 89, Issue 2, Gale, 1990.

Collections:

Kerlan Collection at the University of Minnesota.

Gloria Miklowitz

S urname is pronounced *Mick*-lo-witz; born May 18, 1927, in New York, N.Y.; daughter of Simon (president of a steamship company) and Ella (a housewife; maiden name, Goldberg) Dubov; married Julius Miklowitz (a college professor), August 28, 1948; children: Paul Stephen, David Jay. *Education:* Attended Hunter College (now Hunter College of the City University of New York), 1944-45; University of Michigan, B.A., 1948; New York University, graduate study, 1948. *Politics:* Democrat. *Religion:* Jewish. *Home:* 5255 Vista Miguel Dr., La Canada, Calif. 91011. *Agent:* Curtis Brown Ltd., 10 Astor Place, New York, N.Y. 10003.

■ Career

Writer, 1952—; U.S. Naval Ordnance Test Station, Pasadena, Calif., scriptwriter, 1952-57; Pasadena City College, Pasadena, instructor, 1971-80; instructor for Writers Digest School. *Member:* PEN (Center USA West), Society of Children's Book Writers, California Writer's Guild (member of board of directors, 1968-70), Southern California Council of Literature for Children and Young People.

■ Awards, Honors

The Zoo Was My World was selected one of Child Study Association of America's Children's Books of the Year, 1969, and *Harry S. Truman*, 1975; Outstanding Science Book for Children from the National Council for Social Studies and the Children's Book Council, 1977, for *Earthquake!*, and 1978, for *Save That Raccoon!*; *Did You Hear What Happened to Andrea?* was selected one of New York Public Library's Books for the Teen Age, 1980, *The Love Bombers*, 1981, and *The Young Tycoons*, 1982; Western Australia Young Reader Book Award, 1984, for *Did You Hear What Happened to Andrea?*; Iowa Books for Young Adults Poll, 1984, for *Close to the Edge*, 1986, for *The War Between the Classes*, 1989, for *After the Bomb*, and 1989, for *Goodbye Tomorrow;* "CBS Schoolbreak Special," "The Day the Senior Class Got Married," won the Humanitas Prize for its humanitarian values, 1985; "CBS Schoolbreak Special," "The War Between the Classes," won an Emmy for Best Children's Special, 1986; Recommended Books for Reluctant YA Readers for *Goodbye Tomorrow* and *Secrets Not Meant to Be Kept*, both 1987; IRA Young Adult Choices, 1989, for *Secrets Not Meant to Be Kept*.

■ Writings

Barefoot Boy, Follett, 1964.
The Zoo That Moved (illustrated by Don Madden), Follett, 1968.
(With Wesley A. Young) *The Zoo Was My World*, Dutton, 1969.

The Parade Starts at Noon, Putnam, 1969.
The Marshmallow Caper, Putnam, 1971.
Sad Song, Happy Song, Putnam, 1973.
Turning Off, Putnam, 1973.
A Time to Hurt, a Time to Heal, Tempo, 1974.
Harry S. Truman (illustrated by Janet Scabrini),
    Putnam, 1975.
Parademic Emergency!, Scholastic Book Services,
    1977.
Runaway, Tempo, 1977.
Nadia Comaneci, Tempo, 1977.
Unwed Mother, Tempo, 1977.
Earthquake! (illustrated by Jaber William),
    Messner, 1977.
Ghastly Ghostly Riddles, Scholastic Book
    Services, 1977.
Save That Raccoon!, Harcourt, 1978.
Tracy Austin, Tempo, 1978.
Martin Luther King Jr., Tempo, 1978.
Steve Cauthen, Tempo, 1978.
Did You Hear What Happened to Andrea?,
    Delacorte, 1979.
Natalie Dunn, Roller Skating Champion, Tempo,
    1979.
Roller Skating, Tempo, 1979.
The Love Bombers, Delacorte, 1980.
Movie Stunts and the People Who Do Them,
    Harcourt, 1980.
The Young Tycoons, Harcourt, 1981.
Before Love, Tempo, 1982.
Close to the Edge, Delacorte, 1983.
Carrie Loves Superman, Tempo, 1983.
The Day the Senior Class Got Married,
    Delacorte, 1983.
The War between the Classes, Delacorte, 1985.
After the Bomb (teacher's guide available),
    Scholastic, 1985.
Love Story, Take Three, Delacorte, 1986.
Good-Bye Tomorrow, Delacorte, 1987.
Secrets Not Meant to Be Kept, Delacorte, 1987.
After the Bomb: Week One, Scholastic, 1987.
The Emerson High Vigilantes, Delacorte, 1988.
Suddenly Super Rich, Bantam, 1989.
Anything to Win, Delacorte, 1989.
Standing Tall, Looking Good, Delacorte, 1991.

Contributor to anthologies of children's stories,
and to periodicals, including *Sports Illustrated*,
American Girl, *Seventeen*, *Hadassah*, *Writer*, *Publishers Weekly*, and *School Library Journal*.

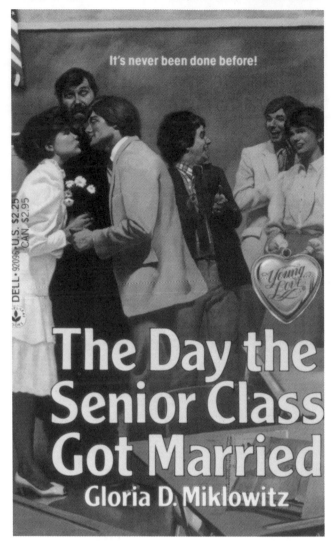

Paperback edition of the 1983 novel.

■ **Adaptations**

"Andrea's Story" (television movie; based on
    Did You Hear What Happened to Andrea?),
    "Afterschool Special," ABC-TV, September,
    1983.
"The Day the Senior Class Got Married"
    (television movie), "Schoolbreak Special,"
    CBS-TV, 1985.
"The War Between the Classes" (television
    movie), "Schoolbreak Special," CBS-TV,
    1986.

■ **Work in Progress**

Shades of Green and *You'll Never Make It to the
Prom.*

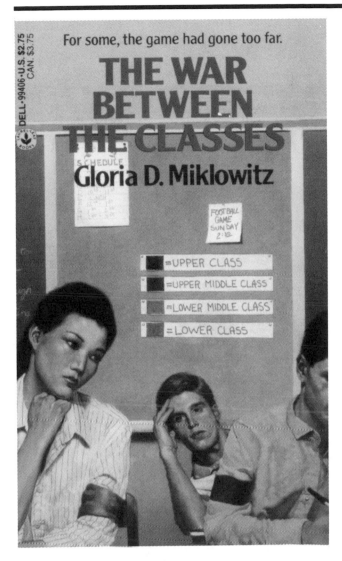

For some, the game had gone too far.

THE WAR BETWEEN THE CLASSES

Gloria D. Miklowitz

SCHEDULE

FOOTBALL GAME SUNDAY 2:12

■ = UPPER CLASS
■ = UPPER MIDDLE CLASS
□ = LOWER MIDDLE CLASS
□ = LOWER CLASS

DELL·99406·U.S. $2.75 CAN. $3.75

Softbound edition of the 1985 book.

■ Sidelights

A successful children's book writer, Gloria Miklowitz creates young adult books that confront such serious issues as nuclear war, religious cults, rape, teen suicide, and AIDS. "Young adults are at a most difficult age—not quite adult, not children. I empathize with their extremes of mood and care about their special problems, their hopes and dreams. I want to be everyone's mom and smooth their way into adulthood in the only way I can—through my books."[1]

Born in New York, Miklowitz was one of five children. "I was a middle child and a dreamer. I was slow to read, but once I learned, I was always reading something, though I can't say anything of great consequence. I was stuck on the 'Nancy Drew' books for a while, and moved to reading adult literature by the age of twelve or thirteen.

"I wrote a composition in the third grade, 'My Brother Goo Goo,' which brought me instant family recognition. I received an 'A' for my effort and got to read it in the auditorium. My family made a big deal out of it, so I said I was going to be a writer. I didn't even really know what it meant, but that label was put on me at an early age."[2]

Miklowitz set out to fulfill that prophecy by joining the newspaper staffs in high school and college. "When I finished college, I moved to New York City to look for an editing job, which I thought was the only option for an English major. I worked at Bantam books for about eight months as a secretary and did graduate work at New York University in education at night. However, I never taught in the public schools.

"I married and moved to California where my husband was hired to work as a researcher at the Naval Ordnance Test Station. The only job available to me was a secretarial position with the Navy. So I took it and persuaded them to train me as a writer when they opened a film branch.

"It was my job to research subjects, develop a script, and become involved in the shooting of the films. We were a small unit, only three people, but we won awards."[2]

With the birth of her second son, Miklowitz decided to stay home to nurture her children. "By the time the boys were two and three years old, I was reading picture books to them—about ten books a week. To satisfy my own need for intellectual stimulation, I took a class at a junior college called 'Writing for Publication,' where I learned about the Follett 'Getting to Read' contest. I had already read most of the 'Beginning to Read' series to my own children. So I read the remaining books in the series and wrote *Barefoot Boy*, which became my first publication. I was looking only to entertain and made no deliberate attempts to include social issues."[2]

"Most of my early [children's] books have dealt with animals, an interest which developed quite accidentally. [I had] read a news item about the proposed move of the Los Angeles Zoo. Curious about how an entire zoo might be moved, I went to the director, asked, and later observed the move over a period of months. From this experience I wrote *The Zoo That Moved* and *The Zoo Was My World*. If I had not been curious, I might not have written either book, nor *The Parade Starts at Noon*, based on what happened to the zoo director years before when he saved a squirrel stuck in a tuba.

"I write for children because the world of children interests me. I am curious, as they are, about everything: insects, animals, people, how things work and why, what it feels like to walk in the rain, or touch the snow. I ask a lot of questions, which most adults are reluctant to do—either because they know the answers, or they are embarrassed to reveal that they don't. But *I* want to know. When I meet strangers, I like to know what they do, how they do it, and what they think about. This curiosity, I think, is almost childlike, and maybe that's why I know what children might find interesting. If it interests me, it should interest them.

"Because I had written amusingly about the zoo, my publisher sent me a clipping about several adventuresome polar bears who escaped from a Chicago zoo and were discovered eating marshmallows and ice cream at the snack bar the next day. *The Marshmallow Caper* grew from that story.

"A friend sent me a news item which began: 'Can Big City Alligators Find Happiness in the Swamps of Mississippi?' The rehabilitation of zoo alligators became *Sad Song, Happy Song*, about an alligator who is forcibly taken from his home, sold as a pet, abused, donated to the zoo, and finally returned to the swamp."[3]

"When my children moved into the middle grades, I started reading middle-grade books. When they moved into high school, I realized that college was looming with its enormous costs. With two boys only fifteen months apart, I began thinking seriously about writing that would sell.

"I stumbled into writing for young adults as a result of conversations I was having with a black cleaning lady who worked for me. We'd have lunch together and she would tell me about all the problems she had with one of her sons involved in drugs. That, combined with talks I'd had with the director of the Los Angeles Zoo about young people involved in animal rescue operations, made me realize that when you reach your hand out to others, you usually don't get into trouble. And that resulted in *Turning Off*, my first novel for young adults.

"From there, the publisher at Berkeley wrote a letter to my agent and asked if I would be interested in writing young adult novels from the

The 1983 "ABC Afterschool Special" "Andrea's Story: A Hitchhiking Tragedy," based on the novel *Did You Hear What Happened to Andrea?*, starred Carrie Snodgress and Michele Greene.

female point of view. He attached a list of problems to choose from, from runaways to girls on drugs."[2]

Miklowitz submitted *A Time to Hurt, a Time to Heal,* about a girl who agonizes over the divorce of her parents and examines especially the resentments she feels towards her mother. "She runs away to be with her father only to discover that he was as much, if not more, to blame for the divorce. She then must take charge of her life and determine what is allowable behavior and what is not.

"I sent the book to the editor at Berkeley and received in return a one line rejection letter which said something like: 'Thank you for submitting this manuscript but we are unable to publish it,' I really felt awful. The teacher in my 'Writing for Publications' class suggested that I write back, asking the editor what she didn't like about the manuscript, reminding her that the president of Berkeley had, afterall, *asked* me to write it. The editor agreed to reread the manuscript and tell me why she'd rejected it. I received an absolutely devastating response. She wrote that the characters were one-dimensional and the plot was hackneyed. I felt like digging a hole and never writing another word.

"In the April issue of the *Writer,* I found a list of publishers who were looking for young adult novels. I sent my manuscript to Tempo Books, a paperback house. I received a very nice letter back saying that while they liked the book, they didn't publish paperback originals. Next I sent it to the Xerox Book Club. They loved it and wanted to use it in the book club. The editor wrote saying she acted as my agent and sent the manuscript to Tempo Books who *now* agreed to publish it with Xerox Book Club's backing. I later wrote two more novels for Tempo, *Runaway* and *Unwed Mother,* also Xerox Book Club selections, as well as non-fiction books: *Nadia Comaneci, Harry S. Truman, Tracy Austin,* and *Martin Luther King Jr.* Each book was an interesting challenge because I had to learn a great deal in a short time. These books helped finance college for both sons."[2]

Miklowitz was looking to have her work reviewed and needed to find someone interested in publishing her books in hardcover. "Tempo expected to publish *Unwed Mother,* but hadn't sent a contract, so I queried Delacorte about their possible interest in that book. They were indeed interested, but couldn't give me an answer soon enough. When the Tempo contract came, I signed it. The next day the head editor of Delacorte called to say he wanted the book—but one day too late.

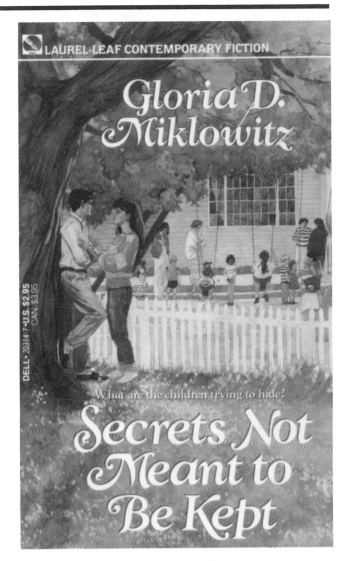

LAUREL-LEAF CONTEMPORARY FICTION

Gloria D. Miklowitz

What are the children trying to hide?

Secrets Not Meant to Be Kept

The 1987 Dell softcover.

"I discussed other book ideas with the Delacorte editor who suggested I consider writing on the issue of rape. I joined a rape hotline and did a lot of research for what became *Did You Hear What Happened to Andrea?* Tempo and Delacorte both wanted the book, but I chose to go with Delacorte who would publish me in hardcover, then paperback."[2]

Research is the quintessential part of Miklowitz's work. "...I live in a quiet suburban community where I rarely meet even a dog on my daily walk. It's so dull here that I go to extremes to bring drama to my life."[1]

Miklowitz spent a weekend with a religious cult for *The Love Bombers.* "I contacted a professor at Berkeley who had spent two years researching the Moonies, and he arranged for me to meet the leaders of the San Francisco and Berkeley groups. I interviewed the professor first, then went to dinner

The 1987 Dell paperback.

"I noticed a young man who I had seen at the Berkeley house, and who, like me, was not a Moonie. He had hiked across the country and was headed for Los Angeles where I lived. We immediately began talking. My group leader tried to draw me away, but I said 'Just a minute,' and kept talking, telling the young man that I was a writer and would be glad to introduce him to former Moonies when he came to L.A. The group leader became very angry and said, 'You have no right talking to anyone outside your group, and you should not have told anyone that you're a writer.'"[2] Miklowitz stood her ground when the Moonie leader tried to persuade her to write only good things about the cult. She said she would not write propaganda, but what she saw, both bad and good.

"For the book I'm working on now, I went to Oregon to do research. I spent many hours with

at the San Francisco house one evening and the Berkeley house the next. From Berkeley I joined a Moonie group for the drive to the camp, two hours north of San Francisco. My husband had objected strenuously to my going, and my writing students feared I might not be allowed to leave, but I never doubted, perhaps out of naivete, that I would be fine."[2]

There were about one hundred people at the camp, all much younger than the writer. The women slept on the floor of one big, empty house, the men in another house. Smaller groups of ten would gather to hear lectures several times each day and sing songs before returning to the *kiosk*-like buildings where they met. "By Sunday afternoon, I was getting very irritated. I had not been alone for a minute. There was always a 'sister' at my side, even accompanying me to the bathroom.

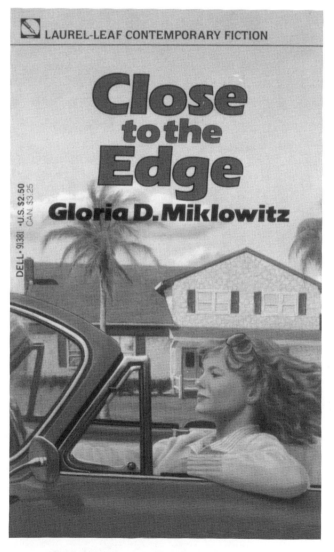

Paperback reprint of Miklowitz's favorite among her novels.

environmentalists and only one with the man representing the logging industry. After returning home, I received an invitation from the logging industry spokesman inviting me back to Oregon to see and understand their viewpoint. I returned and spent two more days meeting loggers, seeing logging operations, asking questions. The result is a good story that shows the complexity of the issue from the environmental *and* logging viewpoints.

"Have I ever been overwhelmed by my research? Obtaining the information I need is always interesting because it taxes my ingenuity in tracking down what I need to know. Sometimes I gather so much material it's hard to keep track of it all. I always fear I may have left some stone unturned and therefore keep digging for all sides to an issue.

"*The Love Bombers* was especially difficult to write because I'd only spent a long weekend with the Moonies and though I'd read a lot and interviewed a number of Moonie drop-outs, it was hard to picture the day to day activities of the group.

"*Standing Tall, Looking Good*, my book about three young people going into the Army, presented much of the same problem. No matter how many people I interviewed, and I interviewed many, it still wasn't the same as living through the experience. I have never taken a rifle apart or held one in my arms. I don't even know what a rifle sounds like when it goes off. It was hard imagining barracks conversation before lights out. What would the men and women talk about? My characters came from different parts of the country, from poor southern kids to northern city slum toughs, to spoiled rich kids living in California. Each talked differently."[2]

Miklowitz faces each of these challenges with a mixture of fact, imagination, and candor. "Delacorte rejected *After the Bomb* because the editors felt the book was too grim for young people. I'm glad Scholastic published it and its sequel, *After the Bomb: Week One*, because they were read by many thousands of children in their book club. Scholastic offered teachers' guides, too, so the issue of nuclear war could be discussed intelligently in the classroom.

"The two boys in those books were based on my own sons at ages fifteen and sixteen. I made my younger son the hero, because, looking back, he had been the underdog in our family and we hadn't recognized his many fine characteristics such as persistence, a sense of humor, courage, and loyalty.

Jacket of the 1989 Delacorte book.

"I'm a very straightfoward person and, as a rule, say what I think. I don't know all the answers and in many of my books I'm searching for answers, too. I don't deliberately create characters to influence the reader's views. Actually, when I was teaching classes in writing, I would encourage my students to know absolutely everything about their characters before starting to write. But I can't write that way. I start out with a general idea of a character who has a problem, and I see where the character takes me. Sometimes the search is like moving through a long, dark tunnel with many wrong turns. I feel my way through, asking at every turn, 'Is this the right turn? Is it natural for the character to do or say this in this situation?' Most of my female characters have a little of me in them, so something from my past will usually come out in every book.

"I think I'm honest and that it comes through in my writing. My readers say so. I truly like young people. I like to think that I guide them a little through my stories. Most times, I'll give both sides of an issue and let the reader decide.

"In only a couple of instances have I deliberately tried to shape the attitude of young people, as in the 'Bomb' books. I deliberately set out to make youngsters activists against nuclear war."[2]

Close to the Edge was written to encourage young people to reject suicide. "I considered doing the book for years before I actually wrote it, because I didn't want to do it until I had a message so positive about life that no child would consider suicide as a way out. In fact, I've had letters from kids who have said that *Close to the Edge* stopped them from committing suicide. One girl from Ann Arbor, Michigan wrote that she had already bought sleeping pills, then read the book and changed her mind. She also enclosed five poems, four of them written before she read the book, and one after. Only the last one showed positive, hopeful signs."[2]

Similarly, in *Close to the Edge*, Miklowitz's personal favorite, the main character, Jenny Hartley, breaks out of her feelings of isolation through volunteer work with a group of senior citizens. This helps her face the tragedy of a friend's suicide and to recognize the extent of her own depression. "...I came to love Hannah and the other old people, and they taught me, as I wrote the book, why people hang onto life even when it seems pointless."[1]

No subject has been too sensitive for Miklowitz. *Good-Bye Tomorrow* explored the tragedy of a teenager with AIDS. "I wanted to show the effect that AIDS had on the main character and on other people. I could have told the story from his point of view, but I found that I enjoyed switching characters from chapter to chapter. It was very much like playing with dolls. One minute I'd be sixteen-year-old Shannon, the next seventeen-year-old Alex and in the next chapter, fifteen-year-old Chris.

"I have played with the idea of doing an adult novel about the transfer of power from husband to wife as we age. I have seen this happen in my own home because of my husband's infirmity. However, this is a project still brewing. Perhaps in years to come I'll write that book."[2]

Miklowitz has recently stopped teaching her writing class. "I had been giving a lot over many years and though I loved my students, I felt the need to replenish myself. I've taken a course in art history and a class in drawing. I'm hoping the latter will help me remember things visually, which will feed into my writing.

"In summing up, it comes as a surprise to find I have written a large body of work on many important social issues, and to realize that what I have written has been enjoyed and has enriched many young people throughout the world."[2]

Footnote Sources:

[1] Delacorte publicity.
[2] Based on an interview with Marc Caplan for *Authors and Artists for Young Adults*.
[3] Anne Commire, editor, *Something about the Author*, Volume 4, Gale, 1973.

■ For More Information See

Writer, August, 1972, March, 1978 (p. 22ff), October, 1979 (p. 15ff).
Publishers Weekly, October 9, 1987 (p. 66).
Los Angeles Times, June 6, 1987.

Collections:

De Grummond Collection at the University of Southern Mississippi.

Gloria Naylor

B orn January 25, 1950, in New York, N.Y.; daughter of Roosevelt (a transit worker) and Alberta (a telephone operator; maiden name, McAlpin) Naylor. *Education:* Brooklyn College of the City University of New York, B.A., 1981; Yale University, M.A., 1983. *Agent:* Sterling Lord, One Madison Ave., New York, N.Y. 10010. *Office:* One Way Productions, Inc., 250 Cabrini Blvd., No. 4A, New York, N.Y. 10033.

■ Career

Missionary for Jehovah's Witnesses in New York, North Carolina, and Florida, 1968-75; worked for various hotels in New York, N.Y., including Sheraton City Squire, as telephone operator, 1975-81; writer, 1981—. Writer in residence, Cummington Community of the Arts, 1983; visiting lecturer, George Washington University, 1983-84, and Princeton University, 1986-87; cultural exchange lecturer, United States Information Agency, India, 1985; scholar in residence, University of Pennsylvania, 1986; visiting professor, New York University, 1986, and Boston University, 1987; Fannie Hurst Visiting Professor, Brandeis University, 1988. Senior fellow, Society for the Humanities, Cornell University, 1988. *Member:* Book of the Month Club (editorial board), National Book Award Foundation (executive board), Black Filmmakers Foundation.

■ Awards, Honors

American Book Award for Best First Novel, 1983, for *The Women of Brewster Place;* Distinguished Writer Award from the Mid-Atlantic Writers Association, 1983; National Endowment for the Arts Fellowship, 1985; Candace Award from the National Coalition of 100 Black Women, 1986; Guggenheim Fellowship, 1988.

■ Writings

Fiction:

The Women of Brewster Place: A Novel in Seven Stories, Viking, 1982.
Linden Hills, Ticknor & Fields, 1985.
Mama Day, Ticknor & Fields, 1988, large print edition, G. K. Hall, 1989.

Nonfiction:

(Contributor) *Centennial,* Pindar Press, 1986.

Also author of unproduced screenplay adaption of *The Women of Brewster Place,* for American Playhouse, 1984, and of an unproduced original screenplay for Public Broadcasting System's "In Our Own Words," 1985. Contributor of essays and articles to periodicals, including *Southern Review, Essence, Ms., Life, Ontario Review,* and *People Weekly.* Contributing editor, *Callaloo,* 1984—; author of column "Hers," *New York Times,* 1986.

■ Adaptations

"Gloria Naylor: Reading and Interview" (cassette), American Audio Prose, 1988.

"Mama Day" (cassette), Brilliance, 1989.

"The Women of Brewster Place" (four-hour miniseries), starring Oprah Winfrey and Jackee Harry, first broadcast on ABC-TV, March 19, 1989.

"Brewster Place" (television series), starring Oprah Winfrey and Brenda Pressley, first presented on ABC-TV, May 1, 1990.

■ Work in Progress

A novel, *Bailey's Cafe*, dealing with "whores, language, and music"; a screenplay for Zenith Productions, London; a film adaptation of *Mama Day*, produced by One Way Productions, Inc., Naylor's company.

■ Sidelights

As author of *The Women of Brewster Place*, Gloria Naylor has assured her place in a body of literature which she has revered since childhood, a reverence owed directly to her mother. "My parents were from the real South. My mother loved to read as a child, but discrimination prevented her from using the public libraries. She came from a family of tenant farmers with nine children and little money for books, so she would hire herself out to work in fields on Saturdays for fifty cents. By the end of the month she saved up two dollars which she sent away to book clubs."[1]

Fulfilling a promise to his wife not to have their children born in the South, Naylor's father moved with his wife to New York in 1949, a month before their first daughter, Gloria's, birth. Three daughters were born to the couple. "Here her children would be raised to have access to public libraries. My mother made it a point to take us for our library cards when we turned six. It was a ritual with us; we had to be able to write our name to get a card. Before I could even do that, my mother would take my younger sister Bernice and me to the library and say, 'You see all these books? Once you can write your name, all these will be yours.' When my other sister came along, my mother did the same with her. The library was a place of magic for me. I recall breaking open books and smelling their bindings before I could decipher words. I was so proud when the moment came that I could finally write my name and get my own card. I'd take out six books at a time, read one a day, bring them back, and take out another six. I would literally fall asleep with books on my chest."[1]

In a strong Southern tradition, Naylor's mother dedicated herself to her family. "Women didn't work in those days, so my mother was confined to being a housewife. I guess most women in the '50s were housewives, but my mother enjoyed being with her children and often read to us.

"My father was a transit worker, a man's man who had wanted sons. It's a pity he didn't have any because he had to survive in a house full of women. Genders were differentiated: women raised the girls and men took the boys under their wing. For the most part, my father let our mother guide us. If he saw any problems, he'd talk to her and then she would come to us. My father wasn't a demonstrative man. He felt that he demonstrated his love by putting up with the humiliation and garbage a black man had to tolerate in those years just to keep a job for his family.

"I was closer to my mother. She taught me to read before I went to kindergarten." This precociousness on Naylor's part had a downside as well. "I was pretty bored in kindergarten. All we learned was socialization, which was playing with other children and singing nursery rhymes. So I would roll up paper and stuff it in the radiator because I knew how to read and we weren't doing that."[1]

Naylor was forced to initiate her own reading program. "Before I was ten, I read predominantly fairy tales. In the library on 113th Street in Harlem, however, I started with Louisa May Alcott and worked my way to Laura Ingalls Wilder, following the lives of Laura and Almanzo. Poetry came next, rhyming 'true' with 'blue' and 'sky' with 'pie.' I was a quiet child, always in the advanced classes. Reading was all it took. Once you master reading well, you can breeze through academics.

"My seventh-grade teacher, Mrs. Abrams, handed me *Jane Eyre* to read because 'every young girl should read it before turning fourteen.' So I read it during the summer of my thirteenth year, and followed it with other English classics. These were the works on which I cut my literary teeth. Their influence is evident even today in how I think about literature. Not to demean what the minimalists and those who are into art for art's sake are doing, I believe that a novel should tell a story. I believe in plot. I also believe in passion in its purest sense. That belief goes back to my early love of language when I discovered that words could affect you. My early reading had been an escape for a very shy child, but when I entered puberty, I began to see that books could also make you cry and think.

"I look back and realize how totally ignorant I was of literature that reflected my experience as a black American. I grew up thinking that black people didn't write books. That benign form of neglect on the part of the educational system was a crime. I, for one, had started scribbling poetry in third and fourth grade. When by fourteen I started worrying about such things as the Cold War and nuclear holocaust, my mother gave me a diary as an outlet for my thoughts, and I began to write in it religiously. My need to write, it seemed to me at the time, was not legitimate, since no one who looked like me had ever written a book. It wasn't until I was much older that I realized that my reading diet lacked books that reflected me.

"That neglect still goes on today, though not to the extent that it did in the sixties. For our children—all American children—to grow up unaware of the literary, political, and economic contribution of various ethnic groups is to deny them enlightenment. That is, afterall, what education should be about: to lead us out of darkness into light. Consequently, we are raising people who are not educated. In my case, because I went on to become a writer, it struck me as more poignant that I had read thousands of books into my twenties and not one by a black writer. Ironically, I had been born in 1950, the very year that Gwendolyn Brooks won the Pulitzer Prize for *Annie Allen*."[1]

Naylor's social consciousness was aroused during the late sixties. "Martin Luther King was assassinated in 1968, my senior year of high school. The media was carefully doing its hatchet job on the Black Panthers. The media told us that the Panthers were about revolution and killing cops, when we knew they were about self-determination. Their whole premise was, 'If someone draws a gun on me, I'm going to defend myself and my family.' This idea was born of a time when people lynched black men and raped their women in full view of a law that simply elected not to enforce itself when it came to the rights of black Americans.

"Black Americans contributed to building this country, at first involuntarily, then voluntarily. No one forced black men to go out and die in the Civil War, World War I, or World War II; they went hoping to secure for themselves and for their families a rightful place in America. The Panthers' response to this was, 'There is a leprosy in this country. We are Americans; we are owed, and we will not have our families demeaned.' The world was going crazy and everyone began to look at America and say, 'I don't care what "Father Knows Best" or "Donna Reed" is saying, this country is not living up to its ideals.'

"The Federal government, on the other hand, set out to destroy and undermine the movements, even to the point of assassinating certain people—Fred Hampton, for example."[1]

Due to the restless atmosphere and Naylor's own feelings, she decided not to attend college after high school. "I had been accepted at several schools but elected not to go. It broke my mother's heart, but I looked around after they assassinated King and said 'This system stinks.' For me to enter college at that time would have been to buy into its corruption. A lot of young people were saying

Dust jacket of the 1982 bestseller.

that—some as activists, others as hippies, but I just opted out.''[1]

For the next seven years Naylor traveled as a missionary for the Jehovah's Witnesses. "My mother had always liked religion. She was a Baptist first, then a Methodist, and a Jehovah's Witness from the time I was thirteen. I had been around Jehovah's Witnesses the longest and liked their philosophy based on the idea that problems can't be solved on a human level and must be tackled by some higher force. So I went around preaching about the coming of a Theocracy where a God would take over the world because men of any shade had not done a decent job of it. I believed that I could make a difference by going around and preaching to people.

"I no longer hope for a cataclysm, but still believe in self-determination and in miracles on small individual levels. I don't believe that we are ever going to see any radical changes in the way human beings relate to each other. The changes will be gradual because that is how progress moves. I have since elected to try and make a difference in other ways. Those years helped to bring me out of my shyness, however, and made me care about something, and I don't think that is ever wasted time.

"The aftermath of the sixties affected only a greater accommodation of black Americans in society. A fair amount of extremely privileged blacks had been going to Ivy League Colleges even in the 1920s and 30s, and there were the black universities, like Howard, called the Harvard of the South. Armed with doctorates from universities and city college, blacks were only able to get Pullman porter jobs. Now, after the broadening of accommodation, some exceptional individual with a Ph.D. can use that degree, but it still hasn't brought about an equitable society where an average black person can gain the same rights as any other working-class person. The 'exceptional' are now allowed some room to exercise their freedom, but for poor people (and in this country we have many poor of all hues) it's not quite the same. I can't really be a die-hard pessimist. I believe that it was Margaret Atwood who said that people without hope do not write books. I'm just a romantic who's been kicked in the heart a lot.''[1]

In 1977, Naylor decided to attend Brooklyn College. "I realized after seven years that I was twenty-five years old with a high-school education and no marketable skills. The time to enter college had come.

"After I entered Brooklyn College, I began to fill the gaps in my earlier reading with loads of courses in the African Studies department where I was able to read black literature for the first time.

"A partial dedication of *The Women of Brewster Place* went to Rick Pearce, my creative writing professor at Brooklyn. His approach to teaching was that writing could not be taught, but that an environment could be created in which the student could find his voice and find the courage to tell his story. No one was coerced into writing in a certain style or with a certain viewpoint. I would never defend my work when the other students tore it apart. My teacher, however, saw something in me and told me that he'd be willing to read my stuff. And that was encouraging.''[1]

Naylor also had the opportunity to work with poet Joan Larkin. "Joan told me to sit in on her graduate, creative-writing workshop. I was scared to death. 'Trust me,' she said, 'the material I'm getting from you is as good, if not better. You can hold your own.' I took her workshop, but didn't officially sign up for it, something Joan didn't realize until it was time to hand out grades. She asked me why I hadn't signed up. 'Are you joking? I'll be darned if I'm going to pull down my grade-point average.' I was extremely ambitious and didn't want to risk my 3.8. I didn't have that kind of confidence.

"But I learned a lot because the workshop was a smaller, a more mature class, and it gave me eyes and ears for my work. I would submit sections of the stories that ultimately became 'Brewster Place' and it forced me to write in order to meet the deadlines for my assignments.''[1]

Despite the fact that she had a publishing contract for *The Women of Brewster Place* in her senior year of school, Naylor decided to matriculate at Yale graduate school in 1981. "I had half the book done and finished it the month I graduated from Brooklyn College. Since I didn't expect to make a living from my writing, my game plan was to parlay my liberal arts degree into a doctorate in English, get one of those high-class union cards with a tenured position somewhere, and develop the financial base from which to write my novels. That was the plan when I entered Yale. The fact was I had no idea of the tremendous amount of energy it took to move from the position of big fish in a small pond to a small fish in a big pond. Everybody was smart, and I had to hold my own.

"I found the tremendous amount of critical theory antithetical to my writing process. They were

The 1989 ABC television mini-series "The Women of Brewster Place" starred Cicely Tyson and Oprah Winfrey, among others.

adamant about teaching you to take apart the creative process. Since much of a writer's work is on a subconscious level, too much critical analysis can be detrimental. Teaching writing can be harmful for that very same reason. Some things, I believe, should not be taken apart. Education should become a more creative and spontaneous process. I left school after I got my masters. Further study would have taken a gamble with my writing. Actually, I was going to leave after my first year, but my grades were good and my progressive-minded director of graduate studies, John Blassingame, allowed me to use my second novel as partial fulfillment for my masters. It was nice to be able to tie that up, but I was committed to do whatever I had to do to make a living from my writing."[1]

The path to success turned out to be smoother than Naylor had anticipated. *The Women of Brewster Place*, the story of the women who thrive on a dead-end ghetto street despite the various paths that led them there, was published in 1982 to significant critical and popular acclaim. One of the few criticisms of the book was a relatively common one to black female writers, namely the maltreatment or absence of significant black male characters. "I've heard, 'Where are the men in *The Women of Brewster Place?*' for the last ten years. My answer, 'Read the title!' I did not perform any sleight-of-hand. I put what the content of that book

YOU DON'T HAVE TO SELL YOUR SOUL
TO LIVE IN LINDEN HILLS.
YOU GIVE IT AWAY, PIECE BY PIECE.

LINDEN HILLS

GLORIA NAYLOR

Author of *The Women of Brewster Place*

Paperbound edition of the 1985 novel.

was right up front. I set out to write about the diversity and richness of the black female experience. That's why the book is structured the way it is, with different chapters, each for a very different woman's life. And all those women come together to form a microcosm on that metaphysical landscape of a dead-end street.

"I refuse to be on the defensive with the question. Instead, I throw it right back with 'Why hasn't anyone ever asked Melville, "Where are the women in *Moby Dick?*" Or "where are the women in Ellison's *Invisible Man*, Mailer's *The Naked and the Dead.*'" We know why those questions are not asked. It is assumed that the woman should be absent when a male is writing and that's because her contributions to American history, until very recently, have been invisible. But it seems as younger women writers found their voices and proclaimed, 'We're talking about this thing defined as life and how it hurts and affects *us*,' all of these questions about the absence of male characters were thrown at us because it was assumed to be *his*

story all along. When women set out to articulate their experience, whatever is peripheral to it will show up as peripheral in their work. Aristotle said that the nature of drama is conflict. Whatever might cause that conflict in a woman's experience, even if it's a man, *her* vision is still central to it. Because we live in a sexist society, that irritates some people."[1] Naylor had little to do with the television series *The Women of Brewster Place*, starring Oprah Winfrey, but expressed satisfaction with the job they did.[1]

"The success of her novel," according to Judith V. Branzburg, reviewer for *Callaloo*, "is in her rendering, in rich, sensuous, rhythmic language, a sense of the reality of Afro-American women's lives while including serious examination of racial and sexual politics. Without being overtly critical of the racism of America. Naylor manages to make the reader understand how the economic and social situation of black lives becomes one with personal lives, with relationships between men and women, women and women, and parents and children, without diminishing the humanity of the individuals involved. She makes it clear that the socio-economic reality of black lives creates black men's tendency to leave their lovers and children. She knows that black children need special training to survive in a society which holds black in disdain. But Naylor is also certain that black men are capable of taking more responsibility than they do, and that mothers of any color will try to do their best for their children.

"Naylor is as successful as she is at presenting the complexity of black lives without reducing the people to types simply because she is an accomplished writer. She is especially good at describing the sensuous and at evoking the sounds, smells, and feelings of any given situation. Her talent for creating rich, emotional characters makes her failings particularly disappointing. Kiswana the Black Power activist and the two lesbians are flat characters, expecially Kiswana. The only time Kiswana seems to come alive is in the few lines when she is thinking of her lover Abshu. The lesbians also fail because Naylor does not invest them with the sensuousness and fullness of feeling that characterizes the other women. The 'Kiswana' chapter is also the only one in which Naylor fails to show the seamless intermingling of the political and personal and resorts to a lecture from Kiswana's middle class and bourgeois, yet very proud mother. Naylor seems to have difficulty portraying women whose life choices or circumstances have separated them from the pain of financial struggle and heterosexual relations that mark all of Naylor's other women. But, taken as part of the whole, these are minor complaints. Naylor's ability to present the pain and love of her characters' lives carries her through.

"So, although at the end of the novel the people leave a dying Brewster Place with their dreams still deferred, there is a sense of hope. The women have, at the very least, gained respect, the readers' and their own."[2]

Her next novel, *Linden Hills*, modeled after Dante's *Inferno*, was published in 1985. It is the story of Willie and Lester, two young black poets who make their way through an upperclass black society. "I wanted to write about the black middle class and about what happens to the hyphenated Americans in pursuit of the 'American Dream,' how they sacrifice whatever is culturally specific to them for the idea of a melting pot and for the notion of success. It is the very force that 'de-sexes' and 'de-racinates' individuals. That's what *Linden Hills* is really all about—what becomes lost in that mad scramble up (which ironically, in the whole topography of the book, is down). I have always been fascinated with Dante's *Inferno* and believed the concept would work well for something like this book, where I turned a society on its head and gave it an inverse mirror-image of itself."[1]

Departing from the strict realism of *Brewster Place* in favor of a stronger touch of allegory, Naylor depicted a society in *Linden Hills* where each member gives up a proportional amount of his soul for each measure of success. "They are forgetting the qualities that have kept black Americans strong through inhuman conditions in this country, qualities like a sense of family, a sense of community, a sense of religious and spiritual value, and ultimately an inner sense of self. Those who held onto those qualities during times of hardship, survived both spiritually and physically. Too many Africans who were stuffed into slave ships committed suicide by jumping overboard or had their spirits broken and their bodies followed. Today's black Americans, however, descended from Africans physically strong enough to endure their bondage, and spiritually strong enough to endure all that came after, more insidious because it went on longer.

"Had my mother been born after the Civil Rights Movement, her life would have been different. In a sense, I'm living the life she would have had because she was a reader and a dreamer. But I also see that attaining some of the crumbs of what we call success often comes at a cost—the cost of being ashamed of our history. I saw the confusion in some of the younger students who came to Yale straight from high school—a confusion over who they were and where they were going. The desire to fit in is universal among the young, but they must examine closely what it is they want to fit *into*, what they must give up, what they must be silent about, and what they must not affirm. I watched them make those decisions day after day. Ultimately you can only make so many decisions and choices before you look back and don't know who you are. So *Linden Hills* is a bit of a cautionary tale, if you will."[1]

Naylor had explored this theme once before in *The Women of Brewster Place* with Kiswana Brown, a radical young woman who had taken on an African name in defiance of everything her affluent parents (who lived in Linden Hills) stood for, ultimately learning a lesson from her mother about pride. This also introduced Naylor's technique of picking up minor characters from a previous book and branching out into a new work. "Kiswana was the flipside of conformity. She tried hard to be unlike the people living in Linden Hills. At that time, black Americans had to look to Africa for a history of anything that was positive and glorious. That was a natural impulse because there was nothing in American history that said blacks were worth anything. All Kiswana saw when she looked back was the slavery and degradation of her people. Mrs. Brown reassured her that she could find pride in her history 'right here on this terra firma. And I don't give a damn what they have said.'"[1]

Education, Naylor feels, is the only key to overcoming this problem, though she is very specific about how she defines that word and doesn't necessarily limit its meaning to formal schooling. "People in the *Hills* understood perfectly how to use the system. I made a point of having them come from Ivy League Schools in the North, South, East, and West, covering all the geographic areas. They were well-versed in getting through the system, but there was something else they had missed—a real education, one that does not lie or slant the truth. It's out there; I found it. If the textbooks are not forthcoming, then go out and do a lot of sifting and researching. Education means parents talking to their children—not only about general history, but also about their own family background. We tend to look for role models in great people, but there are those little, individual stories of courage in all of our families.

"Education is not white; education is just education. All too often it's seen by the street culture as white. Young kids are never taught anything from an early age that is relevant to their own experience, so they come to the disenchanted conclusion, 'What does this have to do with me? This is boring.' Too often kids will opt for nothing. The dropout rate begins at a very early age because they're still too young to exercise any options and consequently become disenfranchised and discouraged. The effort has to be made early on to incorporate a curriculum that serves *all* students. Right now it doesn't."[1]

Naylor also encourages vocal dissent against misleading representations and stereotypes. "When you know that something is amiss in a news program, write the station. Public Broadcasting did a special about welfare in Minnesota highlighting four families, three of which were black. That representation would mean that seventy-five percent of the welfare poor in Minnesota are black. Now, do you know how many black people there are in Minnesota? I would guess no more than two or three percent. Most of the poor people in this country are white, because most of its people are white. The depictions often skew reality.

"For example, I live in Washington Heights where there are a lot of blacks and Dominicans associated with the drug problems. Common sense tells me that there just aren't enough black people to use the tons of cocaine smuggled into the neighborhood. I could look out my window right now and watch the kids from New Jersey drive across the George Washington Bridge to Washington Heights to buy their drugs and return to the suburbs. So it's very much a question of recognizing when reality is being slanted, for whatever reason, and using your common sense."[1]

Naylor has faced her success with realistic self-awareness. "After *Brewster Place* was published, there was a brief time when I was saying, 'Hey, I'm a "Writer," you know!' And working on *Linden Hills*, I had the slight consciousness that I was a 'Writer.' But the work humbles you. I try not to think of myself as a 'Writer' doing this; I'm just somebody facing a blank page. You have to keep yourself rooted in who and what you are. I knew on some instinctive level when I became 'successful' that if I got caught up in the image created around me, my sanity would be doomed. Necessity pulled me away from that kind of ego-tripping and ultimately, it turned out to be a healthy way to live.

"I have challenges I want to meet this year and challenges this very day. I hope to make it through the day, and when I go to bed tonight to say, 'Okay kid, well done for today.' That's about it. I think that goes back full-circle to the way I was raised, coming up as a black female in '50s America when my family taught me to discount whatever the outside world had to say, because ninety-nine percent of it said that I was nothing. So it was kind of hard when I hit my thirties to believe it when they said, 'You're wonderful!' Not that I think that it's hypocrisy, because I think that they believed it, but the point is that you must find your own value and fail or succeed within yourself."[1]

Some critics described Naylor's third novel as "narcotic" and "blessed with excess," a book which treads even closer to that fine line which separates the real from the unreal. Named for it's main character, Miranda Day, *Mama Day* was published in 1988. Naylor took this character from *Linden Hills* and explored new themes around her. "I wanted to talk about love and magic because those are things I really do believe in. Just by living long enough, I've seen examples of the power of love transforming a person's life. I also wondered how I could be a fiction writer and not explore the forces beyond the tangible which can move us."[1]

Her attempt to elevate the love story between Cocoa, Mama Day's grandniece, and the character George to magical heights has drawn comparisons to Shakespeare's *The Tempest*. "I must admit that it wasn't done consciously. Shakespeare influenced me and I have used him in each of my works, but the only thing I consciously took for *Mama Day* was George's love of *King Lear* and the fact that George and Cocoa are the star-crossed lovers of *Romeo and Juliet*. I was not thinking about *The Tempest* at all. The only idea I remember ever taking from *The Tempest* was Caliban telling the fool and the cook after they had overthrown Prospero, 'Burn all he has, but keep his books.' Those words saved my sanity at Yale. I knew that since none of it was built or perpetuated with me in mind, I could burn all that was not intended to serve me, but must keep the books. In other words, I took what was useful for me from that experience and went on."[1] Written in the first person, *Mama Day* was a departure for Naylor. "I started writing the book in the third person, but it just wasn't working. This sort of collected voice of the island kept pushing itself through and I knew that Cocoa and George wanted to talk for themselves, so I just bit the bullet and let them do it."[1]

A reviewer in *Publishers Weekly* found the beauty of Naylor's prose in "its plainness, and the secret power of. . .[*Mama Day*] is that she does not simply tell a story but brings you face to face with human beings living through the complexity, pain and mystery of real life. But *Mama Day* is a black story in particular which is, paradoxically, why it is such a satisfying and all-encompassing experience. A young black couple meet in New York and fall in love. Ophelia ('Cocoa') is from Willow Island, off the coast of South Carolina and Georgia but part of neither state, and George is an orphan who was born and raised in New York. Every August, Cocoa visits her grandmother Abigail and great-aunt Miranda ('Mama Day') back home. The lure of New York and the magic of home and Mama Day's folk medicines and mystical powers pull at the couple and bring about unforeseen, yet utterly believable, changes in them and their relationship. Naylor interweaves three simple narratives—Cocoa and George alternately tell about their relationship, while a third-person narrative relates the story of Mama Day and Willow Island.... Naylor's...skills as a teller of tales are equal of her philosophical and moral aims. The rhythmic alternation of voices and locales here has a narcotic effect that inspires trust and belief in both Mama Day and Naylor herself, who illustrates with convincing simplicity and clear-sighted intelligence the magical interconnectedness of people with nature, with God and with each other."[3]

Naylor finds ideas, inspiration, and help "all over the place." While teaching writing at New York University, she submitted the introduction of *Mama Day* to one of her classes for inspection. "We had gone through their work and had built up a rapport, so I said, 'Okay, now it's my turn,' and gave them the introduction. They tore it apart, and it was loads of fun. My teaching has definitely added to my work because my approach to it goes back to how I was taught. In the very first class, I tell my students that I am not a guru and cannot show them any magic formula, but I *can* offer twenty-something years of avidly reading books and some knowledge of what works and what doesn't. Then it's up to them to make it work. My attitude, as far as their peers are concerned, is that they will criticize in a spirit of constructiveness and love because they have done two very brave things—they have dared to put their thoughts on paper, and they have dared to expose themselves to strangers.

"We all start at the same place. Each day is a new beginning and a blank page is no less terrifying to me than to a freshman creative-writing student. Nothing you've done before matters to that page.

"I don't write a whole novel in the first draft and then go back. I'll write a first chapter and go back until I get it right. Then I'll go on from there. As for my writing style, asking me where that came from is like asking someone what brought about the timber and texture in their voice. I don't really control that."[1]

Naylor is currently working on her next novel, titled *Bailey's Cafe*. "Looking back, I see that each work has been my coming to terms with certain demons within myself. I don't know whether or not I've leaped those hurdles but I've certainly grappled with them. *The Women of Brewster Place* was the emotive work, *Linden Hills*, the cerebral one, *Mama Day*, the spiritual one, and now I'm working on sexuality."[1]

Like Naylor's previous works, this novel will draw from the one before. "It takes place from 1948 to 1949 and the tie-in with *Mama Day* is George and his mother. I expand upon her and the other whores who were with her and deal with the Madonna complex we have in the Western mind when thinking about female sexuality.

David Montiel's jacket painting for Naylor's third book.

"In the beginning, I visualized these books as a quartet upon which to build my career. Once I complete that foundation I can truly say, 'Hey, I'm a writer.'"[1]

Footnote Sources:

[1] Based on an interview with Dieter Miller for *Authors and Artists for Young Adults*.
[2] Judith V. Banzburg, "Seven Women and a Wall," *Callaloo*, spring-summer, 1984.
[3] "Mama Day," *Publishers Weekly*, December 18, 1987.

■ For More Information See

Publishers Weekly, April 9, 1982 (p. 45), September 9, 1983, December 18, 1987 (p. 54ff).
Library Journal, June 15, 1982.
New York Times, July 13, 1982 (p. C10), February 9, 1985 (p. 14), February 10, 1988 (p. C25).
Washington Post, August 13, 1982, October 21, 1983.
New York Times Book Review, August 22, 1982 (p. 11ff), March 3, 1985 (p. 11), February 21, 1988 (p. 7).

New Republic, September 6, 1982 (p. 37ff).
Los Angeles Times, December 2, 1982.
Chicago Tribune Book World, February 23, 1983.
Times (London), April 21, 1983.
Contemporary Literary Criticism, Volume 28, Gale, 1984, Volume 52, Gale, 1989.
Los Angeles Times Book Review, February 24, 1985, March 6, 1988.
Christian Science Monitor, March 1, 1985.
Detroit News, March 3, 1985, February 21, 1988.
Washington Post Book World, March 24, 1985, February 28, 1988 (p. 5).
San Francisco Review of Books, May, 1985.
Commonweal, May 3, 1985 (p. 283ff).
Times Literary Supplement, May 24, 1985.
Ms., June, 1985.
Southern Review, July, 1985.
Women's Review of Books, August, 1985 (p. 7ff).
London Review of Books, August 1, 1985.
Contemporary Literature, Volume 28, number 1, 1987.
Tribune Books (Chicago), January 31, 1988.
Linda Metzger, editor, *Black Writers*, Gale, 1989.

Robert O'Brien

Born Robert Leslie Conly, January 11, 1918, in Brooklyn, N.Y.; died of a heart attack on March 5, 1973, in Washington, D.C.; married Sally McCasin, 1943; children: Christopher, Jane, Sarah, Catherine. *Education:* Attended Williams College, 1935-37, Julliard School of Music, Columbia University, and Eastman School; University of Rochester, B.A., 1940.

■ Career

Worked at an advertising agency, 1940; *Newsweek,* New York, N.Y., staff writer, 1941-44; *Times Herald,* Washington, D.C., rewrite man, 1944-46; *Pathfinder,* Washington, D.C., news editor, 1946-51; *National Geographic,* Washington, D.C., became senior assistant editor, 1951-73.

■ Awards, Honors

Mrs. Frisby and the Rats of NIMH was selected one of Child Study Association of America's Children's Books of the Year, 1971, and *Z for Zachariah,* 1975; Newbery Medal from the American Library Association, Lewis Carroll Shelf Award, *Boston Globe-Horn Book* Award Honor Book for Text, and National Book Award Finalist, all 1972, Mark Twain Award, 1973, and Young Readers' Choice Award from the Pacific Northwest Library Association, and William Allan White Children's Book Award, both 1974, all for *Mrs. Frisby and the Rats of NIMH; A Report from Group 17* was selected one of American Library Association's Best Young Adult Books, 1972, and *Z for Zachariah,* 1975; one of *New York Times* Outstanding Books of the Year, 1975, Jane Addams Children's Book Award Honor Book from the Jane Addams Peace Association, 1976, Mystery Writers of America Best Juvenile Novel, 1977, and one of New York Public Library's Books for the Teen Age, 1980, 1981, and 1982, all for *Z for Zachariah.*

■ Writings

Under Pseudonym Robert C. O'Brien:

The Silver Crown (illustrated by Dale Payson), Atheneum, 1968.
Mrs. Frisby and the Rats of NIMH (ALA Notable Book; *Horn Book* honor list; illustrated by Zena Bernstein), Atheneum, 1971.
A Report from Group 17, Atheneum, 1972.
Z for Zachariah (*Horn Book* honor list), Atheneum, 1975, large print edition, G. K. Hall, 1976.

■ Adaptations

"Mrs. Frisby and the Rats of NIMH" (record; cassette), Newbery Award Records, 1972, (filmstrip with cassette) Miller-Brody, 1973.

"The Secret of NIMH" (motion picture; based on *Mrs. Frisby and the Rats of NIMH*), Metro-Goldyn-Mayer/United Artists, 1982.

Mrs. Frisby and the Rats of NIMH, A Report from Group 17, and *Z for Zachariah* are available as "Talking Books."

■ Sidelights

Shortly after Robert C. O'Brien's birth in 1918, his family moved from New York City to Amityville, Long Island where he attended parochial school. He was both a frightened and difficult child who sought solace in his love of music. He was admired for his singing and piano playing, but he did not adapt well to either school or family life.

His wife, Sally, described the joys and frustrations of his youth: "There is a sign much in evidence these days which proclaims, 'If you aren't nervous, you just don't understand the situation.' My impression of Robert...is that he has, since early childhood, 'understood the situation'—i.e., he was and is a nervous being. On the other hand, he has—also since childhood—had a formidable set of skills or talents for dealing with that nervousness. First, and probably most important, was a talent for music. He could sing before he could talk; his favorite amusement was the family windup Victrola; and he has had a lifelong preoccupation with music both as a listener and as a performer.

"He loved reading and showed an early facility with words, writing rhymed poetry and even a novel about the adventures and exploits of a young boy who traveled around the world.

"[He was not] an endearing, easy-going child. Born a middle child into a literate, sharp-witted, sharp-tongued Irish family, he had an extraordinarily bad case of 'middle-itis.' His younger sister, now his good friend, says frankly, 'We hated him.' His mother, harassed beyond endurance, once threatened to drown him. He was sick a great deal. He despised and feared school and some mornings was literally dragged screaming into the classroom."[1]

By the time he entered Amityville High School, O'Brien's musical talent coupled with a strong sense of humor and athletic ability had made it easier for him to gain the acceptance of his peers. As he became more comfortable socially his need to retreat from the world diminished. "He had a propensity and talent for dreaming," according to his wife. "He could and did regularly create splendid imaginary worlds, with himself in dazzling, heroic roles. While all children do this to some extent, [his] fantasy world was so vivid that he still remembers the place and hour when he (by then a student in high school) made a solemn decision to give it up and to concentrate on living in the real world.

"Another great strength was his self-discipline. In late adolescence he regularly arose at four o'clock in the morning to study, to practice the piano, to walk on the beach while the rest of his family was still asleep. Along with this discipline went a determination and a refusal to compromise almost akin to perversity."[1]

O'Brien served as editor of the school paper, and with his talent for turning out verse, it was soon apparent that he had yet another creative skill. Sally O'Brien recalled: "His respect for language, his talent for dreaming, and his self-discipline were combining to make him a writer."[1]

He entered Williams College in 1935, but the new situation proved too stressful and he left school abruptly during his second year. "He was, for a

Softcover of the multi-award-winning novel.

year, a college dropout when such action was cause for disgrace," wrote his wife. "Still he was not ever drifting. In a hard, uncomfortable-for-those-around-him style he was shaping up; but he was doing it, as he always would, in his own way."[1]

O'Brien returned to his family and suffered what he later referred to as a "breakdown," but following a few months recovery he resumed piano lessons. Determined to become a musician, he studied at the Julliard School of Music while also taking courses at Columbia University. His parents then persuaded him to return full time to college. He continued his study of music at the Eastman School while earning his B.A. in English at the University of Rochester. His desire to write won out over his musical ambitions, and from the time he graduated in 1940 he earned his living as a writer.

O'Brien's career began with *Newsweek* magazine where he quickly advanced from clip desk to researcher to staff writer. While there he met Sally McCasin, then a researcher in the Books Department; they married in 1943. The following year they moved to Washington, D.C. where he worked for the Washington *Times-Herald* and began a family which grew to include one son and three daughters.

In 1951, having covered both national and city news, O'Brien began as an editor and writer for *National Geographic*, a job which was to take him around the world.

In 1964 he was on assignment in Northern Ireland. "A dreadful thing has happened. I've turned partly orange.

"My sainted Grandmother O'Brien, rest her soul, would rise from her grave in wrath if she knew. So would my Great-grandmother O'Leary and a whole army of more distant kinsmen—Carrolls, Fitzpatricks, and Kellys—if they could hear what I am going to admit.

"My grandmother, I should explain, was one for singing and storytelling. She had a memory like an iron safe, and could go on for hours with tales, poems, and songs about the Old Sod, with me sitting on her knee. Now, the gist of most of her songs was this: That Ireland is the finest country in the world, and the Irish the greatest people, but that the North of Ireland is a dreadful, dark, wicked place where a man can be strung up for wearing a green necktie.

"So, the admission: I'm back from a long stay in Northern Ireland and a prettier, friendlier, kindlier country I've never seen. Furthermore, while I was there I attended a massive celebration of North Irishmen, all dressed in orange sashes and fiercely loyal to the Queen....Throughout these ceremonies, which lasted two days, I wore a green necktie, and nobody so much as glanced at it.

"I will continue to wear a shamrock, a green tie, a green sweater, and green socks on St. Patrick's Day, and so will my children.

"I was met at the plane by a pleasant, rather aquiline man in his forties, Mr. Eric Montgomery, Director of Northern Ireland's Government Information Service. He had rolled out the red carpet in the form of a sleek black limousine and a liveried chauffeur to drive me to my hotel.

"His opening remark may not sound particularly significant, but it was, in two ways. In a very British accent, he said:

"'You chose a nice day to arrive.'

"That was my introduction to an Ulster [Northern Ireland] preoccupation that astonished me throughout my stay. Virtually every conversation, every business transaction, starts with comment on the weather. You cannot buy a toothpick without an exchange of meteorological data with the shopkeeper.

"'A fine day it is,' he'll say, though it be gray and foggy. You agree, but you cannot get off so lightly.

"'But a bit close, for the time of year.' Agree again; it will do you no good.

"'However, at least the rain's holding off, so we can't complain, after the terrible summer we've had.' Retreat, clutching the toothpick, and as the door closes he'll be adding, 'Still, we could use a spot of wind to blow the fog away.'

"At the Royal Avenue Hotel, a pleasant and cordial place where the staff quickly learns your name and your idiosyncrasies (mine is that I do not want coffee with my breakfast), I am told that I have a room for three nights but then I must move out. This is not inhospitality. It is Belfast.

"To face facts, the place is bursting at the seams. It has half a million people, but only room for a quarter million, or so it seemed to me. Its bars are crowded, its restaurants jammed, its buses bulge with humanity. Its sidewalks are too narrow for the rush-hour crowds, and they overflow into the streets and dodge the buses.

From the animated movie "The Secret of NIMH," produced by MGM/United Artists, 1982.

"While I was there, the newspapers and city officials were debating on which of several sites to build a new downtown hotel.

"'I wish they'd stop arguing,' a Belfast friend of mine said, 'and build on all of them.' He then offered to put me up at his club, and I accepted gratefully. It was a comfortable place, albeit somewhat creaky at night, with bathtubs about seven feet long and deep leather armchairs in the lounge.

"A waitress comes to your table, sees no food on it, and does not ask if your order has been taken, sir. Instead she says:

"'Are you getting, dear?'

"And when you've been served, she'll come back, look at you searchingly and will not ask if everything is satisfactory, sir. Instead she says:

"'Are you all right, dear?'

"But one breakfast I complained that my egg had been boiled too long, as indeed it had. All she said was:

"'Well, look who got up on the wrong side this morning!'

"I ate the hard-boiled egg.

"You do not read the Belfast newspapers long, nor talk to many people there, before you become aware of an uneasy friction between the one-third of Ulster's citizens who are Irish Catholics (politically 'Nationalists'), and the two-thirds who are predominantly English, Scots, and Protestant (politically, 'Unionists'). No honest discussion of Northern Ireland can ignore this.

"Personally I hope that over the years or decades, the Irish sun and rain will fade the difference between the orange and the green until someday the Irish themselves will no longer be able to tell which is which. As I said, though I'm mostly green, I've turned a little bit orange myself."[2]

Though O'Brien had often spoken of writing a novel, his first fictional work did not appear until 1968. He wrote under his pen name of Robert C. O'Brien because the *National Geographic* did not encourage outside writing by members of their staff.

The Silver Crown is the story of a young girl, Ellen, who receives a silver crown for her tenth birthday and almost immediately thereafter loses her family in a devastating fire. The story employs elements of science fiction and fantasy as it explores the girl's adventures on the way to maturity.

Reviewer Susan Boulanger for *Horn Book* magazine said of the story: "The plot creaks at times under damaging improbabilities and red herrings. All the adult characters are, in fact, noncharacters....Most seriously, however, a desperate talkiness throughout the book undermines the story, leaving it unfocused.

"But interlocking complexities of meaning and reference strengthen the book, giving the adventure substance and significance....It is full of the child-appeal of hidden societies and mysterious, dangerous events. But, primarily, it is a story of testing; Ellen learns to act effectively to defuse a threat, to preserve what she has come to value in the world and in herself. It is a heartening and subtle story of the possibilities for action against the daunting, even overwhelming, personal and public dilemmas of our time."[3]

O'Brien's second book, *Mrs. Frisby and the Rats of NIMH*, achieved both wide popularity and critical acclaim. The novel focuses on a mother fieldmouse attempting to save her child from death and on her encounters with a colony of exceptionally intelligent rats who have escaped from a research laboratory.

In June of 1972 the novel received the Newbery Medal. "After [I was] telephoned [and told] my book had been chosen (...that was the best phone call I ever got), I went out and found a list of all the Newbery titles over the years. I was familiar with quite a few of them, but my youngest daughter knew them all and had read most of them. Obviously the Newbery Medal works. It gets the books to the children and the children to the books.

"Ever since I wrote *Mrs. Frisby and the Rats of NIMH*, I have been asked two kinds of questions, one quite sensible, the other quite incredulous. The sensible one is: Why do you write books for children? The incredulous one is: Why, with all the world to choose from, did you have to write about *rats?*

"One of the first critics to review *Mrs. Frisby* wrote as follows: 'When I first got the book, the title bothered me. Who wants to read about rats? They're filthy, thieving, ravenous and cruel. But once beyond that mental block....' Well, once beyond that mental block the critic went on to write one of the most enthusiastic reviews I have ever read. But the question was valid, and I still

hear it. If you choose rats as heroes, you're going to turn some people off. So why do it?

"Of course, rats are not without precedent in children's books. There is a fine character named Rat in *The Wind in the Willows.* There is a friendly rat named Melchtsedec in *A Little Princess.* There have been others I could mention. Still, it set me thinking. Why *did* I choose rats as subjects for a children's story?

"I regret to say that if there was ever a precise answer to that question, it is lost. I have searched my memory and my files to try to find out how and when the idea first came to me. My files show that I began writing the book in November, 1967, and that by March, 1968, I had finished only two chapters and was debating whether or not to continue. (I was, at the time, also working on another book.) But I have no recollection at all of Mrs. Frisby's initial appearance in my thoughts. I

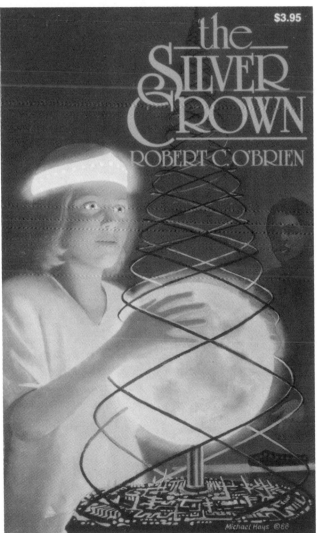

Cover of the Macmillan paperback.

think that may be true of many works of fiction. They are rather like plants. You put a seed under ground. You come back a few days later and find a small green stalk growing. But how often do you actually see the stalk emerge?

"I do know some of the thinking and reading I had done before I wrote about Mrs. Frisby, and I know that these must have been connected with her sudden appearance. I had been, and still am, concerned over the seeming tendency of the human race to exterminate itself—as who is not? I have wondered: If we should vanish from the earth, who might survive us? What kind of civilization might follow ours? I had read in a scientific journal that scorpions were good candidates for survival, since they are resistant to radioactivity. I read the same about cockroaches. But I was unable to imagine a cockroach or a scorpion civilization.

"By coincidence, I had been reading a book by Loren Eiseley called *The Immense Journey.* There was in it a chapter about prairie dogs. It discussed the evidence paleontologists have found that the prairie dogs' ancestors drove our ancestors, the ancestors of the simian primates, out of the prairies and into the woods, in short, the prairie dogs were, millions of years ago, ahead of us in the race toward dominance. While we were still in the trees, they were building little villages. And prairie dogs, as we know, are not dogs at all, but rodents.

"Dr. Eiseley's essay reminded me in turn of another essay—one by Clarence Day called 'This Simian World.' It was required reading when I was in college. That was a long time ago; but, as I recall, it begins by pointing out that many of the things people do—for example, talking a lot and gathering in large groups—are traceable to their simian ancestry. (Monkeys do these things, too.) Then the essay goes on to speculate on what the world would be like if people were descended not from monkeys but from, say, dogs or cats. I remember that Clarence Day thought a cat civilization would be much less gregarious than ours: Cats walk by themselves. Also, a cat culture would be more musical than ours, with a lot of singing.

"Still thinking about survival, I began to speculate: Rats are tough, highly adaptable to a changing environment, and enormously prolific. Maybe, if people should eliminate one another by means of war or pollution, rats would be the survivors. Or if not the only survivors, perhaps the most intelligent.

"What, then, would a rat civilization be like? This, of course, is not precisely what *Mrs. Frisby* is about. In the book there is no war, and the human race has not been exterminated. But it was this *kind* of speculation that led to the birth of *Mrs. Frisby and the Rats of NIMH.*

"I suppose it's a rather grim idea to serve as background for a children's book. But once I got it started, the rats took charge, and they turned out to be much saner and pleasanter than we are.

"To the much more general question—Why do I write books for children?—the honest answer is not very enlightening. I write them because a story idea pops up in my mind; and that really is the way it feels, to me at least. And since I am in the writing business, when I get a story idea I write it down before I forget it. It isn't always for children, of course, but those are the stories I most like to write, because children like a straight-forward, honest plot—the way God meant plots to be—with a beginning, a middle, and an end: a problem, an attempt to solve it, and at the end a success or a failure.

"I would prefer to rephrase the question. Why is it *good* to write books for children? The answer to that is easy: because it is good for children to read books.

"When a child (or an adult) reads a book, I think his mind is getting pretty much the same kind of exercise it gets when it deals with real-life problems, though perhaps less intensely. It is certainly not turned off or lulled. If you watch a child reading—or better, recall your own reading as a child—how often did you put the book down for a minute and wonder: How is the hero going to get out of *this* mess? And try to figure out ways, hoping he would turn right at the next corner, because that's the way the bad guys went.

"As the mind-seed wonders, it grows. Having put down roots, it opens its leaves and looks around. It learns about love, hate, fear, sadness, courage, kindness. All these things are in the world around it. But all of them come to life in books in a way that is peculiarly suitable for examination, for contemplation, and for evaluation.

"Did I mention bad guys? Did I say Long John Silver? Long John is a liar; he is unctuous, greedy, tricky; he is a thief. Then why do we like him better than anybody else in the book? The mind learns that it is not easy to separate good from bad; they become deviously intertwined. From books it learns that not all doors are simply open or shut, and that even rats can become heroes.

"And the lovely thing about a book is that when you finish wondering about these things and pick the book up again, the story is still there, right where you left it. You can't do that with movies or television.

"Not that I am against movies or television when the programs are reasonably good. There are thousands of children who would never read a book anyway—there always were, long before electronics—and a television program can let them know who Romeo and Juliet were, or at least what it's like to go to the moon. And I don't think the medium weans many real readers away from books.

"My own children, who are omnivorous and voracious readers, tend to watch television in spurts which may last an afternoon or two. Then they get tired of it, and I see them back with a book again. They got the reading habit early, and now I think they are hooked for life.

"Which, of course, is why it is good to write books for children."[4]

At the time of his acceptance of the Newbery Medal, O'Brien's wife paid him the following tribute: "In the middle age Robert. . .is a cultured, fastidious, rather solitary man who likes order and quiet, and works by schedule in spite of a busy household. His most long-lasting hobbies, aside from music, have been furniture making (he turns out exquisitely fitted and finished pieces) and growing luxuriant flowers in neatly arranged, weed-free beds.

"He has been married for twenty-nine years to the same wife; and his children have neither turned on nor dropped out, but have gone cheerfully off to highbrow schools where they developed the expensive habit of staying until they graduated.

"In his fiction, though, there is some evidence that [he] has not entirely outgrown influences of his childhood. One finds in his books a fascination with valleys, with hidden worlds, with new societies; he writes with particular sympathy for and perception of children and children's feelings. And children respond. They write him so many letters—smudged, mispelled, tremendously moving documents. A surprising number begin, '. . .I too am writing a book.' These letters he considers extra sacred. They are, he knows, from the special children, from the dreamers. They are from our future writers.

"Writing has been his only profession."[1]

Hardcover of O'Brien's last published novel.

O'Brien was a dedicated and disciplined writer who worked seven days a week. "We make a world, and put people in it, and make things go wrong, all without doing any damage at all to the real world. Then we activate our characters, and they set to work solving the problems we have given them. Readable fiction has to do this. Could Jim Hawkins get along without Long John Silver? Or Tom Sawyer without the murderous Injun Joe, or Frodo without Gollum? Who would want to read about Sara Crewe if her father had not died, if she had just led a happy and protected life as Miss Minchin's star boarder?

"Furthermore, the problems in a book can be much more horrendous than any we would willingly face in real life, and the solutions can be more ingenious. In fact, the characters are quite capable now and then of coming up with solutions better than those the author had planned; unfortunately, they can also develop unexpected new problems of their own. These they toss to the writer to work out."[4]

O'Brien published only two more books before his death on March 5, 1973. Though not a prolific fiction writer, he was admired for his sophisticated exploration of important moral dilemmas. Perhaps as a result of his own unhappy childhood, his writing addressed many of the fears and vulnerabilities experienced in youth. "In college I took a very elementary course in psychology. The professor who taught it was a behaviorist, and one of the ways he explained consciousness, intelligence, awareness—that is, the using of the mind—went something like this. You approach a door, turn the knob; the door opens; and you walk through. You do this a hundred times, it always works, and your mind remains dormant. It is an unconscious act. But the hundred-and-first time something goes wrong—the door sticks, or is locked, or the knob comes off. At this point, consciousness flickers on; the mind comes to work; intelligence awakens, studies the problem, directs the eye and hand to turn the key; and the door opens. The mind may stay active a few seconds longer—wondering who locked it; then it glimmers and goes out. In other words, the mind comes to life when something doesn't work, or when something new comes up. Consciousness, this psychologist said, is merely the pause, the delay between the attempt and the success.

"At this point I disagree with the psychologist—if indeed I understood him correctly. I think the mind is more than a pause, more than a flurry of activity in the brain cells. I think that there is a true dualism here and that the mind continues to exist when it is not being used. I don't know exactly what my mind is, but I am sure that it is more 'me' than my brain is, or my hand, or my endocrine system.

"I also believe that it is improved and strengthened by being used. Putting it the other way around, it seems obvious that the mind would disappear if it were perpetually unused—rather like a vestigial tail. If all of our needs and desires were easily and instantly met all of the time, we would become mindless. It might take a few generations, but it would happen—precisely because the mind *is* a real, living entity and not just a momentary manifestation of brain mechanics. It can starve to death—or fly back into space and look for a better planet.

"Thus we may be happy that our society is not yet perfect. Still, we must not strive for imperfection; it is contrary to our nature. We cannot go around taking the knobs off doors so they won't open, merely because it would keep our minds alert.

"Or can we? Of course we can. That's what books are all about."[4]

Footnote Sources:

[1] Sally M. O'Brien, "Robert C. O'Brien," *Horn Book*, August, 1972.
[2] Robert L. Conly, "Northern Ireland from Derry to Down," *National Geographic*, August, 1964.
[3] Susan Boulanger, "A Second Look: The Silver Crown," *Horn Book*, January/February, 1985.
[4] R. C. O'Brien, "Newbery Award Acceptance," *Horn Book*, August, 1972.

■ For More Information See

National Geographic, September, 1966 (p. 398ff), July, 1970 (p. 69ff).
Horn Book, April, 1968 (p. 174), August, 1971 (p. 385), June, 1975 (p. 277), December, 1976.
Christian Science Monitor, March 23, 1972.
Junior Bookshelf, February, 1973 (p. 49), February, 1974 (p. 28ff), June, 1975 (p. 201ff).
Publishers Weekly, February 5, 1973, January 20, 1975 (p. 77).
Top of the News, April, 1973.
Lee Kingman, editor, *Newbery and Caldecott Medal Books: 1966-1975*, Horn Book, 1975.
Doris de Montreville and Elizabeth D. Crawford, *Fourth Book of Junior Authors and Illustrators*, H. W. Wilson, 1978.
D. L. Kirkpatrick, *Twentieth-Century Children's Writers*, St. Martin's, 1978, 2nd edition, 1983.
Jim Roginski, compiler, *Newbery and Caldecott Medalists and Honor Book Winners*, Libraries Unlimited, 1982.

Obituaries:

New York Times, March 8, 1973.
Publishers Weekly, March 12, 1973.
Library Journal, March 15, 1973.
Time, March 19, 1973.

Collections:

Kerlan Collection at the University of Minnesota.

Janet Quin-Harkin

B orn September 24, 1941, in Bath, England; came to the United States in 1966; daughter of Frank Newcombe (an engineer) and Margery (a teacher; maiden name, Rees) Lee; married John Quin-Harkin (an airline sales manager), November 26, 1966; children: Clare, Anne, Jane, Dominic. *Education:* University of London. B.A. (with honors), 1963; graduate study at University of Kiel and University of Freiburg. *Religion:* Roman Catholic. *Home and office:* 31 Tralee Way, San Rafael, Calif. 94903. *Agent:* Amy Berkower, Writers House, Inc., 21 West 26th St., New York, N.Y. 10010.

■ Career

British Broadcasting Corp. (BBC), London, England, studio manager in drama department, 1963-66; writer, 1971—; teacher of dance and drama, 1971-76. Founder and former director of San Rafael Children's Little Theater. Writing teacher at Dominican College in San Rafael, 1988—. *Member:* Society of Children's Book Writers, Associated Authors of Children's Literature.

■ Awards, Honors

Children's Book Showcase title from the Childrens' Book Council, one of *New York Times* Outstanding Books of the Year, included in the American Institute of Graphic Arts Childrens' Book Show, *Kirkus'* Choice, and one of *School Library Journal*'s Best Books of the Year, all 1976, and one of the American Library Association's Books of International Note, 1977, all for *Peter Penny's Dance;* Children's Choice, 1985, for *Wanted: Date for Saturday Night.*

■ Writings

(Contributor) Lawrence Carillo and Dorothy McKinley, editors, *Chandler Reading Program,* five volumes, Noble and Noble, 1967-72.
Peter Penny's Dance (juvenile; illustrated by Anita Lobel), Dial, 1976.
Benjamin's Balloon (juvenile), Parents Magazine Press, 1979.
Septimus Bean and His Amazing Machine (juvenile; illustrated by Art Cumings), Parents Magazine Press, 1980.
Magic Growing Powder (illustrated by A. Cumings), Parents Magazine Press, 1981.
Helpful Hattie (illustrated by Susanna Natti), Harcourt, 1983.

Young Adult Novels:

Write Every Day, Scholastic, 1982.
(Under pseudonym Janetta Johns) *The Truth About Me and Bobby V.,* Bantam, 1983.
Tommy Loves Tina, Berkley/Ace, 1984.

Winner Takes All, Berkley/Ace, 1984.
Wanted: Date for Saturday Night, Putnam, 1985.
Summer Heat, Fawcett, 1990.
Friends, Harper/Collins, 1991.

"Sweet Dreams" Series:

California Girl, Bantam, 1981.
Love Match, Bantam, 1982.
Ten-Boy Summer, Bantam, 1982.
Daydreamer, Bantam, 1983.
The Two of Us, Bantam, 1984.
Exchange of Hearts, Bantam, 1984.
Ghost of a Chance, Bantam, 1984.
Lovebirds, Bantam, 1984.
101 Ways to Meet Mr. Right, Bantam, 1985.
The Great Boy Chase, Bantam, 1985.
Follow That Boy, Bantam, 1985.
My Secret Love, Bantam, 1986.
My Best Enemy, Bantam, 1987.
Never Say Goodbye, Bantam, 1987.

"Sugar and Spice" Series:

Flip Side, Ballantine, 1987.
Tug of War, Ballantine, 1987.
Surf's Up, Ballantine, 1987.
The Last Dance, Ballantine, 1987.
Nothing in Common, Ballantine, 1987.
Dear Cousin, Ballantine, 1987.
Two Girls, One Boy, Ballantine, 1987.
Trading Places, Ballantine, 1987.
Double Take, Ballantine, 1988.
Make Me a Star, Ballantine, 1988.
Big Sister, Ballantine, 1988.
Out in the Cold, Ballantine, 1988.
Blind Date, Ballantine, 1988.
It's My Turn, Ballantine, 1988.
Home Sweet Home, Ballantine, 1988.
Dream Come True, Ballantine, 1988.
Campus Cousins, Ballantine, 1989.
Roadtrip, Ballantine, 1989.
One Step Too Far, Ballantine, 1989.
Having a Ball, Ballantine, 1989.

"On Our Own" Series:

On Our Own, Bantam, 1986.
The Graduates, Bantam, 1986.
The Trouble with Toni, Bantam, 1986.
Out of Love, Bantam, 1986.
Old Friends, New Friends, Bantam, 1986.
Best Friends Forever, Bantam, 1986.

"Heartbreak Cafe" Series:

No Experience Required, Fawcett, 1990.
The Main Attraction, Fawcett, 1990.

At Your Service, Fawcett, 1990.
Catch of the Day, Fawcett, 1990.
Love to Go, Fawcett, 1990.
Just Desserts, Fawcett, 1990.

Adult Novels:

Madam Sarah, Fawcett, 1990.
Fool's Gold, Harper/Collins, 1991.

Also author of several documentaries and four radio plays and scripts, including "Dandelion Hours," for the British Broadcasting Corp., 1966. Many of Quin-Harkin's young adult novels, including *California Girl, Love Match, Ten-Boy Summer* and *Daydreamer,* have been translated into other languages. Contributor to periodicals, including *Scholastic* and *Mother's Journal.*

■ **Work in Progress**

A mini-series for Harper/Collins, entitled *Senior Year.*

■ **Sidelights**

Growing up in Bath, England, Janet Quin-Harkin did not give much thought to becoming a writer someday, yet writing was very much a part of her youthful activities. "My mother says I wrote my first poem when I was four.

"I was movie-struck during my teens and created a film star persona for myself. Furthermore, I would put out a newspaper for myself reviewing all the movies I was in. I created movies filled with wonderful dramatic stories about lost love, being swept off cliffs, and all sorts of things. I wrote poetry in my teens, too, and saw my first short story published by sixteen.

"I attended a highly academic girls school in England and didn't meet boys until I went off to college, so all the customary emotional upheavals took place at a later age."[1]

After college Quin-Harkin took a job with the BBC and started writing radio and TV plays. "Those plays were fairly highbrow. One was called *Dandelion Hours,* about a little boy who befriended a hobo on a bomb site. From their little microcosm they relived an entire life cycle from birth to death. These works were all for adults, but it's interesting that the main character was a child in several of the plays, which makes me think that probably my interest was in that sphere even then."[1]

Quin-Harkin met her husband while in Australia working for the Australian Broadcasting Company;

the couple married in 1966 and moved to the United States. "That was still the time when your husband said 'move,' you moved. I didn't realize how bleak the broadcast situation was in the States. There was nothing comparable in the television world to the BBC. There was no 'Upstairs, Downstairs' being produced over here. And whatever was being done was being done in Los Angeles. We had moved to San Francisco.

"I wanted to do something creative. My first job was with a textbook company putting out a new series of school readers to replace the 'Here's Dick, here's Jane, here's their dog and we all live in a lovely suburb and we're all white and Daddy washes the car and Dick helps him.'

"The publishers realized that this text didn't apply to the majority of children. Many lived in an urban situation and they didn't have two-parent families and two cars in the driveway. The series was really aimed at big school districts like Chicago and Houston.

"We had a lot of minority folktales and stories about kids living in the city with various ethnic backgrounds—lots of black and white photographs. We also tried to fill in some of the social studies background that children probably didn't get at home; we'd take issues like the first flight across the country.

"It was very interesting as well as challenging because I had to work with a controlled vocabulary. It was like writing a crossword puzzle: you were only allowed to introduce two new words per page, and had to repeat each seven times."[1]

It was during this time that Quin-Harkin began to focus her ideas on her own children's book with *Peter Penny's Dance*. "It came from the lyrics of an old English folk song: 'I've come to claim a silver pound because I've danced the world around.' I liked that notion and worked on it. Farrar, Straus turned it down. Next I sent it to Dial Press, and they accepted it. I thought, 'This is pretty easy.' I didn't sell another thing for about five years, meanwhile learning my craft like everybody else.

"Of course, I was raising children throughout this time, and I was also trying to write picture books, gradually learning by trial and error what was right and what was not.

"*Peter Penny* won several awards and everybody decided I wasn't so bad after all. I started doing other picture books, several for Parents Magazine Press, of which *Benjamin's Balloon* was one. They were fun because Parents Magazine has an enor-

Illustration by Art Cummings from *Magic Growing Powder* by Janet Quin-Harkin.

mous readership, with a book club, and print runs of 100,000 copies. For a hardback, that's rather nice. It also means that kids really read your books.

"When I visit schools and tell kids that 'I wrote this book,' several of them will respond with 'Oh, I've got that.' That's also nice. This was especially the case when I was living in Texas, after my husband had been transferred. I found that you lack the wealth of creative talent that one finds in Marin County. If you talk at a school in California, some child will say, 'my dad works for George Lucas' or 'my mother writes screenplays.' But in Texas, a children's writer really stands out.

"Finding my agent was a real turning point in my career. She phoned one day and asked, 'Do you think you could write a teenage novel in a hurry?' 'Well, I don't know.' I said. 'I'll think about it.' 'You'll need to think fast,' she added. 'I'd like three chapters by next Tuesday.'

"I went to the local bookstore and came home with as many teenage books as I could find. It was relatively a new genre. I spread a couple out on the table. My husband walked past me, looked over my shoulder and said, 'You can't write that sort of stuff.' Something inside me said 'Hah,' and wrote the three chapters.

"They turned out to be the first chapters of *California Girl*, which was one of six books Bantam used to launch a line called 'Sweet Dreams.' It became the most popular series of teenage books ever.

"It was easy to write because it dealt with the experiences that my kids and their friends had gone through. The story involves a girl, living in Santa Barbara, who is training to be an Olympic swimmer. Her coach gets an offer of a really good position in Texas, so her family moves to Texas to be with him. This actually happened to a kid at our swim club.

"In California, swimming is regarded as an important pursuit that is taken quite seriously. But in Texas, where football is the only sport anyone cares about, swimming is considered pretty weird. So she's an outsider, isolated from her teammates, and forced to question her reasons for working at this. She meets a boy whose football career ended with an injury which left him crippled. He's also an outsider and very hostile. The two of them build a relationship, which gives both of them the confidence to overcome their problems. The story ends with her diving off the blocks in the Nationals.

"I found the style of writing teen novels really natural for me. More than half of my books are written in the first person, and I think those come across very fluidly. On the whole, first person is very effective because it doesn't ever become overly dramatic. And of course, when you're first person, you're right there with the character and it's very immediate.

"Sometimes first person is too limiting. You can't reveal things that the main character doesn't know, for instance, and you can't see scenes when the main character is not there.

"Young readers relate incredibly to the characters in these books. All the fan mail I get says, 'I knew just how Jenny felt because I've gone through the same thing'; or, 'that reminded me of the time when we did such-and-such. Would you do another book about so-and-so because I fell in love with what's-his-name just the same as she did.' They really feel these stories.

"Most of my books have an American theme and setting. I've done just a few that have been more international: one in which an English heroine comes to America to attend school, and a couple

that take place in Australia. But mostly they're American. I think that's because I only know American teenagers; I've had four of my own. And everything I know that's current about teenagers is American. Also, my largest audience is American.

"When the 'Sweet Dreams' series came out, it opened up a new direction in publishing. The books were cheap enough to buy once a week, even on an allowance, and they spoke very much to the lives of the readership. The stories were all happening then, to normal people in normal towns. Previously, young adult books had dealt with the darker side of reality—horrendous problems like heroin addiction and suicide. But they were also very severe and not relevant to every girl.

"'Sweet Dreams,' in contrast, was about the sort of lives that Middle America leads. What happens when we move? What happens when my best friends and I break up? What happens when my

Quin-Harkin's 1985 book.

parents break up? All the sort of things lots of kids go through. I've tried always to be very realistic. The ordinary girl never does get the football star. He's not going to look at her; he's going to look at that cute cheerleader instead. She's got to realize that and be happy with what she is.

"What this really meant was that for the first time the reader was buying the books. Until then it had always been a librarian or parent or some adult who bought the book for the child. Now, at last, the readers were dictating what they wanted to buy in books.

"The down side of this, of course, was that every single publishing house cashed in on it instantly. They flooded the market with much mediocrity. It starts with *First Love*, then *First Friends, First Date, Baby Sitters Club* and similar titles, all coming out over and over again. You look at bookshelves now and you have no way of telling from the covers

Cover from the 1989 Ballantine paperback.

what the content is, and too many times the content has been very poor, lacking any depth of characterization.

"Fortunately, I sell better than a lot of authors. Bookstores will buy because of my name, but certainly it's cut the pie very thin. *Ten-Boy Summer* sold more than 500,000 copies. Now, I get just over a hundred thousand in print but not much more.

"I've done, more or less, a book every two months since writing my first teen novel, which amounts to over fifty books now. We've got three children in college which means the economics were slightly important.

"For the past few years I've also done several series of my own: 'On Our Own' and 'Sugar and Spice' and 'The Heartbreak Cafe.' The six books in the series take place around a cafe on the beach and have the same characters. Each book focuses on one character, with the same girl and boy as a common thread.

"One of the books focuses on a girl from an affluent background, whose parents have just split up. Her father has gone to live on a beach to find himself, and her mother has gone back to school to find herself. Suddenly her support group is taken away from her and she has to redefine who she is. The books deal with drugs and runaways as well as lighter moments, but are all relevant situations.

"Writing a series is not as bad as it seems. If each book is 200 pages, it's like writing one very long novel. And you've got the 'givens'—the background and the characters. They're already in your mind. It's not the same as creating something new.

"The big problem is slipping into cliche. You know what a certain character says when they're startled. You know what a certain character always does to get a laugh. It's very easy to switch the cliche on when you bring in the character. I have to fight against that. The other thing I have to fight against is boredom.

"In the 'Sugar and Spice' books, I got really fed up with Chrissy and Caroline. First of all, the series went on much longer than I wanted. I did ten books, when I only wanted to do six. They kept insisting until it was easier to do it than not. I got really fed up with these characters because once you're over the concept that these two cousins are very different and they're each learning something else from the other's approach to life, there's nothing more to say. But I was forced to continue.

The 1989 Ballantine softcover.

"I went on quite happily with the 'Heartbreak Cafe' series because each book was so different. There were so many characters we were dealing with and each had his own set of problems."[1]

Quin-Harkin feels that television and radio influenced her writing. "I did a lot of radio in England and I'm very conscious of the spoken word. In fact, my books are nearly all dialogue. Everyone has said that my strength is my dialogue.

"I tend to think in terms of scenes rather than chapters. I see things almost like a movie storyboard, I see characters getting together in one environment, interacting, then cutting to another environment where something else happens."[1]

As for the future, "I would like to write plays again, and I have several movie script ideas I would love to do. My one problem in life is time. When a publishing house has an author that sells well, it

doesn't want to let that author go. As I'm coming to the end of one project, they'll say, 'Well, it's time to talk about what you want to do next.' Then I'm signed up for another year and a half, which is very nice for a writer, but it also means that I don't have time for other projects.

"I've done a couple of adult novels—something I always wanted to try. *Madam Sarah* came out in spring 1990 and I have finished my second one, *Fool's Gold.* You're not as restricted by length or by the knowledge that your reader gets easily bored. You can spend four or five pages on description if you want to, and you can flashback without confusing your reader. You can go into greater depth.

"Contemporary novels tend to focus on sex and violence. Obviously, I don't go out of my way to do that. It's nice to know that if it's integral to the plot, you don't have to skirt around these things in a dainty way, the way you do in teenage novels. Nonetheless, I haven't shied away from sex and violence in my teen books. When it's appropriate to the plot, I certainly bring it in.

"I don't think there is any moral code or responsibility built into the childrens' market at all. If you read, say, Judy Blume, some of her books carry no message. I personally try and stress responsibility. Obviously, I'm not writing books that deliberately preach. I want my characters to grow up able to make up their own minds. The most important value is a feeling of self-worth which enables you to make correct judgements. I certainly wouldn't say, 'All sex is wrong, remember that,' because obviously that's not going to be true for most of these girls.

"I want them to be able to say: 'I am my own person, I can judge what's best for me and nobody, not my peer group, not my parents, not anybody else can dictate how I feel. If it feels right for me, then it's got to be right.' I think that's how it has to be in these times.

"The 'Sweet Dreams' received a tremendous amount of criticism, especially from librarians who felt that the books were unrealistic. The feeling was that they portrayed girls in stable families getting boyfriends. They were too upbeat and did not show girls as positive role models. They had girls feeling all they needed in life was a boyfriend.

"Of course, I loved that. I point out that my books are not like that. For example, the second book I wrote had a girl who was so good at tennis that she has to play a boy for the number one spot on the boy's tennis team. She really likes this boy and she knows that he's got a very fragile ego and if she beats him, he's not going to like it. And she goes ahead and beats the pants off him. That's hardly a weak little female. I think romance is a very small part in the lives of all the females in my books. They have very full, rounded lives, and are often coping with difficulties.

"Writing these young adult books is as emotionally demanding for me as my adult novels. And, I think that I've been successful because I write what I want to write. I work very hard. Obviously, if I have to do 200 pages in two months, I have to. I work every day from about eight in the morning until I feel I've done enough for the day. When my fingers fly over that keyboard and I finish what I want to say by ten o'clock, that's it. I can't do anymore. After that, it starts to sound stale.

"I find that while driving the car, I can play out an entire scene in my head, almost as if I'm watching a movie. The next day, I find that I've memorized that scene, dialogue and all. If I'm deprived of that process, if I've had a day in which people don't stop bugging me, I find writing more difficult.

"I tend to focus on one project at a time because I really become involved with it. At the moment, I'm in the middle of an adult novel set in the Gold Rush, and in my mind I'm in the Gold Rush with it. It's a slow maturation process and little things dawn on me while I'm working. I might be in a Safeway grocery store and notice an apple and suddenly think, 'Oh, I must bring in the price of apples.'

"I like for everything to be accurate, so research is important. For example, I've set a book in Iowa, and although I've never lived there, I can draw on the knowledge I picked up on Middle America from living in Texas. I also have two friends who were born in Iowa, so I can suggest to them, 'Someone's walking down a road and it's the middle of June, what's blooming beside the road?' or 'What was it like when you were growing up?' I get a lot out of just talking to them."[1]

"Since the first time I crossed Europe alone at the age of thirteen, I feel restless if I don't wander every few months. I have visited most parts of the globe, including a three-month stay in Greece and. . . .four trips to India, which I find fascinating. My love of travel is reflected in everything I write. My characters can never stay in one place."[2]

"Both my adult novels are set in past times, one in Australia in the 1920s. I did a lot of research for both to make them historically accurate.

"My family lives in Australia and I used them quite mercilessly. I'd write to my mother and say, 'Okay, a ship is coming in July 10, 1920. What's it called?' She'd have to go to the old shipping registries and write back and tell me what it was. My brother duplicated pages out of magazines from those years so I could see advertisements, how much everything cost, and what was popular then.

"I'm still waiting for the high point in my career. I have a feeling it's not far out of my grasp now. The young adult books have made my name fairly well known among teens. I would also like my adult work to be well received.

"One of the thrills of producing books is seeing one of my novels in a place I didn't expect. For example, I was once at a news agent's in a small seaside town in Australia and found three of my titles on the book rack. That felt good. I have two friends who write movies and frequently mingle with people like Steven Spielberg and Harrison Ford. One night they began talking about me, when one of their daughters said, 'Janet Quin-Harkin? You know Janet Quin-Harkin?' This is success!

"The one gift I was given was a vivid imagination. I dream in full technicolor involving all my senses. Ideas have never been a problem for me.

"The one piece of advice I can give to an aspiring writer of teen fiction is to be in touch with young people today. It's no good writing from your own childhood. The emotions of your character *will* come from your own emotions, because everybody can remember what it was like to be betrayed by a best friend, and to be misunderstood by a teacher, these are all common experiences. However, it's no good expecting today's youth to be motivated or embarrassed by the same things that we were. So anybody who wants to write for teenagers has got to be in touch with today."[1]

Footnote Sources:

[1] Based on an interview by Chris Hunter for *Artists and Authors for Young Adults.*
[2] *Contemporary Authors, First Revision Series*, Volumes 81-84, Gale, 1979.

Lynne Reid Banks

B orn July 31, 1929, in London, England; daughter of James Reid (a doctor) and Muriel Banks (an actress; maiden name, Marsh); married Chaim Stephenson (a sculptor), 1965; children: Adiel, Gillon, Omri (sons). *Education:* Royal Academy of Dramatic Art, 1947-49. *Residence:* Dorset, England. *Agent:* Sheila Watson, Watson, Little Ltd., 12 Egbert St., London NW1 8LJ, England.

■ Career

Actress in English repertory companies, 1949-54; free-lance journalist, London, England, 1954-55; Independent Television News, London, television news reporter, 1955-57, television news scriptwriter, 1958-62; taught English as a foreign language in Israel, 1963-71; writer, 1971—. *Member:* Society of Authors (London).

■ Awards, Honors

Yorkshire Arts Literary Award, 1976, and selected one of American Library Association's Best Books for Young Adults, 1977, both for *Dark Quartet;* West Australian Young Readers' Book Award from the Library Association of Australia, 1980, for *My Darling Villain;* selected one of *New York Times* Outstanding Books of the Year, 1981, Young Reader's Choice Award from the Pacific Northwest Library Association, 1984, and California Young Readers Medal from the California Reading Association, 1985, Young Readers of Virginia Award, 1988, Arizona Young Readers' Award, 1988, and Rebecca Caudill Young Reader's Books Award from the Illinois Association for Media in Education, 1988, all for *The Indian in the Cupboard;* Parents' Choice Award for Literature from the Parents' Choice Foundation, 1986, selected one of *New York Times* Notable Books, 1986, and Indian Paintbrush Award from the Wyoming Library Association, 1989, all for *The Return of the Indian;* *The Indian in the Cupboard* was selected one of Child Study Association of America's Children's Books of the Year, 1986, and *The Return of the Indian,* 1987.

■ Writings

The L-Shaped Room (first book of trilogy), Chatto & Windus, 1960, Simon & Schuster, 1961, revised edition, Longman, 1977.

House of Hope, Simon & Schuster, 1962 (published in England as *An End to Running,* Chatto & Windus, 1962).

Children at the Gate, Simon & Schuster, 1968.

The Backward Shadow (second book of trilogy), Simon & Schuster, 1970.

The Kibbutz: Some Personal Reflections, Anglo-Israel Association, 1972.

One More River (young adult), Simon & Schuster, 1973.

Two Is Lonely (third book of trilogy), Simon & Schuster, 1974.

Sarah and After: The Matriarchs, Bodley Head, 1975, published as *Sarah and After: Five Women Who Founded a Nation*, Doubleday, 1977.

The Adventures of King Midas (juvenile; illustrated by George Him), Dent, 1976.

The Farthest-Away Mountain (juvenile; illustrated by Victor Ambrus), Abelard Schuman, 1976, Doubleday, 1977, reissued, Doubleday, 1990.

Dark Quartet: The Story of the Brontes, Weidenfeld & Nicholson, 1976, Delacorte, 1977.

My Darling Villain, Harper, 1977, large print edition, ABC-CLIO, 1989.

Path to the Silent Country: Charlotte Bronte's Years of Fame, Weidenfeld & Nicholson, 1977, Delacorte, 1978.

I, Houdini: The Autobiography of a Self-Educated Hamster (juvenile; illustrated by Terry Riley), Dent, 1978, Doubleday, 1988.

Letters to My Israeli Sons: The Story of Jewish Survival (young adult), H. W. Allen, 1979, F. Watts, 1980.

The Indian in the Cupboard (juvenile; Junior Literary selection; illustrated by Robin Jacques), Dent, 1980, (illustrated by Brock Cole), Doubleday, 1981.

The Writing on the Wall (young adult), Chatto & Windus, 1981, Harper, 1982.

Defy the Wilderness, Chatto & Windus, 1981.

Torn Country: An Oral History of the Israeli War of Independence, F. Watts, 1982.

Maura's Angel (juvenile; illustrated by Robin Jacques), Dent, 1984.

The Warning Bell, Hamish Hamilton, 1984, St. Martin's, 1986.

The Fairy Rebel (juvenile; illustrated by William Geldart), Dent, 1985, Doubleday, 1988, large print edition, Cornerstone Books, 1989.

The Return of the Indian (juvenile; sequel to *The Indian in the Cupboard*; Junior Literary Guild selection; illustrated by W. Geldart), Doubleday, 1986, large print edition, Cornerstone Books, 1989.

Casualties, Hamish Hamilton, 1986.

Melusine: A Mystery (young adult), Hamish Hamilton, 1988, Harper, 1989.

The Secret of the Indian (juvenile), Collins, 1988, Doubleday, 1989.

Plays:

It Never Rains (televised, BBC-TV, 1954; produced in repertories), Deane, 1954.

All in a Row, Deane, 1956.

The Killer Dies Twice (three-act), Deane, 1956.

Already It's Tomorrow (televised, BBC-TV, 1962), Samuel French, 1962.

"The Unborn," produced in London, England, at Vaudeville Theatre, 1962.

"The Wednesday Caller" (television play), BBC-TV, London, 1963.

"The Last Word on Julie" (television play), ATV, London, 1964.

"The Gift" (three-act), first produced in London, England, 1965.

"The Stowaway" (radio play), BBC, London, 1967.

"The Eye of the Beholder" (television play), ITV, London, 1977.

"Lame Duck" (radio play), BBC, London, 1978.

"Purely from Principal" (radio play), BBC Radio, 1985.

Author of additional radio and television plays. Contributor to periodicals, including *McCall's, Ladies' Home Journal, Observer, Guardian, Sunday Telegraph, Independent,* and *Marie-Claire.*

■ Adaptations

"The L-Shaped Room" (motion picture), starring Leslie Caron, Davis-Royal Films, 1962.

■ Work in Progress

The Magic Hare, twelve stories for young children; an adult novel.

■ Sidelights

Lynne Reid Banks was born in London, England, on July 31, 1929. "How ungallant to publish one's birthday, but the Library of Congress has it in every blooming book, so I suppose there's not much I can do about it."[1]

"I was the only child of highly contrasted and interesting parents. My father was a Scottish doctor who'd been born in India; my mother was a gifted actress, once a star of the London stage, born in Dublin, she'd lived through the Easter Rebellion, about which—among many other fascinating subjects—she told me exciting stories. Because of those she told me about her stage career, there was never a doubt in my mind that I would become an actress. Drama and English were the only school subjects I cared about or in which I was any good. I was definitely a 'C' student in everything else.

"For some odd reason, my parents sent me to a Catholic convent in the country when I was nine and I spent two strange years there....The location was quite beautiful and, as war approached and strict school routines slackened, the girl-pupils were given a lot of freedom to play in the bluebell woods. We formed a secret society called 'The League of the Deadly Nightshade' whose chief function was to waylay Canadian soldiers from the nearby camp and make them recite or otherwise pay a forfeit. The nuns would have had fits, though it was all entirely innocent and enormous fun."[2]

As for most English children, the war years meant upheaval. "I was evacuated to Canada for five years during the war. In fact, since my mother was evacuated with me, I was very happy, and though we were poor, I hardly noticed it, except that I couldn't have fashionable clothes. I didn't really realise what the war meant, or the terrible things that had been happening, until I got back to England, at the very formative age of fifteen. I found my city in ruins, and learned what had been happening to my family, left behind, and, in Europe, to the Jews. I felt like a deserter."[1] Those feelings left an indelible mark on Banks.

She studied for the stage, acted in repertories for five years, and was then hired by Independent Television News as the first British female news reporter. She worked at Independent Television News for seven years, doing her own writing concurrently as she always had.

Banks published her first book, an adult novel, entitled *The L-Shaped Room* in 1960. The book told the story of a single, pregnant woman rejected by her father, who finds both new friends and a new lover in a dreary boarding house. Banks now feels that the book presented an overly-optimistic view of single parenthood. "Having a baby on your own seemed at the time to me to be rather glamorous....I am still fascinated by...single parenthood—I've written four novels about it. I'm fascinated now I have children of my own, because I don't know how anyone does it."[3]

"My feelings about this are recorded in my book *Letters to My Israeli Sons*, which I wrote as a justification of Zionism. Throughout my late teens and twenties, when Israel was going through its early traumas, I had a great desire to go there. But it was not until my first book was bought that I had

the time or the money—or felt myself properly prepared—to do so.

"My views were simple and perhaps over-romanticised. After centuries of persecution, climaxing with the Holocaust in my own lifetime, the Jews had fought for and established a place from which to defend themselves and create a normal nation. It seemed to me inevitable and right. It also seemed inevitable that I should go there and have some small share of it.

"Through that first visit in October, 1960, I was to meet my husband, and my life was to turn off at a tangent. Perhaps emigrating to Israel, living in a kibbutz, working the land, teaching and having my babies in that 'alien' country that I came to love so much, was a sublimation for my lingering feelings of guilt for having missed the War."[1]

A new career, teaching English to Hebrew-speaking children, occupied her for the following eight years. "Teaching children a new language, when you don't speak theirs, requires one ability above

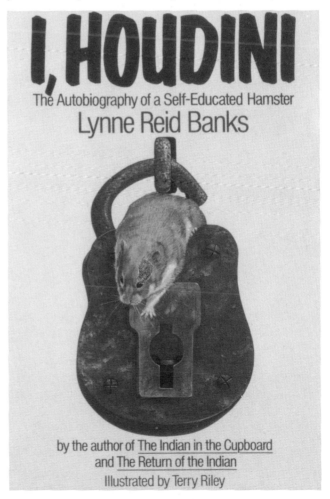

Jacket of the 1988 Doubleday edition.

all: the ability to act. The techniques which had done me so little good when I had tried to earn a living on the stage, now came into their own. And now the techniques I learned as a teacher help me when it comes to talking in schools in Britain and America, which I now do a great deal. Everything I've ever learnt or done has fed into something else."[1]

Banks and her husband returned to England in 1972 with their three little sons. She wrote two sequels to *The L-Shaped Room*, *The Backward Shadow* and *Two Is Lonely*, then began interspersing adult writing with books for younger readers. "Writing for young people is, in some ways, much pleasanter than writing for adults. My mother had a theory that all the ages we have ever been are still shut up inside us. There is the three-year-old you, the ten-year-old you, the teenage you...all of which you can 'tap' for feelings and information if you can just keep in touch with them. All the childme's have been brought out for exercise since I began writing for different age groups. I especially enjoy writing wish-fulfillment tales for younger

Jacket from the 1986 St. Martin's edition.

children in which real, everyday life co-exists with magic."[2]

Banks now divides her time between her country house in Dorset, and a small house in West London. She continues to write books and has done a good deal of journalism, publishing polemical (argumentative!) articles in British newspapers, about politics, the state of British life, travel, Israel, and personal relationships. She travels a lot, having recently visited Zimbabwe, Tanzania, and Nepal. She comes to the United States at least once every year.

"The trick of writing fiction is much akin to the trick of good acting. You have to get into other minds, speak through other mouths, move with other bodies, feel with other hearts. Of course it helps if you can write well. I don't think that's something, basically, that can be taught. You've got it or you haven't, though you can always learn more and improve.

Dust jacket of the multi-award-winning novel.

"The Trumpet Club asked for a quote to put on a personalised bookmark. I said, 'Writing helps me live other lives besides mine.' I've noticed that some people don't understand what this means. They seem to think it's an affectation. But these people are usually non-readers. Readers understand at once, because they know how, through reading, you can live other lives. Doing the creative part of this partnership means living other lives far more intensely, because it's active, not passive.

"I never set out to write a 'message' book, because the function of the novelist is to tell stories, to involve the reader in the lives of made-up characters. But inevitably, my personal philosophy, which basically means what I've learned from sixty years of living, informs everything I do, and occasionally my own opinions and feelings creep in. I can write about people, very different from me—a very religious person, for instance, like Charlotte Bronte in *Dark Quartet,* or a neurotic drunkard like Gerda in *Children at the Gate*—but I couldn't live, for all the months and months it takes to write a book, with a heroine or hero that I found actively dislikable. I have, not only to understand my characters well, but to find them mainly sympathetic."[1]

Banks has found writing for the American market to be slightly different from the British. "In Britain, we make fewer allowances for our child readers. We expect them to accept a good deal of description, to go patiently along with us while we open the story at our own pace. We don't make many concessions in terms of 'long words' or even a little bad language. I have plenty of trouble with that in America, despite the fact that most of my four letter words were learned from American films and television! In schools, everybody is very pure-mouthed. If I have a rough cowboy say, 'Aw, hell,' I get letters from Tennessee saying, 'Please leave all those rude words out because Jesus doesn't like it.' I think Jesus might have more important things to worry about. Writers should write the way people really talk. I realise it's a tricky area. It sounds bad when kids swear. But characterisation seems to me to be more important.

"When *The Indian in the Cupboard* was first published in America, I had to fight for every word over three syllables. I remember a battle royal over the word 'magnanimously.' 'The kids will never know what that means,' the publishers said. 'How will they ever find out if they never read it?' I won that one, but lost others. You'll notice, if you look in that first book that most 'Britishisms' were

The 1988 Doubleday edition.

removed. By the time *Secret of the Indian* came along, eight years later, the publishers had begun to accept that American children are as capable of absorbing differences in culture, long words, and descriptions as children elsewhere. Also, teachers and librarians were beginning to make it clear that they wanted what they called 'whole literature,' so the third book in the series is more or less unexpurgated!

"I don't simplify consciously when I'm writing for young readers, but unconsciously I think I 'tune in' to the age I am writing for. Within those parameters, I use the language I need to describe character and incident. Since English is a very rich language, this means that books written with a twelve-year-old as the hero or heroine, are intended to be read by people of about that age. Not younger. It upsets me when *The Indian in the Cupboard* is read to children of six, seven and eight—they won't get the most out of it. I've written books for younger children, such as *The Fairy Rebel* and *The Adventures of King Midas*, and soon, my book of tales of magic hare. These are stories intended for young listeners.

"My attitude toward writing is very mixed. I regard it as the hardest, loneliest work in the world, and except for those very rare moments when it 'takes off,' I get no satisfaction until it is done. But there is no doubt that, while other forms of writing (such as plays) give more immediate excitement and stimulation because you see their effect on others, and because you get to work with others, still there is nothing to beat holding your own book in your hands. Plays 'fade away,' but books can go on forever. The memory of those that have struck deep into people's minds can go on and on, too. The thought that my books might go on being read after I'm gone is more exciting to me than going to heaven. It's the only kind of immortality I recognise."[1]

Footnote Sources:

[1] Based on an interview by Marc Caplan for *Something about the Author*.
[2] Anne Commire, editor, *Something about the Author*, Volume 22, Gale, 1981.
[3] Deborah H. Straub, editor, *Contemporary Authors: New Revision Series*, Volume 22, Gale, 1988.

■ For More Information See

New Statesman, November 12, 1960 (p. 754), July 26, 1968 (p. 116), April 18, 1975, October 16, 1981 (p. 24ff).

New York Times Book Review, April 9, 1961 (p. 38), May 12, 1968 (p. 40ff), November 8, 1970 (p. 53), October 16, 1977, October 11, 1981, November 9, 1986.
New Yorker, June 8, 1968.
Punch, August 7, 1968.
Books and Bookmen, September, 1968, November, 1976.
Observer, August 9, 1970, April 7, 1974.
Times Literary Supplement, March 22, 1974 (p. 282), December 10, 1976, March 25, 1977, October 2, 1981 (p. 118), August 24, 1984, October 3, 1986, October 17, 1986.
Listener, April 11, 1974.
Horn Book, August, 1977, October, 1977.
Commonweal, November 11, 1977.
Times Educational Supplement, November 24, 1978.
Wilson Library Bulletin, March, 1982 (pg. 632ff).
Contemporary Literary Criticism, Volume 23, Gale, 1983.
D. L. Kirkpatrick, editor, *Twentieth-Century Children's Writers*, 2nd edition, St. Martin's, 1983.
Times (London), August 13, 1984.
Humphrey Carpenter and Mari Prichard, *The Oxford Companion to Children's Literature*, Oxford University Press, 1984.
Washington Post Book World, November 9, 1986.
Los Angeles Times, December 27, 1986.
Paul Schueler and June Schueler, editors, *An Encyclopedia of British Women Writers*, Garland, 1988.
Sally Holmes Holtze, editor, *Sixth Book of Junior Authors and Illustrators*, H. W. Wilson, 1989.

Collections:

Boston University.

Kurt Vonnegut

Born November 11, 1922, in Indianapolis, Ind.; son of Kurt (an architect) and Edith (Lieber) Vonnegut; married Jane Marie Cox, September 1, 1945 (divorced, 1979); married Jill Krementz (a photographer), November, 1979; children: (first marriage) Mark, Edith, Nanette; (adopted deceased sister's children) James, Steven, and Kurt Adams; (second marriage) Lily (adopted). *Education:* Attended Cornell University, 1940-42, and Carnegie Institute of Technology (now Carnegie-Mellon University), 1943; University of Chicago, student, 1945-47, M.A., 1971. *Residence:* New York, N.Y. *Attorney/Agent:* Donald C. Farber, Tanner, Propp, Fersko & Sterner, 99 Park Ave., 25th Floor, New York, N.Y. 10016.

■ Career

Chicago City News Bureau, Chicago, Ill., police reporter, 1947; General Electric Co., Schenectady, N.Y., public relations writer, 1947-50; free-lance writer, 1950—; Hopefield School, Sandwich, Mass., teacher, 1965—; City College of the City University of New York, New York, N.Y., Distinguished Professor of English Prose, 1973-74. Lecturer at University of Iowa Writers Workshop, 1965-67, and at Harvard University, 1970-71; actor in several films, including "Between Time and Timbuktu," 1972, "Back to School," Orion, 1986, "Storytellers: PEN Celebration," 1987, and "That Day in November," 1988. Speaker, National Coalition against Censorship briefing for the Attorney General's Commission on Pornography hearing, 1986. One-man exhibition of drawings, 1980. *Military service:* U.S. Army, Infantry, 1942-45; was POW; received Purple Heart. *Member:* Authors League of America, PEN (American Center; vice-president, 1972), National Institute of Arts and Letters, Delta Upsilon, Barnstable Yacht Club, Barnstable Comedy Club.

■ Awards, Honors

Guggenheim Fellow, Germany, 1967; National Institute of Arts and Letters Grant, 1970; Litt.D., Hobart and William Smith Colleges, 1974; *Slaughterhouse Five* was selected one of American Library Association's Best Books for Young Adults, 1975, and *Jailbird*, 1979; *Jailbird* was selected one of New York Public Library's Books for the Teen Age, 1980, and *Slaughterhouse Five,* 1980, 1981, and 1982; Literary Lion from the New York Public Library, 1981; Eugene V. Debs Award from the Eugene V. Debs Foundation, 1981, for public service; Freedom to Read Award from Playboy Enterprises and the Friends of the Chicago Public Library, 1982, for his support against the suppression of books and his work to preserve First Amendment rights; Emmy Award for Outstanding Children's Program from the National Academy of Television Arts and Sciences, 1985, for "Displaced Person."

■ Writings

Novels:

Player Piano, Scribner, 1952, published as
  Utopia 14, Bantam, 1954, new edition, Holt,
  1966, reissued, Dell, 1981.
The Sirens of Titan, Dell, 1959, reissued, 1967.
Mother Night, Gold Medal Books, 1961,
  (hardcover) Harper, 1966.
Cat's Cradle, Holt, 1963.
*God Bless You, Mr. Rosewater; or, Pearls before
  Swine,* Holt, 1965.
*Slaughterhouse Five; or, The Children's Crusade:
  A Duty-Dance with Death, by Kurt Vonnegut,
  Jr., a Fourth-Generation German-American
  Now Living in Easy Circumstances on Cape
  Cod (and Smoking Too Much) Who, as an
  American Infantry Scout Hors de Combat, as a
  Prisoner of War, Witnessed the Fire-Bombing
  of Dresden, Germany, the Florence of the
  Elbe, a Long Time Ago, and Survived to Tell
  the Tale: This Is a Novel Somewhat in the
  Telegraphic Schizophrenic Manner of Tales of
  the Planet Tralfamadore, Where the Flying
  Saucers Come From,* Seymour Lawrence/
  Delacorte, 1969.
*Breakfast of Champions; or, Goodbye Blue
  Monday,* Seymour Lawrence/Delacorte, 1973.
Slapstick; or, Lonesome No More!, Seymour
  Lawrence/Delacorte, 1976.
Jailbird, Seymour Lawrence/Delacorte, 1979.
Deadeye Dick, Seymour Lawrence/Delacorte,
  1982.
Galapagos: A Novel, Seymour Lawrence/
  Delacorte, 1985.
Bluebeard, Delacorte, 1987, large print edition,
  J. Curley, 1988.
Hocus Pocus, Putnam, 1990.

Short Fiction:

Canary in a Cathouse, Fawcett, 1961.
*Welcome to the Monkey House: A Collection of
  Short Works,* Seymour Lawrence/Delacorte,
  1968.
Who Am I This Time? For Romeos and Juliets
  (illustrated by Michael McCurdy), Redpath
  Press.

Plays:

"Penelope," first produced in Cape Cod, Mass.,
  1960, revised version published as *Happy
  Birthday, Wanda June* (first produced Off-
  Broadway at the Theater de Lys, October 7,
  1970), Seymour Lawrence/Delacorte, 1971,
  revised edition, S. French, 1971.

*Between Time and Timbuktu; or, Prometheus
  Five: A Space Fantasy* (television play; first
  produced on National Educational Television
  Network, 1972), Seymour Lawrence/
  Delacorte, 1972.

Also author of "Something Borrowed," 1958,
"The Very First Christmas Morning," 1962, "EPI-
CAC," 1963, "My Name Is Everyone," 1964, and
"Fortitude," 1968, all produced Off-Broadway or
in summer stock.

Other:

Wampeters, Foma, and Granfalloons: (Opinions)
  (essays), Seymour Lawrence/Delacorte, 1974.
(With Ivan Chermayeff) *Sun, Moon, Star*
  (juvenile), Harper, 1980.
Palm Sunday: An Autobiographical Collage,
  Seymour Lawrence/Delacorte, 1981.
(Contributor) *Bob and Ray: A Retrospective,
  June 15-July 10, 1982,* Museum of
  Broadcasting, 1982.
(Contributor) W. E. Block and M. A. Walker,
  editors, *Discrimination, Affirmative Action,
  and Equal Opportunity: An Economic and
  Social Perspective,* Fraser Institute, 1982.
Nothing Is Lost Save Honor: Two Essays
  (contains "The Worst Addiction of Them All"
  and "Fates Worth Than Death: Lecture at St.
  John the Divine, New York City, May 23,
  1982"), Toothpaste Press, 1984.

Contributor of fiction to numerous periodicals,
including *Saturday Evening Post, Collier's, Galaxy
Science Fiction, Magazine of Fantasy and Science
Fiction, Esquire, Cosmopolitan, McCall's, Playboy,*
and *Ladies' Home Journal.* Editor and contributor,
Cornell Daily Sun, 1941-42.

■ Adaptations

"Happy Birthday, Wanda June" (film), starring
  Rod Steiger and Susannah York, Red Lion,
  1971.
"Slaughterhouse Five " (film), starring Michael
  Sachs and Ron Leibman, Universal, 1972.
"Who Am I This Time?" (film; based on short
  story), Rubicon Films, 1982.
"Slapstick of Another Kind." (film; based on
  Slapstick), starring Jerry Lewis and Madeleine
  Kahn, Paul-Serendipity, 1984.
"Displaced Person" (film; based on short story
  "D.P."), Hemisphere, 1985.
"Slaughterhouse Five" (abridged; cassette),
  Listening for Pleasure, 1985.

"Jailbird" (cassette), Warner Audio Publishers, 1985.

"Breakfast of Champions" (abridged; cassette), Caedmon.

"Cat's Cradle" (cassette), Books on Tape, (abridged; cassette), Caedmon.

"Galapagos" (cassette), Simon & Schuster.

"Slapstick" (cassettes; includes "Mother Night"), Books on Tape.

"The Sirens of Titan" (cassette), Books on Tape.

"Welcome to the Monkey House" (cassette), Books on Tape.

"Vonnegut Soundbook" (record; cassette; includes "Breakfast of Champions," "Cat's Cradle," "Slaughterhouse Five," and "Welcome to the Monkey House"), Caedmon.

"Kurt Vonnegut, Jr. Reads Slaughterhouse Five" (excerpts; cassette), Caedmon.

■ Sidelights

A fourth-generation German, Vonnegut was born into a prominent Indianapolis family. "[My mother] was born very wealthy, a brewer's daughter out there in Indianapolis, and was one of the richest women in town—quite a catch for my father, an architect. Architects customarily don't make that much money and need to marry rich wives—which they usually get, incidentally."[1]

"I was born into a house which was designed and built by my father in 1922, the year of my birth. It was so full of treasures that it was like a museum, and it was meant to be inherited by my brother, my sister, or me. I would not like to live there. Edwardian lives of a sort were conducted there for seven years. That isn't a long period of time, you know. To my parents, who were great lovers of music, it must have been as though a full orchestra had played the first seven bars of a symphony, and then gone home.

"The anti-Germanism in this country during the First World War so shamed and dismayed my parents that they resolved to raise me without acquainting me with the language or the literature or the music or the oral family histories which my ancestors had loved. They volunteered to make me ignorant and rootless as proof of their patriotism.

"This was done with surprising meekness by many, many German-American families in Indianapolis, it seems to me."[2]

Until age ten, Vonnegut was essentially raised by Ida Young, a black woman who cooked and did general housework for the family. "A thing which is not acknowledged when the black problem is discussed is that these people are largely white. They're really relatives of ours and they're part of the white race. She surely was. She was a very bright black woman who must have been aware that she was mostly white. This is never discussed. She was humane and wise and gave me decent moral instruction and was exceedingly nice to me. So she was as great an influence on me as anybody.

"The compassionate, forgiving aspects of my beliefs came from Ida Young...and from my parents, too. They were not vengeful people; that much I've learned. Revenge is a very poor idea. Of course, we have this huge literature which is driven by revenge. So many stories so depend upon revenge as a setting. It's the person who's going to settle old scores. But it's never a good idea and that much I've learned. If it were a good idea I'd be all for it."[3]

"My father had few gifts for getting along famously with me. That's life. We did not spend much time together, and conversations were arch and distant. But Father's younger brother, Uncle Alex, a Harvard graduate and life insurance salesman, was responsive and amusing and generous with me, was my ideal grown-up friend."[2]

"[My mother] was a highly intelligent, cultivated woman....She went to the same high school I did, and was one of the few people who got nothing but A-plusses while she was there. She went East to a finishing school after that, and then traveled all over Europe. She was fluent in German and French. I still have her high school report cards somewhere. 'A-plus, A-plus....' She was a good writer, it turned out, but she had no talent for the vulgarity the slick magazines required. Fortunately, I was loaded with vulgarity, so, when I grew up, I was able to make her dream come true. Writing for *Collier's* and *The Saturday Evening Post* and *Cosmopolitan* and *Ladies' Home Journal* and so on was as easy as falling off a log for me. I only wish she'd lived to see it."[4]

"I got to be a joke-maker as the youngest member of my family. My sister was five years older than I was, my brother was nine years older, and at the dinner table I was the lowest ranking thing there. I could not be interesting to these vivid grownups. My sister was a sculptress and doing extremely well, my brother was a scientist, my father was an architect, and so they had really big time stuff to argue about. I wanted to talk in order to learn how to do it, to engage in give and take, and I must have made accidental jokes at first. Everyone does. It's a chancy thing, it's a spoonerism or something of that sort. But anyway it stopped the adult conversation for a minute. And I understood the terms under which I could buy my way into the conversations, small as I was. So I got awfully good at making jokes, and I became an avid reader of humor books. I listened to radio comedians who were brilliant during the thirties and found out that what made them so damn funny was how their jokes were timed.

"This has slowed me down as a writer, because I can only write jokes. Jokes are efficient things and they must be as carefully constructed as mouse traps. And so for me to write a page of a novel is a very slow business, because the whole thing has to be rigged in order to snap at the end. My books are essentially mosaics, thousands and thousands of tiny little chips all glued together, and each chip is this thing I learned to do—this thing I learned to make as a child—which is a little joke."[5]

The 1929 Depression greatly affected the family fortune. "My mother thought she might make a new fortune by writing for the slick magazines. She took short story courses at night. She studied magazines the way gamblers study racing forms.

"And my father painted pictures in a studio he'd set up on the top floor of the house. There wasn't much work for architects during the Great Depression—not much work for anybody. Strangely enough, though, Mother was right: Even mediocre magazine writers were making money hand over fist."[4]

"But anyway, by 1930 when it was obvious everything was gone and wasn't going to come back, I got pulled out of an elitist private school...and sent to a public high school."[1]

"Was I a sad child, knowing how rich my family had been? Not at all. We were at least as well off as most of the people I went to public school with, and I would have lost all my friends if we had started having servants again, and worn expensive clothes again, and ridden on ocean liners and visiting German relatives in a real castle, and on and on. Mother, who was half-cracked, used to speak of the time when I would resume my proper place in society when the Great Depression ended, would swim with members of other leading families at the Indianapolis Athletic Club, would play tennis and golf with them at the Woodstock Golf and Country Club. She could not understand that

to give up my friends at Public school No. 43, 'the James Whitcomb Riley school,' by the way, would be for me to give up *everything*.

"I still feel uneasy about prosperity and associating with members of my parents' class on that account.

"Henry David Thoreau said, 'I have traveled extensively in Concord.' That quotation was probably first brought to my attention by one of my magnificent teachers in high school. Thoreau, I now feel, wrote in the voice of a child, as do I. And what he said about Concord is what every child feels, what every child seemingly *must* feel, about the place where he or she was born. There is surely more than enough to marvel at for a lifetime where the child is born.

"Castles? Indianapolis was full of them."[2]

While still in high school, "Phoebe Hurty hired me to write copy for ads about teen-age clothes. I had to wear the clothes I praised. That was part of the job. And I became friends with her two sons, who were my age. I was over at their house all the time.

"She would talk bawdily to me and her sons, and to our girlfriends when we brought them around. She was funny. She was liberating. She taught us to be impolite in conversation not only about sexual matters, but about American history and famous heroes, about the distribution of wealth, about school, about everything.

"I now make my living by being impolite. I am clumsy at it. I keep trying to imitate the impoliteness which was so graceful in Phoebe Hurty. I think now that grace was easier for her than it is for me because of the mood of the Great Depression. She believed what so many Americans believed then: that the nation would be happy and just and rational when prosperity came.

"I never hear that word anymore: *Prosperity*. It used to be a synonym for *Paradise*. And Phoebe Hurty was able to believe that the impoliteness she recommended would give shape to an American paradise.

"Now her sort of impoliteness is fashionable. But nobody believes anymore in a new American paradise. I sure miss Phoebe Hurty."[6]

After high school Vonnegut entered Cornell University and majored in chemistry at the insistence of his father. "I wasn't sure I wanted to go to college at all. I had hopes of being a journalist, maybe going to work for the Indianapolis *News*. The problem was, I didn't look old enough to be a very effective reporter. So I had complied with my

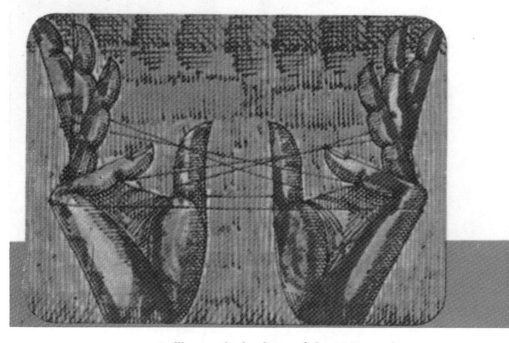

BY THE BEST-SELLING AUTHOR OF
BLUEBEARD

KURT VONNEGUT

CAT'S CRADLE

DELL • 11149-8 • U.S. $4.95 CAN. $6.95

Dell's paperback edition of the 1963 novel.

parents' wishes, but having no gift for science, came close to being ejected from Cornell for academic reasons."[7]

"I'm glad, though, now that I was pressured into becoming a scientist. . . .I understand how scientific reasoning and playfulness work, even though I have no talent for joining in. I enjoy the company of scientists, am easily excited and entertained when they tell me what they're doing. I've spent a lot more time with scientists than with literary people."[4]

"I do see myself as an 'instructed' writer, and there aren't many producing authors who would confess to such a thing. What I mean is: I went to a high school that put out a daily newspaper and, because I was writing for my peers and not for teachers, it was very important to me that they understand what I was saying. So the simplicity, and that's not a bad word for it, of my writing was caused by the fact that my audience was composed of sophomores, juniors and seniors. In addition, the idea of

an uncomplicated style was very much in the air back then—clarity, shorter sentences, strong verbs, a de-emphasis of adverbs and adjectives, that sort of thing. Because I believed in the merits of this type of prose, I was quite 'teachable' and so I worked hard to achieve as pure a style as I could. When I got to Cornell my experiences on a daily paper—and daily high school papers were unheard of back then—enabled me to become a big shot on Cornell's *Daily Sun*. I suppose it was the consistent involvement with newspaper audiences that fashioned my style.

"The people who were senior to me at the *Sun* were full of advice and, again, it had to do with clarity, economy, and so forth. The theory was that large, sprawling paragraphs tended to discourage readers and make the paper appear ugly. Their strategy was primarily visual—that is, short paragraphs, often one-sentence paragraphs. It seemed to work very well, seemed to serve both me and the readers, so I stayed with it when I decided to

Vonnegut wrote the screenplay for "Happy Birthday, Wanda June" which starred Rod Steiger as a man returning after eight years in the Amazon jungle.

make a living as a fiction writer. The magazines were thriving then and the editors knew a good deal about story telling. You could talk to an editor of the *Saturday Evening Post* or *Collier's* and you would find that much of what they were saying was a paraphrase of Aristotle's *Poetics*. And keep in mind that you had to do what they told you to do or you couldn't sell them a story. To a great extent they wanted the same thing a good newspaper wants: an arresting lead, lucid prose, an immediate sense of place. When I teach now I frequently get annoyed when I get four paragraphs into a story and still don't know what city, or even what century, the characters are in. I have a right to be annoyed too. A reader has a right, and a need, to learn immediately what sort of people he's encountering, what sort of locale they're in, what they do for a living, whether they're rich or poor—all of these things make subsequent information that much more marvelous. So I was drilled from the start in basic journalistic techniques and, in a very real sense, my instructors were masters at their craft. I hope I'm making this clear: these editors were neither tyrannical nor contemptible. They were dedicated, knowledgeable professionals. My point, then, is that I was taught to write the way I do. In fact, I've had a lot more lessons than most writers have."[8]

After the Japanese invaded Pearl Harbor, Vonnegut volunteered for military service. "The Army sent me to Carnegie Tech and the University of Tennessee to study mechanical engineering—thermodynamics, mechanics, the actual use of machine tools, and so on. I did badly again. I am very used to failure, to being at the bottom of every class.

"An Indianapolis cousin of mine, who was also a high school classmate, did very badly at the University of Michigan while I did badly at Cornell. His father asked him what the trouble was, and he made what I consider an admirable reply: 'Don't you know, Father? I'm dumb!' It was the truth.

"I did badly in the Army, remaining a preposterously tall private for the three years I served. I was a good soldier, an especially deadly marksman, but nobody thought to promote me. I learned all the dances of close-order drill. Nobody in the Army could dance better than I could in ranks."[2]

In May 1944, Vonnegut obtained special leave to go home for Mother's Day. The night before he arrived, his mother, who had suffered from depression, died of an overdose of sleeping pills. Three months later he was sent overseas and, on Decem-ber 2, 1944, was captured by German troops at the Battle of the Bulge. He spent the rest of the war as a prisoner in Dresden, Germany. "My last mission as a scout was to find our own artillery. Usually, scouts go out and look for enemy stuff. Things got so bad that we were finally looking for our own stuff. If I'd found our own batallion commander, everybody would have thought that was pretty swell.

"We were in this gully about as deep as a World War I trench. There was snow all around, somebody said we were probably in Luxembourg. We were out of food.

"The Germans could see us, because they were talking to us through a loudspeaker. They told us our situation was hopeless, and so on. That was when we fixed bayonets. It was nice there for a few minutes.

"They sent in eighty-eight millimeter shells.... The shells burst in the treetops right over us. Those were very loud bangs right over our heads. We were showered with splintered shell. Some people got hit. Then the Germans told us again to come out. We didn't yell 'nuts' or anything like that. We said, 'Okay,' and 'Take it easy,' and so on. When the Germans finally showed themselves, we saw they were wearing white camouflage suits. We didn't have anything like that. We were olive drab. No matter what season it was, we were olive drab.

"They said the war was all over for us, that we were lucky, that we could now be sure we would live through the war, which was more than they could be sure of. As a matter of fact, they were probably killed or captured by Patton's Third Army within the next few days. Wheels within wheels.

"I tried a few words I knew on our captors, and they asked me if I was of German ancestry, and I said, 'Yes.' They wanted to know why I was making war against my brothers.

"I honestly found the question ignorant and comical. My parents had separated me so thoroughly from my Germanic past that my captors might as well have been Bolivians or Tibetans, for all they meant to me.

"[We were shipped to Dresden] in the same boxcars that had brought up the troops that captured us—probably in the same boxcars that had delivered Jews and Gypsies and Jehovah's Witnesses and so on to the extermination camps. Rolling stock is rolling stock. British mosquito bombers attacked us at night a few times. I guess they thought we were strategic materials of some kind. They hit a car containing most of the officers from our batallion. Every time I say I hate officers, which I still do fairly frequently, I have to remind myself that practically none of the officers I served under survived.

"[Dresden was] the first fancy city I'd ever seen. A city full of statues and zoos, like Paris. We were living in a slaughterhouse, in a nice new cement-block hog barn. They put bunks and straw mattresses in the barn, and we went to work every morning as contract labor in a malt syrup factory. The syrup was for pregnant women. The damned sirens would go off and we'd hear some other city getting it—*whump a whump a whumpa whump*. We never expected to get it. There were very few air raid shelters in town and no war industries, just cigarette factories, hospitals, clarinet factories. Then a siren went off—it was February 13, 1945—and we went down two stories under the pavement into a big meat locker. It was cool there, with cadavers hanging all around. When we came up the city was gone.

"Our guards were noncoms—a sergeant, a corporal, and four privates—and leaderless. Cityless, too, because they were Dresdeners who'd been shot up on the front and sent home for easy duty. They kept us at attention for a couple of hours. They didn't know what else to do. They'd go over and talk to each other. Finally we trekked across the rubble and they quartered us with some South Africans in a suburb. Every day we walked into the city and dug into basements and shelters to get the corpses out, as a sanitary measure. When we went into them, a typical shelter, an ordinary basement usually, looked like a streetcar full of people who'd simultaneously had heart failure. Just people sitting there in their chairs, all dead. A fire storm is an amazing thing. It doesn't occur in nature. It's fed by the tornadoes that occur in the midst of it and there isn't a damned thing to breathe. We brought the dead out. They were loaded on wagons and taken to parks, large open areas in the city which weren't filled with rubble. The Germans got funeral pyres going, burning the bodies to keep them from stinking and from spreading disease. 130,000 corpses were hidden underground. It was a terribly elaborate Easter egg hunt. We went to work through cordons of German soldiers. Civilians didn't get to see what we were up to. After a few days the city began to smell, and a new technique was invented. Necessity is the mother of invention. We would bust into the shelter, gather up valuables from people's laps without attempting identi-fication, and turn the valuables over to the guards. Then soldiers would come in with a flame thrower and stand in the door and cremate the people inside. Get the gold and jewelry out and then burn everybody inside.

"It was a fancy thing to see, a startling thing. It was a moment of truth, too, because American civilians and ground troops didn't know American bombers were engaged in saturation bombing. It was kept a secret until very close to the end of the war. One reason they burned down Dresden is that they'd already burned down everything else. You know: 'What're we going to do tonight?' Here was everybody all set to go, and Germany still fighting, and this machinery for burning down cities was being used. It was a secret, burning down cities—boiling pisspots and flaming prams. There was all this hokum about the Norden bombsight. You'd see a newsreel showing a bombadier with an MP on either side of him holding a drawn .45. That sort of nonsense, and hell, all they were doing was just flying over cities, hundreds of airplanes and dropping everything. When I went to the University of Chicago after the war the guy who interviewed me for admission had bombed Dresden. He got to that part of my life story and he said, 'Well, we hated to do it.' The comment sticks in my mind.

"I think he felt the bombing was necessary, and it may have been. One thing everybody learned is how fast you can rebuild a city. The engineers said it would take 500 years to rebuild Germany. Actually it took about 18 weeks."[4]

"We were empty-headed children in that war, as all ground soldiers are. Anything could be put in our heads and we would believe it. And one idea that was put into our heads was that our enemies were so awful, so evil, that we, by contrast, must be remarkably pure. That illusion of purity, to which we were entitled in a way, has become our curse today.

"The happiest day of my life, so far, was in October of 1945. I had just been discharged from the United States Army, which was still an honorable organization in those Walt Disney times.

"I used to be an optimist. This was during my boyhood in Indianapolis. Those of you who have seen Indianapolis will understand that it was no easy thing to be an optimist there. It was the 500-mile Speedway Race, and then 364 days of miniature golf, and then the 500-mile Speedway Race again.

The 1972 Universal film "Slaughterhouse Five" starred Michael Sacks and was directed by George Roy Hill.

"My brother Bernard, who was nine years older, was on his way to becoming an important scientist. He would later discover that silver iodide particles could precipitate certain kinds of clouds as snow or rain. He made me very enthusiastic about science for a while. I thought scientists were going to find out exactly how everything worked, and then make it work better. I fully expected that by the time I was twenty-one, some scientist, maybe my brother, would have taken a color photograph of God Almighty—and sold it to *Popular Mechanics* magazine.

"Scientific truth was going to make us *so* happy and comfortable.

"What actually happened when I was twenty-one was that we dropped scientific truth on Hiroshima. We killed everybody there. And I had just come home from being a prisoner of war in Dresden. . . .And the world was just then learning how ghastly the German extermination camps had been. So I had a heart-to-heart talk with myself.

"'Hey, Corporal Vonnegut,' I said to myself, 'maybe you were wrong to be an optimist. Maybe pessimism is the thing.'

"I have been a consistent pessimist ever since, with a few exceptions. In order to persuade my wife to marry me, of course, I had to promise her that the future would be heavenly. And then I had to lie about the future again every time I thought she should have a baby. And then I had to lie to her again every time she threatened to leave me because I was too pessimistic."[9]

He enrolled at the University of Chicago to study anthropology. "At last! I was going to study man!

"I began with physical anthropology. I was taught how to measure the size of the brain of a human being who had been dead a long time, who was all dried out. I bored a hole in his skull, and I filled it with grains of polished rice. Then I emptied the rice into a graduated cylinder. I found this tedious.

"I switched to archaeology, and I learned something I already knew: that man had been a maker and

Paperback of the 1982 book.

smasher of crockery since the dawn of time. And I went to my faculty adviser, and I confessed that science did not charm me, that I longed for poetry instead. I was depressed. I knew my wife and my father would want to kill me, if I went into poetry.

"My adviser smiled. 'How would you like to study poetry which *pretends* to be scientific?' he asked me.

"'Is such a thing possible?' I said.

"He shook my hand. 'Welcome to the field of social or cultural anthropology,' he said. He told me that Ruth Benedict and Margaret Mead were already in it—and some sensitive gentlemen as well.

"One of those gentlemen was Dr. Robert Redfield, the head of the Department of Anthropology at Chicago. He became the most satisfying teacher in my life. He scarcely noticed me. He sometimes

looked at me as though I were a small, furry animal trapped in an office wastebasket. (I stole that image from George Plimpton, by the way. God love him.)"[9]

"[In 1947] I left Chicago without writing a dissertation—and without a degree. All my ideas for dissertations had been rejected, and I was broke, so I took a job as a P.R. man for General Electric in Schenectady [New York]. Twenty years later, I got a letter from a new dean at Chicago, who had been looking through my dossier. Under the rules of the university, he said, a published work of high quality could be substituted for a dissertation, so I was entitled to an M.A. He had shown *Cat's Cradle* to the Anthropology Department, and they had said it was half-way decent anthropology, so they were mailing me my degree. I'm class of 1972 or so."[4]

"[At General Electric] I was making about $90 a week then, which was about the norm for people my age....But there was no way anyone could get a significant raise until he was about thirty, and even then the really cosmic raises were reserved for a select few. So because I needed money, and because I was on a very slow escalator, I started looking around. It was at that point that I started writing stories—which was something I hadn't done in high school or college—and an editor at *Collier's* got interested in me and located an agent who was willing to take me on. The two of them gave me a number of tips about fiction writing.

"Actually, they had their reasons. At the time there was a good deal of informal instruction taking place within the profession because every week magazines were being published with as many as six or seven stories in them. If an editor wanted to produce a competitive journal, he simply had to have a stable of writers out there in the wilderness. It's probably not much of an exaggeration to say that anyone with the slightest promise could get as much help and opportunity as he needed because the magazines' needs were so great. Those were good times; there was almost a short story industry.

"There I was making ninety-two bucks a week with two kids to support, and out of nowhere comes a check for $750. Two months take-home pay!...I don't think I'll ever forget coming home to find that check. Needless to say, this caused me to do a bit of thinking about my life-role at General Electric. I wrote another story right away, and this time they paid me $900, because they would give you regular raises to keep you producing. Pretty soon I had money piling up in the corridors and I resigned from General Electric."[8]

Player Piano is a satirical treatment of a corporation, based on the General Electric Research Laboratory in Schenectady, that sacrifices humanity for technology. *Player Piano* attracted no critical acclaim at publication, and although Vonnegut achieved commercial success with his short stories almost instantly, it was nearly twenty years before he started to earn money from his novels. "[Having to support a family] forced me to write for magazines and the sort of fiction they wanted was low-grade, simplistic, undisturbing sort of writing. And so, in order to pay the bills I would write stories of that sort. I would try to accumulate enough capital to allow me to write a book. In effect, I was scrambling pretty hard writing lousy stories for years in order to pay the bills. It wasn't all bad—nothing ever is all bad—I did learn how to tell a story, how to make a story work, so that the thing has a certain flow and suspense and so forth. It is mechanical and it's somewhat worth knowing. Because I went through that apprenticeship I did learn how to tell a story. But every book I ever wrote I wrote with great seriousness, no cynicism at all and no large financial hopes each time. The reason I was living, so far as my professional life went, was in order to write books, simply books I wanted to exist. I was not out to make money. The short stories were going to make my money and after I had accumulated enough I would write as good a book as I could."[10]

"[When I worked for General Electric I was] completely surrounded by machines and ideas for machines, so I wrote a novel about people and machines, and machines frequently got the best of it, as machines will....And I learned from the reviewers that I was a science-fiction writer.

"I didn't know that. I supposed that I was writing a novel about life, about things I could not avoid seeing and hearing in Schenectady, a very real town, awkwardly set in the gruesome now. I have been a soreheaded occupant of a file drawer labeled 'science fiction' ever since, and I would like out, particularly since so many serious critics regularly mistake the drawer for a urinal.

"The way a person gets into this drawer, apparently, is to notice technology. The feeling persists that no one can simultaneously be a respectable writer and understand how a refrigerator works, just as no gentleman wears a brown suit in the city. Colleges may be to blame. English majors are encouraged, I know, to hate chemistry and physics, and to be proud because they are not dull and creepy and humorless and war-oriented like the engineers across the quad. And our most impressive critics have commonly been such English majors, and they are squeamish about technology to this very day. So it is natural for them to despise science fiction.

"But there are those who adore being classified as science-fiction writers anyway, who are alarmed by the possibility that they might someday be known simply as ordinary short-story writers and novelists who mention, among other things, the fruits of engineering and research. They are happy with the *status quo* because their colleagues love them the way members of old-fashioned big families were supposed to do. Science-fiction writers meet often, comfort and praise one another, exchange single-spaced letters of twenty pages and more, booze it up affectionately, and one way or another have a million heart-throbs and laughs.

"I have run with them some, and they are generous and amusing souls, but I must now make a true statement that will put them through the roof: They are joiners. They are a lodge. If they didn't enjoy having a gang of their own so much, there would be no such category as science fiction. They love to stay up all night, arguing the question, 'What is science fiction?' One might as usefully inquire, 'What are the Elks? And what is the Order of the Eastern Star?'

"But listen—about the editors and anthologists and publishers who keep the science-fiction field separate and alive: They are uniformly brilliant and sensitive and well-informed. They are among the precious few Americans in whose minds C. P. Snow's two cultures sweetly intertwine. They publish so much bad stuff because good stuff is hard to find, and because they feel it is their duty to encourage any writer, no matter how frightful, who has guts enough to include technology in the human equation. Good for them. They want buxom images of the new reality.

"And they get them from time to time, too. Along with the worst writing in America, outside of the education journals, they publish some of the best. They are able to get a few really excellent stories, despite low budgets and an immature readership, because to a few good writers the artificial category, the file drawer labeled 'science fiction,' will always be home."[9]

For the next seven years Vonnegut didn't write another book, and struggled to make a living without a regular job. Apart from publishing short stories, he taught English at Hopefield High School on Cape Cod, worked for an ad agency, and opened the second Saab auto dealership in the United States. "It was a hard car to sell. There was no national advertising at the time and I had to start literally from scratch—I had to teach Americans, for example, that Sweden wasn't the same country as Switzerland. It *was* a very good car, but the damn things used to come with a history of the company in the glove compartment. The purpose of the blurb was to persuade you that the manufacturers were a good company, but at the same time they pointed out that they made Stukas and ME-109's for the Nazis during World War II. They're excellent products, but to market an automobile in the United States with this information in the glove compartment is sort of block-headed."[8]

In October of 1957 Vonnegut's father died. He commented in *Jailbird:* "I tried to write a story about a reunion between my father and myself in heaven one time. An early draft of this book in fact began that way. I hope in the story to become a really good friend of his. But the story turned out perversely, as stories about real people we have known often do. It seemed that in heaven people could be any age they liked, just so long as they had experienced that age on Earth. Thus, John D. Rockefeller, for example, the founder of Standard Oil, could be any age up to ninety-eight. King Tut could be any age up to nineteen, and so on. As author of the story, I was dismayed that my father in heaven chose to be only nine years old.

"I myself had chosen to be forty-four—respectable, but still quite sexy, too. My dismay with Father turned to embarrassment and anger. He was lemur-like as a nine-year-old, all eyes and hands. He had an endless supply of pencils and pads, and was forever tagging after me, drawing pictures of simply everything and insisting that I admire them when they were done. New acquaintances would sometimes ask me who that strange little boy was, and I would have to reply truthfully, since it was impossible to lie in heaven, 'It's my father.'

"Bullies liked to torment him, since he was not like other children. He did not enjoy children's talk and children's games. Bullies would chase him and catch him and take off his pants and underpants and throw them down the mouth of hell. The mouth of hell looked like a sort of wishing well, but without a bucket and windlass. You could lean over its rim and hear ever so faintly the screams of Hitler and Nero and Salome and Judas and people like that far, far below. I could imagine Hitler, already experiencing maximum agony, periodically

finding his head draped with my father's underpants.

"Whenever Father had his pants stolen, he would come running to me, purple with rage. As like as not, I had just made some new friends and was impressing them with my urbanity—and there my father would be, bawling bloody murder and with his little pecker waving in the breeze.

"I complained to my mother about him, but she said she knew nothing about him, or about me, either, since she was only sixteen. So I was stuck with him, and all I could do was yell at him from time to time, 'For the love of God, Father, won't you please grow up!'

"And so on. It insisted on being a very unfriendly story, so I quit writing it."[11]

A year later his sister, Alice, died of cancer, and Alice's husband died in a train accident. "'Soap opera!' [Alice] said to my brother and me one time, when discussing her own impending death. She would be leaving four young boys behind, without any mother.

"'Slapstick,' she said.

"Hi ho.

"She spent the last day of her life in a hospital. The doctors and nurses said she could smoke and drink as much as she pleased, and eat whatever she pleased.

"My brother and I paid her a call. It was hard for her to breathe. She had been as tall as we were at one time, which was very embarrassing to her, since she was a woman. Her posture had always been bad, because of her embarrassment. Now she had a posture like a question mark.

"She coughed. She laughed. She made a couple of jokes which I don't remember now.

"Then she sent us away. 'Don't look back,' she said.

"So we didn't.

"She died at about the same time of day that Uncle Alex died—an hour or two after the sun went down.

"And hers would have been an unremarkable death statistically, if it were not for one detail, which was this: Her healthy husband, James Carmalt Adams, the editor of a trade journal for purchasing agents, which he put together in a cubicle on Wall Street, had died two mornings before—on 'The Brokers' Special,' the only train

From the 1984 movie "Slapstick of Another Kind," starring Madeline Kahn and Jerry Lewis. Copyright by S. Paul Co.

in American railroading history to hurl itself off an open drawbridge.

"Think of that.

"Bernard and I did not tell Alice about what had happened to her husband, who was supposed to take full charge of the children after she died, but she found out about it anyway. An ambulatory female patient gave her a copy of the New York *Daily News*. The front page headline was about the dive of the train. Yes, and there was a list of the dead and missing inside.

"Since Alice had never received any religious instruction, and since she had led a blameless life, she never thought of her awful luck as being anything but accidents in a very busy place.

"Good for her.

"My brother and I had already taken over her household. After she died, her three oldest sons, who were between the ages of eight and fourteen, held a meeting, which no grownups could attend. Then they came out and asked that we honor their only two requirements: That they remain together, and that they keep their two dogs. The youngest child, who was not at the meeting, was a baby only a year old or so.

"From then on, the three oldest were raised by me and my wife. . .along with our own three children, on Cape Cod.

"Yes, and our sister's sons are candid now about a creepy business which used to worry them a lot: They cannot find their mother or their father in their memories anywhere—not anywhere.

"For my own part, though: It would have been catastrophic if I had forgotten my sister at once. I had never told her so, but she was the person I had always written for. She was the secret of whatever artistic unity I had ever achieved. She was the secret of my technique. Any creation which has any wholeness and harmoniousness, I suspect, was made by an artist or inventor with an audience of one in mind.

"Yes, and she was nice enough, or Nature was nice enough, to allow me to feel her presence for a number of years after she died—to let me go on writing for her. But then she began to fade away, perhaps because she had more important business elsewhere."[12]

With the publication of *Cat's Cradle* in 1963, Vonnegut hoped to escape the realm of science fiction. Reviewers, however, did not accommodate. The book, concerned with bombing and apocalyptic ends, focuses on the three children of Hoenikker, a so-called innocent scientist and father of "Ice-nine," a device that causes the end of the world. "A man that my brother worked with. . .a Nobel Prize winner named Irving Langmuir, was more or less the model for Dr. Felix Hoenikker.

Langmuir was absolutely indifferent to the uses that might be made of the truths he dug out of the rock and handed out to whomever was around. But any truth he found was beautiful in its own right, and he didn't give a damn who got it next."[13]

After a two-year residency at the University of Iowa Writer's Workshop, Vonnegut received a Guggenheim Fellowship, which included a trip to Dresden where he gathered material for his novel, *Slaughterhouse Five*. The book was named after the building in which he was interned during the war. "It seemed a categorical imperative that I write about Dresden, the firebombing of Dresden, since it was the largest massacre in the history of Europe and I am a person of European extraction and I, a writer, had been present. I *had* to say something about it. And it took me a long time and it was painful. The most difficult thing about it was that I had forgotten about it. And I learned about catastrophes from that, and from talking to other people who had been involved in avalanches and floods and great fires, that there is some device in our brain which switches off and prevents our remembering catastrophes above a certain scale. I don't know whether it is just a limitation of our nervous system, or whether it's actually a gadget which protects us in some way. But I, in fact, remembered nothing about the bombing of Dresden although I had been there, and did everything short of hiring a hypnotist to recover the information. I wrote to many of the guys who went through it with me saying 'Help me remember' and the answer every time was a refusal, a simple flat refusal. They did not want to think about it."[13]

Following the publication of *Slaughterhouse Five*, Vonnegut acquired an audience comprised mostly of university students. He sold the movie rights for $165,000, was hailed by the media as a cult figure, and became much in demand as a campus speaker. "It is strange, but I was just writing books to entertain. I never dreamed of becoming a Pied Piper of the young. I don't want to be a Pied Piper.

"Most students when they see and hear me at campus lectures are blown over with surprise. Some think I'm going to sit around and smoke pot or take dope and give them all the answers to life. I'm not on the dope thing. I don't believe in it. And I don't have all the answers they seek."[14]

Although *Slaughterhouse Five* became required reading in college courses, the novel was banned in several schools and public libraries.

In October 1970, *Happy Birthday, Wanda June*, a play based on one Vonnegut had written some

From "Displaced Person," the Emmy Award winning adaptation presented on American Playhouse, PBS-TV, 1985.

fifteen years earlier, was produced. "Every American author my age has tried a play sometime between the ages of 40 and 60. This is because of loneliness. Families disperse, children become grown, and somewhere during that time writing is an extremely lonesome business. It's physically uncomfortable, it's physically bad for someone to sit still that long, and it's socially bad for a person to be alone that much. The working conditions are really bad. Nobody has ever found the solution to that. Novelists write very bad plays when they are about my age. I write for the stage in order to get to know more people and to become intimately related to them, so I will continue to do that sort of thing. But it is quite obvious from literary history that a person makes a decision very early in life to be either a novelist or a playwright, and the chances of being both are very slight."[5]

As he wrote in *Palm Sunday*, the next year brought a major change in his life. "Jane Cox Vonnegut and I, childhood sweethearts in Indianapolis, separated in 1970 after a marriage which by conventional measurement was said to have lasted twenty-five years. We are still good friends, as they say. Like so many couples who are no longer couples these days, we have been through some terrible, unavoidable accident that we are ill-equipped to understand. Like our six children, we only just arrived on this planet and we were doing the best we could. We never saw what hit us. It wasn't another woman, it wasn't another man.

"We woke up in ambulances headed for different hospitals, so to speak, and would never get together again. We were alive, yes, but the marriage was dead.

"And it was no Lazarus.

"Toward the end of our marriage, it was mainly religion in a broad sense that Jane and I fought about. She came to devote herself more and more to making alliances with the supernatural in her need to increase her strength and understanding—and happiness and health. This was painful to me. She could not understand and cannot understand why that should have been painful to me, or why it should be any of my business at all.

"And it is to suggest to her and to some others why it was painful that I chose for this book's epigraph a quotation from a thin book, *Instruction in Morals*, published in 1900 and written by my Free Thinker great-grandfather Clemens Vonnegut, then seventy-six years old:

"'Whoever entertains liberal views and chooses a consort that is captured by superstition risks his liberty and his happiness.'

"So I left my first wife and Cape Cod home forever in 1971. All our children save for the youngest, Nanette, had lit out for the Territory, so to speak. I became a soldier in what many were calling a sexual revolution. My departure itself was so sexual that a French name for orgasm describes it to a tee. It was a 'little death.'

"There were similar little deaths going on all around me, of course, and that continues to be the situation today. In the case of long marriages, such departures really are make-believe dying, a salute to a marriage in its good old days, sheepish acknowledgment that the marriage could have been perfect right up to the end, if only one partner or the other one had managed to die peacefully just a little ahead of time. . . .

"I left the house and all its furnishings and the car and the bank accounts behind, and taking only my clothing with me, I departed for New York City, the capital of the World, on a heavier-than-air flying machine. I started all over again.

"Somewhere in there my son Mark went crazy and recovered. I went out to Vancouver and saw how sick he was, and I put him in a nut house. I had to suppose that he might never get well again.

"He never blamed me or his mother. . . .His generous wish not to blame us was so stubborn that he became almost a crank on the subject of chemical and genetic causes of mental illness. Talk therapy made sense as poetry but not as a means to a cure, he thought."[2]

Slaughterhouse Five was made into a motion picture. "There are only two American novelists who should be grateful for the movies which were made from their books. I am one of them. The other one? Margaret Mitchell, of course."[2]

In 1979 Vonnegut married the noted photojournalist Jill Krementz, whom he had met while she was on assignment to photograph him. "I work on the top floor of our house, she works on the bottom floor, and we share the two floors in between. And it would be nice to be able to say that I have helped her career in many ways. But advising Jill at 30, her age when I met her, would have been like advising a pinwheel at the peak of its velocity and display.

"To put it another way: only fireworks are as self-propelled as Jill was then, and remains today."[15]

Over the years Vonnegut has had twelve novels published which have sold millions of copies, and appeared in numerous foreign editions. He has topped the bestseller list repeatedly and was made a member of the National Institute of Arts and Letters. Asked about writers who have influenced him, he replied: "Every writer has to set himself for that question because it is asked so often, and almost every writer has worked up a fancy and usually untruthful list of authors to whom he is grateful. I customarily say Orwell, and that is fairly close to the truth, but ordinarily I forget until long after the interview is over a man to whom I am deeply indebted, and he is Robert Louis Stevenson. He seems to be somewhat forgotten now, but as a boy I read an awful lot of Robert Louis Stevenson and was excited by stories which were well-made. Real 'story' stories. . .with a beginning, middle, and end. Because of the early admiration for him I still try to be a storyteller, to tell a story with some shape to it. So basically, Robert Louis Stevenson. Spiritually, I feel very close to Orwell; politically I feel very close to Orwell. But actually Orwell and I are almost of the same generation.

"It is curious that the authors I tend to admire have often been celibate, but I don't know the meaning of that. Orwell was not one of our heavy love makers as nearly as I can tell from his recent biography.

"Most authors are fools about living, as Truman Capote has suggested. . . .Brilliant artists he [knew] are scarcely capable of tying their shoes. And so, if I were to pick any author to imitate, I would likely be imitating someone who had lived very badly but one who had written extremely well.

"One writer I admired a lot was H. L. Mencken. When I was young I knew something about his life—that he had had a very exciting time as a newspaper reporter—and I guess later as a city editor. I read a couple of his autobiographical works, and as a result of this I wanted to be a newspaper man and did a certain amount of newspapering. So, I imitated Mencken to that extent. Again, Mencken was not one of our heavy love makers; he didn't get married, I don't think, until he was about 50.

"There is nothing a living author has written that I wish I had written, and I am sure that is the case for every living author. This is part of the professional stance. This is part of what keeps you going.

"When I write I also act, and I think this is true of most novelists. I will walk around talking to myself, saying out loud what a character is going to say, so that I will become one character and then another one, trying each on for size. So in the process of writing I have identified with every reasonably complex character in any of my books. But there is no carry-over from this. There is no carry-over from a completed book whatsoever."[5]

Footnote Sources:

[1] William Rodney Allen and Paul Smith, "An Interview with Kurt Vonnegut," *New York*, October 17, 1987.
[2] Kurt Vonnegut, *Palm Sunday*, Seymour Lawrence/ Delacorte, 1981.
[3] Hank Nuwer, "A Skull Session with Kurt Vonnegut," *South Carolina Review*, spring, 1987.
[4] David Hayman, David Michaelis, George Plimpton, and Richard Rhodes, "Kurt Vonnegut: The Art of Fiction LXIV," *Paris Review*, spring, 1977.
[5] Frank McLaughlin, "An Interview with Kurt Vonnegut," *Media & Methods*, May, 1973.
[6] K. Vonnegut, *Breakfast of Champions*, Dell, 1973.
[7] H. Nuwer, "Kurt Vonnegut Close Up," *Saturday Evening Post*, May/June, 1986.
[8] Charles Reilly, "Two Conversations with Kurt Vonnegut," *College Literature*, number 7, 1980.
[9] K. Vonnegut, *Wampeters, Foma, and Granfalloons (Opinions)*, Seymour Lawrence/Delacorte, 1974.
[10] Laurie Clancy, "Running Experiments Off: An Interview," *Meanjin Quarterly*, autumn, 1971.
[11] K. Vonnegut, *Jailbird*, Seymour Lawrence/ Delacorte, 1979.
[12] K. Vonnegut, *Slapstick; or, Lonesome No More*, Dell, 1976.
[13] Robert Musil, "There Must Be More to Love Than Death: A Conversation with Kurt Vonnegut," *Nation*, August 2-9, 1980.
[14] William T. Noble, "'Unstuck in Time'. . .a Real Kurt Vonnegut: The Reluctant Guru of Searching Youth," *Detroit Sunday News Magazine*, June 18, 1972.
[15] Jill Krementz, *The Writer's Image*, David R. Godine, 1980.

■ For More Information See

Books:

Current Biography 1970, H. W. Wilson, 1971.
Jerry H. Bryant, *The Open Decision*, Free Press, 1970.
R. H. W. Dillard, George Garrett, and John Rees Moore, editors, *The Sounder Few: Essays from the "Hollins Critic,"* University of Georgia Press, 1971.
Donald A. Wohlheim, *The Universe Makers*, Harper, 1971.
Charles B. Harris, *Contemporary American Novelists of the Absurd*, College and University Press, 1971.
Tony Tanner, *City of Words: American Fiction 1950-1970*, Harper, 1971.
Gilbert A. Harrison, editor, *The Critic as Artist: Essays on Books, 1920-1970*, Liveright, 1972.
David H. Goldsmith, *Kurt Vonnegut: Fantasist of Fire and Ice*, Bowling Green University Popular Press, 1972.

Betty Lenhardt Hudgens, *Kurt Vonnegut, Jr.: A Checklist*, Gale, 1972.

Peter J. Reed, *Kurt Vonnegut, Jr.*, Warner, 1972.

Ihab Hassan, *Contemporary American Literature 1942-1972*, Ungar, 1973.

Thomas R. Holland, *Vonnegut's Major Works*, Cliff's Notes, 1973.

Alfred Kazin, *Bright Book of Life: American Novelists and Storytellers from Hemingway to Mailer*, Little, Brown, 1973.

Jerome Klinkowitz and John Somer, editors, *The Vonnegut Statement: Original Essays on the Life and Work of Kurt Vonnegut*, Delacorte, 1973.

Clark Mayo, *Kurt Vonnegut: The Gospel from Outer Space; or, Yes, We Have No Nirvanas*, Borgo Press, 1973.

Raymond M. Olderman, *Beyond the Wasteland: A Study of the American Novel in the 1960s*, Yale University Press, 1973.

Contemporary Literary Criticism, Gale, Volume 1, 1973, Volume 2, 1974, Volume 3, 1975, Volume 4, 1975, Volume 5, 1976, Volume 8, 1978, Volume 12, 1980, Volume 22, 1982, Volume 40, 1986.

Joe David Bellamy and John Casey, *The New Fiction: Interviews with Innovative American Writers*, University of Illinois Press, 1974.

J. Klinkowitz and Asa B. Pieratt, *Kurt Vonnegut, Jr.: A Descriptive Bibliography and Secondary Checklist*, Shoe String, 1974.

Jean E. Kennard, *Number and Nightmare: Forms of Fantasy in Contemporary Fiction*, Archon Books, 1975.

J. Klinkowitz, *Literary Disruptions: The Making of a Post-Contemporary American Fiction*, University of Illinois Press, 1975.

Thomas D. Clareson, editor, *Voices for the Future: Essays on Major Science-Fiction Writers*, Volume 1, Bowling Green University Popular Press, 1976.

Stanley Schatt, *Kurt Vonnegut*, Twayne, 1976.

Robert Short, *Something to Believe In: Is Kurt Vonnegut Exorcist of Jesus Christ Superstar?*, Harper, 1976.

John W. Tilton, *Cosmic Satire in the Contemporary Novel*, Bucknell University Press, 1977.

Richard Giannone, *Vonnegut: A Preface to His Novels*, Kennikat, 1977.

J. Klinkowitz and Donald L. Lawler, editors, *Vonnegut in America: An Introduction to the Life and Work of Kurt Vonnegut*, Delacorte, 1977.

Michael Chernuchin, editor, *Vonnegut Talks!*, Pylon, 1977.

James Lundquist, *Kurt Vonnegut*, Ungar, 1977.

Dictionary of Literary Biography, Gale, Volume II: *American Novelists since World War II*, 1978, Volume VIII: *Twentieth Century American Science Fiction Writers*, Part 2, 1981.

J. Klinkowitz, *The American 1960s: Imaginative Acts in a Decade of Change*, Iowa State Univerity Press, 1980.

Charles Platt, *Dream Makers: The Uncommon People Who Write Science Fiction*, Berkley Books, 1980, revised edition, 1987.

Dictionary of Literary Biography Yearbook 1980, Gale, 1981.

K. Vonnegut, Jr., *Deadeye Dick*, Seymour Lawrence/Delacorte, 1982.

J. Klinkowitz, *Kurt Vonnegut*, Methuen, 1982.

Jill Krementz, editor, *Happy Birthday, Kurt Vonnegut: A Festschrift for Kurt Vonnegut on His Sixtieth Birthday*, Delacorte, 1982.

Dictionary of Literary Biography Documentary Series, Volume III, Gale, 1983.

Frederick R. Karl, *American Fictions: 1940-1980*, Harper, 1983.

George Plimpton, editor, *Writers at Work: The Paris Review Interviews*, sixth series, Penguin, 1984.

J. Klinkowitz, *Literary Subversions: New American Fiction and the Practice of Criticism*, Southern Illinois University Press, 1985.

Periodicals:

New Yorker, August 16, 1952, May 15, 1965, May 17, 1969, October 17, 1970, October 25, 1976, November 8, 1982.

New York Times Book Review, June 2, 1963, April 25, 1965, August 6, 1967, September 1, 1968, April 6, 1969 (p. 2ff), February 4, 1973, May 13, 1973, October 3, 1976, September 9, 1979, March 15, 1981, October 17, 1982, October 6, 1985, October 18, 1987.

Saturday Review, April 3, 1965, March 29, 1969, February 6, 1971, May 1, 1971, September 15, 1979.

Life, April 19, 1965, August 16, 1968, September 12, 1969 (p. 64ff), November 20, 1970.

Christian Science Monitor, May, 1965, December 5, 1968, September 10, 1979, December 3, 1982.

Times Literary Supplement, November 11, 1965, December 12, 1968, July 17, 1969, November 5, 1976, December 7, 1979, June 19, 1981, September 26, 1980, February 25, 1983, November 8, 1985.

Commonweal, September 16, 1966, June 6, 1969, November 27, 1970, May 7, 1971, December 7, 1973.

Hollins Critic, October, 1966 (p. 1ff), October, 1980.

Esquire, June, 1968, September, 1970.

New York Times, August 18, 1968, March 21, 1969 (p. 41), September 13, 1969, October 6, 1970, October 18, 1970, May 27, 1971, May 13, 1973, October 3, 1975, September 7, 1979, September 24, 1979, October 15, 1979, March 27, 1981, November 5, 1982, February 4, 1983, February 17, 1983, September 25, 1985, January 27, 1987, April 4, 1987.

Book World, August 18, 1968, March 2, 1975, September 2, 1979.

Time, August 30, 1968, April 11, 1969 (p. 106ff), June 29, 1970, June 3, 1974, October 25, 1976, September 10, 1979, October 25, 1982, October 21, 1985, September 28, 1987.

Atlantic, September, 1968, May, 1973, October, 1979, April, 1987.

Spectator, November 9, 1968.

Punch, December 4, 1968.

Critical Quarterly, winter, 1969 (p. 181ff).

Books and Bookmen, February, 1969, February, 1973, November, 1973.

Newsweek, March 3, 1969 (p. 79).

Best Sellers, April 15, 1969, November, 1979.
Boston Globe Magazine, July 20, 1969 (p. 10ff).
Christian Century, August 13, 1969.
Hudson Review, autumn, 1969.
Partisan Review, Number 1, 1970, Volume XLI, number 2, 1974.
Observer Review, March 15, 1970.
Observer, March 22, 1970, November 3, 1985.
New York Review of Books, July 2, 1970, May 31, 1973, November 25, 1976, November 22, 1979.
America, September 5, 1970, December 8, 1979.
Washington Post, October 12, 1970, May 13, 1973, May 15, 1981, February 2, 1982.
Chicago Tribune, November 15, 1970, January 29, 1982.
Critique: Studies in Modern Fiction, Volume XII, number 3, 1971, Volume XIV, number 3, 1973, Volume XV, number 2, 1973, Volume XVII, number 1, 1975, Volume XVIII, number 3, 1977, Volume XXVI, number 2, 1985.
Southwest Review, winter, 1971.
Media & Methods, January, 1071.
New York Times Magazine, January 24, 1971.
Publishers Weekly, March 22, 1971 (p. 26ff), October 25, 1985, January 31, 1986 (p. 263).
Twentieth-Century Literature, January, 1972.
Journal of Popular Culture, spring, 1972, winter, 1973.
American Poetry Review, January 2, 1973.
Modern Fiction Studies, spring, 1973 (p. 57ff), summer, 1975, winter, 1980-81.
Library Journal, April 15, 1973.
Harper's, May, 1973, July, 1974.
World, June 19, 1973.
Playboy, July, 1973 (p. 57ff).
Critic, September 10, 1973.
Extrapolation, December, 1973.
Crawdaddy, April 1, 1974 (p. 42ff).
American Literature, May, 1974.
Western Humanities Review, summer, 1974.

Commentary, July, 1974, November, 1975.
Cleveland Press, July 10, 1974, July 12, 1974.
Novel: A Forum on Fiction, winter, 1975.
Algol, winter, 1978-79.
South Atlantic Quarterly, winter, 1979.
Chicago Tribune Book World, August 26, 1979, November 2, 1980, March 1, 1981, October 10, 1982, November 13, 1983, September 22, 1985, October 4, 1985.
Detroit News, September 16, 1979, October 3, 1982, November 10, 1985, January 5, 1986.
Los Angeles Times Book Review, September 23, 1979, October 31, 1982, March 3, 1984, April 18, 1984, September 29, 1985.
International Fiction Review, summer, 1980.
Horizon, October, 1980.
World Literature Today, winter, 1981.
THOUGHT, March, 1981.
Washington Post Book World, March 8, 1981, October 17, 1982, September 22, 1985, October 4, 1987.
Queen's Quarterly, spring, 1981.
Virginia Quarterly Review, summer, 1981.
London, July, 1981.
Times (London), July 8, 1981, February 17, 1983, May 17, 1986, May 30, 1987.
Progressive, August, 1981.
Antioch Review, winter, 1983.
Wilson Library Bulletin, January, 1983 (p. 379).
Los Angeles Times, February 7, 1983.
Village Voice, February 22, 1983.
Globe & Mail (Toronto), March 17, 1984, February 8, 1986, October 17, 1987.
Film Comment, November/December, 1985 (p. 41ff).
North American Review, December, 1985.
Architectual Digest, May, 1986 (p. 170ff), November, 1987 (p. 76ff).
Tribune Books (Chicago), September 27, 1987.
People Weekly, October 19, 1987.

Meg Wolitzer

Born May 28, 1959, in Brooklyn, N.Y.; daughter of Morton (a psychologist) and Hilma (a novelist; maiden name, Liebman) Wolitzer; married Richard Panek, July 1, 1989. *Education:* Attended Smith College, 1977-79; Brown University, B.A., 1981. *Agent:* Peter Matson, Sterling Lord Literistic Ltd., One Madison Ave., New York, N.Y. 10010.

■ Career

Writer; book reviewer for *New York Times* and *Los Angeles Times. Awards, honors:* Winner of *Ms.* Fiction Contest, 1979, for "Diversions"; MacDowell Colony Fellowship, 1981; *Sleepwalking* was selected one of *School Library Journal*'s Best Books for Young Adults, 1982; Yaddo Residency, 1983; *Caribou* was selected one of Child Study Association of America's Children's Books of the Year, 1986.

■ Writings

Sleepwalking (novel), Random House, 1982.
Caribou (young adult), Greenwillow, 1984.
Hidden Pictures, Houghton, 1986.
The Dream Book (juvenile), Greenwillow, 1986.

This Is Your Life, Crown, 1988.

Contributor to periodicals, including *Ms.*

■ Adaptations

"This Is Your Life" (motion picture), Twentieth Century-Fox, in production.

■ Work in Progress

A first-person narrative of a sixty-five-year-old woman looking back on her life as a well-known child psychiatrist. The novel will include a number of case studies. "The decision to write in the first person was prompted by a friend who is a composer. He knew I was disturbed by the similarities among my first three novels, all written in the third-person, and felt that the switch would be liberating and revealing. The suggestion felt right, particularly since some of my favorite novels are first-person. I've thought often of Frank Conroy, who said, 'If you're going to write in the first person the world has to be larger than the *I* voice.' He's absolutely right. First-person writing can easily devolve into narcissism. The narrator must have an irresistible personal need to tell his or her story; and that story must be deserving of our attention. A first-person book needs an imperative. My own book may rely too heavily on the device of my central character's friends and associates pressing her to tell her story, but I'm hoping her tale is singular."

■ Sidelights

By the time she was twenty-eight, Meg Wolitzer had published three widely acclaimed novels and two books for young readers. A fascination with adolescence is a common thread running through all of her early work. Critics have pronounced her "the chronicler of her generation," a label Wolitzer resists as too confining.

"I was born in Brooklyn, but raised on Long Island in a typical suburban town. What was atypical about my experience was that my mother was writing and had a life outside suburban confines. My friends were creative and artistically active, writing and staging plays. My best friend in high school and I had a radio show called 'Curtains Up,' in which we'd act out all sorts of scenes from classic plays. The two of us would do all the parts, switching from female to male, young to old, whatever was needed. I was also the editor of the junior-high and high-school literary magazines. I was given a great deal of encouragement. It never occurred to me that I wouldn't be able to be a writer when I grew up.

"I read constantly as a child. My mother gave me many of the books she herself had read as a girl. I loved books about foster children and kids in orphanages—adoption fascinated me. I also read as much as I could find about children dying. Death, of course, terrified me, and I think reading about someone else dying had a purgative effect. It enabled me to face those fears from a protective distance.

"I went to the neighborhood library almost every day. The librarian was always putting things aside for me. To this day libraries are crucial to me.

"As you can tell from my books, particularly *This Is Your Life*, I also spent a good deal of time watching television. Because I was such an avid reader, my parents had no rules regarding TV. Television provided me with a rich well of things to draw from. And even though it cluttered my mind with images, I was somehow able to sift through them and keep only what intrigued me. When I first went to college I met people who'd grown up in totally different places and circumstances, but because we'd watched some of the same TV programs we had a real cultural bond.

"I started out at Smith College, but transferred to Brown University because I wanted to write a novel and couldn't get course credit for it at Smith. This project blossomed into *Sleepwalking*, which came out when I was twenty-two. The novel is not autobiographical."

The "death girls" in the novel—much of which takes place on a college campus—are extremely intelligent, bookish, sensitive young women who identify almost entirely with a dead woman poet: Anne Sexton (Laura), Sylvia Plath (Naomi), or the fictional Lucy Ascher (Claire), all of whom had committed suicide. Each young woman has taken on the personal style of her chosen poet. The "death girls" have an undeniable mystique, yet their willed isolation and inability to deal with the day-to-day have a pathological component. The three friends meet every night for a long "seance" in which they read their poets' works and meditate on their lives and deaths. Claire eventually seeks out Lucy Ascher's surviving parents and contrives to live with them as a housekeeper. The novel is concerned not only with the difficulties of discovering and claiming one's identity, but with the complexities of family life and friendship.

"I think to a very great extent my generation has relied on creating 'families' of friends. It seems to me that the traditional nuclear family has failed in many ways, and that our primary relations tend to be with our peers rather than with our relatives. Certainly Laura, Naomi and Claire sought each other out because they needed a family-type security without the judgment, limits and lack of understanding they'd experienced in their respective families. At the time I was writing *Sleepwalking*, I was reading Aeschylus in a college course. I wanted very much for these three characters to form a sort of Greek chorus, to fulfill a symbolic function. Claire is the most fully drawn 'death girl.' There's a labyrinthine quality to her obsession, to the journey she undertakes to overcome that obsession and her efforts to rejoin the world, so to speak. Naomi, whose identification with Plath is not as complete as Claire's with Lucy Ascher, does all she can to bring Claire back. Laura, who goes into a complete withdrawal after a nervous collapse, fades out of the plot."

Sleepwalking was published to enthusiastic reviews citing Wolitzer's ability to capture the feeling of growing up misunderstood; her eye for the telling detail; and her well-developed sense of place. "Virtually every review mentioned my age. I was treated as a sort of *wunderkind*. But the week the book hit the stores I was working as a switchboard operator. 'I'm a novelist,' I complained to myself, 'but here I am working for a temp agency.' That book led to other contracts, freeing me from temporary office jobs. I'm the first to admit I'm

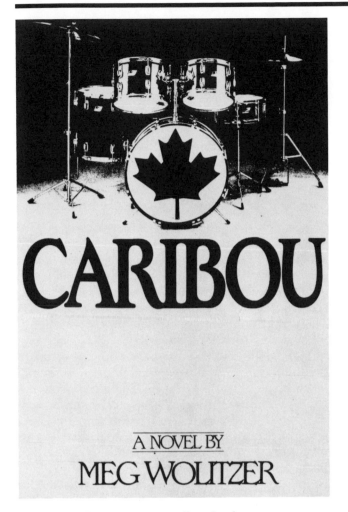

The 1984 Greenwillow hardcover.

very lucky. There are many talented writers in this country who can't support themselves on their writing. I feel enormously grateful.

"One of the first offers I had after *Sleepwalking* was from Susan Hirschman, editor-in-chief of Greenwillow, who asked me to write a children's book. This was something that had never occurred to me, even though my mother had written for younger readers."

Caribou and *The Dream Book*, both for young readers, received mostly favorable reviews. As with her first novel, Wolitzer's storytelling and comical talents, keen insight into adolescents, and firm handle on place were praised. But Wolitzer remains less than satisfied with those efforts. "I really have trouble seeing myself as a children's or young adult writer. I enjoy the work, but I don't write with my whole self as I do when I'm writing for adults. Perhaps as I grow older, I'm becoming less sensitive to the nuances of childhood and adolescence. I've declared a sort of moratorium on childhood in my adult writing, at least for a while.

Certainly fear of repetition plays its part here, but so does a desire to strike out in new directions.

"I suppose I have had difficulty writing for young readers because I don't like to think about an audience as I write. With juvenile books you must ask yourself: Is this word too difficult? Is this concept too abstract? too troubling? I found myself censoring my own work. This was terrifying to me, as self-censorship is the most dangerous kind that exists.

"I'm aware of a paradox here. The best children's books—at least those I most prefer—are wild and exciting. E. B. White comes to mind, so does Maurice Sendak, both of whose books deal with primal, mysterious, frightening things and feelings. *Charlotte's Web* really shook me up; I remember sobbing and sobbing over the death of that spider. For many of us, that was our first hard lesson about death.

"Writing *about* children and writing *for* them are two very different propositions. I'm suspicious of the first-person child's voice written by an adult. Falseness can easily creep in, and a gratuitously ingratiating tone. If I do another book for young readers, I hope it will be in a much more classical storytelling style."

Wolitzer's second adult novel, *Hidden Pictures*, was published in 1986. "Again, my interest here was to take a group of characters, let them scatter, and then see how, and with whom, they resettle." The novel opens on a young New York couple, a doctor, his wife, a fledgling illustrator, and their small son. The marriage lacks a passionate center and not long into the book, the partners separate. The wife becomes romantically involved with another woman, a charismatic photographer. After that relationship ends, and she has come to terms with her desire to live as a lesbian, she enters what proves to be an enduring relationship. She and her lover cement a life together, and her former husband eventually remarries.

"Of course it's important that two of the central characters in this novel are lesbians," said Wolitzer. "But I don't consider that the most important aspect of this book. Of greater weight is the exploration of the ways in which these characters create homes and families for themselves; what they go through to arrive at an understanding of who they are, what they need and how they love. I'd go so far as to say that I'm more interested in the son, than in the relationship between his mother and step-parent. He has an awful lot to deal with: his parents' divorce, their respective domestic situations, his peers' reactions to his having a lesbian mother, the conflicts he feels between his father's urban lifestyle and his mother's suburban move. All of this in addition to growing up, which is complicated enough. I think the adults may have relatively lighter burdens than the child.''

A particularly insightful moment occurred in *Hidden Pictures* when the boy, who had been studying his pensive mother, realized he had absolutely no idea what she was thinking. And then it hit him that maybe he wasn't supposed to know, that his mother was entitled to keep some thoughts to herself. "As adolescents we become obsessed with privacy, particularly our own. That moment for him is a kind of epiphany, a flash of maturity.''

Again the critical response was overwhelmingly positive. "There was one bad review,'' said Wolitzer, "which at first upset me very much. But as I read the piece more closely, I realized the reviewer had his own rather homophobic agenda. Apart from that, I sensed some nervousness regarding the lesbian theme, but no hostility. I think my writing has a lyrical quality that imparts a sort of glaze, perhaps a softer focus that may work to defuse any latent objections to provocative subject matter.''

When asked about the importance of reviews for her, Wolitzer replied, "At the beginning, I thought reviews were the 'Word of God.' I believed everything that was said about my work. With time, of course, that has changed. Now I read reviews in order to get a general idea as to how my books are perceived. For one thing, I want to be sure the work isn't being misconstrued. I never believe writers who say they don't read their reviews. Reviews are kind of like horror movies— you don't really want to see, you cover your eyes and then peek through your fingers. How can you help it? If you're a real writer, your work won't be affected by what the critics are saying. No one worth anything writes to please the critics. But there's nothing wrong with getting a glow from a good review. There's so little instant gratification in writing. It's many months between the time you finish a book and the date it appears. Good writers deserve a little stroking.

"This is particularly important at a time like this, when writing and the arts have become so vulnerable here. It's ironic that just as censorship and other forms of repression are loosening in Eastern Europe, openness is declining here. The current attacks on the National Endowment for the Arts are a prime case in point. We have senators, government officials and parts of the general public

looking at art merely in terms of bald content, merely in terms of what should be 'allowed.' It's very frightening when you stop to think that apparently many people believe the NEA should function as a censorship board. The new requirement that individuals receiving NEA fellowships must sign a waiver that they will not make 'obscene' art is a very dangerous step. It makes me want to push the boundaries, to see just how far the limits can be extended. 'Write as though everyone you know is dead.' That's still one of the wisest things I've ever read about writing.

"By way of comparison, I was part of a group of writers invited to Finland to share in the 500th Anniversary of the Finnish Book. This was a major celebration all over the country. People at all levels of government, including the prime minister, were actively involved. There is a national epic poem called the 'Kalevala,' on which supposedly Longfellow based the cadences of 'Hiawatha.' Everyone in Finland knows this poem, and when I was taken to the National Archives, the librarian suddenly began singing the poem for my benefit. Finland has one of the highest literacy rates in the world; well over ninety percent of the population not only reads and writes, but reads and writes *well*. Our own literacy rate is a disgrace, and it's very hard to imagine our political leaders, let alone the whole country, turning out to celebrate the beginning of U.S. book publishing.''

Wolitzer's most recent novel, *This Is Your Life*, deals wittily with the dark side of television and media culture. The book centers on Dottie Engels, a one-time suburban housewife who, after ending her unfulfilling marriage, packs her two daughters into her station wagon and heads to New York where she becomes a stand-up comic. In her act, Dottie 'roasts' herself as a fat, loud-mouthed misfit in a land where slimness is a sacred ideal. After years of playing tiny clubs, then small ones, then larger ones, Dottie becomes a full-blown nightclub and television star. Suddenly her image is everywhere. She herself is often absent, however, and her daughters grow up watching her on TV and talking with her on the phone.

"Dottie is not modeled on a specific TV personality. I wanted her to be kinder, more motherly than Joan Rivers, without Rivers's sexist streak. Carol Burnett may be closer in spirit to Dottie; she's warm and maternal, though she lacks Dottie's crude, self-deprecating sense of humor. Body image is endlessly fascinating to me. I wanted to explore the dynamics of being fat. On the one hand, being large can be seen as threatening. On the other, fat can lend an image of softness, making it easy to dismiss someone who's obese. Dottie plays all the angles. But she gets caught in the classic trap: believing in her own persona."

Dottie's fat, once her ticket to fame and fortune, becomes life threatening. In order to survive, Dottie must make profound changes not only in her habits but in her identity.

"Interestingly enough, in the movie version (the script for which is co-written by Nora Ephron and Delia Ephron), Dottie is not fat. No studio would take on a fat heroine. It goes to show that Roseanne Barr is an anomaly, not a harbinger.

"When I was a child, television provided access to parts of the adult world from which my parents's behavior shielded me. With Dottie I wanted to explore a woman who is a living representation of all the media taboos, and who triumphs, at least for a while. Much of this book comes from years of watching late-night TV, which can be pretty wild, a freak show. Most of the acts mentioned in *This Is Your Life* are things I actually saw. Mr. and Mrs. Lye, for instance. During their courtship, she wanted to break up with him. He became so enraged he threw lye in her face, blinding and disfiguring her. In his guilt, he vowed to take care of her for the rest of her life. They married, wrote a book and went on television, explaining how they had been shunned by all their friends, how when they went places people threw things at them. As a child, Mr. and Mrs. Lye represented to me all that was terrifying about adult sexuality. The mixture of love and hate, guilt and vengeance, was terribly confusing."

Though Wolitzer's first published fiction was a short story, the winning entry in *Ms.* magazine's College Fiction Contest, she emphatically prefers longer forms. "I wrote stories as a student; even then I favored reading novels. I like to sprawl out, make myself at home. A novel allows you to tell a many-layered story and look at characters and events from a number of angles. In comparison, short stories are like haiku. The form demands too much telegraphing for me. It takes a while to build up a head of steam in a piece of work; by the time a short story is supposed to end, I'm just heating up.

"In a lot of ways, I respond the most to nineteenth-century forms. I'm not trying to reproduce these efforts, but I do respond to that ambition to present the world in all its facets, to tell an irresistible story. There's grandeur to characters facing their problems head-on, struggling against historical, material and moral odds. I relate to this more than I relate to so-called 'post-modern' writing. I'm much more comfortable with 'Reader, I married him!'"

Yet Wolitzer does not feel that she's swimming "against the tide." "There are a number of contemporary writers with whom I feel very much in tune. Mary Gordon, for instance, and Rosellen Brown, John Cheever, and Philip Roth.

"I recently taught a course at the University of Iowa on gender and literature. I've been interested in the critical work done on issues pertaining to a female aesthetic. Admittedly, I'd rather read a primary text than criticism any day, but this seems an important line of inquiry. The idea of a female text, characterized by a circular rather than linear structure, is intriguing, yet I came away from that teaching experience more puzzled than when I began. I'm not sure how much the ideas really have to do with the act of writing. A wonderfully liberating thing about writing is that you can give your imagination free rein—to create male as well as female characters, stories that embrace both genders. There's been speculation as to why most avant-garde or experimental fiction has been writ-

Jacket illustration by Joseph A. Smith.

Softcover edition of the 1988 novel.

ten by men. I've heard it suggested that perhaps women writers are more concerned with stories because men's tales have dominated our culture. Rather than break down stories, or dispense with them, women writers are busy collecting tales, putting the pieces together."

Wolitzer has taught in several university writing programs around the country. "It can be a hard life in that you're sometimes a gypsy, subletting for four or five months at a time. But it's a good way to travel around the States and get a sense of life beyond New York. I have no illusions about being able to teach anyone to write. Nor should students hope to really *learn* to write in a workshop. The greatest value of these programs is that they give you time to hone your material in a supportive environment, develop your craft and acquire some confidence. You also have time to read, which is of capital importance.

"One of the exercises I give my writing students is a version of Twenty Questions. I tell them that they must know more about their characters than what

appears on the page. Even when characters are 'absent' from the story, a writer must have a sense of where they are, what they're doing, what they're anxious about, what they're eating and so on. Among other things, I ask my students to come up with fantasies and dreams for their characters. These details may never appear in the novel or story, but the writer's consciousness of them will lend texture and depth."

When she is not writing fiction, Wolitzer does reviews, interviews and literary essays. "One of my favorite activities is a weekly crossword puzzle. I co-wrote the now-defunct '7 Days.' I've always had an interest in cryptic word games. The one for '7 Days' is nothing like the dull, straight-arrow puzzles you find in more mainstream newspapers and magazines. And, what can I say, my co-author and I have a huge following."

Wolitzer speaks forthrightly about the pressures inherent in early success. "At the beginning, I had a sense of myself as being on the cusp of the adult professional world. True, I was just out of college, but I had an agent, signed a contract, and had an editor. Of course virtually all the reviews of my first two books cited my age. 'Astonishingly mature' and similar evaluations rang out. With my third book, reviewers stopped mentioning my age. I realized, with something of a shock, that my identity in part hinged on being a 'young writer,' with an emphasis on 'young.' If I was no longer young, I feared, perhaps I wasn't 'special.' As a young writer, I was compared with other young writers, as though youth were a separate aesthetic category. I began to be afraid that I'd been 'forgiven' certain shortcomings on account of my youth, and that I wouldn't be able to measure up. It was rocky transition through all of that uncertainty. It's a great relief to no longer be called 'precocious.'

"It's also sobering. Not so long ago it seemed I had all the time in the world. Now I feel strongly that I must focus my energy, concentrate my efforts. There's no way I'll write or read everything I wish to. Priorities are a must, but setting them can be a pleasure."[1]

Footnote Sources:

[1] Based on an interview by Marguerite Feitlowitz for *Authors & Artists for Young Adults.*

■ For More Information See

Library Journal, February 1, 1982, November, 1988.
Village Voice Literary Supplement, June, 1982.
Washington Post Book World, June 8, 1982.

Los Angeles Times Book Review, July 1, 1982.
New York Times Book Review, August 8, 1982,
   March 3, 1985.

Chicago Tribune Book World, August 22, 1982.
Times Literary Supplement, April 1, 1983.
San Francisco Chronicle, October 3, 1988 (p. F4).

Acknowledgments

Acknowledgments

Grateful acknowledgment is made to the following publishers,
authors, and artists for their kind permission to reproduce copyrighted material.

BRENT ASHABRANNER. Jacket of *Morning Star, Black Sun: The Northern Cheyenne Indians and America's Energy Crisis*, by Brent Ashabranner. Dodd, Mead & Company, 1982. Jacket photograph by Paul Conklin. Jacket design by Joy Taylor. Photographs copyright © 1982 by Paul Conklin. Reprinted by permission of The Putnam Publishing Group./ Jacket of *Dark Harvest: Migrant Farmworkers in America*, by Brent Ashabranner. Photographs by Paul Conklin. Dodd, Mead & Company, 1985. Photographs © 1985 by Paul Conklin. Jacket design by Joy Taylor. Reprinted by permission of The Putnam Publishing Group./ Jacket of *Children of the Maya: A Guatemalan Indian Odyssey*, by Brent Ashabranner. G.P. Putnam's Sons. Jacket photograph © 1986 by Paul Conklin. Reprinted by permission of The Putnam Publishing Group./ Jacket of *Into a Strange Land: Unaccompanied Refugee Youth in America*, by Brent Ashabranner and Melissa Ashabranner. G.P. Putnam's Sons, 1987. Copyright © 1987 by Brent Ashabranner and Melissa Ashabranner. Jacket design by Joy Taylor. Reprinted by permission of The Putnam Publishing Group./ Jacket photo from *Always to Remember: The Story of the Vietnam Veterans Memorial*, by Brent Ashabranner. G.P. Putnam's Sons, 1988. Jacket photo © 1988 by Jennifer Ashabranner. Reprinted by permission of The Putnam Publishing Group./ Brent Ashabranner and Russell Davis, "Harvesting Folk Tales," April, 1960, *The Horn Book Magazine*. Reprinted by permission of the Horn Book, Inc./ Brent Ashabranner, *A Moment in History: The First Ten Years of the Peace Corps*, Doubleday, 1971./ Brent Ashabranner, "Did You Really Write That for Children?" November/December, 1988, *The Horn Book Magazine*. Reprinted by permission of the Horn Book, Inc.

BEVERLY CLEARY. Jacket of *Henry Huggins*, by Beverly Cleary. William Morrow & Company, 1950. Copyright © 1950 by Beverly Cleary. Jacket illustration by Alan Tiegreen. Jacket design by Cynthia Basil. Reprinted by permission of William Morrow & Company, Inc./ Jacket of *Beezus and Ramona*, by Beverly Cleary. William Morrow & Company, 1955. Copyright © 1955 by Beverly Cleary. Jacket illustration by Alan Tiegreen. Jacket design by Cynthia Basil. Reprinted by permission of William Morrow & Company, Inc./ Cover of *Fifteen*, by Beverly Cleary. Laurel-Leaf Books, 1956. Copyright © 1956 by Beverly Cleary. Reprinted by permission of Dell Publishing, a division of Bantam Doubleday Dell Publishing Group, Inc./ Cover of *The Luckiest Girl*, by Beverly Cleary. Laurel-Leaf Books, 1958. Copyright © 1958 by Beverly Cleary. Reprinted by permission of Dell Publishing, a division of Bantam Doubleday Dell Publishing Group, Inc./ Cover of *Jean and Johnny*, by Beverly Cleary. Laurel-Leaf Books, 1959. Copyright © 1959 by Beverly Cleary. Reprinted by permission of Dell Publishing, a division of Bantam Doubleday Dell Publishing Group, Inc./ Cover of *Sister of the Bride*, by Beverly Cleary. Laurel-Leaf Books, 1963. Copyright © 1963 by Beverly Cleary. Reprinted by permission of Dell Publishing, a division of Bantam Doubleday Dell Publishing Group, Inc./ Beverly Cleary, "Writing Books about Henry Huggins," December, 1957, *Top of the News*./ Beverly Cleary, "Low Man in the Reading Circle; or, A Blackbird Takes Wings," June, 1969, *The Horn Book Magazine*./ Beverly Cleary, "Regina Medal," July/August, 1981, *Catholic Library World*./ Beverly Cleary, "The Laughter of Children," October, 1982, *The Horn Book Magazine*./ Beverly Cleary, *A Girl from Yamhill: A Memoir*, William Morrow and Company, 1988.

WES CRAVEN. Christopher Sharrett, "Fairy Tales for the Apocalypse," vol. 13, n. 3, 1985, *Literature/Film Quarterly*. Copyright © 1985 by *Literature/Film Quarterly*. Reprinted by permission.

LEN DEIGHTON. Cover of *The Ipcress File*, by Len Deighton. Ballantine Books, 1962. Copyright © 1962 by Len Deighton. Reprinted by permission of Ballantine Books, a division of Random House, Inc./ Jacket of *SS-GB: Nazi-Occupied Britian, 1941*, by Len Deighton. Alfred A. Knopf, 1978. Copyright © 1978 by Len Deighton. Jacket design by S. Neil Fujita. Reprinted by permission of Alfred A. Knopf, Inc./ Hugh Moffatt, "Hot Spy Writer on the Lam," March 25, 1966, *Life* Magazine./ Melvyn Bragg, "Len Deighton: 'The Most Hard-Working Writer I've Met,'" December 22-29, 1977, *Listener*./ Len Deighton, "Introduction," to *Tactical Genius in Battle*, Phaidon Press, 1979./ Len Deighton, "Foreword," to *Battle of Britain*, Jonathan Cape, 1980. Copyright © 1980 by Len Deighton. Reprinted by permission of Penguin Books Ltd./ Len Deighton, "Even on Christmas Day," in *Whodunit? Guide to Crime, Suspense, and Spy Fiction*, edited by H.R.F. Keating, Van Nostrand, 1982./ Edward Milward-Oliver, *The Len Deighton Companion*, Grafton Books, 1987. Reprinted by permission of Grafton Books.

JUDY DELTON. Jacket of *Kitty in High School*, by Judy Delton. Houghton Mifflin Company, 1984. Jacket painting © 1984 by Charles Robinson. Reprinted by permission of Houghton Mifflin Company./ Jacket of *Angel in Charge*, by Judy

Delton. Houghton Mifflin Company, 1985. Jacket © 1985 by Leslie Morrill. Reprinted by permission of Houghton Mifflin Company./ Jacket of *Angel's Mother's Boyfriend*, by Judy Delton. Houghton Mifflin Company, 1986. Jacket painting © 1986 by Margot Apple. Reprinted by permission of Houghton Mifflin Company./ Jacket of *Kitty from the Start*, by Judy Delton. Houghton Mifflin Company, 1987. Jacket painting © 1987 by Charles Robinson. Reprinted by permission of Houghton Mifflin Company./ Cover of *Pee Wee Scouts: Blue Skies, French Fries*, by Judy Delton. Dell Publishing, 1988. Illustrated by Allan Tiegreen. Text copyright © 1988 by Judy Delton. Illustrations copyright © 1988 by Alan Tiegreen. Reprinted by permission of Dell Publishing, a division of Bantam Doubleday Dell Publishing Group, Inc./ Cover of *Pee Wee Scouts: That Mushy Stuff*, by Judy Delton. Illustrated by Alan Tiegreen. Dell Young Yearling, 1989. Text copyright © 1989 by Judy Delton. Illustrations copyright © 1989 by Alan Tiegreen. Reprinted by permission of Dell Publishing, a division of Bantam Doubleday Dell Publishing Group, Inc./ Judy Delton,*The Twenty-nine Most Common Writing Mistakes and How to Avoid Them*, Writers Digest Books, 1985. Reprinted by permission.

ANNIE DILLARD. Cover of *Tickets for a Prayer Wheel*, by Annie Dillard. Harper & Row, Publishers, 1974. Cover painting "Approaching Storm, Beach Near Newport," by Martin Johnson Heade, Museum of Fine Arts, Boston, MA. Cover design © Lynn Dreese Breslin. Reprinted by permission of HarperCollins Publishers./ Cover of *An American Childhood*, by Annie Dillard. Harper & Row, Publishers, 1987. © 1987 by Annie Dillard. Reprinted by permission of HarperCollins Publishers./ Cover of *Teaching a Stone to Talk: Expeditions and Encounters*, by Annie Dillard. Harper & Row, Publishers, 1988. Cover painting "Greenwood Lake," by Jasper Francis Cropsey, 1875, courtesy of the National Museum of American Art, Smithsonian Institution, Gift of Ellen R. Wheeler. Cover design © 1988 Lynn Dreese Breslin. Reprinted by permission of HarperCollins Publishers./ A. Dillard, *Pilgrim at Tinker Creek*, Harper's Magazine Press, 1974. Copyright © 1974 by Harper & Row, Publishers, Inc. Reprinted by permission of the publisher./ "Young, Successful, and First," October, 1974, *The Saturday Evening Post*. Copyright © 1974. Reprinted by permission of *The Saturday Evening Post*./ Robert Lindsey, "Annie Dillard, Far from Tinker Creek," November, 1977, *New York Times Biographical Service*. Copyright © 1977 by the New York Times Company. Reprinted by permission of the publisher./ A. Dillard, *Holy the Firm*, Harper & Row, 1977. Copyright © 1977 by Harper & Row, Publishers, Inc. Reprinted by permission of the publisher./ "A Face of Flame: An Interview with Annie Dillard," May 5, 1978, *Christianity Today*. Copyright © 1978 by Christianity Today, Inc. Reprinted by permission of the publisher./ Harper Barnes, "Millions of Friends Share the Secret of Annie Dillard," May 1, 1983, *St. Louis Post-Dispatch*. Copyright © 1983 by Pulitzer Publishing Company. Reprinted by permission of the publisher./ "Why I Live Where I Live: by Annie Dillard of Middletown, Connecticut," March, 1984, *Esquire*. Copyright © 1984, Esquire Associates. Reprinted by permission of the author and her agent, Blanche C. Gregory Inc./ A. Dillard, "The French and Indian War in Pittsburgh: A Memoir," July/August, 1987, *American Heritage*. Reprinted by permission of Harper & Row, Publishers, Inc./ Annie Dillard, *An American Childhood*, Harper & Row, 1988. Copyright © 1988 by Harper & Row, Publishers, Inc. Reprinted by permission of the publisher.

KEN FOLLETT. Cover of *Eye of the Needle*, by Ken Follett. New American Library, 1978. Copyright © 1978 by Ken Follett. Reprinted by arrangement with New American Library, a division of Penguin Books USA Inc., New York, NY./ Jacket of *The Mystery Hideout*, by Ken Follett. Morrow Junior Books, 1990. Jacket illustration by Stephen Marchesi. Jacket illustration © 1990 by William Morrow and Company, Inc. Reprinted by permission of William Morrow & Company, Inc./ Jacket of *The Power Twins*, by Ken Follett. Morrow Junior Books, 1990. Jacket illustration by Stephen Marchesi. Jacket illustrations © 1990 by William Morrow and Company, Inc. Reprinted by permission of William Morrow & Company, Inc./ Ken Follett, "Books that Enchant and Enlighten," June, 1979, *The Writer*. Copyright © 1979 by The Writer, Inc. Reprinted by permission of *The Writer*./ John F. Baker, "PW Interviews: Ken Follett," January 17, 1986, *Publishers Weekly*. Copyright © 1986 by Reed Publishing USA. Reprinted by permission of the publisher.

RUMER GODDEN. Cover of *The Greengage Summer*, by Rumer Godden. Penguin Books, 1958. Copyright © Rumer Godden, 1958. Cover illustration by Neil Reed. Reprinted by Permission of Penguin Books, a division of Penguin Books USA Inc./ Cover of *The Diddakoi*, by Rumer Godden. Puffin Books, 1972. Copyright © Rumer Productions Ltd, 1972. Reproduced by permission of the British Broadcasting Corporation./ Cover of *The Peacock Spring*, by Rumer Godden. Penguin Books, 1975. Copyright © Rumer Godden, 1975. Cover illustration by Stephen Lavis. Reprinted by permission of Penguin Books, a division of Penguin Books USA Inc./ Cover of *Thursday's Child*, by Rumer Godden. Laurel-Leaf Books, 1984. Copyright © 1984 by Rumer Godden. Cover illustration by Richardson. Reprinted by permission of Dell Publishing, a division of Bantam Doubleday Dell Publishing Group, Inc./ Rumer Godden, *A Time to Dance, No Time to Weep*, Macmillan (London), 1987. Reprinted by permission of the author./ Rumer Godden, *A House with Four Rooms*, William Morrow and Company, 1989. Reprinted by permission of the author.

EILEEN GOUDGE (MARIAN WOODRUFF). Cover of *Kiss Me, Creep*, by Marian Woodruff. Bantam Books, 1984. Copyright © 1984 by Marian Woodruff and Cloverdale Press, Inc. Cover photo by Pat Hill. Reprinted by permission of Cloverdale Press./ Cover of *Night After Night*, by Eileen Goudge. Laurel-Leaf Books, 1986. Copyright © 1986 by Eileen Goudge and Cloverdale Press, Inc. Cover photo by Pat Hill. Reprinted by permission of Cloverdale Press./ Cover of *Deep-Sea Summer*, by Eileen Goudge. Laurel-Leaf Books, 1988. Copyright © 1988 by Eileen Goudge and Cloverdale Press, Inc. Cover photo by Pat Hill. Reprinted by permission of Cloverdale Press.

TONY HILLERMAN. Cover of *The Fly on the Wall*, by Tony Hillerman. Copyright © 1971 by Tony Hillerman. Reprinted by permission of HarperCollins Publishers./ Cover of *Dance Hall of the Dead*, by Tony Hillerman. Harper & Row, Publishers, 1973. Copyright © 1973 by Anthony G. Hillerman. Cover illustration by Peter Thorpe. Reprinted by permission of HarperCollins Publishers./ Cover of *Listening Woman*, by Tony Hillerman. Copyright © 1978 by Anthony

Jacket illustration by Jos. A. Smith. Reprinted by permission of Greenwillow Books, a division of William Morrow & Company, Inc./ Cover of *This Is Your Life*, by Meg Wolitzer. Penguin Books, 1988. Copyright © Meg Wolitzer, 1988. Cover illustration by Amanda Wilson. Cover design by Melissa Jacoby. Reprinted by permission of Penguin Books, a division of Penguin Books USA Inc.

Cumulative Index

Author/Artist Index

The following index gives the number of the volume
in which an author/artist's biographical sketch appears.